This book is dedicated to our clients,
who demonstrate every day that leadership matters.

CONTENTS

FIRST EDITION

AWAKEN, ALIGN, ACCELERATE

A GUIDE TO GREAT LEADERSHIP

EDITED BY

SCOTT E. NELSON & JASON G. ORTMEIER

MDA LEADERSHIP CONSULTING

AWAKEN, ALIGN, ACCELERATE®

ISBN 13: 978-1-59298-391-9

Library of Congress Catalog Number: 2011923353

Printed in the United States of America

First Printing: 2010
Second Printing: 2011
Third Printing: 2013

18 17 16 15 14 13   8 7 6 5 4 3

Cover and interior design by James Monroe Design, LLC.

Beaver's Pond Press, Inc.
7108 Ohms Lane
Edina, MN 55439–2129
(952) 829-8818
www.BeaversPondPress.com

To order, visit www.MDALeadership.com or www.BeaversPondBooks.com
or call (800) 901-3480. Reseller discounts available.

MANAGING SELF

PREFACE

The leadership landscape is changing dramatically, making the work of leaders more challenging than ever. Leaders are being stretched by advances in technology, increased business complexity, and growing market unpredictability. Organizations must build a competitive advantage by investing in the ongoing development of their leaders.

At MDA Leadership Consulting, we have a passion for developing great leaders. We partner with organizations to grow leadership capabilities and talent acumen at all levels of the talent pipeline by providing expert advice in the following areas: identifying potential, accelerating development, and increasing organizational performance.

Our mission is to serve as trusted advisors in helping leaders achieve healthy growth and superior results. Our consultants demonstrate strong expertise in leadership development, combining practical knowledge in psychology and business to deliver increased leadership performance. Collectively, we have accumulated considerable expertise from our client partnerships since we opened our doors in 1981. We have developed our own perspectives on leadership through our consulting work with organizations across industries and companies of all sizes.

Rather than basing this book on a single author's point of view, we pooled our wisdom and insights to create this leadership guide. By making this a collaborative effort, we ensured that you have access to the best insights from our entire team. This guide introduces our unique and powerful framework—Awaken, Align, Accelerate—for enhancing leadership performance at all levels. Filled with practical development suggestions and coaching tips, this guide enables leaders to develop themselves and others.

I invite you to turn the page and connect your aspiration to be a great leader with the tools needed to make it happen.

—Sandra Davis, Ph.D., Founder and CEO
on behalf of MDA Leadership Consulting, Inc.

INTRODUCTION

A Recipe for Great Leadership

Organizations that deliver superior performance have one thing in common: great leadership at every level driving strategy and execution. Leadership practices, employee effort, customer satisfaction, organizational performance, and bottom-line results are all linked. Great leaders connect the moving pieces of a business while engaging and inspiring others along the way. The best leaders help people grow and realize their fullest potential while delivering exceptional business results.

Leadership is an art as well as a science, much like fine cuisine. Different chefs can follow the same recipes—and use the same ingredients—yet produce very different creations. This book is a distillation of what we've learned about leadership, presented in a series of "recipes." These recipes were created with the psychology of how people develop and were refined in the real-world laboratory of our consulting practice. However, the artfulness of how particular leaders infuse these recipes with passion and creative flair will set their leadership apart from another's.

Leaders face a variety of challenges in solving business problems and managing people. Great leaders recognize that ongoing development is vitally important, and they have an appetite for learning. This guide harnesses the art and science of developing leaders into a unique collection of self-assessments, development suggestions, case studies, sample leadership development plans, coaching recommendations, and cross-cultural coaching tips. We offer you our best thinking—packaged with our own passion for developing great leaders.

Developing yourself and coaching others are the central themes of this guide. Increasingly these represent the yin and yang of great leadership—complementary, interacting forces that combine to produce superior outcomes. Our step-by-step approach will help leaders build their strengths while addressing development needs, gain new experience, and engage in robust conversations to maximize their leadership performance and business results.

> " This guide focuses attention on what it takes to develop senior leaders, those who have responsibility for multiple teams inside a function (e.g., sales, marketing, finance) or an entire business within an organization. Additionally, we've designed this guide to be used by managers aspiring upward or even more senior executives facing similar challenges. "

This guide is intended for three distinct groups of leaders:

Self-Developing Leaders

This guide supports leaders who want to develop themselves and coach others. It also provides practical development suggestions that can be used when conducting performance management and development planning conversations.

Coaches

Both leaders who coach other leaders and professional coaches will benefit from this guide. Even seasoned coaches, regardless of theoretical orientation or coaching model, can use our suggestions and tips to expand their coaching toolkits.

Human Resources Leaders

Human resources leaders can use this book to explore a fresh model of core leadership skills based on a set of well-researched behavioral competencies. This guide also provides a comprehensive resource for adding development content to an entire range of human resources initiatives, from leadership development to talent management to succession planning.

Effectively Using This Guide

To get started read Chapters 1–4 to gain a basic understanding of the models that are the foundation for this guide. These will help you better understand how to create powerful development experiences and the necessary components to building strong leadership development for yourself and others in your organization. The guide's core is divided into sixteen chapters, each focusing on a critical leadership competency. Each chapter includes:

- A definition of the leadership competency along with its key core practices.

- A self-assessment that allows leaders to evaluate their strengths, pinpoint specific development needs, and identify potential excessive use.

- Development suggestions that include processes, tools, and conversations to enhance leadership effectiveness and assist with performance management.

- A case study that illustrates how lack of skill can affect one's ability to lead effectively.

- A sample leadership development plan linked to the case study, making the connection from situation to development.

- Specific and actionable suggestions for coaching others.

- Considerations for coaching in the global business environment.

Once you have a good understanding for the models and the guide's layout, getting the most out of the guide and jumpstarting your development requires just a few simple steps:

Step 1: Identify key priorities

Review all 16 competencies using the table starting on page 439. Which are most important to your role? Seek feedback from others, such as your boss or peers, on which competencies they feel are most important and should be your top priority.

Step 2: Assess your strengths

Start with your top three competencies and read the introduction and complete the self-assessment at the beginning of each corresponding chapter. Prioritize the top three, putting the one with the most "Development Need" or "Excessive Use" checks at the top of the list.

Step 3: Review development suggestions

Beginning with your top competency, identify the core practices with the most "Development Need" or "Excessive Use" check marks. Turn to the development suggestions for these core practices within the competency chapter and identify suggestions that you would be comfortable trying or may push you to try new things.

Step 4: Create a development plan

Read the case study and sample development plan at the end of the chapter. Use the template on page 446 to create your own development plan. Complete the Business Context section to ensure that your development goals are aligned and support existing business goals.

Step 5: Work the plan

Work through the development suggestions. Seek regular feedback from others on your progress. Once you, and others, feel as though you've "mastered" a suggestion, move on to another. Continue working through the core practices—returning to Step 4. Once you've mastered all the core practices in the competency, move on to another competency—returning to Step 3.

Development for the Future

Another good development exercise is to rank the sixteen competencies in order of importance for new roles that you may be working toward. Go back to Step 3 and retake the self-assessment while envisioning yourself in a new role. Are there new competencies and core practices where you need improvement? Ask yourself how might this role differ from the one that you are in today? Continue with the process, focusing on the newly identified future competencies to prepare yourself for the future.

1

Leadership Development Fundamentals

Our approach to leadership development is built on the interaction of three proven concepts:

1. **Talent Pipeline**—an overarching context to understanding the leadership requirements at different levels within an organization.

2. **Leadership Competency Model**—a model for defining the knowledge, skills, and behaviors required across different levels of leadership.

3. **Awaken, Align, Accelerate**—a simple but elegant framework (our "secret sauce") to help leaders develop themselves and coach others.

These three concepts can be used in combination to communicate leadership expectations, connect development efforts with business imperatives, and enhance the performance of leaders at all levels. We believe that these concepts are more powerful when used together than when used independently.

Talent Pipeline

Based on the evolving science of leadership in conjunction with our own observations and experience, we know that:

- success looks different at different leadership levels,

- successful transition to a new level involves developing the right skills and behaviors.

A talent pipeline illustrates the skills, knowledge, and values needed in leadership across levels of any organization. To successfully navigate from one level to the next, leaders need to understand the behavior differences and develop strategies for closing the gap.

Our talent pipeline (as illustrated below) is a derivative of the approach presented in *The Leadership Pipeline* (Charan, Drotter, & Noel, 2001). Many companies have used a pipeline framework to guide conversations about succession planning and talent management.

The levels of leadership shown below are based on a natural hierarchy in organizations, where each level calls for different skill and value orientations to handle increasingly complex responsibilities. More importantly, movement up the pipeline involves developing the skills needed to transition through each passage to the next level. Charan and his colleagues take the leader through six passages of learning and experiences as they transition from the role of individual contributor to a role at the top of the organization. Our simplified pipeline highlights the levels of leadership found in most organizations.

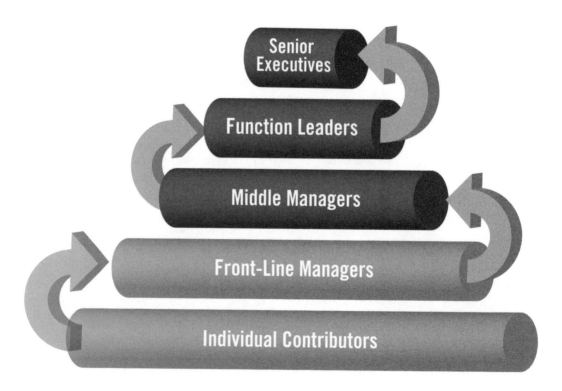

The idea that leadership skills and values vary by level is not unique to our framework. However, the pipeline becomes a compelling illustration for leadership development by promoting the idea that leaders can learn, and it implies that development is necessary for advancement. This view of leadership progression is both optimistic and realistic. As their scope of responsibility increases, leaders must acquire and demonstrate a set of expanding skills—and value the process of managing through others rather than doing things by themselves. The talent pipeline promotes the idea of continuous, career-long learning—especially for people who have leadership aspirations. In this context, leaders always have more to learn as they progress.

The talent pipeline context provides managers with a blueprint of skills and orientations necessary at higher levels. This makes development clear and practical. *The Leadership Pipeline* authors did a commendable job of developing the pipeline concept and highlighting what was involved in transitioning through the leadership passages. Our contribution is to provide insights and recommendations about how to develop specific leadership capabilities that managers and executives need on the job.

Each chapter contains a chart that shows how key leadership skills play out at the manager, function leader, and senior executive levels of the pipeline. While the focus of the guide is on function leaders, the content can be used by leaders at multiple levels, including aspiring executives.

Leadership Competency Model

Leadership is dynamic. The way leadership is practiced today differs from the 1970s and 1980s when competency models were first popularized. Competencies may encompass knowledge, skills, abilities, traits, and attitudes—and these complex skill sets can be defined in many ways. For years we have observed that some sets of leadership behaviors are common across many roles, but they vary by level, which exemplifies the talent pipeline context.

In developing our Leadership Competency Model, we examined dozens of models in the leadership research domain. That analysis, coupled with our own observations of leadership, allowed us to extract the best competencies. MDA's Leadership Competency Model is written in the real-life language our clients use. While many organizations have defined cascading leadership models, few have integrated their models with the pipeline context in as much detail as we present in this guide.

There are many ways to slice the pie of leadership. Our model below is divided into six leadership factors, and then into sixteen competencies that leaders need to perform effectively across multiple leadership levels.

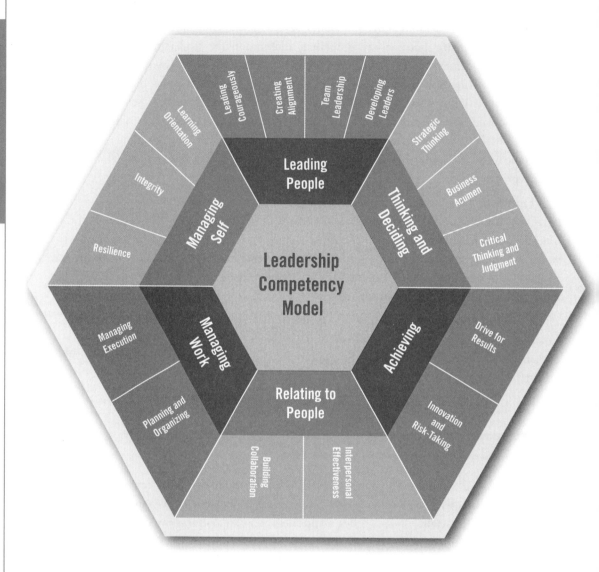

This guide is organized by six leadership factors (Leading People, Thinking and Deciding, Achieving, Relating to People, Managing Work, and Managing Self) and includes a chapter for each of the sixteen competencies. Each competency is broken down into five core practices and corresponding key leadership behaviors. A set of brief definitions for each competency along with its core practices is provided in the Appendix.

Factor	Competency	Core Practice
Leading People	Leading Courageously	Authority
Thinking and Deciding	Creating Alignment	Courage
Achieving	Team Leadership	Assertiveness
Relating to People	Developing Leaders	Independence
Managing Work		Influence
Managing Self		

Utilizing the self-assessment in each chapter, leaders can assess whether each practice is a development need, strength, or overused strength—and find specific development suggestions to enhance their capabilities. Customer focus and global orientation are embedded within each competency rather than presented as separate competencies.

In combining the talent pipeline context with our Leadership Competency Model, we found that thirteen of the leadership competencies differ by leadership level. While higher levels of those competencies build on those below, they also become something greater. For example, when front-line managers are Building Collaboration, this often involves forming personal relationships and encouraging individuals on their teams to cooperate. At higher leadership levels, it means persuading teams to collaborate across functions. The competency transforms from an interpersonal skill to a broader partnering skill at higher levels. Building Collaboration among executives is a higher-order skill where people often need plenty of organizational savvy to form the right coalitions and partnerships.

Likewise, all leaders need to demonstrate some aspect of Strategic Thinking—yet it evolves over time and with experience. Front-line managers need to understand their company's business and the strategy behind the organization's plans. In contrast, senior leaders are typically in charge of monitoring the marketplace and setting a strategic direction. People start by learning how to understand strategy and then develop a stronger external orientation as they learn to analyze markets, industries, competitors, and global factors. As people learn more, that learning transforms their skill in this area.

The three "Managing Self" competencies (i.e., Integrity, Resilience, and Learning Orientation) don't vary much by leadership level. They are fairly stable and don't transform markedly over time or with the demands of the job. Although the underlying ability or capacity may not change with experience, leaders may apply it differently as their roles change—or learn to apply it differently based on situations they encounter during their careers.

Our clients are always looking for practical tools to help individuals become better leaders. It helps when leaders can use a common language for development. The Leadership Competency Model can be used by leaders at all levels to assist with self, team, and organizational development.

2

Awaken, Align, Accelerate

The Awaken, Align, Accelerate framework represents three crucial phases in a leader's growth. Each phase is critical for meaningful and sustained development to occur. Leaders cycle through these phases each time they experience new insights, practices, and results at different levels of the talent pipeline.

Great leaders:

- **Awaken potential** by gaining insight into their leadership impact and aspirations.

- **Align goals** by understanding the business context and connecting leadership development goals with business outcomes.

- **Accelerate performance** by seeking new experiences, gaining additional knowledge, and practicing key leadership skills and behaviors.

Our Awaken, Align, Accelerate framework is a simple and practical approach that helps demystify the development process. It gives organizations a way to link the development process to their business performance. Leaders can use this framework to help people understand that development is part of successful leadership.

Phase 1: Awaken

The Awaken phase is about helping leaders understand their impact through honest assessment. It combines taking stock of their current strengths and development opportunities as well as identifying what they want to achieve. We know that leaders who invest time gaining awareness and committing to improve their performance can realize their full potential and deliver stronger results.

In this phase, leaders gain increased awareness about their leadership style, skills, and values. They also learn how their behavior affects others as well as their own performance and results. Ideally, it should include an assessment of a leader's strengths and development opportunities as well as direct feedback from those with whom the leader interacts. In essence it provides the *clarity* and *motivation* for development.

The Awaken phase can give leaders a comprehensive understanding of how others perceive them and how they see themselves. Leaders gain personal insight and awareness through in-depth exploration and reflection.

The following questions are a great starting point:

- What has shaped you? Think about relationships, education, and experiences.

- What brought you to this point in your career?

- What have you learned about leadership?

- What are your values?

- What is your purpose as a leader?

- What do you bring to the leadership role in your organization?

- How do others view your leadership style, performance, and results?

Leaders can supplement reflection by completing the self-assessments included in each chapter. To deepen the insight leaders can also use additional tools, perhaps using personality assessments, multi-rater feedback surveys, or interviews. A human resources partner can support this effort. After taking stock of who they are and what they aspire to become, leaders can transition to the Align phase.

Phase 2: Align

The Align phase is the intersection between a leader's personal development goals and the business agenda—what the organization needs from that leader to deliver strong results today and into the future. By understanding the business context for the leader's development goals and aligning them with business outcomes, both the leader and the organization are positioned to deliver stronger results and achieve greater potential.

A solid Align phase makes the desired outcomes of development explicit at the individual, team, and organization levels. Alignment involves creating congruence between a leader's awakening and what's expected by the organization. It's critical to know the context of the role—especially the strategic or business context—as well as how stakeholders expect the leader to perform. The outcomes from this phase provide the business *case* and *context* for development.

Key questions for leaders to answer in this phase include:

- How could your strengths contribute to advancing your own goals?
  Your team's goals?

- How will your development needs hinder success in achieving your objectives?
  Your team's objectives?

- How could your development contribute to better business performance and results?

Engaging others to understand how business outcomes and leadership expectations sync up creates additional motivation. This phase creates a supportive development environment for the leader and the organization. Once alignment occurs, leaders and the organization will be more powerfully committed to accelerating their development.

Phase 3: Accelerate

The Accelerate phase entails designing and deploying intentional development strategies that help enhance leadership performance on the most vital priorities. It leverages outcomes from the Awaken and Align phases, focusing development efforts on what is most critical. This phase is about executing the plan to ensure development actually happens through seeking new experiences, gaining additional knowledge, and practicing key leadership skills and behaviors. The Accelerate phase is the *how* and *when* of development.

There are many ways to help people learn and develop. The sheer number of options can be overwhelming to anyone. The best strategies contain the right mixture of challenge and support, balancing learning through new relationships, education, and experiences. The Accelerate phase helps leaders sort through these choices and keeps them on their growing edge—where learning is maximized by being challenged without being overwhelmed.

The Accelerate phase can encompass a number of specific activities, such as targeted skill-building or practical learning applications. Simply performing one activity and gaining experience is usually not enough. A manager or coach can help brainstorm and/or sort through options, if needed. Acceleration involves reflecting on the experience and deciding what to do differently next time. This phase helps get the best return on developmental investment—in the most efficient way possible.

Key considerations in this phase include:

- How do you need to learn?

- What sources of support and challenge are available to you?

- How will your change and growth be obvious or visible to others?

- Who will support and reinforce change?

- How will change be measured?

Without focusing on *awakening*, a leader may lack deep insight into his or her leadership style and how it promotes or impedes effectiveness. Likewise, without *alignment*, a leader may focus on personal development without sufficient attention to how it will affect the results of the team and the organization. Lastly, when *acceleration* is insufficient, a leader may let change happen rather than intentionally make it happen.

The Awaken, Align, Accelerate approach to development is based on six key principles:

1. **Business-oriented:** The business context is critical for development to truly make a difference. Understanding what is necessary for successful business performance and results provides the prioritization of development efforts. Keeping this in mind, leaders can go beyond simply achieving something that is personally satisfying to increasing the impact and return on the investment for the organization.

2. **Insight-oriented:** What does it mean to be a leader in today's world? Leaders are often using outdated perspectives on leadership versus understanding how they can make the greatest impact. Personal insight, insight from others, and insight about the competitive landscape all provide a comprehensive perspective on development efforts. Great leaders who use insight to better understand their impact and incorporate their personal motivation will realize greater results.

3. **Engagement-oriented:** Being vulnerable as a leader can be intimidating; however, it can also be very liberating. Leaders who are transparent around their development goals help to create a supportive development culture. Ensuring that key stakeholders are aligned and involved is a fundamental ingredient for sustaining strong development results.

4. **Action-oriented**: Real-world learning is the most powerful way to develop. Identifying and including meaningful on-the-job activities, experimenting with new behaviors, and reflecting on experiences are all key actions in creating significant development. When leveraging the latest leadership book or online course as the development activity, interpreting and applying the material to the leader's real-world situation is the key to true development.

5. **Measurement-oriented**: Systems, processes, and tools can be powerful allies in reinforcing behavior change. The old adage of "what gets measured and rewarded gets done" remains true today. Strong development cultures hold leaders accountable for creating leadership development plans, measuring progress on goals, and holding routine development conversations.

6. **Systems-oriented**: The organizational environment has a major effect on what, how, and whether leaders learn and develop. Organizations with the strongest focus on individual learning and growth link their talent reviews, succession planning, and development systems together to create an integrated approach. Holding leaders accountable for having solid leadership development plans for their direct reports is a starting point that gets many organizations over the hump.

Take these key principles into account when planning leadership development efforts. When all six principles are used, results are stronger than when fewer are incorporated. Leaders who are development-conscious can act as catalysts for change within the organization, working to concurrently develop themselves while revising internal processes or systems to drive stronger results. Be courageous, make development a priority, and lead the organization to becoming more developmentally oriented.

As you read each chapter, you will learn how to apply the Awaken, Align, Accelerate framework to develop the full range of leadership competencies necessary to navigate today's complex business environment. Great leadership requires a continuous focus on learning and development. We believe this framework will help simplify the process for developing leaders and coaching others.

3

Develop Yourself

Great leaders push themselves to learn, evolve, and adapt. Once leaders stop pushing themselves, their chances of continued success are greatly diminished. Self-development is a key ingredient for leaders who want to stay on the forefront in their professions.

Success can get in the way of people believing they should continue to develop. It may seem counterintuitive, but the best leaders realize they have more to learn as they move up. The most effective leaders continue to see areas of opportunity for themselves. Leaders must commit to ongoing development in the context of being successful. Those who do it well make it part of their everyday lives, not something extra. Great leaders are constantly asking questions, giving and receiving feedback, and assessing whether they are improving. They inspire others by modeling continuous learning and development.

Leaders need to apply their strengths in handling day-to-day challenges and achieving results. However, great performance is based on more than using one's strengths. Leaders must also be aware of their weaknesses and strengths that they overuse. Weaknesses need to be developed and overused strengths need to be toned down. This guide is designed to help leaders develop areas of strength and round out weaker areas that could become liabilities.

How Leaders Develop

Psychologists and social scientists have produced many interesting theories about who or what makes the most effective leader. There was a time when the oldest, the tallest, or those from a certain bloodline or birthright were believed to be the ones to follow. Outdated notions suggesting that "leaders are born" have mostly vanished from contemporary theories of leadership. Research and anecdotal evidence indicate that leaders grow and develop in response to their environments and as a result of choices they make. Personality traits can tell us who might be attracted to leadership positions and who is more or less likely to be successful in those roles. However, personality traits do not fully account for individual differences in motivation or readiness to develop the skills and behaviors indicative of effective leadership, especially as leaders transition into more senior roles.

Leaders who have a strong learning orientation and value self-reflection tend to be able to change or develop at a more rapid pace than those who do not.

Learning-oriented leaders are:

- self-aware—know their own strengths and limitations,

- open-minded—actively consider others' suggestions,

- open to new ideas—adventuresome, curious, and inquisitive,

- flexible—adjust their approach when something doesn't work.

This type of learning orientation allows leaders to:

- Reflect on and learn from mistakes.

- Seek and act on feedback from others.

- Value the perspective of (and learn from) others.

- Seek out challenges and new experiences.

- Actively pursue personal growth and improvement.

- Model a desire to learn and gain new skills.

Predisposition, preference, opportunity, and choice can all play a role in learning. For leaders to learn and develop, they need to be open to information about their styles and decide to change or improve and be open to appropriate ideas and tools for making changes. The degree of organization and manager support for learning or change can be another significant variable in the change process. Balancing support with the challenge of change often creates the most significant results—keeping leaders at their growing edge.

Leadership effectiveness develops over time in response to experiences and challenges that an individual encounters. Effective leaders continually develop, learn, and modify their approaches in response to the ever-evolving leadership contexts in which they find themselves, thereby expanding their range and refining their leadership styles. Leaders develop most effectively when the development occurs:

1. **In the context of business performance.** When development is connected to business performance, we see much greater growth for the leader and the organization. When leaders are sent away to an executive MBA program or leadership training program, they tend to generalize their learnings rather than apply specific insights to their own situations. This is why action learning, learning while working on real business problems, can be so instrumental in sustaining leadership development.

2. **Through on-the-job experiences.** Key research findings conclude that people develop primarily through experiences (70%), people or relationships (20%), and formalized coursework or education (10%). On-the-job experiences found most pertinent to leadership development include situations that involve leading a change or turnaround situation, influencing without authority, or handling unfamiliar responsibilities.

3. **In the community.** Non-work experiences can profoundly affect a leader's development. These may include taking on a role in the community that involves different responsibilities from those faced at work, or personal challenges and peak experiences that provide clarity of individual purpose or leadership values. The more active leaders are in making meaning of key experiences and drawing connections to their leadership style, the more likely those experiences will shape and develop the leader.

4. **Through systemic support.** Many are familiar with the phrase "people join organizations, but leave managers." This rings true for development as well. Manager support for development is crucial—especially as it relates to performance feedback. The degree to which a leader's new practices and behaviors are positively reinforced and rewarded in an organization impacts the sustainability of positive changes and future willingness to grow and learn.

5. **With effective coaching.** Coaching is the most personalized and focused development resource. It provides even the highest-performing leader with an opportunity to leverage the expertise of someone who understands how people change, the context of the business, and fundamentals of leadership. Effective coaching provides the right setting for leaders to examine their own strengths and development needs as they relate to their roles and organizational expectations.

6. **Through developing others.** Coaching or mentoring others helps leaders create a teachable point of view. This experience helps leaders reinforce their own learning. An organization benefits from the cascading effect of leaders teaching leaders as well. The next chapter focuses on coaching others.

Assess your end game. What is your ambition? What is your overall objective? If you want to be a better golfer, you probably need to work on your whole game, not just be the best off the tee or on the green. To be a successful leader, you need to do most things fairly well. You need to tackle things that may be uncomfortable. People aspiring to be great leaders don't want anything to hold them back—and they welcome development to help them improve. Consider how hard world-class athletes train and how willing they are to receive critical feedback and coaching. This represents a mindset about continuing to enhance performance that can apply to leadership development planning as well.

Create a Leadership Development Plan

Although experience is the primary way that leaders develop, research studies have confirmed that leaders need a plan, and they need to write it down. Even the process of creating a plan has been ranked highly as a development experience by some executives. However, low-quality or unachievable plans increase cynicism and can be an impediment to leadership development. For example, ambitious career development plans sometimes raise expectations that can't be fulfilled, especially among high-potential leaders.

It takes effort to construct meaningful, focused, and compelling development plans. Development plans must be dynamic. As the business context changes and leaders are faced with new challenges, there are learning opportunities that should be incorporated. Plans should include experiences, conversations, and tools. Some leaders haphazardly lay out overly broad or vague development strategies or simply restate their performance goals to meet human resources requirements that individuals have development plans in place. Unfortunately, these documents are soon forgotten or the development strategies aren't executed as they lack specifics, support requirements, or success measures to make them compelling.

Development planning creates focus. Concentrate on one or two development areas that will have the biggest impact. Identify challenging goals to push your personal growth. "No pain, no gain"—right? Work on what will make the greatest difference. Write down and share the goals because that will increase the likelihood of accomplishment. Find ways to increase accountability for taking planned actions asking questions such as: How will others notice your attempts at changing? How would you measure your success? Track what you have committed to—because what gets measured gets done. Use a development plan as a compass to keep heading in the right direction.

Explore options for linking your development to formal organizational processes. Think about when managers or others have talked about leadership development. For example, when do development conversations occur? Are there formal channels for doing this? What tools are available?

Following are ten guidelines for creating effective leadership development plans. See these tips in action on the leadership development plan template which follows.

1. **Less is More.** Focus on no more than two to three development areas. A thorough assessment of the leader's context and business goals will help prioritize the most important areas for development. As goals are accomplished, new ones can always be added, but it can be de-motivating and ineffective to spread a leader's development focus too thin across multiple goals.

2. **Use SMART Guidelines.** Goals should be Specific, Measurable, Actionable, Realistic, and Timely. Although crafting goals that meet each of these requirements can feel burdensome, the payoff will far exceed the upfront effort. Qualitative indicators along with appropriate business metrics should be used when specifying how leader behavior change is to be measured.

3. **Link Activities to Individual, Team, and Organization Needs.** Development plans should identify how the leader, team, and organization will benefit from enhanced leadership capability in the targeted areas. Leader behavior has ripple effects throughout the organization. Focus on the link between personal change and leadership effectiveness.

4. **Activate Strengths.** The importance of leveraging strengths to maximize potential and performance has become more relevant in leadership development. Sometimes leaders minimize their strengths or fail to fully apply them in their roles. It can be helpful to identify at least one key strength that has high importance given the business context, in addition to identifying development gaps.

5. **Identify the Business Context.** Focus on the intersection between a leader's development needs and what the business needs are now and in the future. Highlighting the real and immediate business context helps both the leader and the organization achieve their goals.

6. **Use the 70-20-10 Rule.** As noted, research indicates that people develop most through experiences (70%), next through people or key relationships (20%), and lastly through formalized classroom training or education experiences (10%). Weight development plan activities with experiential activities—those that actually engage the leader in new, broader, or deeper experiences.

7. **Live the Plan.** Good plans are ones that live and breathe rather than collect dust on a shelf. Revisit the plan quarterly, assess progress against goals, and revise strategies in light of current business conditions and leadership challenges. Make changes as needed to ensure that the focus of the plan will drive short-term results and long-term learning.

8. **Balance Support and Challenge.** Ensuring sufficient sources of support for the leader (e.g., peers, resources, manager support) will allow the leader to take on more challenges. Activities should challenge a leader to behave in new ways and should

3

DEVELOP YOURSELF

cause the leader to be somewhat uncomfortable—indicating appropriate stretch—but not overwhelming.

9. **Get Feedback from Colleagues.** Feedback from managers, peers, and colleagues can be helpful upfront to build support for development efforts, help refine focus, and generate creative ideas for development. As strategies are implemented, enlisting feedback from stakeholders to assess development can reinforce progress and deepen relationships.

10. **Measure Progress.** Establish measures to evaluate the plan on a regular basis and track progress toward goals. Leaders follow through on their development plans much more when others are informed about the goals and the leader is required to communicate progress updates or gather ongoing feedback from key stakeholders.

Leadership Development Plan

Following is a development plan template that contains the key components necessary for success. You will find sample development plans throughout the guide.

LEADERSHIP DEVELOPMENT PLAN
DEVELOPMENT GOAL
Desired Outcomes—results I want to see from developing this skill
Self: **Team:** **Organization:**
Self Understanding—strengths that I can build on and development needs I can address
Strengths: **Development Needs:**
Business Context—challenges in my business environment that require this skill
DEVELOPMENT ACTIONS
Awaken—activities for gaining personal insight into my impact as a leader • • •

Tip 1: Less Is More.

Tip 2: Use SMART Guidelines.

Tip 3: Link Activities to Individual, Team, and Organization Needs.

Tip 4: Activate Strengths.

Tip 5: Identify the Business Context.

Tip 6: Use the 70-20-10 Rule.

LEADERSHIP DEVELOPMENT PLAN

Align—actions for connecting my leadership development goals with my business outcomes

-
-
-

Accelerate—experiences, people, and education that will provide new concepts, skills, and knowledge

-
-
-

DEVELOPMENT SUCCESS FACTORS

Timeline—when I will accomplish my goals

Tip 7: Live the Plan.

Support Needed—who and what I need to effectively implement my plan

-
-
-

Tip 8: Balance Support and Challenge.

Indicators of Success—how I will measure progress and evaluate my enhanced skill

-
-
-

Tip 9: Get Feedback from Colleagues.

Tip 10: Measure Progress.

4

Coach Others

Great leadership demands ongoing development and drive for personal mastery. However, it isn't enough for leaders to simply develop skills themselves. The best leaders also work to advance others' leadership skills through creating new experiences, setting stretch goals, and providing courageous feedback. Coaching is a critical leadership role that creates powerful learning opportunities when woven into daily interactions for both the coach and the person being coached.

Thousands of books about coaching have been written and countless training programs have been launched, yet leaders still struggle to do it well. The bottom line is that coaching and developing others is a complex skill. Due to the demands on leaders today, it is hard to find time to have meaningful coaching conversations. Coaching should become part of routine interactions and is not reserved for more formal meetings. When senior leaders model receptivity to feedback and encourage a coaching culture, it accelerates the development of other leaders to refine their coaching skills and practice coaching more often.

Coaching is a process by which a leader helps others develop their skills, improve their performance, and adapt their style to achieve greater results.

As a leader, coaching helps you:

- Focus attention not only on "what" needs to be done (performance), but also on "how" people achieve their results (style).

- Do more with less. Coaching others at all levels on ways to think and act independently multiplies the resources available to the leader.

- Deepen the impact of learning for others by providing awareness. It involves helping people think through and reflect on their experiences, style, and impact, and is less "directive" than performance management.

- Conduct high-impact conversations. Leaders need to have conversations about why development is important. Coaching is more than just suggesting activities—it is about connecting new behavior with better results.

While coaching can help anyone improve his or her performance, it's not always the best use of a leader's time. Be clear on where coaching can pay off. Some leaders may try to substitute coaching for performance management. If there are performance issues, it might be more helpful to restructure the job, find a better fit for the person in the organization, or put the person on a performance improvement plan. Accelerating the development of key people with coaching is generally a better use of a leader's time than coaching problem performers.

MDA's process of *awakening* one's potential, *aligning* goals to the business context, and *accelerating* performance through a series of meaningful experiences can also be applied to coaching. The following table shows what leaders can do to support someone's development through coaching at each phase of the Awaken, Align, Accelerate framework. The simple pneumonic in the word IMPACT can help leaders remember six key coaching steps: Insight, Motivate, Plan, Align, Create, and Track.

PHASE	IMPACT Coaching Steps
Awaken	**Increase INSIGHT** as a foundation for growth. Provide feedback using your own observations along with personality or multi-rater feedback to help leaders gain greater self-awareness and understand their effect on others.
	MOTIVATE change by focusing on options and choices available to leaders. Identify what they are truly motivated to change. Help them reflect on what has led to learning in the past. Identify current performance gaps and potential priorities for development along with the consequences of not making any changes.
Align	**PLAN goals** and actions for improvement. Identify possibilities for change that enable leaders to handle current and future business challenges more successfully. Focus on what they could change to improve their performance as well as results. Ask leaders what they would spend time working toward and follow through on. Construct a leadership development plan.
	ALIGN expectations and desired results with business priorities and key stakeholders. Focus on what really matters to improve the performance of leaders, their team, and organization. Get others involved in supporting desired changes.
Accelerate	**CREATE teachable moments** to reinforce learning and actions taken by the leader. Ask powerful questions to encourage novel ways of thinking, solving problems, or behaving. Help them experiment with trying new things. Reflect on impact, successes, mistakes, and learning in order to enhance skills and sustain changes.
	TRACK progress toward goals and results. Evaluate increased effectiveness and measure progress toward outcomes and results. Discuss changes that will be visible to others. Ensure the leader has regular communication with stakeholders regarding goals, experiments, and learning. Invite additional feedback and ask others to support any changes they see.

As you move forward in any coaching conversation be sure to review these simple but helpful coaching tips:

1. **Know yourself,** including what kind of people you work well with versus not. For example, if you are impatient with others' mistakes, you probably shouldn't coach someone who is just learning a new skill.

2. **Assess your own view of the situation.** Ask yourself questions: How did this become a development need or something the person wants to improve? What feedback has the person received? How is the person viewed by others?

3. **Seek to understand what is most important** and meaningful to the person. Connect what is most important with what is expected in the leader's role and what performance changes are sought by the organization. How does this skill/behavior affect the leader's ability to meet his/her goals? What are the implications of the status quo?

4. **Allocate enough coaching time.** Be explicit about when you are coaching versus performing other leadership roles. It's best to make separate time for coaching and development instead of mixing it with performance management.

5. **Focus on the most important thing.** Help the leader prioritize and focus on clear, concrete development goals. Check in on a regular basis. Keep the focus narrow to achieve the desired end result.

6. **Encourage experimentation.** Help the leader figure out new things to try. Debrief attempts to make behavior changes.

7. **Engage in collaborative problem-solving.** Turn off any propensity to direct. Ask questions that get the leader to identify solutions rather than providing solutions. It's a mind shift as well as a behavior shift to do more listening, less telling.

8. **Suspend judgment.** Listen from the perspective of trying to understand the leader's perspective. It means letting go of your own agenda in order to listen.

9. **Be generous in sharing your own experiences**, both good and bad. Leaders often like to hear about your own struggles (e.g., handling your first team or a large project, including mistakes you made). However, they still get to choose what works for them. Be careful not to monopolize coaching time with your own stories.

10. **Monitor the amount of support and challenge** you are providing. If the leader doesn't feel much support, he or she may not change. A leader probably cannot take much challenge if the organization doesn't value development, if resources for development are scarce, or if a premium is placed on getting results. If more challenge is needed, provide more assignments and opportunities that require the leader to stretch.

11. **Provide resources** and connect leaders with other sources of coaching. Identify others who could be good mentors or advisors.

12. **Promote feedback.** Engineer situations for the leader to check perceptions of key stakeholders through interviews or a formalized survey process as well as seeking ongoing feedback.

13. **Be proactive.** Intervene when you observe or sense that problems are occurring. Be flexible and spontaneous. Seize coachable moments to provide feedback and suggestions.

14. **Reinforce progress and celebrate success.** Find something to acknowledge and appreciate in every coaching conversation.

As you continue to refine and develop your coaching approach, here are some reflective questions to ask yourself.

- How is coaching different from managing?

- How is a coaching conversation different from other interactions I have with my staff?

- How do I motivate others to change?

- How do I balance challenging others while supporting them?

- How much do I talk versus listen?

- Am I impatient or patient?

- Am I directive or participative?

- What skills do good coaches need—and do I have those skills?

Review your answers to the questions above with an internal coach, human resources partner, or another leader you believe demonstrates a strong competency in coaching. You can also gather feedback from key reports to ensure your self-awareness of these skills matches the perceptions of others.

Coaching in a Global Environment

The globalization of business means that many leaders are now managing teams consisting of people from a variety of different cultures, nationalities, ethnicities, or geographies. MDA believes that coaching conversations help leaders bridge cultural differences.

When coaching someone with a different background, assume there are important differences that may not be readily apparent—even if you speak the same language. Recognize that the leader you are working with may not be a typical representative of his or her cultural norms. Asking questions and testing your assumptions prevents you from offering suggestions that may not be appropriate or welcome—this is vital to your success as a coach. Find a "cultural informant" and ask what kinds of behavior to expect from people, but always watch for personal biases. Start coaching with an open and interactive dialogue to promote cultural or ethnic awareness. Most importantly, be a student of not only the leader's culture, but also the culture of the organization.

While coaching has become popular globally, it may not be practiced the same way across cultures. For example, in group-oriented cultures, coaching may be seen as a form of teaching and may be practiced in a way that looks more like training or directing. You may need to help other leaders learn about alternative approaches to coaching.

Each of the following chapters contain additional tips for leaders who are coaching others in their organization, as well as across a global environment.

LEADING PEOPLE

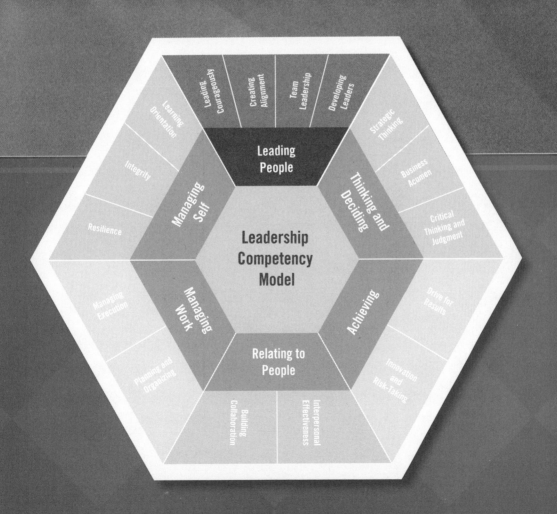

5

Leading Courageously

Successful organizations need courageous leaders at every level who display confidence and skill in the use of leadership, power, and authority. They assume responsibility for tackling tough assignments and pursue difficult challenges. Courageous leaders are assertive and appropriately tough-minded without being insensitive. They take initiative, act with independence, and demonstrate strength of conviction in pursuing their leadership agendas. They shape the thinking of others and actively influence upwards and across the organization.

Factor	Competency	Core Practice
Leading People	Leading Courageously	Authority
Thinking and Deciding	Creating Alignment	Courage
Achieving	Team Leadership	Assertiveness
Relating to People	Developing Leaders	Independence
Managing Work		Influence
Managing Self		

Leading Courageously seems to be in short supply. There are plenty of barriers—from internal voices that caution a leader to "be patient" or "be nice," to the reality that making a tough call or taking a stand can be unpopular. Even the value we place on collaboration in the business world subtly works against taking on the role of being the one in charge. When times are especially difficult, we want to work for leaders who are courageous, who persevere despite the odds, and who relentlessly drive for results. Leaders who act with true courage may listen to a chorus of ideas or suggestions, but ultimately put a stake in the ground. When they aren't right, they acknowledge their mistakes and quickly regroup to make another, better call. They aren't afraid to "tell the emperor he has no clothes."

Courageous leaders step up even when they are uncertain about what needs to be done. They aren't afraid to lead, even when they aren't sure exactly where they are headed. Senior leaders serve as role models in helping others see what behavior is appropriate and desired. By inviting and encouraging others to act courageously, they can build this into the DNA of the organization. Developing your own personal power—the credibility and engaging style that causes others to *want* to follow you no matter what level of the leadership pipeline you occupy—paves the way for greater impact. While the ability to lead courageously is important for all leaders, the most effective behaviors vary by level, as illustrated in the table below.

How Leaders at Different Levels Lead Courageously

	Managers	Function Leaders	Senior Executives
Authority	Displays comfort with managerial power and authority.	Provides direction without smothering creativity and motivation.	Uses personal power to influence, reserving formal authority for specific cases.
Courage	Takes a stand on appropriate issues.	Readily takes on difficult assignments and challenges.	Shows resolve when confronting resistance to unpopular decisions or ideas.
Assertiveness	Confidently asserts own point of view.	Is direct, assertive, and appropriately tough-minded.	Is forceful and persuasive with a wide variety of audiences.
Independence	Defends ideas and positions effectively.	Acts independently and with conviction.	Willingly advocates new or unpopular positions.
Influence	Negotiates successfully with others.	Influences upwards and across the organization.	Actively influences across the entire organization.

Self-Assessment

To evaluate your effectiveness in Leading Courageously, check all boxes below that represent current behavior or performance. Look for patterns: Which core practices represent a development need, a strength, or an excessive use? Recognize that you might have some blind spots. Invite your boss or colleagues to indicate what they have observed in your behavior. Use this assessment to help identify development suggestions that are most relevant to you.

	Development Need	Strength	Excessive Use
Authority	❑ Is uncomfortable using power and authority in a senior leadership role ❑ Is reluctant to provide direction or tell others how to get things done	❑ Uses authority to convey decisions in a manner that enhances commitment to actions and plans ❑ Takes charge readily	❑ Uses authoritarian, command-and-control style that stifles creativity and disempowers people ❑ Relies only on position power to influence, rather than balancing that with personal power
Courage	❑ Avoids or is reluctant to take on challenges outside comfort zone ❑ Sits on issues for fear of failure	❑ Takes on difficult issues and challenges that others won't ❑ Displays firmness and resolve when taking a stand	❑ Leaves projects failed or incomplete because confrontational style alienates others ❑ Pursues only the more difficult solutions and becomes a "lone ranger"
Assertiveness	❑ Is unassertive and hesitant to confront or challenge others ❑ Worries too much about offending others	❑ Is strongly assertive when appropriate ❑ Expresses ideas in a direct, no-nonsense fashion	❑ Turns people off (or away) by being unnecessarily direct and insensitive ❑ Wears assertiveness like a badge of courage
Independence	❑ Is deferent to or overly agreeable with others ❑ Tries to conform first and suppresses ideas that are different or don't have obvious support from others	❑ Demonstrates personal conviction and is resolved in pursuing own leadership agenda ❑ Makes tough calls and takes a stand when others won't; does not wait to see whether others agree first	❑ Appears overly opinionated and rigid about doing things a particular way ❑ Acts as a maverick or contrarian, constantly criticizing or presenting a contentious point of view
Influence	❑ Rarely offers ideas that influence peers or superiors ❑ Stays within boundaries and does not advance opinions outside of own areas of expertise	❑ Uses personal power, not just formal authority, to influence others ❑ Shapes senior executives' agendas—opinions consistently carry weight with peers and superiors	❑ Offers opinions that irritate others ❑ Is self-important—attempts to control things beyond own sphere of influence

Development Suggestions

The following section contains development suggestions for each core practice. Having completed the self-assessment, focus on suggestions that correspond to the core practices you identified as a development need or excessive use. Use these suggestions to create your own development plan, making sure to try one or two from each phase. In addition, feel free to create your own or adapt these to best meet your development needs.

Authority

Provide direction without smothering creativity and motivation.

> *If you wish to know what a man is,*
> *place him in authority.*
>
> Yugoslav proverb

Awaken potential:

- **Accept power.** Become accustomed to thinking of yourself as a powerful person. Explore how you use power and what aspects of having power make you comfortable or uncomfortable.

- **Seek feedback.** Ask your direct reports how clear you are about your expectations of them. Obtain feedback about the kind of clarity you provide.

- **Be ready to respond.** Consider how frequently you are in situations that demand a rapid response and personal expertise. When you are in those kinds of circumstances, be ready to exercise both judgment and control.

Align goals:

- **Define your own accountabilities.** Develop a list of your boss' and your peers' areas of responsibility. Work with your peers and your boss to clearly define your areas of accountability. With your peers, look for areas of shared accountability. Create a shared sense of clarity about who is accountable for what; then demonstrate strong leadership in those areas that are yours.

- **Prepare to take charge.** Talk with your boss about his/her expectations about how you will take charge. Explore how the group has been led in the past and what kind of direction is needed now. Talk with peers about how you or they will take charge under different scenarios. Demonstrate a willingness to fill in the gaps.

- **Set expectations.** Establish the results you expect to see from your staff on a weekly, monthly, and quarterly basis. Communicate those expectations with clarity, and follow up on progress in regular staff meetings.

Accelerate performance:

- **Look for a role model.** Meet with a powerful leader whom you admire. Ask that individual to describe how he/she provides direction without being authoritarian.

- **Borrow from history.** Read about historical leaders whom you admire, especially those who have had to take charge of a difficult situation (e.g., war or economic collapse). Consider how to adapt their approaches to your circumstances.

- **Practice using authority.** Seek out assignments that offer opportunities to demonstrate authority, such as a situation that demands fast action or a novel situation such as a start-up or turnaround.

- **Grab the reins.** When you are with coworkers and no one is taking charge but someone needs to lead, don't hesitate to step forward.

- **Give others a chance to lead.** Don't take over in every situation. Encourage others to lead when it is their accountability.

- **Prepare your followers.** Discover how follower readiness affects the choice of leadership approach by reading *The Situational Leader* by Paul Hersey (Center for Leadership Studies, 1984; 2008). Apply what you learn.

- **Be intentional about your leadership.** Read the classic article "How to Choose a Leadership Pattern" by Robert Tannenbaum and Warren Schmidt (*Harvard Business Review*, 1973). Use their guidelines for being intentional about how much authority you exert.

- **Become certified in sailing;** the course requires you to learn how to give clear directions in the captain's role.

- **Peruse more tips.** Review Chapter 7, "Team Leadership," to learn about Authority as it relates to leading your team, and Chapter 15, "Building Collaboration," for additional insights about the use of informal authority to enhance peer collaboration.

EXCESSIVE USE

As an example, if you use a controlling style, this may stifle your team's creativity.
Find out from others what you do that restrains them.
Where do they want more freedom to act?

Courage

Readily take on difficult assignments and challenges.

> *Courage is what it takes to stand up and speak. Courage is also what it takes to sit down and listen.*
>
> Winston Churchill

Awaken potential:

- **Size up your reputation.** Find out from your manager whether he/she would come to you when there is a difficult challenge ahead. Why might you be someone who is not called upon? When are you asked?

- **Ask peers for advice.** Have conversations with your peers about the challenges in your current work setting. Seek feedback on what they believe you can do to act with more courage.

- **Play in your learning zone.** Read *Monday Morning Leadership* by David Cottrell (Cornerstone Leadership Institute, 2002). Pay special attention to Chapter 8. Consider what activities are in your comfort zone, which are in your learning zone, and which are in your "panic" zone. Ask yourself whether you avoid stretching yourself just because it is uncomfortable? What could you do to "play" more in your learning zone?

- **Bite the bullet.** Ask yourself whether you tend to neglect or put off issues that seem difficult or troublesome in favor of new or exciting projects. What tends to hold you back from tackling the tough challenges?

- **Face your fears.** Ask yourself whether you are willing to try something even when the outcome is unknown. Sometimes individuals hold back because they are afraid of making a mistake. Trial and error learning is invaluable in new situations or when innovation is needed.

- **Confront your demons.** Delve into the barriers that stop you from taking action when you are uncomfortable or afraid. Is it perfectionism, fear of looking stupid, worrying about what others will say, or something else? Do you care too much about what that voice in your head says?

Align goals:

- **Tackle difficult challenges.** Make a list of the most difficult challenges facing your function or division in the next six months. Have a conversation with your manager about the expectations of your role to address the challenges.

- **Deal with important problems.** Ask your team and other peers whether there are issues or problems they believe your group is not facing or dealing with. Decide which ones are most important to the business, and delve into them.

Accelerate performance:

- **Learn from the best.** Identify some leaders who truly thrive in tough situations and may even seek them out. What do they do that you do not? What is holding you back?

- **Serve on a task force.** Volunteer to lead the group or be part of it when you hear that a small group or task force is being formed to deal with a big problem in the organization.

- **Ask for help if you procrastinate.** If your issue is procrastinating or not following through when something becomes more difficult, go to your manager or a peer and talk about what you will do to keep the challenge on your radar screen.

- **Collect examples of survivors.** Read books about people who handled difficult challenges, either at work or in their lives. Make notes about what they did and what you could try. Start with one of the many books or films documenting the survival story of Sir Ernest Shackleton.

- **Push your limits.** Consider challenging yourself physically. Learn a new sport like scuba diving, rock climbing, or skiing. Or, push yourself on weekends to do some things out of your comfort zone; use these experiences to know what to expect when you feel scared and to learn how to manage yourself.

EXCESSIVE USE

As an example, if your confrontational style has alienated others, your reputation may limit your advancement potential. Ask your manager for feedback and suggestions.

5

LEADING COURAGEOUSLY

Assertiveness

Be direct, assertive, and appropriately tough-minded.

Standing in the middle of the road is very dangerous; you get knocked down by the traffic from both sides.

Margaret Thatcher

Awaken potential:

- **Look in the mirror.** Would others describe you as too aggressive? If you pride yourself in being demanding and direct, consider whether there are times when you go overboard. If so, when?

- **Figure out when you are assertive.** Even people who are unassertive in some circumstances are assertive in others. Remember situations and people you have faced. When do you hesitate to confront others vs. express your opinions?

- **Check your reputation.** Ask people around you how they would describe you—as unassertive, assertive, or aggressive. Why do they say that, and what can you learn from their observations?

- **Pay attention to how you communicate during meetings.** After meetings do you find yourself thinking about things you wish you would have said? Did you articulate your ideas effectively, wait too long to speak up, or did you not speak up at all?

Align goals:

- **Set priorities for advocacy.** Write down your primary challenges and accountabilities. Which ones require you to be especially strong in standing up for your views or advocating for what your area needs? Find out from your team in what areas they would like you to be more of an advocate for their needs or points of view with your peers. Are you a strong enough voice?

- **Assert your needs.** Consider your peers' areas of responsibility and how they overlap with yours. What do you need from them to be successful? What do they need from you to be successful? Initiate a dialogue with each of your peers about what you need from each other. Be clear.

- **Confront performance issues.** Determine how you deal with performance problems in your group. Make a list of those problems. When do you provide feedback? What action could you take to deal with each item more quickly?

Accelerate performance:

- **Toughen up.** Read *How to Grow a Backbone: 10 Strategies for Gaining Power and Influence at Work* by Susan Marshall (Contemporary Books, 2000) for tips and exercises to help you act more courageously.

- **Develop a point of view** for your area as it relates to company strategy. What is important for other managers to know and use? Find venues to communicate that point of view.

- **Eliminate words that soften your position** such as "I guess," "maybe," or "I'm not sure, but." Replace them with phrases such as "in my opinion," "I believe that," or "I have noticed."

- **Prepare to be assertive.** Every time you attend a cross-functional meeting, think about the agenda in advance and write down one or two key points you want to get across. Make sure you bring them up.

- **Tackle a tough issue.** Volunteer for a turnaround experience where you know that being tough-minded will be critical.

- **Confront issues right away.** Make sure you provide your team members with real-time feedback—both positive and for change—on a regular basis.

- **Practice assertiveness** off the job as well as on the job. Say what you think while continuing to keep an interest in others' points of view.

- **Keep seeking feedback.** Once you demonstrate more assertiveness, seek regular feedback from trusted peers. How did you come across in your last meeting? How could you be even more effective?

EXCESSIVE USE

As an example, if you are overly aggressive about an issue, you may dominate conversations, discourage feedback and idea-sharing, and intimidate others. Ask your manager and team about their observations and suggestions for changes you can make in your behavior and communication.

Independence

Act independently and with conviction.

"Do what you feel in your heart to be right—
for you'll be criticized anyway."

Eleanor Roosevelt

Awaken potential:

- **Don't wait to take a stand.** Reflect on the extent to which you seek approval for your ideas before advancing them. How often do you ask others to confirm what you are thinking when that may not be necessary? Do you wait to take a stand until you are sure others will like it? Do you always make sure your boss will approve? Do you try to find out what your boss wants and thinks before you state an opinion or make a decision?

- **Stop second-guessing.** Consider how much you second-guess yourself on major decisions. Thinking independently and a willingness to stand alone are part of being a good leader.

- **Stop hedging your bets.** Finish this sentence: "If I were more self-assured and convinced about my ideas, I would…" To what extent do you hedge your bets when you state an opinion? For example, do you rely on someone else in authority to give weight to your ideas?

Align goals:

- **Practice informing instead of seeking approval.** Talk to your manager about how frequently he/she observes you looking for guidance or approval. Ask what things should be brought forward for approval and where the manager wants to be kept informed *after* the fact. As new things come up that don't fit those criteria, email your manager that you will proceed with your decision unless you hear otherwise in the next twenty-four hours. Better yet, practice informing after the fact instead of asking for approval before you finalize.

- **Develop your team to act independently.** Have a conversation with your team about when they think it is important to check with others at higher levels in the organization and when it is better to simply move ahead and inform, rather than ask for approval.

Accelerate performance:

- **Look for a mentor** who is highly independent, willing to make tough calls, and able to take an unpopular stand. Talk about situations you face and learn how that individual might approach them.

- **Just do it.** Stop before you ask for additional input on a decision or idea. Ask yourself, "To what extent am I just playing it safe, or will additional input really change my mind?"

- **Make educated guesses.** Don't let your lack of experience hold you back from making educated guesses—as long as you label them as that. Make a list of areas in which you are expert, areas in which you are still learning, and areas in which you have no experience. State opinions boldly in areas where you know you are experienced, and state an opinion along with the fact that you are still learning in other areas.

- **Determine when to consult peers.** Find out from your peers when they want you to check in with them and when they just want you to decide. When do they expect to hear your independent opinion?

- **Clarify your interest in input.** Tell people how open you are to other ideas when you make a pronouncement, especially if you tend to decide on a course of action that others then take as an absolute.

- **Audit your actions** once per month, rating them in terms of how well you made a tough call, stated your views, or confronted performance issues.

- **Keep a journal** of your progress, noting particularly when you have overcome a tendency to hesitate or second-guess yourself.

EXCESSIVE USE

As an example, if you come across as if your mind is completely made up and there is no room to influence you, read *The Seven Habits of Highly Effective People* by Stephen R. Covey (Free Press, 1989). Practice the fifth habit: "Seek first to understand, then to be understood."

Influence upwards and across the organization.

"Eagles don't flock, you have to find them one at a time."

Ross Perot

Awaken potential:

- **Take an inventory.** Reflect on how you deal with your manager or other senior leaders when you have to influence, convince, or dissuade. How comfortable are you stepping forward; how often do you do that? How does your style of influencing superiors differ from how you lead your team?

- **Reflect on your influence.** Think about a time when you were not as influential with senior leaders as you wanted to be. What was the situation? What did you do or not do? What could you have done to be more effective?

- **Ask for what you want.** To what extent do you wish your manager would "let" you do things differently? Why not have that conversation? People who lack influence may spend considerable time talking with others about how ineffective their managers' actions are. If that sounds familiar, what conversations are you hesitating to have?

Align goals:

- **Test your manager.** Find out how much your manager wants you to push back. Talk with your manager at a time when things are not in crisis about how much you are expected to challenge, test ideas, and raise conflicting points of view.

- **Invite dissent.** Encourage your own team to bring you information that is contrary to your thinking. Explain that you want them to help prevent you from following an ineffective path. Engage in constructive dialogue about which path will lead to better results.

Accelerate performance:

- **Prepare to influence key stakeholders.** Create a list of key stakeholders in the organization. What do you know about them that can help shape your influence strategy? Develop tactics based on their styles.

- **Learn how to use multiple styles of influence.** "Push" strategies mostly entail logic and authority (e.g., "Believe me because I know more," or "Believe me, I have thought this through."). "Pull" strategies require figuring out "What's in it for me?"—how your audience will benefit if they accept your idea.

- **Gather stories.** Ask those with more tenure in your organization about how they have seen others successfully manage up in a way that had impact. What have others done to make this work?

- **Cultivate your point of view.** Decide what is most important to convey in advance of a group meeting with your peers and your manager. For something that may be controversial, plan to draw on ideas beyond your own.

- **Express your opinion.** If there is something that you believe a peer is doing that will lead to failure or a sub-par result, make a point to bring out your opinion. You can do this in a way that is non-judgmental such as, "I see potential negative effects from this action, and I wonder whether you have considered it."

- **Don't stand on the sidelines.** Don't let your peer fail while you stand by and watch. If you hear a lot of talk about something not working well in your peer's area, find a way to bring him or her that information without breaching confidentiality. Ask yourself, "If I were in that position, what would I want to know?"

- **Manage your boss.** Read the classic article "Managing Your Boss" by John Gabarro and John Kotter (*Harvard Business Review*, 2005). Use the ideas to create an action plan for yourself.

- **Don't give up** just because you raised an idea once and it was dismissed. Sometimes influence takes several tries. People may resist until they see how much you really believe what you are conveying.

EXCESSIVE USE

As an example, if you are constantly critiquing or presenting a contentious point of view, others may not listen. Ask others how this behavior affects the impact you make. How valuable is it, and when is it irritating? Who else could take on that role?

5

LEADING COURAGEOUSLY

Coach Others on Leading Courageously

When coaching others, focus on the core practices that were identified as either a development need or excessive use in the self-assessment at the beginning of this chapter. Identify and adapt any relevant development suggestions. Additional coaching tips are provided in the following table for some adverse leadership behaviors. For more information review Chapter 4, "Coach Others."

Coaching Suggestions

Behavior		Awaken	Align	Accelerate
Authority	Is insecure in a leadership role	• Discuss how others ascribe power or expertise to an individual based on role. Help the individual understand that the more senior the role, the more visible and observed one is. Probe to better understand the person's discomfort. • Talk about the parts of the job where setting a direction is highly necessary.	• Discuss how much direction or expectation-setting the most effective leaders do. How does that help achieve results? • Find someone whom you both agree is an effective leader and clearly in charge. How does the person complement formal authority with personal power? What can the person model from the behavior of that leader?	• During your one-on-ones, talk about your own experiences with power and leadership authority. Use real examples to help illustrate the choices you make. • Pick a specific project or initiative that will be more successful if the person takes more authority. Identify specific behavior for the person to practice, and observe it in action.
	Is reluctant to provide direction	• Discuss how people actually want their managers to lead, set a direction, and provide a sense of confidence about the future. • Brainstorm specific situations where teams spun their wheels or were inefficient because they had no direction. Have conversations about how direction-setting can solve or prevent problems.	• Encourage the person to discuss with the team specific situations where he/she made no progress or was inefficient due to a lack of direction. What consequences were observed? • Identify current situations where people may need more direction. Ask for current or upcoming instances.	• Work together to formulate a plan for providing more direction. Use specific projects identified by the team. • Provide real-time feedback when you see the person taking charge and when you see the person holding back.

Behavior		Awaken	Align	Accelerate
Courage	*Avoids challenges*	• Together examine what prevents the person from stepping up. How can these barriers be minimized? • Rate situations or issues with which the person is dealing in terms of the amount of courage needed to address them.	• Help the person build a game plan for addressing the simplest, the next hardest, and the most difficult. • Identify an internal mentor of someone who takes challenges in stride. What observations can the person make from observing that mentor?	• Find an assignment you can give that will demand operating in a gray area, outside of the person's comfort zone. Keep the challenge realistic and doable, but deliberately choose a situation that will be uncomfortable. • When you are aware that people are making decisions with which the person does not agree, point out what you see happening and ask why the person is being silent.
	Sits on ideas	• Discuss individuals whom the person observes having courage and how/why that helps the business succeed. • Talk about the positive things that happen when someone does not let an issue languish. Provide some examples of when you observed the person holding back. What were the consequences?	• Have the person invite peers and you to draw out his/her participation in conversations. Sometimes a prompt will help the person express an idea that he/she was considering. • Have the person observe a key peer who offers insight regularly. How does that person communicate so that others are receptive? What can be modeled from that person?	• After meetings, ask what the person wished he/she would have said. Ask the person to figure out what the obstacle was. • Create a plan to circle back with key stakeholders to voice the unsaid opinion after the fact. How will the person influence them?
Assertiveness	*Is unassertive*	• If you don't have much opportunity to observe the person in action, suggest that the person keep a record of situations and his/her responses. • Show how a person who does not receive tough performance feedback is actually hurt in the long run (e.g., lack of respect from others or inability to grow).	• Be careful of accepting upward delegation. Sometimes people who lack assertiveness try to hide behind their managers' actions or directives. • Leverage your human resources business partner to role-play difficult conversations that the person needs to have with direct reports or peers.	• Help the person prepare for key conversations. During your interactions with this person, encourage him/her to express thoughts and concerns. • Provide feedback at every opportunity regarding whether the person is not assertive enough or too aggressive. Real-time feedback is needed to be able to understand the impact of one's behavior.

Behavior		Awaken	Align	Accelerate
Assertiveness	*Worries about offending others*	• Have a conversation about the implications of being "nice" and how it prevents others from performing to the best of their ability. • Talk about the value of courageous conversations. Point out the positive outcomes for the organization when people have made their points of view clear.	• Have the person circle back with peers about times when they felt the person was less courageous than needed. What held the person back? • Identify an internal mentor who is known for being firm but fair. Have the person review upcoming situations where demonstrating toughness may be needed.	• Encourage the person to practice providing difficult performance feedback. Practice a specific situation during your one-on-one. • Have the person practice the technique of being "overly harsh" or "overly offensive" then pare it back to acceptable. Plot any natural tendency to be soft on a continuum.
Independence	*Is overly deferent*	• Have a discussion about confidence and independent actions. Why does the person believe checking with you first is appropriate? • Brainstorm what can happen if the person only pays attention to managers' thinking or constantly defers to others. Discuss how that behavior could affect career options.	• Describe your role and what you need in terms of the person's independent decision-making so you don't have to make all of the calls. • Talk about some visible examples of individuals standing up for what they think and why that was good for the business.	• Rather than giving your opinion first when asked, put the person in the position of having to reveal his/her thinking first. Then ask, "Is this your best judgment?" to see how the person adapts. • Probe to see if the person has any other opinions or options or just seems to be second-guessing what you want (e.g., ask "What solution did you discard because you thought I might not like it?").
	Tries to conform	• Explore what it means to the individual to "do things right." How does that constrain good ideas? • Talk about how conformity is a moving target and in the eye of the beholder. With whom or what is the person trying to conform?	• Talk about someone in the organization who is a non-conformist. When is that of value, and under what circumstances does it go too far? • Have the person review with peers when they believed the person's conformity inhibited success. What were the consequences they observed?	• Give the individual an assignment for which you will not provide direction to promote independent thinking. Monitor your own need for providing strong and clear expectations. • Encourage the person to promote ideas for doing things differently. Set a challenge for the person to bring one "breakthrough" idea to your one-on-ones. Reinforce the importance by taking time to review the impact of those ideas together.

Behavior	Awaken	Align	Accelerate
Fails to influence	• Provide feedback about instances you have seen when the person could have stepped up to influence. Discuss what actions the person could have taken. • Explore what it means to have personal power and to influence without authority. Provide feedback about where you think the person's gaps are.	• Explore what is required of senior leaders in being influential up and across the organization. Help the person see those responsibilities as much broader than what was required before. • Identify specific projects or initiatives in which the person's influence will promote success. Together develop a plan for the person to be more influential within those.	• Help the person create an influence map to better understand strategies and tactics for adapting an influence style based on the people the person is trying to influence. • Provide an opportunity for cross-functional leadership where direct lines of authority are not a given. Debrief the person's learning regularly so that adjustments to influence style can be made throughout.
Stays within own comfort zone	• Talk about the progression from being successful by having expertise to being successful by being a good leader who relies on others to have expertise. Explore the negative aspects of having only one area of expertise or of not offering an opinion because "it's not my job." • Talk through the negative aspects of "silo" mentality or actions in a vacuum. With whom does the person need to be most closely aligned?	• Encourage the person to meet with individuals in other areas of the organization who have completely different responsibilities and expertise. Identify things that might be learned from them or areas in which they overlap. • Encourage the person to circle back with peers. Where do they feel that the person could offer more insight or opinions?	• Have the individual lead or participate in a task force on a topic in which the person does not have expertise. Give the person a chance to lead when it is not possible to rely on expert power. • Figure out the situations that occur on a regular basis where an opinion can be offered even though the person does not have functional expertise. Identify them specifically.

5

Tips for Coaching in a Global Environment

Leading Courageously may be practiced or expressed differently within other cultures. This might affect how you approach coaching. Try to keep an open mind, avoid generalizations, and continue gathering data as you gain experience with another culture. Consider these suggestions:

Authority: Explore how leaders in that culture effectively take charge and set direction. How does personal power get expressed? What is acceptable behavior for confronting one's superiors or making demands on team members? When you see behavior that is overly aggressive or too controlling from a chain of command perspective, have a dialogue about what your expectations are for enhancing engagement or empowerment. You may need to provide training to individuals who need to find other ways to lead and influence others.

Courage: Sometimes there is an element of risk in confronting difficult issues. Risk-taking is not encouraged in all cultures. The practice of "begging for forgiveness rather than asking for permission" may not be welcomed by managers who expect their people to obey rules. Ask the person you are coaching what the environment for risk-taking is like in that culture and organization.

Assertiveness: Consider how assertiveness and tough-mindedness may vary based on whether one is dealing with corporate headquarters or with local teams or customers. Offer suggestions and provide examples for using different approaches to handle these situations. Be careful about making the assumption that because someone is quieter in team meetings, he or she is not assertive or not a strong leader. Have a conversation about leadership and exchange ideas about what effective leadership looks like in your culture and in that individual's culture.

Independence: Learn all you can about the culture of the individual with whom you are dealing—is it collectivistic or individualistic? Does it promote security and predictability or entrepreneurial risk-taking and change? Those elements will affect what constitutes effective leadership in those cultures. Help the person understand your expectations for speaking up or speaking out. Sometimes you may not see a high degree of participation simply because the expectations are not understood.

Influence: Influence can take many forms, particularly when trying to influence the opinions of senior leaders. It is often done informally, outside of regular meetings. Access to senior leaders may be extremely restricted in some places, whereas leaders in other places may be more visible and approachable. Find out what forms of influence are available to the people you are coaching. Help them understand the politics of influence in their culture.

A Case Study in Leading Courageously

Leading Courageously provides clarity to your own team as well as influencing peers or upper management. However, influence doesn't just happen; it requires action. As you read about David Wang's situation, reflect on what you've learned about Leading Courageously in this chapter and consider how you could help David demonstrate greater skill in Leading Courageously and be successful in his leadership role.

Influencing Up With Intention

David Wang had a problem. The vice president in charge of research and development was an intense, passionate leader who handled everything with confidence and assuredness. David had never worked for someone like him before; his previous managers had been more approachable and supportive. Things were going along fine between the two of them until David ran into a roadblock with one of the products he supported that was scheduled for launch within two months. David had stepped into the role of leading the product design teams halfway through the process.

The more he understood about the new product technically, the more problems he saw. Twice in his biweekly one-on-one with his manager, he mentioned that it was not going to be easy to meet the product release date. His manager bristled at the suggestion that there could be a delay and said, "To get around obstacles, you just have to be creative; that's why you are here." Each time David tried to raise the possibility that there was a flaw in the design that needed to be corrected, his manager brushed him off, telling David that he was just new to the product.

Yesterday two of David's team members came to him with data showing just the flaw that David had feared. Clearly they were expecting David to take the problem up the chain. He took the data to his boss, who started grilling David about the information. The boss told David that his team members were being overly analytical and simply succumbing to analysis paralysis. "You have to be decisive in product design. Just keep things moving—this is a critical launch for us."

David left discouraged. When his team members asked how the conversation went, he merely shook his head. His manager was discounting his message, and David was uncertain what to do. As he reflected on the interactions, trying to figure out why he wasn't being heard, he realized that all he had brought to his manager were suggestions or complaints. Had he ever really said, "This is what I believe and we have to change course"? He had to admit he was afraid to be direct; there was something about his vice president's intensity that intimidated him. Therefore, he was hinting at the issues and expecting his manager to read between the lines and reach the conclusion that David was afraid to voice.

David realized that it was time to be more courageous and probably not just with his manager.

David's Leadership Development Plan

Following is a sample development plan for David Wang. Research on leadership development has shown that leaders learn through experience and that this learning is optimized through the use of an individual development plan. A successful plan includes new experiences and introduces the leader to new conversations and tools. Suggestions included in previous sections may stimulate your thinking about additional possibilities for David's development.

LEADERSHIP DEVELOPMENT PLAN FOR DAVID WANG

DEVELOPMENT GOAL

Goal: To strengthen my skills in Leading Courageously

Desired Outcomes—results I want to see from developing this skill

Self: I will find new ways to have an effect on and persuade my manager or my peers.

Team: My team will have increased confidence in my ability to be an advocate for our business.

Organization: We will spend product development resources on the highest value-add ideas.

Self-Understanding—strengths that I can build on and development needs I can address

Strengths: My business acumen and ability to get things done.

Development Needs: Learn to work with powerful people who can be intimidating or are in a position to make decisions about me.

Business Context—challenges in my business environment that require this skill

Challenges I face in my business setting include advocating for new products throughout the organization, gaining resources or support from my manager or others, and moving viable products through the pipeline.

DEVELOPMENT ACTIONS

AWAKEN

- Keep a weekly journal in which I track ideas or opinions that I wanted to tell my peers or my boss but did not. Figure out how much I am sitting on ideas and why. Is it out of fear or from telling myself, "That's not my job"? Or, did I once know someone who did that so much that I have inadvertently cut all of those behaviors out of my repertoire?

- Compare myself objectively to Deborah, who is really strong in this area. Where do I fall short, and why? What does she do that I don't? Am I letting her carry the contrary opinions when I should be taking on some of them myself?

- Determine how often I use push versus pull strategies.

LEADERSHIP DEVELOPMENT PLAN FOR DAVID WANG

ALIGN

- Have a conversation with my boss about the assumptions I have about what he expects of me. I especially need to know how he would like to handle it when I have an idea or opinion that diverges from his thinking or ideas.

- Figure out another setting in which I need to influence or speak my mind even when I am not invited or am not comfortable.

ACCELERATE

- Do some reading on the topic, including *Power and Influence* by John Kotter (Free Press, 1985). Use the ideas in his book to create additional action steps for myself.

- Talk to Deborah, who is highly influential and always willing to put her opinion out there. Find out whether she worked on this or comes by it naturally. How does she make the choice to speak up or not? Does she ever feel she is out on a limb?

- Don't give up just because others disagree. Raise my ideas again. Others might be debating because they want to see how much I really believe in my ideas. I will try bringing it up in a different way—like trying for a pull rather than a push strategy.

- Observe how others influence, debate, and voice contrary opinions. I'll try them more than once since it takes more than one experiment to discover how something works.

DEVELOPMENT SUCCESS FACTORS

Timeline: Within the next six months

Support Needed:

- My own team to the extent I tell them what I intend to do or try.

- Deborah's willingness to help me and even step in behind me when I am the one out on a limb.

Indicators of Success:

- There are fewer times when I keep my opinions and ideas to myself for fear of irritating my boss.

- My peers like to debate and exchange ideas with me because it is energizing and helpful.

- There are no instances of a project or business failing where I knew better but said nothing.

5

LEADING COURAGEOUSLY

An Example of Coaching to Lead Courageously

David Wang's goal was to strengthen his skills in Leading Courageously. Here are some steps David's manager could take using the Awaken, Align, Accelerate framework to coach David in this area:

AWAKEN	**Increase INSIGHT**	Encourage David to complete a multi-rater feedback assessment. Look together for any gaps in his perceptions. Help him understand the effects and implications of his behavior, especially on peers. Provide feedback about David's lack of directness in conversations with you.
	MOTIVATE change	Help David reflect on previous projects where taking a stand or being more direct could have produced a different outcome. Explore the consequences of not making any changes; identify consequences for him personally as well as his projects.
ALIGN	**PLAN goals**	Ask David what would enable him to handle the current product launch more successfully. Focus on what he could change to improve his performance and effectiveness on future projects. Work together to construct a leadership development plan similar to the sample provided in this chapter.
	ALIGN expectations	Focus on observing David's interactions in meetings with others on the team. Provide feedback afterward about actions he took that influenced others positively or negatively. Coach him on making necessary changes to improve his effectiveness and influence.
ACCELERATE	**CREATE teachable moments**	Introduce David to Peter, who might be a good mentor in this area. Invite David to debrief each stage-gate meeting one-on-one to discuss where he could have shown more courage and how he could have been more effective.
	TRACK progress	Discuss what kinds of changes will be visible to others. Work with David to evaluate progress toward his goals. Express appreciation for his courage—especially when he succeeds in presenting an alternative point of view that wins your support.

Results: Measuring Impact

David Wang made rapid progress on his plan during the first few months, fueled by his desire to get the product design fixed and the project back on track. He didn't try every action step, and he found some activities were more helpful than others. However, he got the new product launched and made progress on becoming more direct. His new skills in Leading Courageously allowed David to:

- Advocate for course correction successfully, winning more confidence and trust from his team.

- Express his opinions and ideas without hesitation, especially in conversations with his manager.

- Exercise greater persuasiveness with senior leaders in other functions.

- Debate with peers about where research and development resources should be invested in the next cycle.

- Win support for his favorite proposal.

6

Creating Alignment

Leaders who drive organizational alignment direct the work of their functions or areas of responsibility in support of overall business strategy and goals. They create a shared understanding and commitment to the organization's direction and plans. They see opportunities and initiate changes in the culture, systems, structure, or processes that better integrate teams and departments to improve overall operating effectiveness and organizational performance. They communicate a vision for the future and provide a clear rationale for change. Ultimately, they are clear about where the organization is going, and what it needs to do to get there.

Factor	Competency	Core Practice
Leading People	Leading Courageously	Direction
Thinking and Deciding	Creating Alignment	Diagnosis
Achieving	Team Leadership	Change
Relating to People	Developing Leaders	Motivation
Managing Work		Coordination
Managing Self		

Many leaders have difficulty translating well-crafted business strategies into tangible results. The challenge for some is their inability to align the strategic direction with the systems, structure, resources, skills, and culture to ensure execution and achievement of results. People cannot align their actions with the organization's priorities if they lack an understanding of the strategy, its performance, and the ways in which their actions affect business results.

Moving the organization and its people toward an ever-changing state of alignment is central to the work of leaders. Creating Alignment means gaining commitment from, and coordinating the activities of, the people the organization depends on to achieve its objectives. The work of alignment is about improving the organizational fit between the business strategy and its market, between an individual and the organization's goals, and among internal systems and processes that reinforce the work to be done. Alignment requires specifying and creating a shared mindset around the change needed to improve internal effectiveness and external competitiveness. It also means gaining commitment and coordinating the activities of people. When a company's activities are designed and combined in a way that is unique and difficult to imitate, this provides a competitive advantage that is both valuable and potentially sustainable. Achieving deep alignment so that all organizational activities support and reinforce its strategic position can be a powerful source of differentiation.

How Leaders at Different Levels Create Alignment

	Managers	Function Leaders	Senior Executives
Direction	Establishes a clear line of sight between individual roles and organizational objectives.	Focuses people on the organization's strategy, goals, and priorities.	Shapes a compelling vision for the organization as a whole.
Diagnosis	Evaluates structure and process of teams against desired results.	Analyzes fit between activities and goals to ensure they support and reinforce each other.	Serves as an organizational "architect," ensuring that the structure and culture support the overall strategy.
Change	Enrolls team members when implementing change efforts.	Pursues change plans that align structures, systems, and processes in support of the organization's goals.	Sponsors crucial change initiatives.
Motivation	Creates a sense of enthusiasm and ownership in team members for their work and responsibilities.	Inspires people to make changes and improvements.	Inspires commitment to the organization's direction, priorities, and plans for change.
Coordination	Facilitates efforts to synchronize work unit activities.	Integrates efforts to improve alignment across teams and functions.	Optimizes the contributions from all parts of the business to achieve desired results.

Self-Assessment

To evaluate your effectiveness in Creating Alignment, check all boxes below that represent current behavior or performance. Look for patterns: Which core practices represent a development need, a strength, or an excessive use? Recognize that you might have some blind spots. Invite your boss or colleagues to indicate what they have observed in your behavior. Use this assessment to help identify development suggestions that are most relevant to you.

	Development Need	Strength	Excessive Use
Direction	☐ Allows staff to operate with an incomplete understanding of the organization's direction. ☐ Spends very little or no time clarifying organizational priorities or line of sight.	☐ Ensures direct reports and others focus their time and effort on accomplishing the organization's key priorities. ☐ Helps staff see how their work contributes to implementing the organization's strategy and goals.	☐ Overemphasizes top-down organizational direction; allows little or no opportunity for bottom-up change recommendations. ☐ Treats everything as a high priority, leaving others with little sense of what is most important.
Diagnosis	☐ Ignores or seems unaware of the conflict among competing goals, activities, systems, structures, or processes. ☐ Doesn't recognize the issues and allows the organization to under-perform or work at cross-purposes.	☐ Understands and uses good diagnostic models to aid analysis of fit. ☐ Accurately diagnoses and interprets the fit, or lack of fit, among organizational activities and goals; recommends changes or improvements.	☐ Overanalyzes or over-studies problems; too slow to convert diagnoses into an action plan for change. ☐ Readily sees the business need for change and moves too quickly without considering culture or other intangibles.
Change	☐ Supports activities in isolation from or that are inconsistent with the overall business strategy. ☐ Accepts the status quo.	☐ Aligns change plans and activities with the business strategy to improve performance. ☐ Sees opportunities and leads change in a way that improves the organization's competitive advantage.	☐ Creates unnecessary duplication and overlap of effort. ☐ Creates confusion and instability by making constant changes.
Motivation	☐ Focuses primarily on short-term goals and objectives. ☐ Communications about need for change are vague, uninspired, and unrelated to business needs.	☐ Achieves commitment to a direction for the future. ☐ Communicates a compelling and rational business case for change and improvement.	☐ Makes assumptions that others are prepared and eager for change. ☐ Communicates messages about need for change that sound threatening and create fear or resistance.
Coordination	☐ Allows teams and departments to work in silos or at cross-purposes. ☐ Is unwilling to consider tradeoffs or make compromises to improve overall alignment.	☐ Coordinates activities of different teams and departments so they support and reinforce each other. ☐ Actively engages other teams and functions to learn how change in one's own area can improve overall alignment.	☐ Creates an overly complex structure with too many interdependencies. ☐ Proposes a vision or direction that is too lofty and ignores reality.

Development Suggestions

The following section contains development suggestions for each core practice. Having completed the self-assessment, focus on suggestions that correspond to the core practices you identified as a development need or excessive use. Use these suggestions to create your own development plan, making sure to try one or two from each phase. In addition, feel free to create your own or adapt these to best meet your development needs.

Direction

Focus people on the organization's strategy, goals, and priorities.

A leader takes people where they want to go.
A great leader takes people where they don't necessarily
want to go but ought to be.

Rosalynn Carter

Awaken potential:

- **Get in sync.** Discuss the organization's strategic direction with your manager to help you deepen your understanding and get in sync with what the organization is trying to accomplish. If you need more information, ask your manager for additional background, reading material, or to recommend other people with whom to discuss these issues.

- **Get aligned.** Reflect upon your area of responsibility. How can your function best support the overall direction of the organization or contribute to business results? How can you involve your staff in this discussion? Develop a succinct, clear description of the organization's goals and strategy—and the role your function plays. Test this with your manager, and use any feedback that will sharpen your thinking.

- **Shape your role.** Reflect on your role in facilitating the organization's direction. Review Chapter 5, "Leading Courageously," for additional suggestions for powerfully shaping others' thinking about your role.

- **Revitalize your vision.** Learn what should be included in your vision statement and get some tips about how to proceed. Develop a vision of what a better-aligned organization looks like and discuss with key stakeholders. Read "Building Your Company's Vision" by James Collins and Jerry Porras (*Harvard Business Review,*

1996) or the "Envision the Future" chapter in *The Leadership Challenge: How to Keep Getting Extraordinary Things Done in Organizations* by James Kouzes and Barry Posner (Jossey-Bass, 2007).

Align goals:

- **Set direction.** Read *Morrisey on Planning, A Guide to Strategic Thinking: Building Your Planning Foundation* by George Morrisey (Jossey-Bass, 1995). How might you set direction for your function? Share your ideas with your manager.

- **Articulate direction.** Know and understand the strategic direction of your organization so that you can communicate this to others and articulate the impact on your function. Is your organization's goal to grow? If so, how? Does the organization intend to enter new markets or geographies? Will there be a particular emphasis on productivity, efficiency, or increasing margins? What initiatives is the organization undertaking to increase engagement of the workforce?

- **Develop a shared mindset.** Facilitate strategic planning with your staff to clarify your function's vision, mission, and priorities. Talk with your staff to build a shared mindset about the direction of your organization and create clear line of sight. Review the core practices "Long-Term Perspective" and "Strategic Scope" in Chapter 9 along with "Participation" in Chapter 16 for tips on getting this accomplished.

- **Reinforce goal alignment.** Make time in your regular staff meetings to talk about business goals and how your area supports that direction. Help your direct reports broaden their view and deepen their understanding.

Accelerate performance:

- **Learn together.** Develop a better understanding of strategy with your direct reports. Select and distribute pre-reading to your direct reports, such as *Blue Ocean Strategy: How to Create Uncontested Market Space and Make Competition Irrelevant* by W. Chan Kim and Renée Mauborgne (Harvard Business Press, 2005) or *Competitive Strategy: Techniques for Understanding Industries and Competitors* by Michael Porter (Free Press, 1998). Devote staff time to discuss what you learned and implications for your function.

- **Analyze time allocation.** Assess where your direct reports are spending their time. If necessary, help them shift the amount of time they are giving to various responsibilities so their time allocation reflects the priority or importance of the activity.

- **Test your communication.** See if you and your staff can pass the "What's in it for them?" test. Does your communication clearly convey and convince others of the value of the organization's direction? Do people see how they directly contribute and the difference they can make?

- **Provide coaching** to your direct reports who manage others about how they can discuss the organization's direction with their staff. Coach them to help their staff see the link between what your function or area does (including what they specifically are responsible for doing) and the organization's performance and success.

- **Maintain focus.** Keep the organization's direction and priorities top of mind. Invite staff to question or challenge you whenever they suspect this focus is becoming blurred or diluted.

EXCESSIVE USE

As an example, if you treat everything as a high priority, others will not know what is most important. Continuously communicate, clarify, and reinforce the most important goals.

Diagnosis

Analyze fit between activities and goals to ensure they support and reinforce each other.

"At general management's core is strategy: defining a company's position, making trade-offs, and forging fit among activities."

Michael Porter

Awaken potential:

- **Reflect upon the alignment** among the key elements in your organization's design and business strategy. Read "What is Strategy" by Michael Porter (*Harvard Business Review*, 1996) to learn more about understanding these elements. Then map activities in your function or area that are designed to deliver or support the organization's strategy. Where could re-design strengthen your strategy implementation and effectiveness?

- **Study organizational fit.** Read *Organizational Development and Change* by Thomas Cummings and Christopher Worley (South-Western College Pub, 2004) to learn about the design components that comprise organizational fit at different levels (e.g., individual, group, and organization).

- **Engage your staff in diagnosing the culture** within your function to assess its fit with the business strategy. Meet with staff to analyze current strengths and weaknesses of your business strategy. What aspects of the culture can be reinforced or altered to achieve improved, sustainable results?

- **Find a useful model.** Learn about how experts view and diagnose organizational alignment. Look for a model that can help you think more systemically about analyzing organizational alignment (e.g., Weisbord's Six-Box Model, Galbraith's Star Model, or Kotter's Organization Dynamics Model).

Align goals:

- **Assess internal alignment.** Involve your direct reports in a discussion of the internal factors that affect your group. What are the key employee competencies? Are they aligned with current business goals? If not, how can you leverage strengths or minimize weaknesses? Are people working cooperatively toward a common strategic goal, or is there internal competition? Compare group strengths, weaknesses, and goals with those of your organization. Identify any gaps.

- **Align your teams.** Evaluate whether you have aligned *team* or *group-level* design components (e.g., team goals, tasks, task structure, team or group composition, and team dynamics) with each other and with the overarching organizational-level design to maximize the output and performance of your function.

- **Align jobs.** Diagnose whether design components for each job (e.g., tasks, task significance, variety, autonomy, and performance feedback at the individual level) are aligned with the organization's design as well as the individual's personal characteristics, motivations, and skills.

Accelerate performance:

- **Engage your key talent** in a discussion of whether and how overall organization design components (e.g., strategy, technology, structure, measurement, systems, and culture) are aligned with each other and the external environment.

- **Assign staff to critically analyze routines** and eliminate or modify inefficient or outdated procedures. Ask, "What is the purpose of this procedure?" and "Where is this procedure failing to meet its objectives?"

- **Benchmark best practices,** both inside and outside your organization. What practices can you apply to your own work and use as a basis for analyzing what and how you might change?

- **Research other operations.** Study how things are done in organizations that don't compete with yours. Arrange to visit people who work in the same function you do. Discuss what you learn with your team and explore what changes could be implemented.

EXCESSIVE USE

As an example, if you over-analyze problems, you may not be taking action in time to make a difference. Don't study the situation to death.

Change

Pursue change plans that align structures, systems, and processes in support of the organization's goals.

*"Management is about coping with complexity.
Leadership, by contrast, is about coping with change."*

John P. Kotter

Awaken potential:

- **Remember transitions.** Reflect upon your personal experiences with change. Read *Managing Transitions: Making the Most of Change,* by William Bridges (Da Capo Lifelong Books, 2009).

- **Assess your ability to effectively lead change.** Thinking in terms of these steps: (1) identify the need for change; (2) communicate and engage others in the change process; (3) plan and oversee implementation of change activities; and (4) integrate successes from change initiatives.

- **Ask your manager for feedback** about what to develop to be most effective as a change leader.

- **Consult with others** who have been successful in leading significant change initiatives either inside or outside your organization. What advice do they have about what change leaders need to do to be effective? What worked? What failed? Make a list of what can be learned from past efforts. Apply lessons from past experience to your own change effort.

Align goals:

- **Create a guiding coalition** of key leaders who support the need for change and will help you establish momentum and motivation in the broader organization. Identify key stakeholders who will be most affected by change, and explore the need for change to gain their support early on.

- **Establish a change management team** to help with your initiative. Talk with peers who lead areas that will be affected; ask for suggestions about people to include on the core team.

Accelerate performance:

- **Provide a clear team charter.** Be specific about the rationale behind the change you want the team to manage and activities you believe they must undertake.

- **Educate the change team** on critical components for effectively leading change. Read "Leading Change: Why Transformation Efforts Fail" by John Kotter (*Harvard Business Review*, 1995) to learn more about preparing the organization for change and involving the right people in the process.

- **Develop a realistic timeline.** While some simple changes can be accomplished quickly, you need to continue action steps over a longer time period if you really want to see different behavior from people. Put a project plan in place to sustain the change effort over time.

- **Create a good communications strategy** so that information about activities, successes, and benefits are shared and understood by an increasingly larger audience.

- **Stay involved with the change team.** Ask for regular status reports and updates. Serve as the coach. Help the team by removing obstacles and providing financial, human, or other resources.

- **Find a mentor** who has implemented change successfully and ask for his/her feedback on your efforts.

EXCESSIVE USE

As an example, if you make constant changes in your organizational structure or processes, you may create confusion and instability. Ask someone to observe your pacing and monitor the organization's tolerance for change.

Motivation

Inspire people to make changes and improvements.

"If you do not change direction, you may end up where you're heading."

Lao Tzu

Awaken potential:

- **Learn how to overcome the immunity to change** in yourself and others. Read *Immunity to Change: How to Overcome It and Unlock the Potential in Yourself and Your Organization* by Robert Kegan and Lisa Laskow Lahey (Harvard Business Press, 2009).

- **Conduct a competitive analysis** to sensitize your team to pressures for change. Research what competitors are doing and how they are winning in the marketplace.

- **Conduct a trend analysis.** Consider the trends that are affecting or likely to affect your business, and discuss their probable impact. Use the STEEP approach to identify societal (e.g., demographic changes or consumer trends), technological, economic, environmental, and political trends that may impact your organization. Convert your findings to a presentation that you can share and discuss with others to heighten their awareness of the need to change.

- **Compare perceptions.** Conduct a gap analysis with your manager or staff to examine how the organization is currently performing compared to its goals or other expectations about how the group *ought* to be performing. Are your perceptions similar? If so, this data can often motivate the need for change.

Align goals:

- **Paint a picture.** Demonstrate the gap between the current state and what your organization could become, to help people understand the need for change. Sensitize people to pressures for change. Involve your team in developing the vision of a better, more positive future for the organization.

- **Look for opportunities to involve others.** The need for change requires communication and involvement (e.g., in conducting gap or trend analyses, or creating a vision). Strive to conduct, expand, and continue your efforts with others whose support you need to implement those changes.

- **Consult senior management.** Seek inspiration from your senior management group. Ask your manager for insights and suggestions about how to align with broader change initiatives that top management may be considering. What information will they need from you? Your manager may also be able to counsel you about the best way to gain their buy-in for initiatives you want to undertake.

Accelerate performance:

- **Develop your voice.** Ask your manager or a colleague for feedback and ideas about how you can improve your message and communicate your ideas persuasively. Strengthen your personal communication and presentation skills to enhance your ability to motivate the need for change.

- **Engage a coach.** Enlist an external communications coach to help you refine your message, speak powerfully, communicate through stories, and build and deliver the most effective presentations.

- **Enroll others.** Develop a plan for approaching, engaging, and involving people who will be most affected and may see things differently. What might they feel they would lose if a change were to occur? Try to articulate what you believe they (and the organization) would gain. Listen to their positions, and search for ways to incorporate their suggestions about how your change can be implemented most effectively.

EXCESSIVE USE

As an example, if your change messages sound threatening, you may create resistance. Focus on the benefits of changing more than the negative consequences of not changing.

Coordination

Integrate efforts to improve alignment across teams and functions.

"Of all the things I have done, the most vital is coordinating the talents of those who work for us and pointing them towards a certain goal."

Walt Disney

Awaken potential:

- **Analyze alignment.** Use an organizational alignment model to reflect upon how your organization is performing and what should be improved or changed. Ask your staff what organizational factors (e.g., systems, structure, skills, staff, style, culture) keep them from performing their work to the best of their ability and why.

- **Consider your culture.** Create an environment where people are encouraged to critique the status quo and suggest improvements. Invite your associates to question policies or procedures that are outdated or out of alignment. Start by questioning them yourself. What improvements are needed in your own area?

Align goals:

- **Make alignment a priority.** Elevate the importance you give to the need for change, alignment, and integration. How do you communicate this now? Set aside time during regular staff meetings to discuss changes and improvements to your function, area, or responsibility.

- **Align with peers.** Talk with your peers about the organization's direction and how your function supports it. Do they understand or see things the same way you do? Can they articulate the roles they (and their areas) will play in advancing the direction and accomplishing the organization's priorities?

- **Focus on interdependencies.** Identify the areas or functions that are most interdependent with yours. Develop a stakeholder map to identify your most critical partners in terms of workflow. Who does your area depend on most to accomplish overall results and achieve success for the company? Meet with your peers to ensure that all are pulling in the same direction, that they understand their parts or roles, and appreciate yours.

Accelerate performance:

- **Evaluate current operations.** Assess the effectiveness and efficiency of your existing systems and processes. Challenge the procedures you have in place. Do other options exist to achieve the results you need?

- **Identify tradeoffs.** Consider where you can make tradeoffs to achieve larger organizational goals. Where can you shift resources or assign staff to accomplish key objectives?

- **Seek customer feedback.** Establish regular feedback mechanisms with your key internal customers. Focus on what they recommend to improve the ways your area could work with theirs.

- **Propose joint projects** co-sponsored by a peer that would improve operating effectiveness and the organization's ability to align, implement strategy, or create a source of differentiation.

- **Maintain focus and attention.** Keep the issue of creating and improving organizational alignment on the table in meetings you attend. Ask others how they believe greater alignment can be achieved or accomplished faster.

- **Increase your contribution.** Ask your manager to assign you to a project or task force that is specifically aimed at improving coordination and alignment among two or more functions or units. If that doesn't exist, volunteer to organize and lead a task force in an area that suffers from a lack of alignment.

- **Learn about participation.** Review the "Participation" core practice in Chapter 16 for ideas about how to engage and coordinate your plans with others outside your area of the business.

EXCESSIVE USE

As an example, if you create overly complex structures with too many interdependencies, people may have difficulty figuring out how to coordinate their efforts—especially when key players change. Strive for a cleaner structure that can be more easily understood and managed.

Coach Others on Creating Alignment

When coaching others, focus on the core practices that were identified as either a development need or excessive use in the self-assessment at the beginning of this chapter. Identify and adapt any relevant development suggestions. Additional coaching tips are provided in the following table for some adverse leadership behaviors. For more information review Chapter 4, "Coach Others."

Coaching Suggestions

	Behavior	Awaken	Align	Accelerate
Direction	*Allows staff to operate in a vacuum*	• Identify a time when the person could have influenced the team to work more closely in accordance with the organization's strategy. • Review the consequences you observed. What could have been avoided or achieved if the person had acted differently?	• Create the opportunity for the person to discuss his/her team's work with your manager. • Pay particular attention to the questions your manager asks. Review together what underlies those questions.	• Encourage the person to assess how staff members are spending their time to ensure time is allocated according to goals and priorities. • Promote regular communication with the person's peers to ensure the team's work supports more than just the person's goals.
	Spends no time clarifying organizational direction	• Review together how the person makes connections between the work of the team and the broader vision or strategy. • Talk together about when and how he/she then connects for staff the work of the team to the broader vision or strategy.	• Use a grid to identify which of the organization's strategic imperatives are goals for your team and ask the person to do that for the team. • Have the person's team complete the grid for their own work. Do all parties see things the same? Facilitate a conversation to promote alignment.	• Model effective aligning communication. Make connections with your team between their work and the organization's strategy. • Have the person create a segment in team meetings in which he/she regularly reviews this for new projects or initiatives that arise.

	Behavior	Awaken	Align	Accelerate
Diagnosis	*Ignores system conflict*	• Have the person identify gaps in organizational alignment using Weisbord's Six-box Model, Galbraith's Star Model, or Kotter's Organization Dynamics Model. • Review the person's findings and discuss your perspective on the subject—how aligned are the two of you?	• Create a review process during the planning process to discuss alignment of each goal with broader strategy. • Involve several key stakeholders in a discussion to widen the person's perspective and provide other input.	• Reinforce regular evaluation and prioritization based on the organizational alignment model. • Facilitate discussion with others to encourage regular dialogue and shared priorities.
	Allows organization to underperform or work at cross-purposes	• Assess what happens when the person evaluates team performance toward alignment. What indicators does the person use for evaluation? • Provide a recent example of where you observed his/her team working at cross-purposes. What were the consequences?	• Identify the cycles you personally use to review performance on organizational alignment goals. Have the person sit in on one with you. • Create a future cycle to evaluate performance toward alignment goals with other key stakeholders.	• Routinely discuss alignment in quarterly performance reviews. Provide the person with an opportunity to review challenges and successes. • Reinforce when you observe the person making distinct choices to facilitate alignment.
Change	*Allows people to work in isolation*	• Identify an event in which the person's teams worked in isolation, creating negative consequences. Discuss what the person did that reinforced this. • Brainstorm other approaches to driving change that the person could have taken to prevent this.	• Help the person use a matrix to identify overlaps and intersections of goals, priorities, and key teams. • Together, regularly consult this matrix when new teams or goals are created.	• Create a change team designed to facilitate collaborative change within the organization. Have the person serve as a key member. • Regularly review how the person is facilitating others working more cross-functionally. Have the person bring examples of successes and challenges.

Behavior		Awaken	Align	Accelerate
Change	*Accepts the status quo and misses opportunities for change*	• Help the person to assess his/her own comfort level with leading change. What areas does the person identify as strengths? As development needs? • Provide feedback from your perspective on instances in which you have seen the person excel as well as be challenged.	• Reinforce times when taking a stronger leadership position toward change would be helpful. Share why this situation is particularly important. • Identify a current priority in which the person can focus behavior change. Provide specific examples of how the person can positively impact the change.	• Pair the person with someone who has complementary change skills. Have them co-lead a project to learn from each other. • Create a "cabinet" of people with whom the person can consult on change leadership, serving as a go-to for support as well as a source of feedback on the person's leadership.
Motivation	*Is primarily focused on short-term goals*	• Evaluate together the timeline for his/her goals. Which are integral for driving longer term change? Which meet an important tactical need? • Define what short-term and long-term mean in the organization. Creating consistent time horizons may be necessary.	• Have the person audit organizational systems (e.g., incentives) that impact goal-setting. Are they well aligned with both short- and long-term goals? • Make necessary changes to align the systems. Discuss the process together and encourage the person to do something similar within the team.	• Advocate for broadening the person's time perspective. • Reduce the frequency or intensity with which you inquire about short-term needs. Model a shift in your own thinking to facilitate change in his/hers.
	Communicates about change in a vague, uninspiring way	• Ask who inspires the person. What about that person's communication is motivating? • Read *Inspire, Persuade, Lead* by Paul Batz (Beaver's Pond Press, 2001) together and debrief the learning.	• Create opportunities for the person to get feedback from others after speaking about change efforts in front of a group or team. How is the person inspiring others? • Have the person observe and learn from another leader in the organization who does this well. What behavior does the person observe that could be modeled?	• Provide coaching for the person from a specialist in executive presence or public speaking to push the practice of new behavior. • Target a specific change initiative to hone the person's ability to be clear and specific in communication.

Behavior		Awaken	Align	Accelerate
Coordination	*Allows teams to work in silos*	• Discuss how the person keeps team members collaborating on goal setting. What mechanisms has the person put in place to reinforce this? • Review the benefits of cross-functional collaboration. When have you observed the person missing an opportunity? What was lost because of it?	• Suggest that the person and team review stakeholders with whom they actively communicate. List key stakeholders to keep informed. • Create a plan to keep those stakeholders informed; how should they be communicated with and how frequently?	• Advise the person to practice regularly seeking feedback from other teams prior to moving plans forward. • Model this behavior by bringing together the person's peers during informal meetings that reinforce communication.
	Is unwilling to compromise or make tradeoffs	• Brainstorm questions for the person to ask himself/herself (e.g., "What is the implication of my decision?", and "Whose goals are being impacted by my team?"). • Discuss where some of the person's results could be sacrificed to help others. Reinforce a current situation where you believe this would be helpful.	• Have the person ask key peers which tradeoffs they wish the person would have made. How did those tradeoffs impact their teams? • Use a current project as an example. Help the person weigh a tradeoff that will affect others within the organization.	• Encourage the person to seek feedback from key stakeholders prior to making important decisions. • Debrief feedback from others during your one-on-one meetings. How is the person working to adapt behavior using their input?

Tips for Coaching in a Global Environment

Creating Alignment may be practiced or expressed differently within other cultures. This might impact how you approach coaching. Try to keep an open mind, avoid generalizations, and continue gathering data as you gain experience with another culture. Consider these suggestions:

Direction: Everyone should know what the organization's goals, strategy, and priorities are. This can be a challenge for people who are interacting at work in a non-native language. Encourage people you are coaching to check the understanding of people on their teams. During a meeting, ask everyone to write down the goals and priorities, and then compare notes. Encourage subgroups to confer about the goals and priorities in their native language so that people can come to a good understanding.

Diagnosis: Context plays a greater role in some cultures than others. The need to define things clearly and explicitly is not seen as a need in all cultures. Written rules and procedures may not exist (or be followed in the same manner) in some parts of the organization. Creating Alignment often involves making things more explicit. You may need to help the leader understand what is required to diagnose fit among goals, activities, structures, systems, and processes. Provide examples to illustrate your explanation.

Change: Alignment depends on agreement. Agreement is not obtained or expressed in the same way in all cultures. For example, people in some cultures may say "yes" to indicate that they understand what you are saying—but that doesn't necessarily mean that they agree with what you said. Help the people you are coaching identify how to gain agreement and commitment from others. Apply these insights to your coaching conversations as well. Ask people to summarize their understanding of what was discussed, along with what actions they are committing to take. Send an email afterward to restate key points.

Motivation: While people may recognize a need for improvement, they may be constrained from taking action by a variety of factors of which you may not be aware—including beliefs about their own efficacy as well as beliefs about whether their roles entitle them to initiate changes. Some cultures are more formal than others about prescribing appropriate behavior for people in different circumstances. Try to learn about factors that may influence someone's motivation and ability to exercise independent initiative in that culture.

Coordination: People working in multinational companies may face very different challenges based on local conditions. Do not assume that people mean the same thing when using words like "coordination" or "integration." A lack of coordination in some areas may be seen as largely a technical issue resulting from having to rely on lots of manual processes with limited information technology support. In other areas, a lack of coordination might have more of a human or political dimension. Ask whether there is a lack of coordination and whether efforts need to be better integrated to improve alignment. Probe for examples and encourage people to reflect on possible improvement scenarios.

A Case Study in Creating Alignment

Most organizations invest a great deal of effort in developing and communicating their missions, visions, and values. Many also work hard to align their systems and processes to these. Alignment must be monitored, adjusted, and improved to prevent slippage and deterioration.

As you read about Chris Taylor's situation, reflect on what you've learned about Creating Alignment in this chapter and consider how you would help Chris demonstrate greater skill in Creating Alignment and be successful in her leadership role.

Creating a Case for Change

Chris Taylor was frustrated. As one of the managing partners in a large professional service consulting firm, she was struggling to understand why people in the firm weren't acting in line with the firm's core values (quality, respect, integrity, responsibility, and collaboration to achieve results). Chris was proud of those values and the work done by her partners to embed the values in the organization.

The collaboration value reflected the partners' beliefs about working together to serve clients. Last year, they developed a new incentive system to reward a shared process of business development. When the system was devised, they paid attention to reinforcing the collaborative efforts the firm wanted to promote. People in each office were encouraged to make joint sales calls with other people in that office. The managing partners modeled this by bringing others along to visit their clients without ever asking, "What's in it for me?" when asked to accompany junior staff members.

Despite various efforts to promote collaboration, Chris saw that business development was still too often being conducted by individuals working on their own. There was an undercurrent of competition for leads, business development opportunities, and new clients. Some consultants were almost secretive at times, rather than being collaborative. Chris was particularly bothered by the practice of splitting credit for new business development. While some consultants shared credit equally, others had begun to recognize that they could keep 100 percent of the credit if they operated alone—so they tended not to include others on new business calls. There was also a mix of skills among the staff in their ability to effectively conduct sales meetings.

Things came to a head for Chris one day. During a major client presentation, she was taken aback when one of the colleagues she had invited to join the discussion took center stage. That person used a lot of "I" rather than "we" language and promoted himself rather than the client team as a whole.

Chris realized that some action had to be taken before the situation got any worse. How could they assess and strengthen the skills of staff members to effectively sell as a team? How could they realign the reward system with the core values to promote collaboration and minimize competition?

Chris' Leadership Development Plan

Following is a sample development plan for Chris Taylor. Research on leadership development has shown that leaders learn through experience, and that this learning is optimized through the use of an individual development plan. A successful plan includes new experiences and introduces the leader to new conversations and tools. Suggestions included in previous sections may stimulate your thinking about additional possibilities for Chris' development.

LEADERSHIP DEVELOPMENT PLAN FOR CHRIS TAYLOR
DEVELOPMENT GOAL

Goal: To strengthen my skills in Creating Alignment

Desired Outcomes—results I want to see from developing this skill

Self: I will be able to implement new initiatives more effectively in the future.

Team: Other partners and consultants will operate more collaboratively, in accordance with our values.

Organization: Our clients will view our organization as a collaborative partner for their businesses.

Self-Understanding—strengths that I can build on and development needs I can address

Strengths: Exceptional knowledge of our industry, professional consulting expertise, client relationships

Development Needs: Must overcome reluctance to challenge colleagues and deal with conflict

Business Context—challenges in my business environment that require this skill

Changes in our customer base where internal staff are now doing many of the things we used to do in consulting; economic downturn that reduced corporate spend on consulting

DEVELOPMENT ACTIONS

AWAKEN

- Read "What is Strategy" by Michael Porter (*Harvard Business Review*, 2009), then map activities in the firm that are designed to deliver or support the firm's strategy. Identify places where re-design could strengthen strategy implementation and effectiveness.

- Ask consultants what organizational factors keep them from performing business development to the best of their ability and why.

- Diagnose whether design components for each job (e.g., tasks, task significance, variety, autonomy, and performance feedback) are aligned with the firm's design as well as individual capabilities.

- Help people understand the need for change. Show gap between current state and what the firm could become.

- Use a gap analysis to examine how the firm is currently performing compared to its goals. Discuss my conclusions with other partners. Do we have similar perceptions?

LEADERSHIP DEVELOPMENT PLAN FOR CHRIS TAYLOR

ALIGN

- Talk with my peers about the firm's direction and how we support it. What role can each of us play in advancing the direction and accomplishing key priorities?

- Analyze internal factors that affect consultants in my local office. Where is there internal competition?

- Create a guiding coalition of key leaders who will help me establish momentum for the change. Identify partners or consultants who will be most affected by change and try to gain their support early on.

ACCELERATE

- Analyze whether managing partners can pass the "What's in it for me?" test when discussing business development opportunities.

- Survey key internal customers. What suggestions do they have?

- Benchmark best practices, both inside and outside the firm. What practices can we apply? Specifically, how do other firms share business development responsibilities and credit?

- Study how things are done in consulting firms that don't compete with ours. Discuss what we learn.

- Develop a plan for approaching, engaging, and involving people who will be most affected.

DEVELOPMENT SUCCESS FACTORS

Timeline: Within the next six months

Support Needed: Time and cooperation from my business partners

Indicators of Success:

- Changes in the firm that lead to an increase in joint client and business development calls
- A corresponding decrease in individual sales activities

An Example of Coaching to Create Alignment

Chris Taylor's goal was to strengthen her skills in Creating Alignment. Here are some steps her manager could take using the Awaken, Align, Accelerate framework to coach Chris in this area:

AWAKEN	**Increase INSIGHT**	Provide feedback using your own observations if possible. Identify an event, such as the recent client presentation in which Chris worked in isolation that potentially created negative consequences. Discuss what Chris did that reinforced this. Brainstorm other ways she may have been more effective in teaming to lead the meeting.
	MOTIVATE change	Focus on options and choices. Find out how she prefers to learn. Ask about the consequences of not making any changes. Identify what Chris is motivated to change.
ALIGN	**PLAN goals**	Ask Chris what would enable her to handle current alignment challenges more successfully. Ask what she would spend time working toward and follow through on. Work together to construct a leadership development plan similar to the sample provided in this chapter.
	ALIGN expectations	Ensure that organizational systems (e.g., incentives) are well aligned with the behavior Chris is hoping to change. Discuss with Chris how she sees the incentives aligning with what the organization is expecting of her. Coach Chris on making necessary changes to improve alignment and team performance.
ACCELERATE	**CREATE teachable moments**	Pair Chris with someone who has complementary change skills. Have them co-lead a project or new client relationship to learn from each other. Consider forming a change team, designed to facilitate collaborative change (such as the new incentive system) within the organization. Have Chris serve as a key member. Schedule periodic coaching sessions to debrief Chris on her new experiences, discuss obstacles, and brainstorm additional possibilities.
	TRACK progress	Discuss expected outcomes and results. Work with Chris to evaluate progress toward her goals. Encourage her to invite additional feedback and ask other people to support the changes they see. Acknowledge and celebrate her efforts.

Results: Measuring Impact

Chris Taylor took almost six months to work through her plan. She didn't try every action step, and she found some activities were more helpful than others. However, she made tremendous progress on improving her own skills and increasing alignment within the firm. Her new skills as a change agent allowed Chris to:

- Make organizational changes that facilitated an increase in joint business development calls.

- Help other partners and consultants operate more collaboratively, in accordance with the firm's values.

- Strengthen existing relationships with key clients.

- Win some significant business from new clients who valued their collaborative style of working.

- Implement new initiatives more effectively in the future.

7

Team Leadership

Great team leaders are attuned to and insightful about the dynamics of groups. They assemble effective teams with the right mix of talents and perspectives. They capitalize on interdependencies and draw on people and resources from across the organization to be successful. They harness the energy of the group and involve others in decisions and plans that affect them. They empower and trust team members and help others to put the team first. They build consensus and cohesion within and across their teams.

Factor	Competency	Core Practice
Leading People	Leading Courageously	Utilization
Thinking and Deciding	Creating Alignment	Orchestration
Achieving	Team Leadership	Involvement
Relating to People	Developing Leaders	Empowerment
Managing Work		Cohesion
Managing Self		

The workplace has changed dramatically over the past twenty years and will continue to change as pressure mounts to be more competitive, agile, and customer-focused. Team Leadership is a critical leadership skill, more so than ever before. Virtual teams are now operating across widely dispersed geographies. Continual changes in technology, social networking, and globalization bring people into team environments with different backgrounds and expectations for communication. The nature of teams has changed and is likely to continue evolving. Leadership is a team sport. Learn the rules so you can play the game!

Effective teamwork can produce incredible results. However, effective teamwork does not just happen automatically; it takes a great deal of effort and hard work. To build high-performing teams, leaders must be effective team sponsors, team leaders, and team members—simultaneously, on different teams—as well as contribute to the efforts of other teams in different ways. It is a great compliment these days to be seen as an effective team player. Wouldn't it be great if you and everyone on your team deserved that recognition?

People may play a variety of roles when they participate on different teams (e.g., team member, team project manager, team leader, team sponsor, and team advocate). Each of these roles requires people to be team players as well as exhibit leadership behaviors. A strong team leader assembles the right talent, maximizes cross-functional resources, practices group decision-making, empowers others to lead, and builds a sense of team. In more senior-level leadership roles, the need to demonstrate effective Team Leadership only increases as leaders contribute to, sponsor, and manage more and more teams at higher levels in an organization. While the ability to lead teams is important for all leaders, the path to Team Leadership often varies by level, as illustrated in the following table.

How Leaders at Different Levels Lead Teams

	Managers	Function Leaders	Senior Executives
Utilization	Considers everyone's talent when assigning and accomplishing work.	Forms productive teams; assembles the best people to meet the function's goals.	Optimizes talent and resources for the entire organization.
Orchestration	Brings people together to work on problems or projects.	Builds teams' capacity by skillfully managing group dynamics.	Maximizes inclusion of people and resources from across the entire enterprise.
Involvement	Encourages everyone to actively participate on the team.	Involves people in decisions that affect them.	Maximizes others' participation in planning and decision-making.
Empowerment	Provides direction to team members while maintaining appropriate controls.	Gives team members real responsibility and authority.	Fully trusts yet holds people accountable for their responsibilities.
Cohesion	Ensures relationships among team members are constructive and positive.	Builds agreement and trust within and across teams.	Actively fosters consensus and cohesion within and across the business.

7

TEAM LEADERSHIP

Self-Assessment

To evaluate your effectiveness in Team Leadership, check all boxes below that represent current behavior or performance. Look for patterns: Which core practices represent a development need, a strength, or an excessive use? Recognize that you might have some blind spots. Invite your boss or colleagues to indicate what they have observed in your behavior. Use this assessment to help identify development suggestions that are most relevant to you.

	Development Need	Strength	Excessive Use
Utilization	☐ Assembles teams with little thought regarding their membership ☐ Doesn't add talent or build capacity of the team	☐ Creates effective teams by carefully matching and balancing members' skills ☐ Assembles the right team to meet the function's goals	☐ Turns teams loose without developing their charter ☐ Assumes that each team is working effectively without checking in
Orchestration	☐ Over-relies on a limited number of staff ☐ Misses opportunities to utilize people and resources from other areas	☐ Leads teams in a way that builds their capacity ☐ Skillfully manages group dynamics	☐ Casts a wide net and includes too many people to be productive ☐ Informs a wide variety of people who are not associated with the team outcome
Involvement	☐ Solves problems without involving the right people ☐ Makes decisions unilaterally and doesn't utilize team members effectively	☐ Artfully knows when and how to involve others in decisions such that people feel uniquely valuable to the team ☐ Practices effective team decision-making processes	☐ Involves so many individuals in decision-making that people question whether they are adding value ☐ Involves only a core group on the team and doesn't expand involvement
Empowerment	☐ Micromanages performance of others; is unnecessarily involved in aspects of team members' work ☐ Abandons the team and abdicates leadership responsibility	☐ Continuously expands direct reports' responsibilities, while providing guidance and helpful feedback ☐ Supports the actions and decisions of his/her direct reports	☐ Empowers in a hands-off manner that leaves people floundering ☐ Sets such high standards that teams are not motivated
Cohesion	☐ Fails to build consensus or contributes to tension within teams ☐ Allows teams to operate when they are dysfunctional	☐ Establishes trust by modeling effective conflict resolution ☐ Builds agreement among people with differing views	☐ Mandates cohesion and is overly concerned about achieving unanimous agreement ☐ Delays taking action until everyone agrees

Development Suggestions

The following section contains development suggestions for each core practice. Having completed the self-assessment, focus on suggestions that correspond to the core practices you identified as a development need or excessive use. Use these suggestions to create your own development plan, making sure to try one or two from each phase. In addition, feel free to create your own or adapt these to best meet your development needs.

Utilization

Form productive teams; assemble the best people to meet the function's goals.

*"If we are to achieve a richer culture,
rich in contrasting values, we must recognize the whole
gamut of human potentialities and so weave a less
arbitrary social fabric, one in which each diverse human
gift will find a fitting place."*

Margaret Mead

Awaken potential:

- **Learn about strong teams.** Read *The Wisdom of Teams: Creating the High-Performance Organization* by Jon Katzenbach and Douglas Smith (HarperBusiness, 2003) to learn about team basics, including optimum team size and criteria for selecting team members.

- **Learn about your team members.** Do you know the skill levels of team members so you can staff project teams effectively? What motivates them? Learn more about their skills, abilities, and aspirations in performance management and career development discussions.

- **Talk to peers or customers.** If you are leading an established team, talk to peers or customers who may have insights about team members' relative strengths and limitations. Consider coaching, re-assignment, or replacement for any team member who you learn needs to make a stronger contribution.

Align goals:

- **Develop a team charter.** Make sure you provide new teams with a clear charter that defines their purpose, scope of responsibility and authority, and the outcomes or results you expect them to produce.

- **Define elements of team effectiveness.** Do you know what your team looks like at its best? Work with the team to determine charter, goals and objectives, roles, responsibilities, and accountabilities. Use responsibility charting with your team to clarify who is responsible for what.

- **Learn about other teams' goals.** To resolve conflicting goals with other teams, find out what is important to the other team. What are their main concerns? What are they doing to achieve their goals? If several teams appear to have overlapping responsibilities, make sure you clarify who is doing what and where the different teams need to coordinate to accomplish overarching objectives.

Accelerate performance:

- **Focus on team member selection.** Determine team needs, assess team member capabilities, and identify any gaps. Meet with each team member individually to identify the person's strengths and relevant knowledge or experiences. Discuss how to use those strengths to achieve team goals. Ask a mentor what he/she did to select the right team members based on competence and motivation.

- **Look for diversity when building teams to come up with the best solutions.** Homogenous teams with similar members collaborate better and more efficiently, but may not examine all possible alternatives.

- **Identify and remove roadblocks.** In leading new teams, schedule a meeting to talk about goals, share the proposed schedule, give an overview of the work, and make team assignments. Allow time for discussion with all participants to identify obstacles to successful team collaboration. Make a note of these roadblocks, and decide how they will be managed if they occur, or if adjustments can be made to avoid them.

- **Establish ground rules for what is expected from each team member and for how items should be resolved.** For example, when a team needs to operate in a highly interdependent way, clarify what will happen if one person does not follow through with his/her commitments.

EXCESSIVE USE

As an example, if you carefully assemble teams but then turn people loose without developing a charter, they may waste time getting focused. Start them off with a charter.

Build teams' capacity by skillfully managing group dynamics.

"Unity is strength…when there is teamwork and collaboration, wonderful things can be achieved."

Mattie Stepanek

Awaken potential:

- Assess your Team Leadership capabilities by participating in a multi-rater (360-degree) feedback process with your team members to explore your impact on the team.

- Evaluate your team membership. Do you have the right representation of the various functions and perspectives from across the organization? Consider what skills or interests could help take the team to the next level.

- Assess your perspective. Ask a colleague who is not on the team to look at your project and offer ideas about how it could function better. Ask, "Are there any issues that we are not addressing? Is anything slipping through the cracks?" Try to evaluate your project objectively to catch things that may have been missed from the perspective of other parts of the organization.

Align goals:

- **Clarify individual goals and expectations.** When a team forms, meet with each team member to discuss his/her experience, skills, interests, and role on the team. Discuss the importance of the role and how that person's contributions will affect the ability of others to complete their work and meet the team's goals.

- **Establish a team concept in your organization.** Use the processes and tools in *Tools for Team Leadership* by Gregory Huszczo (Davies-Black, 2004) to effectively structure teams and create a culture where cooperation and collaboration are the norms.

Accelerate performance:

- **Teach people about teamwork.** Read *The Discipline of Teams: A Mindbook-Workbook for Delivering Small Group Performance* by Jon Katzenbach and Douglas Smith (Wiley, 2001) to gain ideas for including people and improving small-group performance. Propose and support training programs for managers that emphasize the benefits of teamwork and teach the specific competencies required to implement company-wide teamwork successfully.

- **Promote cooperation.** Tell people that you want to promote cooperation across different work groups and are willing to provide assistance by facilitating the process. If you suspect that specific members are having difficulty cooperating, meet with them individually to discuss the issues and work through potential problems.

- **Encourage people to engage the whole group when speaking in meetings.** When someone directs a message only to you, rather than to others in the group, try to redirect the person's attention to the group.

- **Require open communication.** Encourage team members to follow up with each other, not just with you. At the same time, clarify your own need for information. If there are individuals with whom you need to follow up directly, tell them.

- **Diagnose team dysfunction.** Read *The Five Dysfunctions of a Team: A Leadership Fable* by Patrick Lencioni (Jossey-Bass, 2002) to analyze whether your team may have those dysfunctions (e.g., absence of trust, fear of conflict, lack of commitment, avoidance of accountability, or inattention to results). Complete an assessment with your team. Discuss team strengths and opportunities for improvement, and then initiate action planning.

- **Create cross-organizational team practices.** Establish an action team with employees from different sites to identify ways to enhance teamwork across departmental lines.

- **Monitor team effectiveness.** Periodically ask team members for specific suggestions to improve the system in place. Ask, "Is this the most efficient way to do things?" Where appropriate, implement those suggestions.

- **Celebrate team successes.** Once you have completed a major project or team effort, schedule a lunch, breakfast, or special event to celebrate the team's success. Make an extra effort to recognize contributions of everyone involved; you are likely to need their contributions in the future.

EXCESSIVE USE

As an example, if you include too many people on teams, the groups may become unwieldy and waste time. Evaluate the productivity of teams you have chartered.

Involve people in decisions that affect them.

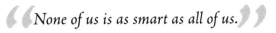
None of us is as smart as all of us.

Ken Blanchard

Awaken potential:

- **Reflect upon your ability to communicate** the team's rules, goals, expected duties, and decision-making authority. Are there ways that you can strengthen your communication skills?

- **Assess your decision-making practices.** Participate in a leadership assessment to understand your preferred decision-making style both individually and in teams.

- **Analyze team decision-making.** Read "What Makes a Decisive Leadership Team," by Bob Frisch, et al., (*Harvard Business Review*, 2008). Analyze whether your team suffers from any obstacles (e.g., endless bickering) and how to address each of them.

Align goals:

- **Seek buy-in from all team members** by giving a big-picture overview of where the organization is going and how the team will contribute.

- **Involve team members in setting team goals.** Enlist help from the team in taking on responsibilities and determining how team members should work together to attain their goals.

Accelerate performance:

- **Facilitate rather than direct your team.** Effective facilitation on your part will increase engagement, and therefore productivity, of your team members Consider rotating tasks and process roles among team members (e.g., meeting facilitator, team development).

- **Encourage cooperation of all team members** by advocating a "we" mentality. Identify the benefits to each member if the team succeeds, as well as the consequences of failure.

- **Provide meeting agendas.** Send out the team meeting agenda ahead of time so team members can come prepared to actively participate in decisions.

- **Educate your team on decision-making.** Ask team members to read *Making Meetings Work: Achieving High Quality Group Decisions* by John Tropman (Sage, 1996).

Circulate a copy of *Harvard Business Review on Decision Making* (Harvard Business Press, 2001). Lead a discussion about the effectiveness of the team's decision-making style.

- **Clarify decision-making authority and responsibility.** Use responsibility charting with your team to determine in advance with whom decisions will rest.

- **Promote communication and idea sharing among team members.** Set aside time to allow for meetings and discussions. Support changes initiated by others by listening to their suggestions attentively. Do they seem like viable options? If so, ask what you can do to support them and help implement the changes.

- **Practice active listening.** Practice listening by summarizing what people say during meetings. Your goals are twofold: (1) to communicate your understanding of what they are saying, and (2) to resist offering your opinion in a way that might prevent the team from coming to their own conclusions.

- **Recognize team efforts and accomplishments** during meetings; emphasize accomplishments that resulted from teamwork. Encourage teams to reward themselves when they excel. Reward individuals who consistently provide good team outcomes.

EXCESSIVE USE

As an example, if you involve so many individuals, people may question whether they are adding value. Analyze the composition of each team and restructure as needed.

Give team members real responsibility and authority.

> *The great leaders are like the best conductors—*
> *they reach beyond the notes to reach the magic*
> *in the players.*
>
> Blaine Lee

Awaken potential:

- **Examine accountability.** Read *The OZ Principle: Getting Results Through Individual and Organizational Accountability* by Roger Connors, Tom Smith, and Craig Hickman (Prentice Hall, 1994). Analyze the extent to which you and others on your team accept responsibility for outcomes rather than blaming others or outside circumstances.

- **Understand what drives people.** Use surveys or focus groups to collect data about what is motivating and satisfying to your workforce; bring the data to a task force or senior decision-making team to determine what changes are possible. Pay attention to the types of tasks and projects in which individuals excel. People will be more satisfied and committed to work if they are given assignments based on personal interest and expertise.

- **Evaluate how you support and advocate change** within your team. Describe your present efforts to foster change. What have you done in the last year to support change? Reflect upon your ability to motivate your team members. How are you inspiring them through your enthusiasm and energy?

- **Look for opportunities to delegate.** Think about how you are balancing your priorities. Where can you do more delegation? How can you manage your time and your team members' time more effectively?

Align goals:

- **Set priorities.** Clarify the importance of a team charter, and determine if members will be able to commit sufficient time to participate. If a team assignment is an "add on" to existing responsibilities, it may not be given sufficient priority.

- **Create a clear line of sight** between the organization's strategic goals and the roles of individual team members. Support them in making decisions on their own as long as they are aligned with the organization's direction.

Accelerate performance:

- **Match control to readiness.** Read *The Situational Leader* by Paul Hersey (Center for Leadership Studies, 2008). Analyze the experience and capability levels of people you lead, and determine what leadership style will work best for each person.

- **Hold a "Think Out Loud" session** to involve team members in the process of delegation. Let them know what tasks need to be accomplished and how. Ask who would be interested in each task and how team members think the work could be accomplished most efficiently and effectively.

- **Use responsibility charting.** List all team activities on a chart, plot the activities and names of team members on a matrix, and reach consensus as to which person or group is responsible for each activity.

- **Be an equal opportunity delegator.** Develop a checklist to avoid continuously delegating to the most capable people. Delegate responsibilities broadly to develop a strong team. Provide instruction and coaching according to team member capability.

- **Encourage leaders to teach leaders.** Identify an individual on the team who has a particular skill that may benefit others. Ask that person to serve as a coach or mentor for others who are lacking that skill.

- **Help teams to evaluate their performance** as a team through an honest feedback process (e.g., survey). Identify strengths and improvement opportunities, and then brainstorm how to address trouble spots.

EXCESSIVE USE

As an example, if you delegate and empower in a hands-off manner, you may leave people floundering. Clarify your expectations. Follow up to ensure those expectations are met.

Build agreement and trust within and across teams.

> *Focus and attention convey genuine respect,*
> *which is the cornerstone of trust.*
>
> Frances Hesselbein

Awaken potential:

- **Take stock of how you lead.** Reflect upon how you are building trust and confidence with your team. People need to feel that you, as their team leader, have the knowledge and expertise required to lead them in the right direction, and that you have the confidence to lead them through any challenges that may arise.

- **Solicit team feedback.** Periodically, ask team members if they feel you are surfacing all the important points-of-view when discussing issues. Invite their ideas about how you and your team can be sure you are getting all important ideas and views on the table before making decisions.

- **Review the development recommendations within Conflict Resolution** in Chapter 15, "Building Collaboration," for additional suggestions. Pay particular attention to better understanding your own style and tendencies of managing conflict.

Align goals:

- **Seek common ground.** When in conflict, talk to individuals personally and listen carefully to how they perceive the issue. Focus on the goals of the organization, and keep the discussion aimed at finding the best ways to accomplish overarching business objectives.

- **Encourage collaboration.** To build trust within your team, check in with members regularly. Communicate your willingness to help on specific tasks. Keep them informed about your availability. Discuss upcoming tasks and deadlines during meetings; as a group, identify areas where someone might need help. Work together to complete the tasks. Build a norm where members feel safe to ask each other for help.

Accelerate performance:

- **Emphasize interdependence.** Clarify issues that team members may not see in quite the same manner as you. Identify issues on which the team should focus attention. Communicate the need to operate by way of consensus, if appropriate. Emphasize that interdependence will lead to greater success than working independently.

- **Facilitate participation.** When you observe team members withdrawing from a discussion or struggling with an issue, step in and facilitate the discussion. Encourage people to interact with each other. Create ground rules with your team for what is expected from each team member, what behaviors will facilitate trust, and what behaviors will hinder it.

- **Use a facilitator.** Assign a person who is good at facilitating conversations to lead team discussions, and then try to implement some of the recommendations the group makes.

- **Surface issues early.** Develop the habit of articulating the pros and cons of ideas to help team members see potential disagreements at the outset. When conflict surfaces early, it is easier to work through it.

- **Resolve conflict within the larger context.** When issues arise, meet with representatives from other teams and describe what is happening in terms of the bigger picture.

- **Express confidence in the team.** Publicly support decisions made in collaboration with the team. Give public and individual praise for a job well done. When appropriate, share the success of the team with other parts of the organization.

- **Create time for building relationships.** If you can, plan team-building activities once or twice a year that include a focus on how team members interact with each other. These are often most effective if they are off-site, include some team activities that are not directly focused on the business problems at hand, and include time where team members can relax socially with each other. Refer to the core practice "Motivation" in Chapter 6 for behaviors that will help you assert your position while building buy-in in a timely way.

EXCESSIVE USE

As an example, if you overemphasize consensus and delay taking action until everyone agrees, you may miss key milestones and jeopardize your credibility. Work behind the scenes to foster agreement.

Coach Others on Team Leadership

When coaching others, focus on the core practices that were identified as either a development need or excessive use in the self-assessment at the beginning of this chapter. Identify and adapt any relevant development suggestions. Additional coaching tips are provided in the following table for some adverse leadership behaviors. For more information review Chapter 4, "Coach Others."

Coaching Suggestions

Behavior		Awaken	Align	Accelerate
Utilization	Has wrong team mix	• Help the person analyze the outcomes needed and the skills required by team members. How well are the existing team members' strengths and experience aligned with the needs of the team? • Share resources such as articles or Belbin's Team Role Inventory. Debrief the person's learnings and share how you incorporate the inventory into your own team.	• Encourage the person to hold a team session where together they review current needs and roles, and then assess team strengths and development needs. Have the person present the findings and action plan to you. • Have the person review the team matrix with peers. Have the person solicit the team's feedback on own observations of team make-up.	• Recommend creating an accountability map for roles and responsibilities. Focus on getting the right people to play the right roles at the right time. Debrief regularly. • Coach the person in creating a team profile, assessing potential resources, and matching required skills with individuals who possess those skills.
	Under-utilizes team members	• Encourage the person to self-reflect on the impact individual members have on the team. Discuss barriers to impact. • Discuss how he/she believes the team could function better—not just how it is already functioning. If there were no boundaries, what changes would the person like to see made?	• Ask the person to select an internal mentor who excels in this area. Have that person explain how to draw out and utilize the best capabilities of people. • Propose that the person engage the team in a discussion about utilizing all/other members. Brainstorm solutions together to maximize consensus and engagement.	• Encourage the person to establish a norm of "maximum utilization" and develop a feedback loop with the team. Agree on a feedback mechanism for individual team members to bring up utilization issues. • Make the person's change plan a regular discussion during your one-on-one meetings. Hold the person accountable for maximizing all aspects of the team, not just favorites.

Behavior		Awaken	Align	Accelerate
Orchestration	*Plays favorites; over-relies on particular staff*	• Suggest mapping how tasks have been assigned; also look at who received the most emails or phone calls. Ask if that was the person's intention. • Discuss your observations of the person favoring a small group of staff. Talk about the consequences of those actions.	• Together, discuss what an ideal mix would look like to optimize everyone's contributions. • Present that ideal mix to key internal customers. Do they believe their needs will be satisfied?	• Help the individual with team charters, team roles, objectives, and outcomes. Work to establish team ground rules and levels of accountability. • Support the person in planning a kick-off to share the team charter and action plan.
	Has team functional bias	• Help the person identify who else in the organization could help (outside of people on the team). Who needs to be influenced? Whose commitment is needed? • Review a previous project that did not go as well as expected. Who could the person have involved to improve results? What prevented that from being done at the time?	• Recommend talking to key influencers about how to involve other people. What do they see as the benefits or positive consequences? • Suggest the person add a "divergent voice" from another area to the team to encourage cross-functional points of view.	• Debrief major current or future project plans, asking who is missing to accomplish goals? Who would make them easier to achieve? Create a plan for how to involve the right people. • Help the person look for opportunities to support development of people from other functions by adding them to teams where they can also contribute expertise.
Involvement	*Plays lone ranger*	• Review any employee engagement or multi-rater feedback data that has recently been collected. What behavior can the person imagine doing that facilitates collaboration? Inhibits it? • Talk together about motivations. How motivated is the person by collaboration? Perfection? Discuss the person's level of trust with others in the organization. Where are there gaps? How does this reinforce the need to go at it alone?	• Suggest the person partner with someone to facilitate a project planning process to educate and engage more people. • Encourage the person to get the right people involved. Use RACI model to explore who should be responsible, accountable, consulted with, or informed.	• During your one-on-one meetings, monitor the person's decisions and determine whether he/she optimized the involvement of others. Help the person create plans to be more proactive in doing so. • Propose using Myers-Briggs Type Indicator® to help the person identify problem-solving and decision-making preferences.

Behavior		Awaken	Align	Accelerate
Involvement	*Makes autocratic decisions*	• Invite the person to participate in a multi-rater feedback process. What does the data say about his/her ability to achieve optimal engagement and commitment from others? • Discuss decisions that others have made that excluded the person, yet had adverse impact on him/her, the team, or results. How did that make the person feel?	• Recommend that the person work with the team to establish a decision-making charter where the whole team is in agreement about what decisions should be made by whom. • Review which decisions affect the ability of other functions, teams, or groups to achieve their goals. Help the person build them into a decision-making process.	• Help the person develop methods for getting input and insights from others. • Discuss the process of situational decision-making. Assign research into multiple decision-making models that could be implemented or executed based on the situation.
Empowerment	*Micromanages*	• Invite the person to conduct a workflow analysis of all tasks in which he/she is involved. Discuss how micromanaging limits the ability to be involved in the right places, at the right levels. • Help assess and understand why the person is over-diligent and needs a high level of control. Is it perfectionism? Lack of trust with team members? What has prompted this?	• Discuss how others on your team operate with different styles. Identify a peer role model who delegates effectively. Have the person partner in a peer coaching relationship with that person. • Ask how often people are waiting outside his/her office. Encourage asking for feedback from the team.	• Encourage the person to experiment with letting go more. Recommend putting together a delegation plan for the next time he/she goes on vacation or select a key project to begin this plan. • Help the person create effective scorecards and measurement systems for team performance that reinforce individual accountability. Use them as tools for robust conversations during one-on-one meetings.

7

TEAM LEADERSHIP

	Behavior	Awaken	Align	Accelerate
Empowerment	*Abandons the team*	• Recommend reading *Zapp! The Lightning of Empowerment* by Bill Byham and Jeff Cox (Random House, 1997). • Learn the situational leadership model. Have the person take the Leader Behavior Analysis II® to determine natural style and tendencies. Help the person understand how people on the team might need more ongoing involvement, direction, or support.	• Facilitate a team Town Hall session where they are able to provide feedback on what they would like the person to keep doing, start doing, stop doing. • Together with the team, help the person create an action plan for increasing his/her engagement and consistency of interaction.	• Use the situational leadership model to analyze what each member might need. Help the person adapt a style to meet their needs. • Regularly debrief how the person is interacting differently with team members. What results are achieved because of this flexibility?
Cohesion	*Fails to build consensus or leaves conflict unaddressed*	• Suggest getting feedback about what's working and what isn't from trusted team members. Discuss the issues and their consequences. Is the person okay with them? Are you? • Convey the importance of consensus on a current project. Why is it so vital? What might not be achieved if consensus is not reached?	• Identify who in the organization addresses conflict well. Have the person observe that person in action. What does he/she do that is different? What behaviors can be adopted? • How is consensus reinforced as a team or organizational value? Ensure you are modeling this behavior yourself.	• Work together to improve ability and comfort in dealing with conflict. Coach the person to build more trust by committing to specific actions and consistent behaviors. • Regularly seek ongoing feedback from the team. Help translate that data into action steps for resolution.
	Doesn't deal with team dysfunction	• Help the person reflect on personal leadership style and assess his/her courage as a leader. What promotes that self-confidence? What inhibits it? • Review a project or initiative in which you observed the person not addressing dysfunction. What was the obstacle? What consequences could have been avoided?	• Have the team complete the Thomas-Kilmann Conflict Assessment. What styles are predominant? • Facilitate a working session to review the data and develop a shared plan for addressing conflict.	• Encourage the person to stay in contact with team members, regularly review their roles and responsibilities, and hold them accountable. • Have the team offer real-time feedback when they observe the person not addressing conflict head on.

Tips for Coaching in a Global Environment

Team Leadership may be practiced or expressed differently within other cultures. This might impact how you approach coaching. Try to keep an open mind, avoid generalizations, and continue gathering data as you gain experience with another culture. Consider these suggestions:

Utilization: Try to understand what teams and teamwork mean and typically look like in that culture. Some development suggestions presented earlier in this chapter call for making many aspects of team functioning more clear and explicit (e.g., establishing team charter, roles and responsibilities, ground rules, etc.). Such explicit communication might seem strange to people who come from a "high context" culture, where many things are left unsaid. Ask the person you are coaching about the relevancy of your suggestions for the way teams operate in that culture.

Orchestration: The practice of bringing the best people and resources together on projects works well when you know where to look—and when people speak the same language. It may not work as well when talented people in other countries cannot be located due to the absence of a skills database—or where people's inability to communicate with others on the project team could be a liability. Many organizations have adopted English as their global corporate language. When coaching people whose English is not proficient, help them recognize the importance of networking as well as improving their communication skills if they want to be included on global projects. Have a frank discussion about the challenges and obstacles of getting people to work together cross-culturally. Also talk about the benefits. Seek out a trusted advisor to help you understand potential barriers to cross-cultural teamwork.

Involvement: Some cultures have a more structured, hierarchical approach to decision-making than others. Find out if participation in decision-making is the norm in the person's culture. Help the person you are coaching seek divergent viewpoints, invite negative feedback, and welcome input from junior people.

Empowerment: While delegation is a common managerial practice, empowerment is not as widespread. People from different cultures may have different expectations about performance commitments (e.g., setting stretch goals or meeting particular project milestones). These differences may impact empowerment. Come to a common understanding of empowerment. If the leader you are coaching is working in a non-native language, use examples to illustrate what you mean. Check for understanding.

Cohesion: Building agreement and trust takes time particularly when people have different levels of experience and come from diverse backgrounds. Read articles about team leadership and teamwork written by people from that culture (if you can find copies available in your own language) to understand the broader context of team leadership. Ask about the history of the local organization, including how decisions are made and communicated.

A Case Study in Team Leadership

Team Leadership requires assembling the right talent, maximizing cross-functional resources, practicing group decision-making, empowering others to lead, and building a sense of team.

As you read about Ron Johnson's situation, reflect on what you've learned about Team Leadership in this chapter. How does Ron sound like you, or one of your team members? What experiences or tendencies do you share? Finally, consider how you might help Ron demonstrate greater skill in Team Leadership and be successful in his leadership role.

Trusting in Teams

Last year, Ron Johnson became the head of medical operations for a national healthcare company that was planning to launch significant global initiatives. His direct reports resided in eight cities, where they managed multiple facilities at many different sites. In addition to being a key member of the senior executive team, Ron belonged to five other teams that were working on different strategic initiatives. He was sponsoring several of those initiatives himself. These teams were all at different phases of team development; some were not well managed, and there was a general lack of integration and collaboration among the teams. These teams did not all report to Ron, yet all were critical in meeting his objectives.

The senior executive team met twice a month, with some members habitually absent. Ron brought his direct reports together quarterly and conducted monthly staff meetings by teleconference. The different physical locations of his teams were proving to be quite a challenge. Ron was used to operating face to face, but now needed to work remotely via email and conference calls instead. This would become even more of a challenge when the organization went global. People on his teams also had different levels of experience and motivation. His style worked well with experienced, motivated team members, but had not produced consistent results with less-experienced or less-motivated members.

Early on, he attempted to ensure that all teams had established charters, outcomes, and measurements. However, many meetings were ineffective because trust had not been established. Conflict was avoided in the meetings, but came out in different ways afterward. This frustrated Ron, who wondered why people didn't say what they meant openly and resolve conflict constructively.

Ron was committed to being the best team leader and team player that he could be. He needed to influence the various teams in different ways based on the different roles he played. While Ron always handled teams well when they reported to him, he found it challenging to achieve results when he played other roles on the team. Authoritative by nature, Ron was used to driving team performance by setting high expectations and then allowing the team to perform up to these expectations. This style didn't work well when he was the team sponsor or simply a team member. His style tended to promote independence and fear rather than collaboration and trust. Ron got feedback that he must demonstrate better Team Leadership skills. He wondered where to begin.

Ron found that he needed Team Leadership more than ever, to:

- Identify the many types of teams he was leading,

- Clarify the matrix of teams with shared accountability,

- Learn how to navigate the various teams to gain support for his initiatives and drive performance,

- Gain new Team Leadership skills and coach others, and

- Work with others to build trust and promote collaboration.

Ron's Leadership Development Plan

Following is a sample development plan for Ron Johnson. Research on leadership development has shown that leaders learn through experience and that this learning is optimized through the use of an individual development plan. A successful plan includes new experiences and introduces the leader to new conversations and tools. The suggestions included in the previous sections may stimulate your thinking about additional possibilities for Ron's development.

LEADERSHIP DEVELOPMENT PLAN FOR RON JOHNSON

DEVELOPMENT GOAL

Goal: Strengthen my Team Leadership skills.

Desired Outcomes—results I want to see from developing this skill

Self: Have more impact and influence in numerous settings.

Team: Achieve more with less during times of constricting resources.

Organization: High-performance outcomes from high-performing teams.

Self-Understanding—strengths that I can build on and development needs I can address

Strengths:

- Relationship-building skills
- Results focus
- Communication skills
- Technical competence and established reputation

Development Needs:

- Authoritarian leadership style
- Collaborative and trusting relationships

Business Context—challenges in my business environment that require this skill

Dynamic complex environment. Do more with less in many physical locations. On teams where I am not the team leader, I share the accountability for the outcomes.

DEVELOPMENT ACTIONS

AWAKEN

- Read *The Wisdom of Teams* by Jon Katzenbach and Douglas R. Smith. (Harvard Business Press, 1992).
- Obtain multi-rater feedback from team members about my impact on the team.
- Gain a better understanding of my personal influence style and situational leadership tendencies.
- Conduct a team analysis to determine strengths and weaknesses of the team.

ALIGN

- Develop the habit of articulating the pros and cons of ideas and recommendations in group and one-on-one discussions.
- Explain strategic objectives in enough detail to provide my team members with direction, and discuss my general expectations.

ACCELERATE

- Ask a mentor what he/she has done to successfully navigate Team Leadership issues.
- Read *The Situational Leader* by Paul Hersey (Prentice Hall, 1986) and evaluate the experience and capability levels of team members to determine what leadership style will work best for each person.
- Check in with team or group members regularly. Let them know I am willing to help on specific tasks. Keep them informed of my availability.
- During team meetings, discuss upcoming tasks and deadlines and, as a group, identify areas where someone might need help. Work together to complete the tasks. Try to build a norm for the group where members feel safe to ask for help from each other.
- Encourage teams to take time to evaluate their performance as a team and reward themselves when they excel. Help team members identify areas where the team works well and areas where they could improve.
- Set an appropriate example for others to follow.

DEVELOPMENT SUCCESS FACTORS

Timeline: Within the next six months

Support Needed:

- I will need corporate support for analytics and business intelligence to inform me and my team.
- I will need a corporate-level leader or external mentor to bounce ideas off of and learn from their experiences.

Indicators of Success:

- I will have a strong plan for dealing with current business challenges, including long-term plans and contingencies.
- My team will feel engaged and involved in the decision-making process and committed to the ultimate plan.
- I will gain credibility with corporate leadership and respect for my thought processes.

7

TEAM LEADERSHIP

An Example of Coaching for Team Leadership

Ron Johnson's goal was to strengthen his Team Leadership skills in order to foster greater involvement, collaboration, and trust among team members. Here are some steps Ron's manager could take using the Awaken, Align, Accelerate framework to coach Ron in this area:

AWAKEN	**Increase INSIGHT**	Help Ron brainstorm what it takes to develop and lead high-performing teams. Analyze his strengths and areas of development against that model. Work with Ron to take an inventory of his participation on different teams and determine which people should be included in his 360-degree feedback assessment. Debrief Ron's 360-degree feedback and discuss implications for different teams. Provide feedback using your own observations. Help him assess where people on various teams could become more involved.
	MOTIVATE change	Discuss Ron's style of setting high expectations and how that style impacts his own enthusiasm as well as the motivation of others. Encourage Ron to visualize the kind of team leader he wants to become. Help Ron reflect on his previous experience as a team sponsor, team leader, or team member when he did not achieve the desired outcomes. Explore the consequences of not making any changes; identify consequences for him personally as well as his teams.
ALIGN	**PLAN goals**	Focus on what Ron could change to improve his team performance and results. Ask what would enable Ron to handle his current team commitments more successfully and how he could best prepare to lead global teams. Ask what Ron would spend time working toward and follow through on. Work together to construct a leadership development plan similar to the sample provided in this chapter.
	ALIGN expectations	Help Ron focus on aligning expectations and desired results with key stakeholders. Focus on what could improve the performance of his team/organization. Encourage Ron to get more people involved in supporting proposed changes. Observe Ron's interactions in meetings with the senior team. Coach him on making changes to improve his influence with others on the team.
ACCELERATE	**CREATE teachable moments**	Help Ron experiment with trying new Team Leadership approaches. Help Ron reflect on impact, successes, mistakes, and learning to enhance skills and sustain changes. Encourage Ron to assign others to perform developmental activities that will get them more involved with teams (e.g., managing several related projects simultaneously or leading task forces that are tackling cross-functional issues). Ask Ron to serve as a coach and sounding board for these activities.
	TRACK progress	Discuss what kinds of changes will be visible to others along with expected results. Debrief together periodically to see if he is becoming more comfortable involving others and working virtually with people on different teams. Provide feedback as you see Ron making progress toward his goals. Acknowledge and celebrate his efforts.

Results: Measuring Impact

Ron took almost a year to develop and work through his action plan. He found that some changes were needed on his plan after seeing his multi-rater feedback results. He added some action steps after reading the books about teams. Overall, he made tremendous progress on increasing the involvement of others wherever he served as sponsor, leader, or member of teams. His new Team Leadership skills allowed Ron to:

- Clarify his interest and accountability in playing different roles on teams.

- Become more comfortable using virtual teams and communicating with others during and after conference calls.

- Engage each one of his direct reports in planning and decision-making much more successfully than before.

- Gain enthusiastic support and collaboration from people on different teams as they worked on various issues.

- Enhance his credibility, trust, and influence with people at all levels, including other senior leaders.

8

Developing Leaders

Developmentally oriented leaders identify, deploy, and develop talented team members and trust them to lead and manage. They understand, plan for, hire, and develop the talent needed to support function and business objectives. They create and place staff in stretch assignments. They hold managers accountable for developing the leadership skills of their reports.

Factor	Competency	Core Practice
Leading People	Leading Courageously	Talent Assessment
Thinking and Deciding	Creating Alignment	Stretch Assignments
Achieving	Team Leadership	Development Culture
Relating to People	Developing Leaders	Feedback
Managing Work		Succession Planning
Managing Self		

Leadership development is the future of your organization. As Jack Welch said, "The team with the best players wins." This simple but telling statement highlights the importance of talent in every organization. Over time, without the development of leaders, an organization struggles. Apathy sets in, ideas dry up, the thrill of winning fades, and the organization's best talent seeks out the competition, where they feel they can win again. To minimize this risk, organizations are focusing significant energy on developing diverse talent to meet the needs of their customers today *and* in the future.

Many organizations consider developing talent to be one of their most important business strategies. This way of thinking about leadership is what gets them on the "Best Places to Work" list and keeps them at the top of their industry. Leadership—not necessarily innovation—is spurring the success of these top organizations. How have you prepared your organization's talent for the future? Are those at lower levels in the organization ready to take over if a leader moves on? What are you doing to develop talent across all levels of your organization? An organization's talent is often the difference between mediocrity and excellence. Research consistently shows that those who invest in and develop their talent succeed.

The ability to assess and develop talent is central to the long-term success of every organization. Managerial activities such as assessing talent, coaching others, and mentoring high-potential team members are clearly needed at all levels of leadership, whether you are a first-time manager, a director, or a senior executive. At more senior levels, the leader's role changes, and there is a need to think more broadly and consider how talent affects success across the organization. The table below illustrates how Developing Leaders varies according to leadership level.

How Leaders at Different Levels Develop Leaders

	Managers	Function Leaders	Senior Executives
Talent Assessment	Makes good hiring decisions.	Identifies, hires, or promotes top talent to achieve the organization's objectives.	Routinely assesses the organization's talent to meet current and emerging business demands.
Stretch Assignments	Assigns challenging tasks that help people learn and grow.	Provides relevant stretch assignments to develop others' leadership skills.	Provides stretch assignments to develop others' leadership breadth.
Development Culture	Encourages people to develop themselves and others.	Holds leaders accountable for developing talent.	Helps leaders see the value of talent development as a strategic lever.
Feedback	Actively coaches reports on their performance.	Provides feedback to strengthen leadership skills in others.	Creates a culture that supports open exchange of feedback.
Succession Planning	Identifies and develops leadership potential in direct reports.	Conducts regular reviews of leadership talent.	Champions the need to build key talent bench strength across the organization.

Self-Assessment

To evaluate your effectiveness in Developing Leaders, check all boxes below that represent current behavior or performance. Look for patterns: Which core practices represent a development need, a strength, or an excessive use? Recognize that you might have some blind spots. Invite your boss or colleagues to indicate what they have observed in your behavior. Use this assessment to help identify development suggestions that are most relevant to you.

	Needs Development	Strength	Excessive Use
Talent Assessment	☐ Displays poor understanding of the skills people need to succeed in the role and the group ☐ Misjudges the talent of others	☐ Identifies, assesses, and deploys top talent to achieve business objectives ☐ Makes sure the best people are in the right positions	☐ Constantly reorganizes, moving people around so much that they never gain traction ☐ Creates systems by which people are evaluated too regularly, not allowing sufficient time for change
Stretch Assignments	☐ Rarely assigns growth opportunities to team members ☐ Believes that having adequate experience is a necessary precursor for new opportunities	☐ Customizes developmental assignments to maximize reports' learning and growth ☐ Has a development assignment in mind for each team member	☐ Puts people in stretch assignments before they are ready—inadvertently sets them up to fail ☐ Is not thoughtful about which assignment would promote growth, feeling any rotation is acceptable
Development Culture	☐ Underemphasizes or de-values the importance of developing others ☐ Believes that development within a role is nonexistent and that development will only occur by promotion	☐ Involves direct reports in developing plans and strategies for filling the talent pipeline ☐ Ensures that all leaders have development plans for each direct report	☐ Focuses on reports' responsibilities for developing others, but neglects developing them ☐ Creates too many development goals for each report; focuses too much on learning for the sake of learning only
Feedback	☐ Avoids giving feedback or provides it in an ineffective manner ☐ Requires that employees figure it out themselves, keeping a hands-off approach	☐ Provides insightful, balanced, and challenging feedback that pushes people to a new level of performance ☐ Values coaching others, makes time for high impact conversations	☐ Comes across as critical, blaming, and never satisfied ☐ Leaves people feeling demotivated rather than challenged or supported
Succession Planning	☐ Allows function to operate without having key successors ready ☐ Protects own talent, preventing high-potentials from leaving the group to maintain talent	☐ Conducts regular reviews of leadership talent ☐ Ensures talent is in place to support changes in leadership; puts the right people in the right roles at the right time	☐ Develops unrealistic expectations for advancement among reports ☐ Promotes unhealthy competition pitting peers against each other for aspirational roles

Development Suggestions

The following section contains development suggestions for each core practice. Having completed the self-assessment, focus on suggestions that correspond to the core practices you identified as a development need or excessive use. Use these suggestions to create your own development plan, making sure to try one or two from each phase. In addition, feel free to create your own or adapt these to best meet your development needs.

Talent Assessment

Identify, hire, or promote top talent to achieve the organization's objectives.

> *If human beings are perceived as potentials rather than problems, as possessing strengths instead of weaknesses, as unlimited rather than dull and unresponsive, then they thrive and grow to their capabilities.*

Barbara Bush

Awaken potential:

- **Understand your direct reports' capabilities.** Regularly assess your direct reports against key knowledge, skills, and abilities (KSAs) determined for each departmental role, completing this task at least twice per year.

- **Complete a rigorous talent review.** Sort your direct reports into a nine-block talent grid (i.e., plot people by evaluating their performance as high-medium-low on one axis and their potential as high-medium-low on the other axis). This tool can provide insights about the readiness of particular people for broader roles or more responsibility—as well as comparing the performance and potential of everyone in your group.

- **Actively participate in talent review meetings.** Come prepared to talk about your own talent and provide feedback about others. Listen to all reviews and take notes. Later on, you may need to recruit some of those people for your organization. Your advance knowledge could lead to faster on-boarding.

Align goals:

- **Obtain team members' assessments.** Ask each of your team members where they feel most suited. Seek their input about where other team members might be most suited as well. Have them address their own and others' performance using objective criteria and not gut feeling.

- **Ask for others' evaluation.** Discuss with your peers and their teams the performance and potential of your team. Calibrate your ratings with other key stakeholders who observe their work.

- **Match resources to goals.** Review the goals set for your team this year. Will the positions you have in place facilitate the achievement of set goals? What other resources would help?

Accelerate performance:

- **Learn about leadership transitions.** Read *The Leadership Pipeline: How to Build the Leadership Powered Company* by Ram Charan, Stephen Drotter, and James Noel (Jossey-Bass, 2000) for some excellent guidance on nurturing and developing leaders through the six critical leadership passages.

- **Create robust job descriptions.** Ensure that each position within your organization has a clearly articulated job description, including KSAs necessary to execute the role well.

- **Provide honest feedback on capability.** Talk with direct reports about where they align with most relevant KSAs for their roles and what gaps they must close to facilitate a promotion or a move into a broader or more desired role.

- **Implement a multi-rater feedback tool** as part of your standard leadership development activities. Use this feedback to drive development recommendations.

- **Support development for the future.** Ensure that each direct report has a powerful development plan focused on more than just the achievement of this year's goals.

- **Promote for potential as well as performance.** Push yourself to promote not just the best performers, but those who have been identified as having significant potential as well. Remember, for instance, that the best sales person may not have the potential to be the most effective sales manager.

- **Beef up your selection process.** Use behavioral interview questions to identify the best candidates for each role. Try using leadership assessment from a reputable provider to calibrate and provide further insight to your internal ratings.

EXCESSIVE USE

As an example, if you constantly reorganize and shift leaders around, they may never gain traction. Try to leave people in place for longer periods of time so they can make more significant contributions where they are and also experience the consequences of their decisions.

Provide relevant stretch assignments to develop the leadership skills of others.

> *You cannot hope to build a better world without improving the individuals. To that end each of us must work for his own improvement, and at the same time share a general responsibility for all humanity, our particular duty being to aid those to whom we think we can be most useful.*

Marie Curie

8

DEVELOPING LEADERS

Awaken potential:

- **Learn from your own stretch experiences.** Reflect on stretch assignments you have had. How did you feel when your manager took a risk and trusted you with more responsibility? Such assignments offer tremendous learning opportunities. Ask yourself why you haven't stretched your own people more. Then start doing more.

- **Assess others' development needs.** Complete a leadership assessment to understand skill gaps of each member of your team.

- **Learn about "the growing edge."** Ask yourself whether you push your team members out of their comfort zones enough. Are they successfully "feeling the burn" of the stretch assignments you are asking them to do? Remember that the best development occurs when challenge and discomfort are strong enough, but not overwhelming.

- **Keep a ready resource of mentors.** Determine who might be strong internal mentors based on stretch assignments. Maintain an active list of internal mentors based on each mentor's strengths and expertise as well as the requirements of your team.

Align goals:

- **Identify growth roles.** Identify key roles that offer stepping stone growth opportunities, providing employees with significant growth and preparation for future roles. Ensure that you rotate your top talent through these roles to broaden their experience.

- **Customize developmental assignments** to maximize the learning and growth. Ensure that the experience is aligned with their development needs and plans.

- **Clarify developmental intent.** Make sure to discuss with your direct reports what development you believe stretch assignments will provide. Ensure they see these as opportunities, rather than your unloading something from your own plate.

Accelerate performance:

- **Learn to create meaningful development experiences.** Read *88 Assignments for Development in Place* (Center for Creative Leadership, 2003) to find out how to create stretch assignments for developing leaders from within.

- **Stretch yourself and others.** Read *Bootstrap Leadership: 50 Ways to Break Out, Take Charge, and Move Up* by Steve Arneson (Berrett-Koehler, 2010). Challenge yourself to find some ways to stretch yourself and your team.

- **Delegate for development.** Evaluate the tasks you perform for the organization. Which of these might provide stretch opportunities for team members if you delegated them? Match tasks with development opportunities for your team.

- **Match development to readiness.** Work to place key talent in developmental stretch assignments as they show readiness. Make a commitment to do so.

- **Vary developmental assignments.** Add onto the roles of team members incrementally. Remember that stretch assignments can be time-bound, project-focused, and short-term as well as more permanent.

- **Leverage internal expertise.** Assign internal mentors who are experts in the tasks you have selected for stretch assignments to provide support to your staff. Ensure that they focus on coaching rather than telling people what to do.

- **Balance challenge with support.** Imagine a scale with support on one side and a challenge on the other. Evaluate each stretch assignment you have assigned on this scale. Are you pushing your staff hard enough? Are you providing adequate support to ensure their success? Remember that balancing support and challenge is optimal in stretch assignments.

- **Encourage others to learn by doing.** Avoid taking control over situations in which you are the expert, expecting others to learn from you. Let others take the lead while you help them in a supporting role. Communicate when you are doing this.

EXCESSIVE USE

As an example, if you have put people in stretch assignments before they were ready and they failed, evaluate why. Was it due to lack of readiness? Support? Skill set? What could you have done differently to promote their success? Who might need that kind of attention now?

Hold leaders accountable for developing talent.

> *My main job was developing talent. I was a gardener providing water and other nourishment to our top 750 people. Of course, I had to pull out some weeds too.*
>
> Jack Welch

Awaken potential:

- **Seek feedback** from direct reports on how well you hold them accountable for developing talent. Ask them where you could refine or improve.

- **Learn what motivates you to develop others.** Reflect on a situation in which you felt inspired to develop those on your team. What promoted this motivation? What was done to help you reinforce this development?

Align goals:

- **Look upward for feedback** from your manager and peers about the degree to which you set stretch, yet realistic, goals for your team. Are you pushing them hard enough? Expecting too much?

- **Learn from others.** During talent review meetings, pay attention to how others develop their talent. Ask your peers about their approaches to talent development. Where do they identify strengths? Development opportunities? Ask for recommendations about where to focus more of your attention.

- **Involve your direct reports** in developing plans and strategies for filling the talent pipeline. Test your ideas for development recommendations, and seek their input.

Accelerate performance:

- **Model development.** Push yourself to learn and grow as well. Start by creating your own development plan and make it public. Lead the development charge with authority and by example.

- **Hold leaders accountable for developing talent** within their organizations. Ensure that development planning is part of each leader's annual performance goals. Make it a regular part of your ongoing one-on-one discussions.

- **Leverage group learning opportunities.** Aggregate development recommendations from each leader to provide targeted skill-building opportunities that can be generalized across the group. Use regular staff meetings or off-sites for group development.

- **Separate coaching from performance management.** Schedule regular coaching sessions, ones in which you "take off" your performance management hat, and "put on" your coaching hat. Clarify which hat you are wearing so that the person is clear about the message you are trying to convey.

- **Practice coaching conversations** with your human resources partner. Debrief how the conversations went and ask for feedback. Have him/her identify areas of strength or needs for refinement.

- **Provide internal mentors.** Identify possible role models for the behavior change you seek in your direct report. Pair him/her with an internal mentor—someone whom he/she can observe, discuss challenges with, etc.

- **Rate yourself as a developer of others.** Once a month, do an audit of your actions, rating them in terms of how well you held others accountable for growth and took adequate time to focus on the development of your organization.

- **Track development follow-through.** Implement a tool such as Fort Hill's *ResultsEngine* (www.forthillcompany.com) to help leaders track their people's progress against development goals.

- **Require timely performance feedback.** Encourage everyone to hold at least quarterly performance review sessions rather than saving their feedback for the annual review. Timeliness is an important aspect of any feedback.

EXCESSIVE USE

As an example, if you focus on their responsibility for developing others, but then neglect to develop them yourself, your credibility may be jeopardized. Become a better role model.

Provide feedback to strengthen leadership skills in others.

"Leadership is unlocking people's potential to become better."

Bill Bradley

Awaken potential:

- **Learn about coaching.** Reflect on your most and least powerful coaching experiences. What about it made an impact? What did not?

- **Consider why and how you give feedback.** Think through your approach to giving feedback. Do you use a framework or model? What is your philosophy? Why is feedback so important? Is it performance-related? Behavioral? Emotional?

- **Videotape yourself giving feedback**; analyze your approach. What would you appreciate if you were sitting in the other chair? What would you be adverse to?

- **Develop empathy.** Identify a time when you felt surprised or blindsided by feedback. How did that feel? How could the situation have been avoided?

Align goals:

- **Target your feedback.** Ensure that your feedback is always tied to the items most relevant to the team, department, or organization's goals.

- **Link feedback to organization performance.** Make links to the team or organization's goals in the context of giving feedback. Show how your direct report's actions help support or inhibit progress on these goals.

- **Focus on the precious few.** Ensure your coaching is focused on the things that will have the most effect on the organization—the "need-to-haves" versus the "nice-to-haves."

- **Ask for immediate feedback after providing coaching.** What are others seeing you try to accomplish? How are they reacting to the style you are using?

- **Share your own development goals.** Let your team know that you are focusing on improving your ability to coach and provide courageous and balanced feedback.

Accelerate performance:

- **Learn the DESC method** (describe, express, specify, consequence) of providing feedback. DESC helps minimize defensiveness and increase the receptivity of the person receiving feedback.

- **Practice giving feedback to a trusted mentor or coach.** Assess your areas of strength and development needs in providing feedback. Use this information to develop your own coaching plan.

- **Motivate with carrots, not sticks.** Use positive consequences rather than negative ones to motivate behavior change. They tend to be more inspiring and help people see what they could achieve with the behavior change you are seeking.

- **Focus on behavior.** Describe your observations in an unemotional way. This will help prevent the recipient from getting defensive and tuning out your feedback.

- **Track feedback suggestions, and monitor progress.** That which gets followed up on, also gets followed through. Ensure there is an adequate follow-through mechanism.

- **Practice a no-surprises feedback policy** as no one likes to be blindsided by feedback, especially in a performance review.

- **Use electronic reminders to help you remember to give feedback.** Others may need more feedback or reinforcement than you do. Ensure they receive enough feedback to stay motivated.

- **Don't overcomplicate.** Remember to keep coaching action plans simple; focus on one or two things rather than a laundry list. This ensures that the changes you are coaching toward will be sustainable and not just temporary.

EXCESSIVE USE

As an example, if your feedback leaves people feeling demotivated, establish a "catch them doing well" policy. Provide as much positive feedback as critical feedback. Keeping things balanced will ensure that your direct reports seek regular feedback from you instead of being intimidated.

Conduct regular reviews of leadership talent.

"Someone's sitting in the shade today because someone planted a tree a long time ago."

Warren Buffett

Awaken potential:

- **Learn about succession management.** If you are relatively new to succession management, read *Grow Your Own Leaders: How to Identify, Develop, and Retain Leadership Talent* by William Byham, Audrey Smith, and Matthew Paese (Prentice Hall, 2002) for suggestions about developing pools of leadership talent.

- **Evaluate how and when you promote others.** How many people have you promoted in the past year? What did you do to ensure they were ready for a broader role or more responsibility?

- **Gain insight from your own promotions.** Think through your own promotions. What prompted the organization to consider you for a bigger job?

- **Learn from when you were not promoted.** Talk with your manager about a time when a peer was promoted ahead of you. Seek insight about what made that person more ready.

- **Understand organizational rules and process.** Learn from the rationale used to make promotion decisions within your organization. What are the criteria today? What could make promotion decisions easier?

Align goals:

- **Ask about your company's succession planning process.** Talk with your human resources partner about the organization's philosophy and history regarding succession planning, especially if you are relatively new to the organization. (Some organizations have more visible policies and practices than others.) Find out how succession planning is linked to the talent review process. Ask for guidance about how you can maximize your contribution to the succession planning process.

- **Ask yourself if you are using succession planning strategically.** Is it more of replacement planning in case of an emergency or are you using it to grow and develop individuals and the organization?

- **Seek feedback from your peers.** How are they using succession planning differently from you? What about their strategy is working? What isn't?

Accelerate performance:

- **Identify "A" players.** Read *Topgrading: How Leading Companies Win by Hiring, Coaching and Keeping the Best People* by Bradford Smart (Prentice Hall, 1999). Talk with your organization about "A-B-C players" and work on recruiting and developing more "A" players.

- **Do your own succession planning.** Identify a list of potential successors for each role that reports to you. Expand your view to include enterprise-wide talent for successors. Don't limit yourself to only those within your own organization. Get to know others' talent as well.

- **Take on a mentee or two across the organization.** Broaden your understanding of high-potential talent in the organization. Actively seek out a high-potential person from another area to mentor.

- **Keep a journal of your progress** in developing successors, particularly noting what happened when you provided stretch experiences to others.

EXCESSIVE USE

As an example, if you raise people's expectations about succession or promote unhealthy competition, you may be operating with more transparency than necessary. Decide what level of investment you want to have in developing successors while considering the price of possible employee turnover.

Coach Others on Developing Leaders

When coaching others, focus on the core practices that were identified as either a development need or excessive use in the self-assessment at the beginning of this chapter. Identify and adapt any relevant development suggestions. Additional coaching tips are provided in the following table for some adverse leadership behaviors. For more information review Chapter 4, "Coach Others."

Coaching Suggestions

Behavior		Awaken	Align	Accelerate
Talent Assessment	Doesn't understand skill requirements	• Walk through the organization's competency model together. Demonstrate how to effectively measure a leader against it. • Review job descriptions within the person's organization. How well does the person believe current talent meets these requirements? What is missing?	• Ensure the person is committed to the organization's talent review/succession planning process. • Push the person to think more broadly about the future needs of the group. Based on the strategic plan, what will their needs be one year from now?	• Suggest other strategies (e.g., use of assessment, behavioral interviewing, etc.) that may enhance the person's ability to put the right people in the right roles. Have the person experiment and debrief progress. • Review current talent pipeline against needs of the organization together. Highlight opportunities to close the gap.
	Misjudges talent	• Discuss the person's strategy for assessing talent within the organization. What tools are being used? How are talent decisions being made? • Provide your own feedback and observations on talent within the person's organization. How does that align with the person's own perspective?	• Use peer review to discuss the performance and potential of the person's team. Have the person calibrate his/her own ratings against those of others. • Provide the person with an internal mentor who actively assesses talent well. Review with him/her how he/she has become an effective judge of talent. What tools does the person use to do so?	• Have the person experiment using multiple techniques (e.g., multi-rater feedback or talent reviews) for assessing talent. Multiple raters usually mean better perspective. • Debrief mid-year or year-end reviews together prior to the person delivering them to the team. How is the person making progress?

Behavior		Awaken	Align	Accelerate
Stretch Assignments	*Rarely assigns growth opportunities*	• Remind the individual that 70 percent of development occurs through experience. As you review development plans, make sure they are focused on more than just education or mentorship. • Review stretch assignments you have given the person. What has been gained from that experience?	• Ensure the person is thinking about assignments and opportunities that are broader than his/her group, team, or function. • Encourage conversations with other leaders about opportunities for their team members.	• Push the person to give up something meaningful from his/her own plate to provide a key developmental experience for another team member. Create a plan to do so, and monitor it with the person. • Model this by using experiences effectively as stretch assignments for your own team.
	Doesn't move people along	• Assess how frequently the person's team members are promoted. Discuss what the person is doing to hold others back. • Offer feedback regarding your own observations of instances the person showed protective behavior. What were the consequences?	• Brainstorm with your human resources partner opportunities for your team across the enterprise. • Hold career planning discussions with each direct report, reviewing which other areas or opportunities he/she may have interest in.	• Advocate for one of your staff members to take a rotational experience, even within your own team. • Facilitate networking with the person's team members and other cross-functional leaders. Take pride in making connections across the enterprise.
Development Culture	*Downplays the importance of developing others*	• Discuss the person's philosophy on development. How does the person believe development occurs? How has he/she been developed in the past? • Review a key time when your own development was facilitated by one of your managers and a time it was stifled. Ask the person to review how he/she has shown similar or different behavior to your examples.	• Advocate for an active role and model how you hold yourself accountable for others' development. Make this a part of each major discussion, at least quarterly. • Partner the person with the organization's chief talent officer or head of learning and development to review development plans for the team.	• Ensure the person is holding self and teams accountable for developing talent. Set this as a development goal for the person. • During your one-on-ones, ask how others are progressing on their development goals and what the individual is doing to facilitate their growth.

Behavior		Awaken	Align	Accelerate
Development Culture	*Believes that development occurs through promotion*	• Take time to review the development plans the person has put together with his/her team. What is the person doing to help the team grow and develop? Discuss how the person has used his/her development resources over the past few years. What has the person found valuable in programs, conferences, courses, or other opportunities? • Have the person review best practices literature on talent development. How would the person rate the organization and himself/herself based on the findings?	• Provide insight into how others (e.g., peers) are developing their team members. What best practices are you observing within the organization? Connect the person with someone in the organization who is actively demonstrating strong coaching of others. • Have the person present best practices findings to peers at a staff meeting. Have them discuss how they would change the organization's focus on development based on these findings and the organization's strategic goals.	• Debrief coaching sessions with the person's team members to provide real-time feedback on making the conversations more effective. • Hold the person accountable for enrolling team members in organizational leadership development programs, learning opportunities, etc.
Feedback	*Avoids giving feedback*	• Learn how to give feedback in a way that promotes listening rather than defensiveness, such as DESC (describe, express, specify, consequence). • Ensure the person understands when you are providing performance feedback or development feedback. Convey how you adjust your own style to meet the person's needs.	• Link team progress with results as well as successes and challenges. Demonstrate the correlation between feedback, adapting the approach, and results. • Have the person consult with team members. How would they rate the person's ability to give feedback? What could the person improve upon?	• Practice tough coaching sessions with the individual. Have the person experiment using positive consequences, not just negative ones. • Use positive consequences with the person. Show the positive implication of this investment in the person's team.

8

DEVELOPING LEADERS

Behavior		Awaken	Align	Accelerate
Feedback	*Is too hands-off*	• Discuss when the person engages with his/her team. What are the triggers? Are there routine opportunities being missed? • Provide an example of when you believed the person could have taken a more active role. What were the consequences?	• Help the person seek feedback from others on his/her involvement and ability to effectively coach others. How does the person's team or other stakeholders believe he/she could improve? • Have the person observe the one-on-one meetings of others. How do they actively coach during these sessions? Create a plan together for what behavior the person plans on experimenting with during his/her own meetings.	• Sit in on the person's team meeting. Provide active and open feedback about his/her style and agenda. Debrief team meetings regularly together. How are they evolving? What is the person experimenting with? What is working? What is not? • Encourage the person to work with a master coach to begin targeted skill building on coaching.
Succession Planning	*Fails to develop successors*	• Seek to understand the rationale behind the person's succession plan. Has the person adequately assessed the performance, potential, and readiness of the organization? Challenge thinking to establish or refine the person's process. • Provide your own insights on his/her talent to validate or challenge perspective.	• Seek out other leaders from across the organization to talk about the person's talent. Suggest the person talk to other leaders for whom his/her team serves as a resource or provides support. • Implement a departmental talent review process where staff can share their experiences and discuss the talents of each other.	• Model being a mentor to others within the organization on succession and suggest the person do that as well. • Review the person's succession plan together. Ensure the person is taking both a strategic and tactical approach. How has the person planned for both immediate and future needs of staff and the organization?
	Protects own talent	• Assess how frequently the person rotates team members to other parts of the business. Discuss what the person is doing to hold others back. • Provide an example of when you let one of your key team members move on. Explain the difficulty you had with the situation, but also what was achieved from the opportunity.	• Collaborate with the internal human resources partner to brainstorm opportunities for the person's team across the enterprise. • Together, create a plan to move strong talent on and cultivate new, emerging high-potentials.	• Advocate for one of the person's staff members to take a rotational experience. Make it a development goal for the person in the upcoming year. • Foster and model opportunities as a strong talent manager yourself.

Tips for Coaching in a Global Environment

Developing Leaders may be practiced or expressed differently within other cultures. This might impact how you approach coaching. Try to keep an open mind, avoid generalizations, and continue gathering data as you gain experience with another culture. Consider these suggestions:

Talent Assessment: Consult with human resources to find out local practices before doing much coaching in this area. Countries have different employment laws and customs that must be considered along with corporate practices. Some cultures do not value diversity and may not prohibit discrimination. Others have established affirmative action practices (e.g., the United States) or positive discrimination policies (e.g., India) to provide equal opportunity or address social imbalances. Cronyism and familial connections are still rampant in some places. The practice of using standardized tests and other validated measures is not universal; for example, people in some countries may use blood typing, university prestige, or homemade testing to screen candidates. Find out what practices the leader is currently using to identify, assess, and deploy top talent before coaching any changes.

Stretch Assignments: Singling out an individual for stretch assignments or special treatment is more common in some cultures than others. Recognize that this type of attention may not be motivating for some individuals. When you see behavior that may be too controlling (e.g., not allowing other team members to take advantage of a development opportunity), have a dialogue about what your expectations are for stretching and empowering people on the team. You may need to help people stretch their definition of leadership and find other ways to lead.

Development Culture: Learn all you can about the culture of the leaders you are coaching. Does the culture promote individual development, or is it more focused on group training? Help the leaders understand your expectations for developing the people around them. Be clear about how you will measure their success and what incremental indicators will look like. If leaders are not actively championing the development of their teams, you cannot simply assume that they are not strong talent developers. Have a conversation about development, and ensure you fully understand what has been expected of them in the past.

Feedback: The responsibility for coaching has become an important part of the managerial role in some cultures, but not in others. Some people may associate coaching with sports rather than business. Find out how coaching is practiced in the culture with which you are working. Be cautious about the directness of your feedback. Some cultures are less forthright than others, and this may prevent some people from hearing the point you are trying to make.

Succession Planning: Some countries have such high turnover among high-potential leaders that the notion of succession planning is almost laughable. In some cultures, the promotion of talent is up to the senior executives and is not the role of line management. Other countries have had what amounts to a life-long employment system where companies took care of their people—rotating them among departments and promoting them based on seniority. Leaders in such cultures were not invited to think about personal career goals. They learned to take care of their employees in a paternalistic manner. Globalization and the fast pace of change have radically altered these systems. However, mid-career and senior leaders who grew up in those systems may not have a good appreciation of the role individual aspirations or individual performance can play in achieving career or business success. Such people may need extra help to identify and develop successors.

A Case Study in Developing Leaders

Developing Leaders requires you to effectively identify talent, create a development culture, promote succession planning, challenge others, and provide coaching and support. As you read about Grant's situation, reflect on what you've learned about Developing Leaders in this chapter. How does Grant sound like you or one of your team members? What experiences or tendencies do you share? Finally, consider how you would help Grant demonstrate greater skill in Developing Leaders and be successful in his leadership role.

Stretching Successors

Grant Peters was a successful, high-potential general manager. Leading the flagship plant in a highly profitable organization for the past ten years, he was in an enviable position. His results were strong and he reached all of his major goals. Grant grew up in the business and worked just about every role within his division. This made him extremely valuable to the organization. Having first-hand knowledge of many important tasks and roles, his advice came from experience; he wasn't shy about telling others what to do. He considered himself the epitome of plant leadership.

While he enjoyed his success over time, he always yearned to do more—to be able to take on a larger role within the enterprise. When Grant asked the president of his division about his next opportunity within the organization, he was taken aback by what he heard. His boss saw him as having a hub-and-spoke style of leadership in which all decisions came through him, rather than empowering his team to lead on their own. Grant was told that if he wanted to take a different role, he had to build leadership skills across his team to prepare the organization for his eventual succession.

Knowing that he would need to "show up differently" to his team and manager, Grant realized he had to reposition his leadership role in the organization and change the culture he had established within his team. He needed to give more feedback, provide assignments that would stretch people, and develop a strong succession plan to fully develop the leaders below him. Yet, he could not afford to lose the results they were achieving just to make the changes. He wondered how that would go.

In consultation with his boss, Grant decided to seek support from an executive coach to develop his organization for the impending change. This would involve defining and communicating the shift in his leadership role, clarifying the roles and responsibilities of his team, and identifying specific changes necessary for the team to grow (e.g., replacing his hub-and-spoke leadership with a more empowering style and changing how he would hold his team accountable). He also wanted to focus on closing development gaps of his team through specific and targeted development plans to ready them for transition into broader roles.

Grant found that he needed skills in Developing Leaders more than ever, in order to:

- Create rigorous development plans for his direct reports.

- Promote stretch assignments for team members to learn on the job.

- Empower his team to make decisions rather than over-relying on him.

- Establish a solid succession plan to prepare the organization for his transition.

- Hold others, not just himself, accountable for developing leaders throughout the organization.

Grant's Leadership Development Plan

Following is a sample development plan for Grant Peters. Research on leadership development has shown that leaders learn through experience and that this learning is optimized through the use of an individual development plan. A successful plan includes new experiences and introduces the leader to new conversations and tools. The suggestions included in the previous sections may stimulate your thinking about additional possibilities for Grant's development.

LEADERSHIP DEVELOPMENT PLAN FOR GRANT PETERS
DEVELOPMENT GOAL
Goal: To strengthen my skills in Developing Leaders
Desired Outcomes—results I want to see from developing this skill
Self: Be a strong developer of talent across the organization, allowing opportunity for future promotion.   **Team:** Be promotable, having a core foundation of development, strong execution, and results.   **Organization:** Bench strength will improve, allowing greater results and less investment in hiring.
Self-Understanding—strengths that I can build on and development needs I can address
Strengths: Direct and forthright; seen as an expert within the organization; history of strong results   **Development Needs:** Can be critical; tendency to take over and do it myself; focused on quarterly results versus the long term
Business Context—challenges in my business environment that require this skill
The challenges I face in my business environment include a strong focus on short-term, quarterly results; my team tends to look to me for direction, and I provide it rather than pushing them to think critically; our history of strong results—if it ain't broke, why fix it?

LEADERSHIP DEVELOPMENT PLAN FOR GRANT PETERS

DEVELOPMENT ACTIONS

AWAKEN

- Review the development plans I currently have for my staff. Evaluate how much is focused on goal execution and how much is focused on development. Identify areas to strengthen.

- Read *88 Assignments for Development in Place* by Michael Lombardo and Robert Eichinger (Center for Creative Leadership, 1989) for ideas.

- Use a multi-rater feedback tool (e.g., 360-degree) to gather insight on myself. Show others how I will lead by example and use that feedback to provide development activities for myself.

- Learn about succession management. Read *Grow Your Own Leaders: How to Identify, Develop, and Retain Leadership Talent* by William Byham, Audrey Smith, and Matthew Paese (Prentice Hall, 2002) for suggestions about developing pools of leadership talent.

- Evaluate how and when I promote others. How many people have I promoted in the past year? What did I do to ensure they were ready for a broader role or more responsibility?

- Gain insight from my own promotions. What prompted the organization to consider me for a bigger job?

- Learn from when I was not promoted. Talk with my manager about a time when a peer was promoted ahead of me. Seek insight about what made that person more ready.

ALIGN

- Share and compare my succession plan with those of my peers. Ask ourselves if we are effectively thinking about each other's talent as we strive to strengthen our bench?

- Actively participate in the organization's talent review—and not only when talking about my own talent.

ACCELERATE

- Create development plans with each key direct report and high-potential.

- Secure mentors for direct reports, allowing them to have another perspective, rather than just my own.

- Take on a mentee or two across the organization. Broaden my understanding of high-potential talent in the organization. Actively seek out a high-potential from another area to mentor.

- Keep a journal of my progress in developing successors, particularly noting what happened when I provided stretch experiences to others.

DEVELOPMENT SUCCESS FACTORS

Timeline: Within the next six months

LEADERSHIP DEVELOPMENT PLAN FOR GRANT PETERS

Support Needed:

- Ongoing feedback from my manager on the strength of my team.

- Insight and reactions from my team on the way I provide feedback. Is it positive or does it make them feel hurt or defensive?

Indicators of Success:

- I will have rigorous development plans for each direct report and high-potential in my organization.

- At least quarterly, I will provide regular feedback to my team on their progress toward development goals. I will practice a no-surprises approach to feedback.

- I will learn and effectively use the DESC (describe, express, specify, consequence) method for providing feedback.

- Direct reports will say that I am more effective at providing clear, direct, and supportive feedback.

8

DEVELOPING LEADERS

An Example of Coaching to Develop Leaders

Grant Peters' goal was to strengthen his skills in Developing Leaders in order to be promoted himself. Here are some steps Grant's manager could take using the Awaken, Align, Accelerate framework to coach Grant in this area:

AWAKEN	**Increase INSIGHT**	Debrief Grant's multi-rater feedback. Focus on any items or comments related to how he provides feedback or develops others. Take time to review the development plans he has put together with his team. What is he doing to help his team grow and develop?
	MOTIVATE change	Help Grant reflect on previous promotions as well as times when he wasn't promoted. Ask how his motivation was impacted. Suggest that he try to imagine how and why people on his team might be motivated to develop their skills. Explore the consequences of not developing other leaders. Encourage him to become a role model in this area.
ALIGN	**PLAN goals**	Plan goals and actions for improvement. Identify possibilities for change that would enable Grant to develop others more successfully. Focus on how Grant could improve the way he provides feedback to others. Work together to construct a leadership development plan similar to the sample provided in this chapter.
	ALIGN expectations	Discuss Grant's expectations about what will happen when he completes his development plan. Reinforce succession planning and developing others as the right things to do—not just what will help him get promoted. Link progress his team is making with results, successes, and challenges. Demonstrate how developing leaders is correlated with results.
ACCELERATE	**CREATE teachable moments**	Push Grant to give up something meaningful from his own plate to provide a key experience for another team member. Model this by using experiences effectively as stretch assignments for your own team. Try to observe how Grant provides feedback to people on his team. Coach him on making changes to improve the clarity and directness of his feedback.
	TRACK progress	Encourage Grant to review his development goals, experiments, and learnings with leaders on his team who are engaged in their own development. Discuss how the development of his people could become visible to others. Work with Grant to evaluate progress toward his goals. Invite feedback from others, and ask them to support the changes they see. Acknowledge and celebrate his efforts.

Results: Measuring Impact

Grant Peters sped through his development plan in record time, recognizing that this was a precondition for his promotion. He was conscientious in trying out every action step, although he found some activities were more useful than others. He experimented with approaches recommended in some of the resources. After six months, his manager informed Grant that he was back on track for promotion as long as his people kept developing. His new skills in Developing Leaders allowed Grant to:

- Implement rigorous development plans for each of his direct reports and all high-potentials.

- Provide regular, clear, direct, and supportive feedback on people's development.

- Hold other leaders accountable for developing their talent.

- Create stretch assignments and become a mentor for several high-potentials.

- Establish a solid succession plan.

THINKING
AND
DECIDING

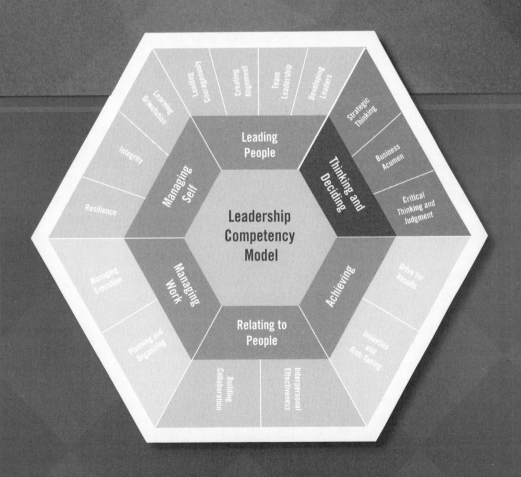

Leadership
Competency
Model

Leading
People

Thinking and
Deciding

Managing
Self

Achieving

Managing
Work

Relating to
People

Learning
Orientation

Creating
Alignment

Team
Leadership

Developing
Leaders

Strategic
Thinking

Business
Acumen

Integrity

Critical
Thinking and
Judgment

Resilience

Drive for
Results

Managing
Execution

Innovation
and
Risk-Taking

Planning and
Organizing

Building
Collaboration

Interpersonal
Effectiveness

9

Strategic Thinking

Strategic leaders bring a broad and longer-term perspective to bear on issues and problems. They possess a strategic mindset and an external focus, and consider industry, market, customer, and competitor information when developing plans. They evaluate the strategic fit of decisions and actions, and their impact on the entire business. They identify and advocate state-of-the-art practices that improve profitability and competitive advantage.

Factor	Competency	Core Practice
Leading People	Strategic Thinking	Long-term perspective
Thinking and Deciding	Business Acumen	External Focus
Achieving	Critical Thinking and Judgment	Strategic Scope
Relating to People		Growth Orientation
Managing Work		Competitive Advantage
Managing Self		

In the midst of emails, tasks, and tweets, it's easy to miss the future. A successful leader takes the time to imagine the future and strategize for the organization. Strategic Thinking is the competency successful leaders apply to uncover potential opportunities that will chart the future course of their functions or the entire organization. Strategic thinkers bring perspective to the potential opportunities and threats facing the business, create strategies that support the organization's direction, and assess the implications of different approaches. Strong Strategic Thinking results in improved capability, measurable growth, and increased profitability.

To think strategically, a leader must understand the internal operations of the organization and how it connects to the external competitive landscape. A continual analysis of internal and external factors will uncover potential opportunities or threats in the current decisions and actions being executed. Leaders who think strategically will play a key role in designing the direction and shaping the future of their organizations. Without clear strategy, organizations waste valuable time, energy, and resources—they lose their ability to compete effectively.

Thinking strategically involves visualizing the future, understanding the external business environment, considering the strategic impact of decisions and choices, creating new strategies to grow the business, and improving the overall competitive position of an organization. Senior leaders must understand how the business is positioned in its industry as well as market, customer, and competitive factors that influence its performance. Developing the organization's strategic orientation and considering the impact of decisions on the future direction of the organization is key to sustainability. While the ability to think strategically is important for all leaders, the most effective behaviors vary by level, as illustrated in the following table.

How Leaders at Different Levels Think Strategically

	Managers	Function Leaders	Senior Executives
Long-Term Perspective	Makes decisions that reflect both short-term and long-term thinking.	Brings a long-term perspective to planning and problem-solving.	Identifies the long-term implications of different strategic approaches.
External Focus	Stays abreast of the marketplace, competitors, and customer needs.	Demonstrates a well-developed understanding of the external business environment.	Evaluates business strategies relative to the competition and industry.
Strategic Scope	Understands the implications of decisions and plans for the organization's strategy.	Considers the strategic impact of decisions and choices on the business.	Critiques and develops corporate business strategy
Growth Orientation	Embraces and focuses on implementing key growth initiatives.	Creates ideas and strategies to grow the business.	Focuses growth initiatives on new markets or unaddressed customer needs.
Competitive Advantage	Integrates best practices into plans and decisions.	Promotes ways of doing things that increase differentiation and competitive advantage.	Consistently considers how to enhance differentiation and competitive advantage.

9

STRATEGIC THINKING

Self-Assessment

To evaluate your effectiveness in Strategic Thinking, check all boxes below that represent current behavior or performance. Look for patterns: Which core practices represent a development need, a strength, or an excessive use? Recognize that you might have some blind spots. Invite your boss or colleagues to indicate what they have observed in your behavior. Use this assessment to help identify development suggestions that are most relevant to you.

	Development Need	Strength	Excessive Use
Long-Term Perspective	☐ Lacks insight around potential solutions or future opportunities ☐ Unable to see a broader vision of the future; fails to recognize future impact of decisions	☐ Considers longer-term implications when planning and problem solving ☐ Thinks and plans for a two to three year time horizon	☐ Focuses too much on the future and loses touch with the current state of the business ☐ Spends too much time anticipating and countering different possibilities
External Focus	☐ Has an internal focus and fails to consider external influences when developing plans ☐ Fails to solicit input from external sources	☐ Develops strategies relative to the marketplace, industry, and competition ☐ Clearly understands the external business environment and its impact on the organization	☐ Overemphasizes external orientation ☐ Fails to give sufficient attention to internal issues
Strategic Scope	☐ Fails to consider the business' strategy when making decisions ☐ Decisions and plans reflect primarily short-term, operational thinking	☐ Thinks about business strategy as well as tactics ☐ Consistently ensures that decisions and actions are aligned with and support business strategy	☐ Overanalyzes; prefers thinking or talking about problems at a higher level more than taking action ☐ Lacks patience when handling tactical details
Growth Orientation	☐ Plans are primarily operational and show little focus on growth ☐ Is not in tune with the market; doesn't understand customer needs	☐ Develops ideas and strategies to grow the business ☐ Anticipates and understands the current and emerging needs of customers	☐ Proposes ideas that are odd, too unconventional, or otherwise not grounded in reality ☐ Allows day-to-day operations to suffer by too much focus on doing things differently
Competitive Advantage	☐ Maintains the status quo and rarely considers new or different approaches for the department ☐ Is not in tune with profit or loss of the business or department	☐ Is focused on improving the organization's differentiation and competitive advantage ☐ Ensures best-in-class practices are regularly considered and implemented	☐ Jeopardizes productivity by introducing too many improvement ideas ☐ Spends too much time outside the organization researching competitors

Development Suggestions

The following section contains development suggestions for each core practice. Having completed the self-assessment, focus on suggestions that correspond to the core practices you identified as a development need or excessive use. Use these suggestions to create your own development plan, making sure to try one or two from each phase. In addition, feel free to create your own or adapt these to best meet your development needs.

Long-Term Perspective

Bring a long-term perspective to planning and problem-solving.

"Vision without action is a daydream.
Action without vision is a nightmare."

Japanese proverb

Awaken potential:

- **Consider how actively you have contributed to strategic decisions.** Critique yourself and identify things to do differently. Think back to a time when you had a strategic idea. What were the circumstances that prompted you to think strategically? What did you do with that idea? Keep a journal to record strategic ideas. Discuss your ideas with a trusted colleague and brainstorm how to bring them forward.

- **Evaluate how well you know the long-term strategy.** What are the long-term goals and strategies of your business unit or company? How do the plans or objectives for your current responsibilities relate to the long-term strategies?

Align goals:

- **Gain perspective from others.** Talk with your manager about how to take a longer-term view in looking at plans and decisions. What are the expectations for your role? Make sure the way you are thinking about strategy aligns with the organization's priorities. Obtain your manager's perspective on important decisions. Other colleagues can also help you see possibilities from a fresh perspective.

- **Develop a stakeholder map,** and figure out how to more fully engage key stakeholders in what the future might look like. Having them engaged with you will help you understand the levers for their success when developing your own objectives.

Accelerate performance:

- **Identify the strategic thinkers in your organization.** Arrange to interview them over coffee or invite them to join a team meeting to share how they think and what they think about. What kinds of questions do they ask? What comments do they make? How does their thinking differ from yours?

- **Review customer data** that illustrates opportunities for improvement in quality. What changes would be needed to make these improvements?

- **Recognize the long-term implications of different strategic approaches.** Think about the conditions of success and identify the results or mileposts you would like to see at each interval or time frame.

- **Keep a long-term mindset.** When others present ideas, be sure to ask how their ideas connect to the long term and to company strategy. Create a list of three to five key questions that can help put you and others into a long-term mindset.

- **Challenge your long-term view.** Ask yourself what time span is best to identify and weigh future forces, develop options, and play out the implications of your strategy. Read "Strategy Under Uncertainty" by Hugh Courtney, Jane Kirkland, and Patrick Viguerie (*Harvard Business Review*, 1997) to help you think differently about long-term solutions. You will need to increase the time horizon of your thinking as you move to higher levels.

- **Study other industries.** Attend industry trade shows, including some that are not directly related to your field. Trends that revolutionize an industry often come from another field. Industry players can become too insular. Avoid reliance on simply extrapolating current trends into the future. Imagine how your own industry could be disrupted. What could change the current portfolio of products and buyers in the future?

- **Get a mentor.** Ask your manager who could serve as a mentor, or be a sounding board for you in this area.

EXCESSIVE USE

As an example, if you spend too much time thinking about the future, you may miss the chance to correct present problems. Don't neglect short-term thinking and action.

Demonstrate a well-developed understanding of the external business environment.

> *To satisfy the customer is the mission and purpose of every business. The question 'What is our business?' can, therefore, be answered only by looking at the business from the outside, from the point of view of customer and market.*

Peter F. Drucker

Awaken potential:

- **Assess your sense of the business environment.** Do you continually review business models being used by competitors? How are their operations different? What are they electing to outsource? Study a variety of business models.

- **Evaluate your customer knowledge.** Rate yourself on the depth of your knowledge about your customers. Who are your customers? What are their buying trends? How are they influenced? When was the last time you interacted personally with them? If the answer is rarely, you need mechanisms for staying in touch with them.

Align goals:

- **Talk to customers** about buying trends and other critical data. Review findings with key stakeholders and evaluate how your goals and objectives align with where your customers are going.

- **Stay current.** Ask your manager to help you keep up-to-date with industry and company developments. Discuss implications for key initiatives in your part of the business. Use your understanding of external forces to establish objectives for your team.

Accelerate performance:

- **Learn to analyze industries and competitors.** Read *Competitive Advantage* by Michael Porter (Free Press, 1998) for information about strategic analytic techniques. Porter's five forces concept (rivalry, threat of substitutes, buyer power, supplier power, and barriers to entry) provides a useful model for understanding what influences an industry.

- **Analyze trends that may impact your organization.** Complete an External Environment Analysis (a template is included in the appendix) to understand key

9

STRATEGIC THINKING

factors, opportunities and threats related to societal, technological, economic, environmental, and political impacts. What is your current competitive advantage? What external factors affect your competitive positioning? What trends could impact your future strategy? Prepare a presentation of your findings that you can share with others to heighten their awareness of the need to change.

- **Learn about the competition.** Identify all key competitors. Assemble a grid that captures your competitors' strategies, strengths, and weaknesses.

- **Subscribe to industry magazines and e-newsletters.** Also read about broader areas of business and economics through popular sources such as *The Wall Street Journal*. Keep a monthly log of what you have learned, especially conclusions about the challenges and pressures affecting your industry

- **Request information on market trends.** Find new ways to analyze and leverage information. Seek out and use all of the resources that are available to you in terms of technology and expertise.

- **Meet your customers.** Find ways to interact with external customers at least annually even if your role does not include customer contact. This will help you gain a better understanding of how others view your organization.

- **Be an active student of business.** Focus both in your field and throughout the business world. Learn about individuals and organizations that have developed innovative business ideas.

EXCESSIVE USE

As an example, if you overemphasize an external orientation,
you may fail to give sufficient attention to internal issues and opportunities.
Make sure you take a balanced approach.

Consider the strategic impact of decisions and choices on the business.

> *I skate to where the puck is going to be, not to where it's been.*

Wayne Gretzky

Awaken potential:

- **Challenge your understanding of the company's strategy.** What are the fundamental assumptions behind it? Are you trying to achieve a low-cost advantage or differentiate in some way you believe the market (customers) will value? Can you articulate the difference between your business' strategy and your function's strategy? Do all members of your team understand what the company is trying to do strategically?

- **Rate yourself on strategic thinking.** Create two rating scales: (1) detail orientation and tactical, and (2) strategic and big picture. Ask your manager, peers, and team members to rate you on both scales. Effective leaders can do both.

- **Rate yourself on strategic talking.** Can you describe the organization's strategy and initiatives in a compelling and motivating way? Solicit feedback to check your assessment. Ask other leaders and peers for suggestions.

Align goals:

- **Align your function with the organization's overall strategy.** Develop a clear understanding of how your work impacts the business and contributes to the bottom line. Talk to peers or managers in the areas with which you intersect. Ask how your work affects their operations. Work with your team to "connect the dots" between daily activities and strategy by helping them translate broader strategies into specific implications for everyone's work. Review Chapter 6, "Creating Alignment," for ideas on how to create a shared understanding and commitment to the organization's strategic direction.

- **Review the business strategy regularly** with your team. Use the strategy to guide decisions and prioritize action steps. Identify how strategy could be impacted if an initiative is altered.

9

STRATEGIC THINKING

Accelerate performance:

- **Expand your knowledge** of strategic marketing or strategic analysis by attending courses or seminars to gain exposure to models that could guide your thinking about strategy.

- **Stay current on your organization.** Periodically review corporate documents such as mission and values statements. Read press releases, articles, and investor presentations. Practice communicating about these topics with your team.

- **Clarify your assumptions.** Maintain a clear, overall view of the operational and financial parameters of the organization so that your strategies are based on assumptions that are realistic, practical, and financially feasible.

- **Vet strategies with others.** Develop a formal process for reviewing and fine-tuning proposed strategies. Invite people from different parts of the organization to participate in critiquing your strategies. Volunteer to reciprocate.

- **Plan scenarios.** For critical decisions, map the short-term and long-term implications of various alternatives. List the conditions or changes that would disrupt current business strategies. What risks are associated with your planned approach?

- **Do contingency planning.** For every implementation schedule you create, spend time looking at what could go wrong and what you would do if that happened. Incorporate contingency thinking into your execution plans.

- **Consider the talent implications of your strategies.** Learn to project workforce needs for the future by analyzing the strategic initiatives of your department.

- **Analyze strategically.** Refer to the "Diagnosis" core practice in this chapter for additional recommendations that could help you analyze situations more strategically.

EXCESSIVE USE

As an example, if you go overboard in developing elaborate strategies, you may procrastinate on important decisions. Surround yourself with people who are great at execution.

Growth Orientation

Create ideas and strategies to grow the business.

*"Don't judge each day by the harvest you reap,
but by the seeds you plant."*

Robert Louis Stevenson

Awaken potential:

- **Assess your outside perspective.** Evaluate whether you are keeping well-informed about customer preferences, competitors, the dynamics of your industry, and the economy in general. You need this background to make choices about how to do things that customers will pay for. This requires crisp thinking and bold decisions so a firm doesn't end up with a vague or unworkable strategy.

- **Compare yourself to a recent MBA graduate.** Compare your strategic knowledge repertoire to that of new MBA graduates. Have you been staying up-to-date with the latest thinking on strategy being taught in leading business schools?

- **Evaluate what you are doing to grow the business.** To what extent are you simply maintaining or managing programs that have worked well in the past rather than making changes and improvements?

Align goals:

- **Talk with your manager** to better understand how your initiatives will contribute to the growth of the organization. Make time to communicate the growth strategies to your team.

- **Connect with key stakeholders** across the organization to discuss opportunities for growth. How could you adjust your goals and objectives to take advantage of new opportunities? For example, ask people in the marketing function what you could do to capitalize on growth prospects. Become involved in the broader organization through task force assignments and company meetings. Network with other leaders to stay current on issues in other areas.

Accelerate performance:

- **Swim in a different pond.** Read *Blue Ocean Strategy: How to Create Uncontested Market Space and Make Competition Irrelevant* by W. Chan Kim and Renée Mauborgne (Harvard Business Press, 2005) to learn about a different approach to developing strategies for growth.

- **Conduct a SWOT analysis** to identify opportunities to pursue a new strategy. How do some of the anticipated future needs of your customers differ from what you are providing them today?

- **Establish an ongoing customer feedback system.** Talk regularly with key customers to gather information about their current and future needs. Review potential new products/services with customers (internal or external) through focus groups or other processes to solicit their reactions and insights.

- **Encourage "what if" thinking.** Model and develop a culture where "what if" thinking is reinforced and valued. Add players to your team who will come up with innovative ideas for growing the business.

- **Ask "what if" questions.** Identify what would need to change in the current structure if the strategy was altered. To learn more about ways to engage others in evaluating the need for change and ensuring alignment across functions, review the "Coordination" core practice in Chapter 6.

- **Examine your assumptions** regarding what is possible within a given framework and the information you have available. Some of the best strategic innovations are later viewed as obvious or simple. Developing distinctive new strategies requires courage and creativity in taking calculated risks. In Chapter 5 the "Courage" core practice provides suggestions for challenging your view of the status quo. The "Creativity" core practice in Chapter 13 provides techniques and behaviors that will help you step outside your comfort zone to embrace new possibilities.

- **Debate future strategies regularly.** Surround yourself with individuals who have different perspectives, think in new ways, and will challenge your own thinking.

- **Practice compelling communication.** Selling a new strategy requires you to communicate in language that will speak to the individuals and departments who will implement those plans. Figure out what they will be most interested in or most skeptical about. Plan and practice your communications accordingly.

EXCESSIVE USE

As an example, if you are too focused on the next new thing, you may fail to leverage what is already working well. When facing new challenges, consider approaches that were effective in addressing similar problems, even if they were used in different businesses or situations.

Competitive Advantage

Promote ways of doing things that increase differentiation and competitive advantage.

Don't be afraid of opposition. Remember, a kite rises against, not with, the wind.

Hamilton Wright Mabie

Awaken potential:

- **Assess your objectivity.** Be honest about what you believe the business could do differently. What do you think the organization should stop doing? Start doing? What would you do if you owned the business? Do you see ways to help the organization manage cash flow better? What does your team think the organization could do differently? Ask the question, "How could we beat ourselves?"

- **Rate your knowledge of competitors.** Compare yourself to someone who is more knowledgeable about competitors. What is missing from your skill set? Can that person serve as your mentor? Identify what you want to learn.

Align goals:

- **Check your knowledge of the fundamentals.** The most common sources of differentiation and competitive advantage comprise a short list: efficiency (low cost); quality (reliable or best-in-class products and services); innovation; and customer responsiveness. Do you know which of these provides the foundation for your company's business strategy and how your team or function contributes to it?

- **Research best practices.** Find out how others in the company have used best practices to improve what they do. Talk to your manager about what he/she thinks might be possible in your area.

Accelerate performance:

- **Conduct an industry analysis** using Michael Porter's five forces to evaluate sources for competitive advantage. What differentiates you from the competition? Where could you gain market share?

- **Keep informed about best practices** for your function and in your industry. Read magazines like *Business Week*, *Fortune*, and *The Economist* to spark your thinking. Where do you have opportunities for improving on the status quo?

9

STRATEGIC THINKING

- **Expand your perspective.** Propose or volunteer to serve on a task force that will examine alternative approaches to an issue or opportunity relevant to your company's future.

- **Organize a benchmarking trip** and invite peers in other functions to come along. Visit organizations that have experienced changes similar to those that are affecting or will affect your organization.

- **Canvass customers.** Ask customers about future needs and requirements. Discover how they are planning to go to market. What can you do to help them realize their future state? Find out what features of your current products or offerings are most valued.

- **Find out why customers buy.** Read customer satisfaction reports or reach out to customers to understand why they continue to do business with you. Review customer feedback, product return reasons, or other data that could reveal operational issues that need to be addressed.

- **Tap other viewpoints.** Bring individuals into your team (regularly or on a periodic basis) who have different ideas about how the business should look in the future. Choose people who can spark fresh thinking on your team. Employees who are newest to the company or function will likely provide helpful insights.

- **Foster continuous improvement.** Develop key performance indicators for your organization, and review them regularly. Establish expectations for continuous improvement. Develop a strong culture of brainstorming, constructive debate, and a sense of continual competition with past achievements and results. Use team brainstorming sessions to help people test their assumptions and challenge each other's thinking.

- **Test your ideas with key stakeholders.** Work to position and present your ideas for growth and profitability improvement in a positive, constructive manner that respects organizational history.

EXCESSIVE USE

As an example, if you introduce too many improvements, you may jeopardize productivity. Use key performance indicators to help you monitor the pace of change.

Coach Others on Strategic Thinking

When coaching others, focus on the core practices that were identified as either a development need or excessive use in the self-assessment at the beginning of this chapter. Identify and adapt any relevant development suggestions. Additional coaching tips are provided in the following table for some adverse leadership behaviors. For more information review Chapter 4, "Coach Others."

Coaching Suggestions

	Behavior	Awaken	Align	Accelerate
Long-Term Perspective	*Is short-term, operationally focused*	• Invite the person to analyze and discuss the longer-term implications of specific strategies. • Provide an example of when you observed the person making a decision that impaired a long-term opportunity in favor of short-term results. Review the rationale in making that decision.	• Coach the person to develop a stakeholder map and get key stakeholders more engaged at critical times during the business cycle. • Pair the person with a peer who has a clear, long-term game plan.	• Ensure that there is at least one longer-term goal represented in the person's goals. • Hold the person accountable for progress toward this goal in your one-on-one meetings.
	Lacks insight about future opportunities	• Ask the person to review what is planned after current projects/initiatives are completed. • Seek to understand what the person would work on if he/she currently had more time.	• Suggest that the person meet with the corporate head of strategic planning. Help to create an interview guide that will expand the person's current thinking on future possibilities. • Have the person translate a future corporate goal into one for his/her own team, filling the future pipeline.	• Create a future-focused committee to keep the idea pipeline full. • Have the person co-lead the group with someone who excels at keeping the future in mind when developing strategy.
External Focus	*Is internally focused*	• Ask the person to read Michael Porter's books or articles and conduct an industry analysis. • Help the person understand the components of a SWOT analysis as it relates to customers and competition. Focus on your position in the industry against other competitors.	• Suggest the person research best practices of a business that is well recognized for innovation. • Have the person create a presentation and review it with a group of peers. Debrief this meeting together. What ideas did the group believe were transferable to your organization?	• Work together to select an idea for pursuing a new strategy relative to the marketplace, industry, or the competition. • Regularly provide the person with articles or relevant materials that may provoke thinking more broadly. Debrief these with him/her during your one-on-one conversations.

Behavior		Awaken	Align	Accelerate
External Focus	*Does not seek or share external input*	• Find out whether and how the person actively seeks input from outside the organization. Develop a list of who might help expand his/her thinking. • Review with the person how you expand your own thinking. What resources do you leverage to do so?	• Identify which industry groups would provide solid experience and relationship potential. Encourage the person to join at least one industry group. • Have the person co-lead a focus group of key customers with marketing when developing a potential new product or service idea.	• Discuss attendance at industry meetings, focusing specifically on with whom the person is actively communicating and what is being learned. • Facilitate sharing of information from all team members' external involvement in quarterly brown bags or summits.
Strategic Scope	*Fails to consider business strategy when making decisions*	• Assign the person to conduct a cost-benefit analysis of alternative choices to meet the future business strategy. • Help the person develop a process by which to evaluate options. How does the person generate ideas? With whom?	• Ask the person to present the team's initiatives to key stakeholders. The presentation should include the alignment with the strategic direction of the organization. • Debrief together how to change the plan/strategy based on their feedback. What advantage would this offer the organization short term? Long term?	• Review your own team's strategic priorities together during a one-on-one meeting. • Seek the person's feedback on ideas for enhancing the strategies along with his/her ideas for executing them.
	Lacks a broad future vision	• Ask the person to read "Building Your Company's Vision" by Jim Collins and Jerry Porras (*Harvard Business Review*, 1996). Debrief the article and discuss how the person might use that approach to develop a vision for his/her area. • Discuss what the person's time horizon is. How far out does his/her planning go? What factors would cause the person to think further out?	• Review the organization's vision together. What are the key components? Encourage the person to translate this into his/her team's goals. • Have the person co-lead or participate in the project when the organization re-visits its strategic vision.	• Create a task team to develop some BHAGs (big hairy audacious goals). Assign the person to lead the team. • Provide feedback when you observe the person making a short-term decision that may be in conflict with the long-term vision. Evaluate the tradeoff.
Growth Orientation	*Plans lack strategic alignment*	• Have the person review his/her understanding of the organizational strategy with you. With what key aspects is the person aligned? Which are questionable? • Discuss what the person believes are the emerging growth opportunities to meet customer needs.	• Review together how the person's priorities are aligned (or not) to support the growth of business. • Together develop a plan to better align the work of the person's team to key organizational strategies or priorities.	• Have the person conduct an open brainstorming discussion aimed at sharing ideas for new growth levers within the function. • Stop the person when you observe focus on problems and not solutions. Create a signal for you to give feedback without others knowing.

Behavior		Awaken	Align	Accelerate
Growth Orientation	*Is not in tune with customer needs*	• Review the person's mechanisms for staying connected to the customer. What streams of communication does the person regularly use? • Discuss how regularly information is gathered. What kind of information does the person find helpful? Provide feedback on where the person might be missing opportunities to gather relevant data.	• Assess the customer needs the person is hearing about against the team's strategic priorities. Are they aligned? What would need to occur to make them more aligned? • Pair the person with a key leader in sales or marketing. Schedule a few customer visits where the person is able to hear direct feedback on how the team impacts the customer.	• Have the person develop a plan to implement a "voice of the customer" program, involving the person and other peers. • Assign the person to lead an improvement team to execute on critical issues discovered in the process.
Competitive Advantage	*Rarely considers new approaches*	• Engage in a discussion about how the person identifies best practices. What resources does the person regularly review to expand thinking? • Who does the person look to for inspiration on innovation? Why are they meaningful to the person? How does the person model himself/herself after those people? • Discuss what prevents the person from pursuing new ideas? Is he/she satisfied with the status quo? Does the person fear making a mistake?	• Have the person facilitate regular brainstorming sessions with key stakeholders to fill the idea pipeline. Pre-select team members you know will expand his/her thinking. • Pair the person with a key innovator within the organization. Have him/her present new ideas to this person for evaluation and refinement before bringing them to you.	• Have the person read *Fast Company* and review IDEO's innovation and design materials (www.ideo.com). Debrief these together during your one-on-one meetings. • Establish a goal of selecting one new idea per quarter to develop further. Hold the person accountable for not just bringing the ideas, but engaging with others to implement them.
	Is not in tune with financial drivers	• Review the department's profit and loss together. Make key correlations between recent or upcoming decisions and their impact on the data. • Provide an example of when you observed the person making a decision that demonstrated a lack of awareness of the profit and loss. What were the consequences?	• Secure an internal mentor for the person in the Finance Department. Create regular dialogue to gain or broaden his/her perspective. • Encourage the person to not only anticipate the external results/ implications of decisions, but also how the organization will have to adapt to fully realize the financial benefit.	• Attend a presentation that the person makes to the team about the organization's financial levers. Provide feedback. • Develop a plan to better balance the person's focus on the external market with focus on the internal levers. Help the person pay more attention to the internal impacts of decisions. Debrief the successes the person is able to champion with this shift in priority.

9

STRATEGIC THINKING

Tips for Coaching in a Global Environment

Strategic Thinking may be practiced or expressed differently within other cultures. This might impact how you approach coaching. Try to keep an open mind, avoid generalizations, and continue gathering data as you gain experience with another culture. Consider these suggestions:

Long-Term Perspective: Some cultures tend to have a much longer time horizon than others. The quarterly focus driven by Wall Street doesn't incentivize long-term planning. Great strategists set aside time to think—especially about the future. The need for creating time to do that may not be well understood by leaders in other cultures, especially when turnover is high and their currencies are devaluating so rapidly that short-term survival becomes paramount. Educate your leaders about the value of reflection along with maintaining a long-term perspective. Encourage them to be proactive in addressing strategic challenges.

External Focus: The external business environment is changing everywhere more rapidly than before. Some countries (e.g., Singapore) have reached out to embrace new ideas and technologies in order to raise their economic level, while others tend to remain more inwardly focused. Review Chapter 18, "Resilience," for suggestions about coaching people who are experiencing uncertainty, stress, and setbacks.

Strategic Scope: If your direct reports see the world in a hierarchical fashion, they may believe that you do all the Strategic Thinking, not them. You may need to clarify your expectations before you can expect them to embrace getting involved with strategy. Differences in governmental regulations, infrastructure, resource availability, and supply chains in other markets need to be factored into the strategic planning process. Keep these differences in mind as you brainstorm strategies and tactics with people you are coaching.

Growth Orientation: As the authors discuss in *The Alchemy of Growth* (Basic Books, 2000), some businesses may operate on a three-tier strategic horizon with operations categorized as cash cows, entrepreneurial ventures, or strategic bets for the future. The leaders you are coaching in other countries may not view their businesses the same way that you do. Help them see what phase of the "S" curve they are in. Otherwise they may not understand your reluctance to approve capital investments, which they believe are vital to growing their businesses. Discuss your assumptions, and probe to understand their expectations while you coach them through the strategic planning process.

Competitive Advantage: Invite bottom-up Strategic Thinking in your organization to promote a sense of ownership. Encourage people to focus on external competitiveness and implement emerging best practices. In *The Art of War* (El Paso Norte Press, 2009), Sun Tzu offers a timeless approach to competitive advantage based on military strategy. For more information on building business in emerging economies see: (1) *The Fortune at the Bottom of the Pyramid* by C.K. Prahald (Wharton School Publishing, 2004); and (2) *Capitalism at the Crossroads* by Stuart Hart (Wharton School Publishing, 2010). By figuring out how to profitably serve the four billion people at the base of the pyramid, you could transform other parts of your business.

A Case Study in Strategic Thinking

Strategic Thinking is required to bring a broad, longer-term, and informed perspective to bear on issues and problems, and to grow the business and compete in the market.

As you read about Michele's situation, reflect on what you've learned about Strategic Thinking in this chapter. How does Michele sound like you or one of your team members? What experiences or tendencies do you share? Finally, consider how you would help Michele demonstrate greater skill in Strategic Thinking and be successful in her leadership role.

Exploring the Competitive Environment

Michele Newman was a newly hired regional manager of the Eastern Region Distribution Centers for a large consumer electronics and appliance retailer. The distribution centers handled the delivery of all large-sized products, such as big-screen televisions and refrigerators. Profit margins were dropping and customer complaints were rising. Michele had previous retail distribution center experience and was directed to implement ideas that could improve profitability. She began her analysis internally by learning about the strategic objectives of the organization and its distribution process.

Two critical strategic objectives of her company were achieving high customer satisfaction and growth through improved profitability. As Michele began reviewing customer satisfaction and product return claims, the data revealed a growing problem with damaged product. Further external focus exposed an opportunity to determine when in the distribution process the product was becoming damaged. Michele implemented a new process that required vendor-shipped merchandise to be checked for damage as it was received. Implementing this new process began to solve the problem. In turn, customer satisfaction increased and profitability went up with the reduction in product return claims.

Michele also researched the external competitor landscape. She gathered data about all competitors in the big-screen television and appliance space. Michele focused on some of the distribution center processes, including the delivery schedule offered to customers and delivery driver contracts. Her organization outsourced the delivery, and her research validated that this arrangement was still a best-in-class practice. The research also revealed that other retailers were offering more evening and weekend delivery times to customers. Although her data showed the potential opportunity for the business, Michele was unsure if changing delivery hours was a feasible strategy for her organization to pursue.

9

STRATEGIC THINKING

Michele found that she needed to develop skills in Strategic Thinking more than ever, in order to:

- Develop a new distribution strategy aligned to support the broader business.

- Evaluate the long-term implications of a different distribution approach.

- Assemble ideas for creating innovative functions for the distribution center that would align with the new distribution strategy.

Michele's Leadership Development Plan

Following is a sample development plan for Michele Newman. Research on leadership development has shown that leaders learn through experience and that this learning is optimized through the use of an individual development plan. A successful plan includes new experiences and introduces the leader to new conversations and tools. Suggestions included in previous sections may stimulate your thinking about additional possibilities for Michele's development.

LEADERSHIP DEVELOPMENT PLAN FOR MICHELE NEWMAN
DEVELOPMENT GOAL
Goal: To strengthen my Strategic Thinking skills
Desired Outcomes—results I want to see from developing this skill
Self: Bring a longer-term perspective on issues for the business. **Team:** Engage my team in innovative thinking focused on the customer. **Organization:** Improved profit margins, reduced customer complaints, and a stronger competitive distribution strategy.
Self-Understanding—strengths that I can build on and development needs I can address
Strengths: • Ability to think with a strategic purpose that in turn creates a vision for the future • Passion for learning • Knowledge of the organization and the function **Development Needs:** Tendency to just solve today's problem and not see other opportunities
Business Context—challenges in my business environment that require this skill
In the process of improving profit margins and reducing customer complaints, we discovered that our competitors are offering extended delivery hours in the evenings and weekends. There is an opportunity for us to change some of our distribution strategies and gain market share.

LEADERSHIP DEVELOPMENT PLAN FOR MICHELE NEWMAN

DEVELOPMENT ACTIONS

AWAKEN

- Seek the history around current operating procedures and the process for making changes.
- Meet with key stakeholders in the distribution process and engage them in a conversation about the current and future state of distribution. Summarize these discussions to document their viewpoints.
- Communicate development plan with my manager and other key stakeholders over the next three weeks, and ask for input.

ALIGN

- Conduct a SWOT analysis on the impact of changing delivery hours.
- Build relationships with individuals in sales, operations, and marketing to keep our functions aligned.
- Continue learning about the competition to evaluate how a new delivery strategy would build a competitive advantage.

ACCELERATE

- Build time into my calendar on a weekly basis and into my ongoing team meetings to think or talk about strategy, innovation, and ideas for better serving our customers. Make sure I hear from people throughout the ranks.
- Read *Learning to Think Strategically* by Julia Sloan (Butterworth-Heinemann, 2006).
- Attend an external strategic seminar on new developments in distribution strategy or on broad-based Strategic Thinking. Bring back ideas from those seminars to benefit my team.
- Look for webinars and podcasts about Strategic Thinking and planning.
- Ask myself key questions such as, "What are the primary changes that will be implemented?" and "Who will be most affected, and how are they likely to react?" Identify and interview these individuals to confirm or disconfirm my assumptions.
- Complete a change blueprint to outline current state and identify change implications for altering the future state.
- Identify a format for presenting the new delivery strategy. Update content as I gather additional findings.
- Solicit ideas from my manager and others about the most effective communication process for the new strategy.

DEVELOPMENT SUCCESS FACTORS

Timeline: Within the next six months

9

STRATEGIC THINKING

LEADERSHIP DEVELOPMENT PLAN FOR MICHELE NEWMAN

Support Needed:

- Advice and perspective of my manager, peers, and team to gain insight into the vision and create alignment.
- Coaching and feedback from my manager on effective strategic planning.
- Potentially, time and dollars to support my attending an external seminar.

Indicators of Success:

- I have connected with key stakeholders and can articulate how aligned they are with our new strategic choices.
- I personally feel more confident in the new business strategies I create.
- I have a new strategy for our distribution center that gives us a competitive advantage.

An Example of Coaching to Think Strategically

Michele Newman's goal was to strengthen her skills in Strategic Thinking. Here are some steps Michele's manager could take using the Awaken, Align, Accelerate framework to coach Michele in this area:

AWAKEN	**Increase INSIGHT**	Talk with Michele about how her assimilation into the new role is going. Ask about her progress in developing relationships with key stakeholders and identifying new strategies. Provide feedback using your own observations. Propose that she conduct a cost-benefit analysis of the alternative distribution strategies she is considering. Discuss the long-term implications of each choice. Suggest that she learn about value chains and conduct a value chain analysis as well.
	MOTIVATE change	Applaud Michele's motivation to strengthen her Strategic Thinking skills. Encourage her to contact other people to discuss the current and future state of distribution. Reflect together on her learnings. Ask about the consequences of not making any changes.
ALIGN	**PLAN goals**	Ask what Michele would spend time working toward and follow through on. Focus on what she could do to build her confidence as well as improve her results. Work together to construct a leadership development plan similar to the sample provided in this chapter.
	ALIGN expectations	Review your own strategic priorities with Michele. Ask what ideas she has to enhance the strategies, and her ideas for executing them. Ensure she has a good understanding about business priorities and desired results. Discuss how Michele sees her incentives aligning with what the organization is expecting from her.
ACCLERATE	**CREATE teachable moments**	Help Michele experiment with trying new things. Encourage Michele to get her team involved in brainstorming innovative functions for the distribution center. Assign Michele to lead a task force to conduct an industry analysis and develop BHAGs that would improve your competitive position. Ask Michele to present her team's initiatives to key stakeholders. Her presentation should include the alignment with the strategic direction of the organization. Schedule periodic coaching sessions to debrief Michele on her new experiences, discuss obstacles, and brainstorm additional possibilities.
	TRACK progress	Work with Michele to evaluate progress toward her goals. Encourage her to invite additional feedback and ask other people to support the new strategy. Work with Michele to evaluate progress toward her goals. Express appreciation for her efforts and success in developing a new distribution strategy.

9

STRATEGIC THINKING

Results: Measuring Impact

Michele Newman took almost six months to work through her plan. She didn't try every action step, and she found some activities were more helpful than others. However, she made tremendous progress on improving her Strategic Thinking skills and approach to developing strategy. Her new skills allowed Michele to:

- Connect and align with key stakeholders.

- Develop a new distribution strategy that produced a competitive advantage.

- Evaluate the long-term implications of a different distribution approach.

- Create innovative functions for the distribution center that aligned with the new strategy.

- Feel more confident about the process of creating future business strategies.

10

Business Acumen

Leaders with solid Business Acumen understand the organization and the business environment in which it competes. They are astute about the organization's business model, its strategic direction and goals, and its internal dynamics. They think like a business owner rather than a function expert and use key operational data and financial information to make decisions. They are able to consider tradeoffs and make choices that support the business strategy. They use data to measure and analyze the function's performance and contribution to the business.

Factor	Competency	Core Practice
Leading People	Strategic Thinking	Business Context
Thinking and Deciding	Business Acumen	Operating Models
Achieving	Critical Thinking and Judgment	Financial Drivers
Relating to People		Tradeoffs
Managing Work		Performance Metrics
Managing Self		

A leader with strong Business Acumen understands why a company is making money or losing money. Do you know what drives the profitability of your business?

The outcome of any sports game depends on a strategy that capitalizes on the team's strengths while exploiting the opponent's weaknesses. Fans understand winning and losing when they look at the scoreboard. In business, that "scoreboard" reflects revenue and profitability. To be competitive, leaders must demonstrate solid Business Acumen by making the right decisions to positively affect financial performance and influence the competitive position of the business. Business leaders must know how to apply the right strategy and assess the effect of every play to produce a positive outcome for shareholders. Without this type of thinking from their leaders, any business is likely to lose more often than it wins.

Leaders must appreciate the global environment, business model, and key drivers of the organization and leverage this understanding to recommend alternatives and drive performance. Senior leaders, in particular, must understand the societal, technological, economic, environmental, and political factors at a level that allows them to make quick adjustments to their short-term plans, as well as spot potential business opportunities for the future. While Business Acumen is important for all leaders, the required behaviors vary by level, as illustrated in the following table.

How Leaders at Different Levels Use Business Acumen

	Managers	Function Leaders	Senior Executives
Business Context	Knows what the business is trying to accomplish.	Understands the global business environment.	Looks for opportunities in global trends and economic conditions.
Operating Models	Recognizes how their areas of responsibility contribute to the bottom line.	Knows the organization's business model and how it operates.	Enhances and evolves business models that fuel profitable growth.
Financial Drivers	Focuses their team on key financial measures.	Concentrates on key financial drivers and their impact on profit and loss.	Conveys and maintains a strong profit and loss perspective.
Tradeoffs	Considers possibilities and implications when making recommendations.	Makes tradeoffs that support growth and/or profitability objectives.	Assesses alternatives and makes effective choices about where to invest in the business.
Performance Metrics	Uses key metrics to assess and improve performance.	Uses data to monitor performance and measure results.	Bases decisions about investments and resources on key metrics.

10

Self-Assessment

To evaluate your effectiveness in Business Acumen, check all boxes below that represent current behavior or performance. Look for patterns: Which core practices represent a development need, a strength, or an excessive use? Recognize that you might have some blind spots. Invite your boss or colleagues to indicate what they have observed in your behavior. Use this assessment to help identify development suggestions that are most relevant to you.

	Development Need	Strength	Excessive Use
Business Context	☐ Views the business in isolation and fails to appreciate the larger business environment ☐ Lacks knowledge of the global environment and its effect on the business	☐ Understands how the global business environment affects the organization ☐ Stays current with industry trends and dynamics	☐ Is more versed in the global competitive landscape than on the current state of the business ☐ Imagines or scopes a plan that has little bearing on the current organizational issues
Operating Models	☐ Focuses only on own area and does not fully appreciate how the entire business operates or makes money ☐ Lacks knowledge of industry benchmarks	☐ Understands how the entire business operates and sees synergies that contribute to profit or growth ☐ Knows the operational strengths and opportunities compared to the competition	☐ Sees so many interconnections and relationships that it is difficult to maintain focus and prioritize action ☐ Suggests operational changes that are unrealistic for the organization
Financial Drivers	☐ Makes plans and decisions without concern for their effect on the bottom line ☐ Is unable to articulate the profit levers of the department or organization	☐ Uses financial analyses to make decisions and improve business performance ☐ Supports the overall profitability of the business first, then considers implications for own area	☐ Focuses on maximizing short-term profitability and ignores longer-term implications ☐ Loses touch with the day-to-day operations due to a sole focus on financial reports
Tradeoffs	☐ Protects own area at all costs; shows no willingness to make tradeoffs that would benefit the overall business ☐ Misses key implications for the business when analyzing an alternative option	☐ Understands the upside as well as the downside of alternatives for increasing profitability and growing the business ☐ Actively supports others' plans, initiatives, or projects to accomplish broader organizational objectives	☐ Identifies too many alternatives without qualifying risks and setting priorities for tradeoffs ☐ Goes overboard in analyzing tradeoffs; becomes paralyzed by alternatives and fails to take action
Performance Metrics	☐ Has an inadequate or incomplete understanding of performance data ☐ Does not utilize metrics to assess performance	☐ Knows the key performance indicators of the department and their link to the goals of the organization ☐ Monitors performance against goals on a regular basis	☐ Implements changes based on overall results prior to analyzing the detailed data ☐ Analyzes detailed issues at a deep level but misses the bigger picture

Development Suggestions

The following section contains development suggestions for each core practice. Having completed the self-assessment, focus on suggestions that correspond to the core practices you identified as a development need or excessive use. Use these suggestions to create your own development plan, making sure to try one or two from each phase. In addition, feel free to create your own or adapt these to best meet your development needs.

Business Context

Understand the global business environment.

"You have to combine instinct with good business acumen. You just can't be creative, and you just can't be analytical."

Andrea Jung

Awaken potential:

- **Assess your knowledge of the business.** Reflect on important questions about national and international trends. What is happening in business around the world today? What are the trends in your industry? Who drives the strategy in your firm? What is the national and international strategy for your business? How does your organization compare to competitors?

- **Analyze your awareness of societal changes.** What are the primary demographics of your customers (age, education, mobility, race, religion, gender, etc.)? What are the up-and-coming lifestyles, contemporary culture, consumer tastes, employee expectations, social movements, etc.?

Align goals:

- **Expand your understanding of the business strategy.** Ask your manager and other senior leaders about the organization's strategy for addressing the competition and existing opportunities. Invite one of them to lead a discussion at one of your team meetings.

- **Meet with colleagues** to discuss business challenges and opportunities. Take advantage of their experience and insight to help you see more opportunities in your own area. Establish goals that align with others'.

10

BUSINESS ACUMEN

Accelerate performance:

- **Stay informed.** Keep on top of general business developments by reading publications such as *Business Week, The Economist, Fortune, Financial Times,* or *The Wall Street Journal.* Consider implications for your organization.

- **Read trade journals** and other professional publications to gain more industry and function-specific knowledge. Subscribe to online newsletters or other communications provided by competitors.

- **Become active in a professional organization** or association where you can learn more about global trends, emerging issues, and best practices in your industry and function.

- **Conduct regular online research** on global trends to stay up-to-date. Follow or create a blog for professionals who want to discuss topics of mutual interest.

- **Identify emerging technologies.** Identify three emerging technological advances that will most likely have an impact on your field or industry. Develop an action plan to learn more about these areas.

- **Learn more about the global business environment.** Read *The World is Flat 3.0: A Brief History of the Twenty-first Century* by Thomas Friedman (Picador, 2007) to learn about global supply chains, uploading, and innovations that may disrupt your business.

- **Learn from the successes of others.** Analyze successes of your competitors and related businesses. Identify ways to apply similar approaches to your business.

- **Expand your point of view.** Seek diverse opinions by obtaining input from a wide range of people, including people outside your own area. Ask for help in understanding their experience, perspectives, and cultures.

- **Gain a global perspective.** Look for an opportunity to tackle a project or assignment in a different geography or seek a mentor with international work experience.

- **Broaden your thinking.** Look beyond what you know and use the ideas in the "External Focus" and "Competitive Advantage" core practices in Chapter 9 to learn new ways to enhance your understanding of your organization's external business environment.

EXCESSIVE USE

As an example, if you pursue your global interests instead of addressing critical organizational issues, you risk becoming marginalized.
Invest in addressing current priorities first.

Know the organization's business model and how it operates.

> *Secret operations are essential in war; upon them the army relies to make its every move.*
>
> Sun Tzu

Awaken potential:

- **Assess your understanding of business fundamentals.** How does the business make money? What are the key drivers? What are the unique features of your business model relative to others in your industry? What is your value chain? How are decisions made? What is emphasized, and why? How does your work impact the business and contribute to the bottom line?

- **Evaluate your knowledge of how other functions operate.** What do you know about the strategic plans and goals of the organization, including the goals of other departments? How does your work impact them? How do your functional area, your work as a team, and your individual job fit into the overall business plans of your organization?

Align goals:

- **Understand your area's impact.** Make an effort to meet with leaders and key stakeholders from other departments on a regular basis. Ask about their challenges and opportunities. Ask how your work affects their areas. Ask for specifics about what creates problems, what makes things run more smoothly, and what suggestions they have for improvement. Explore possible areas of mutual support and collaboration.

- **Collaborate across functions.** Look for synergies where your function can collaborate with others on common business goals. Establish formal liaisons with these different functions in order to pursue your goals.

Accelerate performance:

- **Learn best practices.** Read *Good To Great: Why Some Companies Make the Leap... and Others Don't* by Jim Collins (HarperBusiness, 2001) or *Jack: Straight from the Gut* by Jack Welch and John Byrne (Business Plus, 2003) for stories about engaging employees in business reinventions. Welch was also famous for requiring key data for

10

each business to be summarized on a single page. Can you summarize key business levers at a glance?

- **Use MBWA (management by walking around)** to stay current with the day-to-day operations and finances of the organization. Work to maintain a clear, overall view.

- **Compare your company to the competition.** Analyze the operational strengths and weaknesses of your organization compared to the competition. Review customer feedback. Look for obstacles that might be hindering your company's performance. Identify process improvements to incorporate into your company's practices.

- **Become an active student of business success**—both in your field and business at large. Read *Fast Company* or *Harvard Business Review* articles to learn about individuals and organizations that have developed innovative business ideas.

- **Be a leader teaching leaders.** Obtain case studies, online simulations, or interactive exercises (see *Harvard Business Online*) to analyze and discuss with your team. Invite one or more members to prepare a case study about your business. What are the key challenges and issues in your industry, your market niche, and your organization? What differentiates you, or has the potential to differentiate you, from the competition? How can you best respond to ambiguity and ever-changing information?

- **Work outside your function.** Volunteer for a project or team opportunity that exposes you to operations across the organization.

- **Find a mentor.** Ask someone who seems particularly savvy about the organization to be your mentor. Learn about the sources of power and influence in your company and how the most senior leaders make decisions.

- **Keep learning.** Pursue continuing education, independent reading, and new developmental challenges to refresh your thinking, stay up-to-date, and learn about emerging business models.

EXCESSIVE USE

As an example, if you spend too much time analyzing operations,
it may be difficult to prioritize action. Work to identify the most important problems
and root causes to focus on.

Concentrate on key financial drivers and their impact on profit and loss.

"If you don't drive your business, you will be driven out of business."

BC Forbes

Awaken potential:

- **Consider your organization's key financial drivers.** What are the key drivers of financial performance? What drives the top line or the organization or your area? What affects the bottom line? What levers would you pull today if you had to cut your budget? What business levers would you pull if you were given additional budget dollars to spend today? Where are there opportunities to negotiate agreements or leverage relationships?

- **Evaluate what you know about how the organization really makes money.** How could your business become more efficient or profitable? What changes are possible, given your current market? If you are in a low-margin business, your options will be different from if you are in a high-margin business.

Align goals:

- **Understand your finances.** Talk to the person in charge of finance for your business unit. Ask what could be done in your area to improve profitability, reduce costs, or add growth. Ask for feedback on how you think about the bottom line.

- **Learn more about unfamiliar functions.** Connect with peers who are experts in their functions to expand your understanding of the whole organization, and adjust your goals accordingly. Make sure their plans do not include activities that would adversely affect your costs, and vice versa.

Accelerate performance:

- **Enhance your business knowledge.** Read *What the CEO Wants You to Know: How Your Company Really Works* by Ram Charan (Crown Business, 2001) to learn more about basic business philosophy.

- **Refresh or strengthen your financial analysis skills.** Make sure you are conversant with the various terms and calculations commonly used to discuss and interpret financial information. These include ratios such as profit, liquidity, activity, leverage, and shareholder-return. A good test of your knowledge is how well you believe you understand the financial information on your company's annual report.

10

BUSINESS ACUMEN

- **Gain external perspective.** Learn more about how financial analysts such as Barron's and Standard & Poors evaluate industries, companies, and products. Study their forecasts for your industry and the global economy.

- **Analyze the financial implications of a special initiative or project before implementation.** Review the actual effect with your team afterward. Invite your manager to participate in some of the reviews.

- **Help others act like business owners.** Focus on getting people to think about every action taken and the end result for the business. For example, customer service directly affects customer loyalty. Discontinuing products with a negative margin could add more to the bottom line than their sales were adding to the top line.

- **Ask good questions, and promote this behavior in others.** This will lead to increased efficiency, innovation, and collaboration across the company, positively impacting both top and bottom line. For example, will we have enough cash flow to cover the bills next quarter? What's an appropriate return on investment for a new product? How much inventory is too much? Too little?

- **Identify a finance tutor.** Ask someone who seems particularly savvy about the business to be your mentor. Ask your manager to suggest someone who could be helpful in this role.

EXCESSIVE USE

As an example, if you focus on maximizing short-term profitability and ignore longer-term implications, your business may not survive in the long run. Balance the attention you pay to day-to-day operations with time spent thinking about where you want the organization to be heading in three years.

Make tradeoffs that support growth and/or profitability objectives.

To open a shop is easy, to keep it open is an art.

Chinese proverb

Awaken potential:

- **Keep overall business goals front and center.** Review your company's annual and longer-range goals. How do the activities and responsibilities of your team or function support them? What role do other functions play in accomplishing these objectives? Are there projects, initiatives, or efforts others are responsible for that deserve more support from you or your team?

- **Assess what you know about company performance and profitability.** How is the company making money? What services/products are the least profitable? Most profitable? What must the company do to stay competitive? How can you and your team help?

- **Improve your knowledge of the marketplace.** What are your key competitors doing? How are their product mixes different? What are the differences in their operational models? Is there anything you should consider applying in your organization?

Align goals:

- **Connect with peers who are experts in their functions.** Learn about their operations, key business levers, and the contributions they make to the business as a whole. Use what you learn to better align your own objectives with the overall business strategy.

- **Make form follow function.** Invite your team to join you in brainstorming how the structure of the organization could change to be more efficient and effective. Know what you would trade off or what you believe is not helping the organization succeed and why. Discuss tradeoffs that could enhance performance or profitability.

- **Talk with your manager to establish priorities and consider what tradeoffs you can make.** Are there areas of focus for you that don't align well with the rest of the organization?

Accelerate performance:

- **Expand your thinking about sales.** Read *What the Customer Wants You to Know: How Everybody Needs to Think Differently About Sales* by Ram Charan (Portfolio

10

Business, 2007) to learn about orienting your employees to your customers' profitability and competing with aggressive price cutters.

- **Analyze the value chain for your business.** Use Michael Porter's value chain analysis (see his book *Competitive Advantage*) to understand how each primary activity (inbound logistics, operations, outbound logistics, marketing, sales, and services) and support activity (administrative infrastructure, human resources, research, and procurement) operate in your organization. Consider discussing this with your team so you are certain they understand how the business operates as a whole.

- **Make tradeoffs within your function.** Talk to your reports about how each of their teams works with the others. Where are the strongest connections? Where are the weakest? Solicit their recommendations about where or how resources could be re-deployed to improve workflow between groups.

- **Discuss new ideas early.** Talk with your peers when you have new ideas you would like to propose. Who do they believe would be best served to implement your ideas? Develop and support budget requests with others if your idea is best implemented by another team or function.

- **Support others' highest priorities.** Make sure you stay informed about others' critical priorities and projects. Are they on track? Where do they need help? Offer support (e.g., resources, temporary re-assignments of staff, etc.) if you can afford to do so.

- **Evaluate whether the right people are in the right jobs.** Think about possibilities for changing the organization design or permanently relocating people or teams to improve organizational performance. The core practice "Diagnosis" in Chapter 6 contains ideas for engaging your team in finding ways to better align the organization for the results you need.

EXCESSIVE USE

As an example, if you spend too much time brainstorming alternatives and discussing opportunities, you might be perceived as indecisive or paralyzed by analysis. You may need to become more comfortable with taking risks and making tough decisions.
Tips for trying out ideas and either adopting or discarding them quickly can be found in the core practice "Experimentation" in Chapter 13. "Resource Management" in Chapter 16 can help with ways to anticipate and successfully request the resources you need to get the results expected of you.

Use data to monitor performance and measure results.

> *The world is changing very fast. Big will not beat small anymore. It will be the fast beating the slow.*

Rupert Murdoch

Awaken potential:

- **Identify key business metrics.** What are the most important operational and financial metrics in your company? What financial data is most important to your role? Your function? How does your function add to the top line? To the bottom line? What are the performance indicators for your role? Your team? What internal or external factors could impact the numbers?

- **Quiz yourself and your team.** What are the key performance indicators for the organization? What are the key department performance indicators? What do they measure? How are they calculated? How are the indicators used? How do key performance indicators relate to department activity and goals?

Align goals:

- **Link outcomes.** Identify which of your performance goals are directly related to key business metrics.

- **Discuss financial performance.** Share department and organization performance and financial results with your team. Seek their input on how to improve your department's performance.

Accelerate performance:

- **Brush up on basics.** Attend a "Finance for Non-Financial Professionals" course to learn more about reading financial statements and using terms such as COGS (cost of goods sold), EBITA (earnings before interest, taxes, and amortization), depreciation, P/E ratio (price/earnings ratio), ROI (return on investment), and net income.

- **Review financial data on a regular basis.** Know the activities that affect performance indicators. Know which measures are the most sensitive (i.e., have the biggest effect on profitability when they fluctuate).

10

BUSINESS ACUMEN

- **Use external benchmarks.** Use your industry contacts, trade association, or professional organization to request information on performance indicators for your function or industry. Obtain benchmarking or survey data if available.

- **Compare predictions to actual results.** Develop your own hypotheses about what you expect to see in your business reports. For example, if dollar volume against goals has increased steadily for three months, do you expect it to increase in the fourth month? Test and revise your hypotheses and predictions with your associates. Compare assumptions and predictions. Do they think yours are reasonable? Why or why not?

- **Learn from trends.** Use historical data to identify a "normal" range for key performance indicators, and then pinpoint seasonal variations. This will help you to distinguish variations that are insignificant versus those that bear further investigation. When a significant variation occurs, determine the cause and whether it represents a meaningful change, a one-time aberration, or a possible miscalculation.

- **Leverage technology for data collection and analysis.** Software systems can enable you to gather, manipulate, and analyze data in multiple ways, allowing for more meaningful interpretation of data.

- **Learn from the success of others.** Research an example of a successful product or company. What are the measures of success? Do the same for a poorly performing company or product. How does the analysis compare to your business?

EXCESSIVE USE

As an example, if you spend too much time analyzing detailed metrics,
you might miss the bigger picture. Step back periodically to examine the impact of your
analysis on the business.

Coach Others on Business Acumen

When coaching others, focus on the core practices that were identified as either a development need or excessive use in the self-assessment at the beginning of this chapter. Identify and adapt any relevant development suggestions. Additional coaching tips are provided in the following table for some adverse leadership behaviors. For more information review Chapter 4, "Coach Others."

Coaching Suggestions

Behavior		Awaken	Align	Accelerate
Business Context	*Views function in a silo*	• Review the SWOT framework together. Ask the person to complete a SWOT analysis based on what he/she knows or thinks about the organization/function. • Challenge the person to look more broadly or beyond his/her own area. How does the function fit into the broader business context?	• Discuss the SWOT analysis. Point out how the information may be helpful as a reference for others. • Select two key functional areas where the person could explore the initial analysis further.	• Create a cross-functional review team to discuss functional alignment on a regular basis. • Assign the person to co-lead a sub-team focused on internal communication and collaboration.
	Lacks knowledge of global business environment	• Ask what mechanisms the person has to gather insight into the global environment and economy. How does the person regularly assess the landscape? • Explain how you keep abreast. What resources do you use, read, or follow?	• Demonstrate for the person how global factors affect your business drivers. Make direct correlations between the external data and internal levers. • Pair the person with someone who integrates this information well into his/her own function. Facilitate a discussion to broaden perspective.	• Regularly debrief the global factors during your one-on-one meetings. Ask about the person's ongoing learning. • Provide feedback when you observe the person making connections to global business or when he/she misses the opportunity to do so.

Behavior		Awaken	Align	Accelerate
Operating Models	*Doesn't fully appreciate how the business operates*	• Review how the person's team's performance affects the success of the organization. What facilitates success? What impairs it? • Provide a recent example of when a decision the person made either facilitated or impaired success. Why was this important?	• Facilitate working sessions with the finance team to better understand key functional interactions. • Brainstorm together about how to more effectively capitalize on these interactions.	• Create a plan together to regularly review synergies with the finance team and close identified gaps. • Promote cross-functional collaboration by routinely inviting someone from finance to the team meeting as a guest. Encourage the person to comment when he/she observes the team making aligned choices or not.
	Lacks knowledge of industry benchmarks	• Discuss the competitive landscape with your top customers. Do they use others like your organization? Why do they choose to work with your organization? • Have the person's team evaluate what sets your organization apart from your top five competitors.	• Assign the person to obtain market research data and make a presentation at one of your staff meetings. • Pair the person with a key marketing leader to expand the tools he/she has to benchmark.	• Facilitate a roundtable discussion highlighting key findings for the sales and marketing teams. • Create a plan to regularly solicit this information, and discuss it with key stakeholders.
Financial Drivers	*Makes decisions without concern for effect on bottom line*	• Review a time when the person clearly made a decision that favored his/her own area without concern for the bottom line. What were the implications for other aspects of the business? • Volunteer an example of a time when you personally made a similar mistake. What did you learn? How have you adapted your behavior since?	• Have the person circle back with the peers who were affected and review the learning. • Together create a plan for how the person might avoid the issue in the future. What checks and balances might be instituted to prevent it?	• During your one-on-ones, ask about the broader business implications of the person's decisions. • Check the person's knowledge of key performance indicators and their link to the goals of the organization.

Behavior		Awaken	Align	Accelerate
Financial Drivers	*Cannot articulate profit levers*	• Discuss the key measures of success for the department and the business. What changes in the metrics would cause concern? Why? • Review the implications of favoring one metric over another. What might those decisions lead to?	• Schedule time with a key finance person to jointly review how the person's function affects profitability. • Together create a plan for how the person could strengthen his/her unit's contribution.	• Assign the person to lead a task team to implement a continuous improvement project. Set clear expectations for how the person can measure the effect. • Sit in on a meeting in which the person reviews financial reports with the team. Provide feedback on the person's clarity and linkage to the key business levers.
Tradeoffs	*Protects own area at all costs*	• Provide an example of when you have observed the person making a protective decision. How did this limit the success of the project, initiative, or task? • Brainstorm ways to conduct business in the person's unit differently. Pay close attention to ideas that make broad gains as well as more incremental functional ones.	• Encourage the person to team with key peer stakeholders to develop a business case for change. • Ask the person to present information to other key leaders. Encourage the person to shape the plan with new information they provide.	• Model commitment to the ideas that show strong overall business performance, rather than those that will affect merely your area. • Provide feedback and reinforcement when you see the person modeling positive behavior.
	Is unwilling to make tradeoffs	• Present a key problem affecting the business. Ask how he/she would solve the problem if there were no restrictions. • Help the person evaluate what criteria he/she would use to develop a solution. Provide some recommendations for how to expand his/her thinking.	• Have the person lead the team through a similar solution session, asking similar questions. Pay particular attention to how they prioritize ideas. What criteria do they use? • Pair the person with another leader you believe makes tradeoffs well. Have the person review issues at critical junctures with this leader to expand thinking and perspective.	• Assess the reality of proposed solutions and challenge the person to implement any positive change that would be realistic for the business. • In your one-on-ones, review the person's learning and how his/her perspective has changed.

Behavior	Awaken	Align	Accelerate
Performance Metrics *Has inadequate understanding of financial data and analyses*	• Review together the financial analyses the person uses to make decisions or measure progress. What holes do you see in the analysis? • How are those tools and analyses similar or different from your own? What might he/she begin using to be more comprehensive in the evaluation?	• Partner the person with an internal mentor with expertise in data analysis. • Have the person review financial data for a successful product/service and another one that is underperforming. Review the findings and recommendations.	• Together, create a plan to improve the performance of the underperforming product/service. Execute the plan and then evaluate its effect. • Regularly review the person's analyses during one-on-ones. Encourage the person to cascade this learning downward, facilitating learning deeper in the organization.
Doesn't use metrics to assess performance	• Review together the operational data and financial metrics the person uses to measure progress. How regularly is measurement necessary? • Provide your observation on an occurrence where better use of metrics could have driven a stronger business result. What were the implications?	• Coach the person to team with key stakeholders to create a balanced scorecard. Identify shared business metrics that powerfully tell the unit's story. • Create a task team of cross-functional advisors to offer divergent views on measurement.	• Review the scorecard regularly together. Reinforce the importance of leveraging this data in driving business decisions. • Model how you use this information in your own decisions. Make connections between evaluation and decision-making processes.

Tips for Coaching in a Global Environment

Business Acumen may be practiced or expressed differently within other cultures. This might affect how you approach coaching. Try to keep an open mind, avoid generalizations, and continue gathering data as you gain experience with another culture. Consider these suggestions:

Business Context: The external business environment is changing rapidly everywhere. It is shifting faster in some countries than others, especially where currency fluctuations, changing government regulations, and high turnover add to the unpredictability. If you are coaching leaders in other countries, their external forces may differ from yours. Ask what external opportunities and threats apply to doing business in their countries. Also try to understand the cultural context around taking business risks there.

Operating Models: Through coaching, you can encourage people to imagine different operating models. You may uncover new models through your coaching that could benefit other parts of the organization. Invite leaders to share best practices.

Financial Drivers: Some leaders you are coaching might have had limited exposure to multinational business practices before joining your organization. They may also lack the kind of added value that comes from having an MBA. Meanwhile, they may not view their businesses the same way you do. They may try to use different financial drivers from the ones you would see as appropriate in moving their businesses forward. As you are coaching, try to understand how leaders view their businesses. Help them recognize all of the financial drivers under their control and take steps to manage those drivers in a systematic manner.

Tradeoffs: Some countries lack sophisticated infrastructure. Supply chains do not operate the same everywhere. Differences in the level of mechanization, transportation logistics, and resource availability may need to be factored into the financial planning process. Understanding cultural differences and knowing the ins and outs of how to accomplish things in different geographies is imperative to managing execution as well as financial performance. Keep these differences in mind as you are coaching people and brainstorming alternatives.

Performance Metrics: While the use of metrics is a standard business practice in most countries, standard practices in multinational firms (e.g., the use of balanced scorecard metrics) may be unfamiliar to people from some cultures. Such people may need more explicit and regular communication to establish protocols that conform to the expectations of headquarters. Provide examples as part of your coaching.

A Case Study in Business Acumen

Business Acumen is not just an understanding of the numbers on a financial statement. Leaders with strong Business Acumen understands what levers will influence the numbers on a financial statement and impact the competitive position of the business. This ability involves a deep understanding of the business model and the ability to size up options that exist to impact the bottom line and support the goals of the organization.

As you read about Jeff's situation, reflect on what you've learned about Business Acumen in this chapter. How does Jeff sound like you or one of your team members? What experiences or tendencies do you share? Finally, consider how you would help Jeff demonstrate greater skill in Business Acumen and be successful in his leadership role.

Accumulating Acumen

Jeff Miller was the top salesperson in his region, selling industrial copying and printing equipment. He was recently promoted from field sales management to the corporate VP of Sales and Service. Jeff welcomed the opportunity to direct sales force activity on a wider scale. Having developed good relationships with all of the service managers while in sales, he was also excited about managing the service area.

The first big request for Jeff came from one of his direct reports, who asked him to approve offering a one-year service agreement at no cost. For the past ten years, the company had required a minimum purchase of a one-year service agreement with every sales contract. Jeff recalled how the previous VP rarely approved any reduced pricing or special offers, even if it meant losing the sale. He believed that offering free maintenance for the first year would have little or no effect on the service department because the equipment was new and functioning well during the first year. Jeff was under pressure to improve the profitability of sales engagements, so he developed a new contract offering that included a free one-year maintenance plan with a small price increase to help offset the maintenance cost. Jeff was determined to help the sales team succeed and believed this new offer would help drive overall sales and improve profitability.

Instead, Jeff soon learned that the company had a greater profit margin on service call revenue than on the sale of equipment. He had mistakenly assumed that decisions that would be good to drive the top-line of his department would be good for the business. As he moved away from direct field sales, Jeff had also lost touch with how competitive pricing had become and how hard it would be to sell any price increase, even with the value-added maintenance agreement. Jeff had always focused on delivering a top-line number, but suddenly his new position was requiring him to focus on the top and bottom line.

Upon reflection, Jeff realized that he needed to understand more about the key operational levers across both sales and service. He also recognized the importance of assessing the impact of his decisions throughout the company and against the marketplace. In order to develop competitive sales and service options, he would need to focus more on Business Acumen to:

- Understand the operations of the business beyond generating sales revenue.

- Learn how to evaluate the long-term impact of his ideas vs. only looking at short-term results.

- Proactively seek input and feedback from other key stakeholders to make the best decisions possible for the organization as a whole.

Jeff's Leadership Development Plan

Following is a sample development plan for Jeff Miller. Research on leadership development has shown that leaders learn through experience and that this learning is optimized through the use of an individual development plan. A successful plan includes new experiences and introduces the leader to new conversations and tools. Suggestions included in previous sections may stimulate your thinking about additional possibilities for Jeff's development.

LEADERSHIP DEVELOPMENT PLAN FOR JEFF MILLER
DEVELOPMENT GOAL
Goal: To strengthen my Business Acumen
Desired Outcomes—results I want to see from developing this skill
Self: Understand how my actions affect the business.   **Team:** Know how my department fits in the business.   **Organization:** Gain enough knowledge about the industry and business to influence my use of levers.
Self-Understanding—strengths that I can build on and development needs I can address
Strengths: • Knowledge of the sales function   • Relationships with sales and service teams   • Desire to help others succeed   **Development Needs:**   • Complete knowledge of the organization's business model from a profitability perspective   • Tendency to resort to what I know vs. taking time to assess what I need to know
Business Context—challenges in my business environment that require this skill
In an attempt to increase top-line sales, I inadvertently made decisions that negatively affected the results of the department. There is an opportunity to better understand the metrics and the critical levers that drive the end result.
DEVELOPMENT ACTIONS
AWAKEN   • Think of all I know about the sales department and the impact it has on the business. Review the history of the service department. How does the revenue from this area affect the top-line?   • What effects the profit margin in service?   • How do competitors position sales and service in their businesses?

LEADERSHIP DEVELOPMENT PLAN FOR JEFF MILLER

ALIGN

- Meet with my boss and other key stakeholders. What experiences have they had with sales and service? Review my thoughts with them. What are their insights?

- Consider the bigger picture when talking with other leaders. What are their thoughts about sales and service in the organization?

- Review customer service logs or meet with customers. What insights can I gain about sales and service needs?

ACCELERATE

- Review financial reports on a regular basis to understand all top-line indicators and factors affecting the bottom line. Meet with a member of accounting or finance if there are items on the report I do not fully understand. What are the key indicators I plan to watch?

- Complete a SWOT analysis on sales and service. Where are the opportunities? Threats?

- Join a national association for my industry. Review the industry publications. What are the current trends?

- Read *What the CEO Wants You to Know: How Your Company Really Works* by Ram Charan.

DEVELOPMENT SUCCESS FACTORS

Timeline: Within the next six months

Support Needed:

- Insight from the accounting/finance and customer service departments.
- Input from sales and service team members, peers, and my manager.
- Time with customer base to grasp what is working and not working.

Indicators of Success:

- Know how the department is doing financially.
- Have ideas that impact the top and bottom line of the department.
- Be able to give a presentation about the business.

An Example of Coaching to Build Business Acumen

Jeff Miller's goal was to strengthen his skills in Business Acumen. Here are some steps Jeff's manager could take using the Awaken, Align, Accelerate framework to coach Jeff in this area:

AWAKEN	**Increase INSIGHT**	Ask Jeff to study the profit margin on each product and service offered by the company and make a presentation to your team. Discuss questions such as: Where is the organization the strongest? Weakest? Where are customer demands the strongest? Weakest? What trends are people seeing in customer data?
	MOTIVATE change	Help Jeff reflect on previous times when sales and service were at odds; evaluate those situations from an overall business standpoint. Explore the consequences of not improving his Business Acumen; identify consequences for him personally as well as his departments.
ALIGN	**PLAN goals**	Ask Jeff what would enable him to handle his new role more successfully. Focus on what he could change to improve his Business Acumen. Ask what Jeff would spend time working toward and follow through on. Work together to construct a leadership development plan similar to the sample provided in this chapter.
	ALIGN expectations	Invite Jeff and your finance leader to a meeting to discuss the status of key financial metrics. Identify additional indicators that might be useful in preventing a similar situation from happening in the future. Align expectations and desired results with business priorities and key stakeholders. Focus on what would make a difference in improving the business performance of Jeff's organization.
ACCELERATE	**CREATE teachable moments**	Encourage Jeff to create a cross-functional team to review and strengthen the margin on a high-demand product/service. Work with Jeff to orchestrate a kaizen event to reduce overall cost based on key findings from the cross-functional team. Coach Jeff in developing a plan to implement and communicate those changes.
	TRACK progress	Review key indicators with Jeff on a regular basis. Debrief what he is learning. Evaluate increased effectiveness and measure progress toward outcomes and results. Encourage him to invite additional feedback, and ask other people to support the changes they see. Acknowledge and celebrate his efforts.

Results: Measuring Impact

Jeff Miller took longer than six months to work through his plan. Along the way he toyed with applying for an evening MBA program. However, he decided to ask the CFO for mentoring instead. By the end of the year, he had made significant progress on improving his Business Acumen. His new skills allowed Jeff to:

- Better understand the operations and profitability of the business.

- Recognize cross-functional and financial interdependencies.

- Consult with key stakeholders in making decisions about the business.

- Evaluate the long-term impact of proposed strategies.

- Make presentations about the financial health of the business.

11

Critical Thinking and Judgment

Leaders who think critically are inquisitive and dig below the surface to understand underlying issues. They are able to efficiently analyze, synthesize, and manage complex information to develop well-reasoned solutions to problems. They are holistic thinkers and consider multiple variables and options in problem solving. They readily see patterns and make connections that others miss. They handle ambiguity well. They reach decisions with effective timing, and can decide in the face of uncertainty.

Factor	Competency	Core Practice
Leading People	Strategic Thinking	Investigation
Thinking and Deciding	Business Acumen	Analysis
Achieving	Critical Thinking and Judgment	Systems Thinking
Relating to People		Navigation
Managing Work		Decision-Making
Managing Self		

Critical Thinking and Judgment is central to great leadership. Leaders must be decisive. With indecisive leadership, organizations lack direction and the ability to move forward. This is not to say that leaders make decisions and employees don't, but ultimately the tough calls that determine the direction of the business fall on those in leadership positions. The quality of judgment shown by leaders has a tremendous impact on the success or failure of an organization.

Leadership in organizations is an increasingly complex and demanding enterprise. It is easy for even the best and brightest to be overwhelmed, confused, or distracted. The volume of information, the pace of business, and the sheer number of decisions a leader faces in the course of a day, week, month, quarter, or business cycle requires a keen sense of what is, what could be, and what matters. Great leaders are able to consistently make the tough calls and provide direction in the face of complexity, ambiguity, and risk.

Strong analytical and problem-solving skills characterize leadership effectiveness at all levels in an organization. More senior leaders are asked to think more expansively, make more connections, and excel within ambiguity. Indeed, the focus of judgments and decisions tends to change as a leader's scope of responsibility increases. Perhaps most importantly, a leader's perspective must expand to stay ahead of increasing responsibility. The five core practices of Critical Thinking and Judgment vary by level as illustrated in the following table.

How Leaders at Different Levels Use Critical Thinking and Judgment

	Managers	Function Leaders	Senior Executives
Investigation	Asks probing questions to get at root causes.	Investigates underlying issues when solving problems.	Insists on investigation to uncover root causes of problems.
Analysis	Examines different variables and options when solving problems.	Takes an analytic approach to complex issues.	Develops logical and well-reasoned solutions to problems.
Systems Thinking	Looks for trends or relationships among issues.	Thinks systemically—sees how a decision or action affects other parts of the organization.	Identifies systemic factors that could lead to overly narrow solutions.
Navigation	Views unknown situations as opportunities.	Balances the need for action with patience to let ambiguous issues evolve.	Successfully directs problem-solving in complex, volatile, and ambiguous situations.
Decision-Making	Makes timely decisions.	Makes good decisions in a timely manner.	Balances thorough research with determined action and speed.

Self-Assessment

To evaluate your effectiveness in Critical Thinking and Judgment, check all boxes below that represent current behavior or performance. Look for patterns: Which core practices represent a development need, a strength, or an excessive use? Recognize that you might have some blind spots. Invite your boss or colleagues to indicate what they have observed in your behavior. Use this assessment to help identify development suggestions that are most relevant to you.

	Development Need	Strength	Excessive Use
Investigation	☐ Too often takes problems at face value; asks too few questions to get at root causes ☐ Is too quick to rely on old approaches in solving problems	☐ Digs below the surface to uncover root causes ☐ Gathers data to make decisions; does not leap to conclusions	☐ Keeps challenging or digging past the point of practical value; pursues curiosities at the expense of key priorities ☐ Is restless and unfocused in pursuing new thoughts and ideas
Analysis	☐ Misses underlying issues or complexity when analyzing issues ☐ Values expedience over accuracy and assumes information is complete	☐ Demonstrates expertise in critical thinking and analysis ☐ Spots errors and discrepancies in data in reports and analyses	☐ Overanalyzes problems, misses the bigger issues, and unnecessarily slows decision-making ☐ Endlessly evaluates everything, even minor details
Systems Thinking	☐ Typically considers only a narrow range of perspectives ☐ Views details and facts in isolation; fails to identify trends or recognize relations among components	☐ Recognizes the implications of decisions and actions on other parts of the organization ☐ Sees relationships among issues that are not obviously related	☐ Loses focus and overwhelms others with excessive range of possibilities ☐ Speculates about connections that don't really exist; is impractical and unrealistic
Navigation	☐ Is overwhelmed or ineffective in ambiguous situations ☐ Misreads situations with limited data; fails to identify and analyze assumptions	☐ Excels in ambiguous situations and consistently finds a way forward ☐ Demonstrates patience; lets complex issues evolve before making decisions	☐ Moves too quickly; ignores complexity of situations ☐ Consistently pursues a middle road rather than taking conclusive action
Decision-making	☐ Is too slow in making decisions; misses emerging opportunities ☐ Is too quick to make decisions; acts prematurely	☐ Effectively balances thorough analysis with decisiveness ☐ Makes sound decisions in a timely manner	☐ Is overly intuitive; doesn't give adequate attention to the facts that are available ☐ Plays hunches and takes unnecessary risks

Development Suggestions

The following section contains development suggestions for each core practice. Having completed the self-assessment, focus on suggestions that correspond to the core practices you identified as a development need or excessive use. Use these suggestions to create your own development plan, making sure to try one or two from each phase. In addition, feel free to create your own or adapt these to best meet your development needs.

Investigation

Investigate underlying issues when solving problems.

> *He who asks a question is a fool for five minutes. He who does not ask a question remains a fool forever.*
>
> Chinese proverb

Awaken potential:

- **Review your history.** List the biggest problems you have faced in the recent past. Identify times when asking more questions or digging deeper might have produced a better outcome. Where can you apply those insights in addressing current problems?

- **Model inquiry.** Do you push others to think things through carefully? Wherever possible, encourage active debate and discourage premature agreement. Set aside time at your regular staff meeting to fully discuss ideas so that people will feel free to inquire, examine, and dig deeply into issues.

Align goals:

- **Investigate with others.** When issues or problems have an obvious interest to or impact on others, seek out their perspective and solicit their input.

- **Check with your manager.** If problems you identify are particularly difficult to understand, talk to your manager. How would he or she explain things? Who else does he or she recommend you speak with?

Accelerate performance:

- **Make a habit of asking multiple questions** when you are trying to understand an issue or make a judgment call. Try to view problems from multiple perspectives and find at least one or two new sources of information for each significant issue.

- **Use open-ended questions.** Ask questions that start with "Tell me about..." or "Describe for me..." to draw out others' thinking and encourage them to share broadly.

- **Ask questions from others' perspectives.** To broaden the types of questions you ask, consider how other functions would think about the issue—how would sales, marketing, finance, operations, etc. view the problem we are trying to solve?

- **Balance inquiry and advocacy.** Read Peter Senge's *The Fifth Discipline Fieldbook* (Crown Business, 1994) to develop an understanding of the difference between inquiry and advocacy, and when and how to use them in combination to most fully explore issues and ideas.

- **Search for root causes.** Study and apply the "root cause analysis" problem-solving technique to ensure you are finding and addressing the real causes of problems, not just responding to symptoms.

- **Make time to think broadly** about what types of products or services your organization will need to remain viable in the future. Monitor what's happening in competitor organizations. Question people about what new technologies or consumer shifts could disrupt your business over the next few years.

- **Involve your team in brainstorming sessions.** Be sure to address specific, important issues. Review the rules with everyone first: (1) refrain from evaluating ideas as they are generated, (2) encourage any and all ideas, (3) generate as many ideas as possible, and (4) build on or modify other's ideas to generate new ideas. Follow through with a process for refining, testing, and implementing the best ideas.

- **Invite a subject matter expert** to your organization to help you and your team think about issues more deeply. Prepare a list of questions in advance.

EXCESSIVE USE

As an example, if you have the tendency to ask an overwhelming number of questions, stay focused on what matters to the business. You may benefit from a trusted colleague who can help you evaluate the relevance of your inquiries.

Analysis

Take an analytic approach to complex issues.

"Get in the habit of analysis—analysis will in time enable synthesis to become your habit of mind."

Frank Lloyd Wright

Awaken potential:

- **Assess your problem-solving style.** Do you focus on the big picture and miss important details? Do you get lost in the details and lose sight of the big picture? Do you rely too much on your intuition or gut feelings in solving problems? Do you focus too much on logic and neglect the human element?

- **Examine your ability to evaluate complex data.** Work with a coach to take the Watson-Glaser Critical Thinking Appraisal to analyze and develop your approach to recognizing assumptions, evaluating arguments, and drawing accurate conclusions.

- **Seek out feedback** from colleagues, peers, and customers to ensure that analyses coming out of your group are consistently meeting or exceeding expectations and adding value.

Align goals:

- **Determine priorities.** Explore with trusted colleagues the key priorities or issues in your part of the organization that require careful analysis because of their importance to the business. Confirm with your manager.

- **Use checks and balances.** Put precautions in place when delegating responsibility for thinking through complex issues. Make sure you let others know the degree of importance you place on their analyses. Find ways to ensure that your group's best thinking is reflected.

Accelerate performance:

- **Understand the root cause.** Read the classic work *The New Rational Manager* by Charles Kepner and Benjamin Tregoe (Princeton Research Press, updated edition 1997). Before you attempt to conduct complex analyses or look for relationships, make sure you develop a clear understanding of the central problem involved. Work to understand the root cause rather than simply the signs or symptoms of problems.

- **Find the right tools.** Learn about the analytical approaches used in your business or industry. There are a wide range of analytical tools at your disposal. These can include ways of structuring or understanding problems, developing solutions, or evaluating performance.

- **Practice taking a consistent approach to problems** by following this seven-step model: (1) recognize and define the problem, (2) gather facts and make assumptions, (3) define end states and establish criteria, (4) develop possible solutions, (5) compare possible solutions, (6) select and implement solution, and (7) analyze solution for effectiveness.

- **Try the Zig-Zag Problem Solving Model** by Gordon Lawrence in working with your team to solve problems. The model addresses the importance of tapping different personality types to solve problems more effectively.

- **Provide recommendations.** Put more personal effort into forming conclusions and offering solutions. If being more analytical in your approach is a development need, you may be simply summarizing the information you have gathered without thinking critically or drawing conclusions of your own.

- **Find a trusted advisor** or expert who can help you think through more complex issues. Make sure you do your homework so that you have questions and issues prepared to discuss.

EXCESSIVE USE

As an example, if you tend to overthink things or make problems into something bigger or more complex than they actually are, focus your problem solving on defining your desired outcome early and determine the simplest way to reach that outcome. Avoid becoming caught up in analysis paralysis. Set some limits on how extensively to search for information.

Systems Thinking

Think systemically—see how a decision or action affects other parts of the organization.

> *The test of first-rate intelligence is the ability to hold two opposed ideas in the mind at the same time, and still retain the ability to function.*

F Scott Fitzgerald

Awaken potential:

- **Ask others whether you have difficulty thinking systemically** and considering multiple factors. Do others view you as too narrow in your thought process or approach to issues? Do you tend to get lost in complex issues? The next time you have difficulty, seek help from trusted colleagues to broaden your perspective and view issues in a more interconnected manner.

- **Consider the types of problems you solve.** Do you prefer certain kinds of problems? For example, some people excel at solving technical problems, but are uncomfortable with people problems. Try thinking in terms of relationships—seeing complex information as patterns and trends over time.

- **Identify forces and barriers** in your part of the organization that may contribute to overly complex problems or overly narrow solutions.

Align goals:

- **Gain a good understanding of complex issues.** Who and what are involved? Before proceeding with a course of action, consider the implications and work through the chain of possible consequences. Start with your own area, but also evaluate how this action could affect the work of other individuals and departments. Take a big picture view. Make sure you are looking at issues and making decisions with the long term in mind and from the perspective of the whole organization, not just your area.

Accelerate performance:

- **Learn how systems thinking applies to organizations.** Peter Senge (MIT Sloan School of Management) and his colleagues at the Society for Organizational Learning illustrate how systems archetypes can trigger persistent, long-term problems that affect an organization's growth, stability, and performance. Try to view your world as a complex system in which events are interconnected.

- **Learn to identify weak signals** in your environment. The ability to anticipate and think ahead is often helped by knowing how to spot the trends and patterns that others miss.

- **Experiment with perspective-taking** in order to broaden your view. Putting yourself in another person's shoes will help you see relationships you may typically overlook.

- **Take multiple positions.** Practice thinking about every complex issue in at least two ways. Consider the problem from a different point of view, and see whether you reach the same or different conclusions.

- **Draw relationships** among factors, concepts, or issues on paper. Use visuals or diagrams to give yourself and others a better understanding of an issue when there are many factors and concerns.

- **Research the TRIZ approach** developed by Genrikh Altshuller to learn about a series of algorithmic rules that can be used to solve complex problems and invent solutions.

- **Seek consultation and assistance** in handling complex issues by creating task forces to tackle larger issues. Have others help you generate alternative solutions. With what issue could you start?

EXCESSIVE USE

As an example, if you tend to focus on the big picture and neglect important details, you may need to do more to test the validity of the relationships or trends you are seeing in the business and bring a realistic, practical perspective to your analysis.

Navigation

Balance decisiveness with patience when dealing with complex and ambiguous issues.

"The quest for certainty blocks the search for meaning. Uncertainty is the very condition to impel man to unfold his powers."

Erich Fromm

Awaken potential:

- **Take stock of your tolerance for ambiguity** and whether a desire for certainty causes you to delay or avoid action. Consider what information you typically need to make a decision quickly. Separate what information you tend to think you need from what information would be "nice to have."

- **Check your gut.** If you tend to be heavily reliant on concrete data and facts for decision-making, you may benefit from honing your intuitive reasoning skills. The more experienced you are, the more reason you have to trust your instincts, especially when dealing with familiar challenges.

- **Test your ability to think quickly under pressure** by imposing arbitrary, imaginary deadlines on real problems. For example, if an issue requires an answer in five days, imagine that the deadline is tomorrow and write down the decision you would have reached after only one day. Later you can check the quality of your quick reaction. You may find that your initial analysis was on track.

- **Enhance your decision-making ability.** Review Chapter 5, "Leading Courageously," for some suggestions for enhancing your confidence in your ideas and ability to make decisions in the face of crisis or uncertainty.

Align goals:

- **Evaluate options in light of your broader strategy and culture** to help you rule out your least-effective options. A frequent test of leadership is the need to establish direction when facing complex or even overwhelming situations. These instances are particularly good times to revisit the organization's mission, vision, and values.

- **Hold a meeting to discuss how decisions are made on your team.** When people are uncertain about who owns the problem, they may not take any responsibility or react quickly enough. Discuss what kinds of decisions tend to "fall through the cracks" in your organization.

Accelerate performance:

- **Make critical thinking part of your life.** Read *Critical Thinking: Tools for Taking Charge of Your Professional & Personal Life* by Richard Paul and Linda Elder (Prentice Hall, 2000).

- **Set the direction and fine-tune later.** When faced with a situation for which there does not appear to be an ideal solution, it may make sense to make a broad, directional decision and set things in motion with a plan; empower yourself to adjust your thinking along the way.

- **Practice the Pareto principle.** Be willing to experiment with a course of action or a solution with less than 100 percent of the supporting data.

- **Gather people with varying perspectives** together when dealing with more ambiguous problems. When faced with a decision that needs to be made despite continuing uncertainty, group decisions tend to be stronger than individual decisions.

- **Prioritize your decisions.** Look at pending decisions and see if they can be broken down into categories (e.g., need additional information, will affect the bottom line, or will affect someone else's deadline). Evaluate which of those decisions can be made immediately and which ones can be delayed as appropriate.

- **Consider using a consultant or external advisor** to help you solve an issue or move forward on a project. This may be especially helpful when the issue lies beyond the scope of any one department.

EXCESSIVE USE

As an example, if you tend to play hunches and take unnecessary risks, learn to appreciate the complexity of issues. Make time to think and consult with others.

Decision-Making

Make sound decisions in a timely manner.

The most difficult thing is the decision to act, the rest is merely tenacity. The fears are paper tigers. You can do anything you decide to do. You can change and control your life; and the procedure, the process is its own reward.

Amelia Earhart

Awaken potential:

- **Assess the timeliness of your decisions.** Some leaders postpone decisions because they are overly concerned about the possibility of making a mistake. Others have the tendency to move too quickly and underestimate the complexity of situations. Which "watch out" most applies to you?

- **Consider how your emotions may influence your decision-making.** The ability to effectively monitor and control your affective reaction when dealing with problems and issues is critical to your ability to draw accurate conclusions. What role did emotion play in your last major decision?

- **Ask people for feedback** about how well you utilize others in decision-making. If you are not doing enough to check with others, raise the issue directly and ask your manager and your peers for input.

Align goals:

- **Focus on the most important issues for the business.** Learning to correctly identify and quickly deal with the less important issues will allow you to devote more time to the truly important decisions. Leverage others and delegate such issues downward when you can.

- **Test your decisions against your organization's strategy.** Evaluate the tradeoffs of critical decisions in terms of which option addresses the most critical outcomes, and spend less time on the other options.

- **Establish criteria based on the business needs.** Identify a general set of standards or criteria to improve the consistency of your decision-making. Do this before encountering specific situations. General criteria might be things such as profitability, cost, or relevance to business goals and needs.

Accelerate performance:

- **Identify the problem before making a decision.** One of the most common mistakes of decision makers is to misdiagnose a situation.

- **Evaluate where decisions are made.** Read the article "Who Has the D?" by Paul Rogers and Marcia Blenko (*Harvard Business Review*, 2006) and evaluate where decisions are made in your organization and within your team. Who makes the decisions? Are they made at the right level or in the right locations?

- **Conduct a cost-benefit analysis when making tough choices.** Taking time to brainstorm and weigh expected benefits against expected costs can frequently identify the most desirable action to take.

- **Ask others what they would do.** Don't over-rely on others or abdicate your own responsibilities, but use the judgment of people you trust as a barometer of when to move from analysis to decision.

- **Take the time to inform affected parties of your decisions**, particularly in advance of a less-than-ideal solution. Previewing the decision with them may yield additional data or perspectives that might enable you to fine-tune the solution to make it more workable for all.

EXCESSIVE USE

As an example, if you tend to make decisions too quickly, learn when to let some complex situations evolve. With the types of broader, more complex issues encountered at higher levels, the effect of poor judgment is often greater. Assess the cost of a possible mistake versus the cost of waiting to decide until the problem is better defined or additional information is available.

Coach Others on Critical Thinking and Judgment

When coaching others, focus on the core practices that were identified as either a development need or excessive use in the self-assessment at the beginning of this chapter. Identify and adapt any relevant development suggestions. Additional coaching tips are provided in the following table for some adverse leadership behaviors. For more information review Chapter 4, "Coach Others."

Coaching Suggestions

	Behavior	Awaken	Align	Accelerate
Investigation	*Accepts problems at face value; doesn't look for root causes*	• Work with the person to explore organizational bias or established ways of doing things. • Help the person see where there are opportunities to challenge some of the current assumptions.	• Create an environment where the person will feel comfortable sharing thinking, and invite the person to do so. • Identify the issues or problems that seem most critical for the organization to figure out.	• Encourage the person to think more deeply about issues. Recommend probing others' ideas and assumptions as they are offered and discussed. • Recommend that the person try to ask more questions of others to ensure they are getting to the real issues and root causes.
	Relies on old approaches to solve problems	• Audit the person's exposure to new ideas or innovations in the external environment. Who does he/she talk to? What does he/she read? What professional events does he/she attend? • Together read and debrief *Change By Design*, by Tim Brown. Identify new opportunities to use design thinking in your organization.	• Ensure an understanding of the organization's basic business model so that exploration is relevant versus tangential to the organization's success. • During a team meeting, pair team members together to generate novel solutions. Identify one to explore further.	• Provide stretch assignments or look for other opportunities to broaden the person's exposure and open the mind to other possibilities. • Brainstorm possibilities together for new ideas and approaches.
Analysis	*Misses underlying issues or complexity*	• Help the person assess his/her problem-solving style. Does the person have a methodology for approaching issues? • Ask the person about when he/she may have mishandled large, complex problems in the past.	• Counsel the person to involve others when tackling larger, complex issues and be willing to listen to alternative approaches. • Advise the person to talk with others in advance when proposing an idea to help improve his/her thinking.	• As you work together, make a habit of explaining the approach you typically take to solve a problem. • Talk about the types of situations where it makes sense to slow down and take a more analytical approach to issues.

THINKING AND DECIDING

198

Behavior	Awaken	Align	Accelerate
Analysis — *Values expedience over accuracy*	• Talk about what sources of information the person uses to help inform his/her analyses. Are potential sources being overlooked? • Identify one real world situation in which you have observed him/her overlooking potential important information. What were the consequences?	• Recommend that the person classify decisions in terms of the risks involved and gather input or involve others when appropriate. • Have the person review their decision-making criteria with another team member. Debrief this experience. What were their take-aways?	• Emphasize the value and importance of the person's role in making logical, sound recommendations to move the business forward. • Create an opportunity to review how analysis leads to decision-making for you. Work independently then come together to review each other's decision criteria.
Systems Thinking — *Considers only a narrow range of perspectives or possibilities*	• Discuss the person's ability to put himself/herself in others' shoes. • Assess the person's ability to articulate how the whole is greater than its parts.	• Explain how the person's role or function is related to other parts of the organization. • Have a big picture discussion about where things might be heading.	• Ask the person to flowchart or map the entire business process to develop a visual of the relationships involved. • Create opportunities for ideation and discussion with key groups identified.
Views facts and situations in isolation	• Challenge the person to connect the dots. What key patterns and trends does the person see? • When reviewing new opportunities, ensure that you highlight connections that you see, or that you expect them to explore.	• Help the person appreciate things from your perspective. What key relationships do you see? • Ask them to identify another person who they feel thinks broadly in the organization. Have them review a situation together to understand their point of view.	• Encourage the person to meet with others in adjacent parts of the organization to better appreciate how things are connected. • Provide immediate feedback when you see they are narrowly focused. Determine what caused them to miss this important connection.

Behavior		Awaken	Align	Accelerate
Navigation	*Is overwhelmed by ambiguity*	• Assess the person's tolerance for risk. What kinds of issues worry him/her the most? • Help the person appreciate past experiences and where to rely more on intuition.	• Discuss together where the organization has more or less tolerance for risk. • Talk about how you compartmentalize aspects of the business and how this focuses your thinking.	• Have the person practice the 80/20 rule and encourage him/her to experiment with making decisions with the idea that they can be fine-tuned later. • Work together to narrow the scope of the issue or decision to more manageable parts. Help them sort out that which is non-essential.
	Misreads situations with limited data	• Review times when the person felt forced to make a decision or set a direction when information was limited. What helped him/her draw conclusions? • Identify when you see them over-valuing certain data points. Do they favor a particular metric? What are the implications of this?	• Recommend that the person work with the team to establish criteria in advance for making judgment calls in different types of situations. • Work together to create decision trees for routine decisions. Create plans for reviewing exceptions together.	• When the relationship allows, tell the person about examples of times when you blew it, and ask what you could/should have done differently. • Recognize them when you observe them reading the situation well. Highlight their ability to make strong assumptions and good judgment.
Decision-making	*Makes decisions too slowly*	• Talk about the person's decision-making style. When has the person been able to act quickly? Moved too slowly? • Identify a specific example of when you believe their pace has hindered the outcome. Where were there opportunities for change?	• Help the person see the cost or benefits to the business of moving too quickly or too slowly in decision-making. • Have them seek feedback from other peers that may have been impacted by decisions they have made. Work together to develop checks and balances to minimize this moving forward.	• Coach the person to push minor decisions down to others so that he/she can focus on making the bigger decisions more quickly. • Hold them accountable for pace. Set targets by which you will review their decision-making. By putting parameters on this stage you can help them better understand how to optimize their decision-making.
	Makes decisions too quickly	• Ask about the person's approach to specific types of problems; ask questions to gain a sense of the person's decision-making skills. • Have them reflect on a decision they wish they could take back. What would they do differently? Why?	• Work together on your expectation or understanding of how you would approach making key decisions. • Identify who they admire for the thoroughness of their analysis. Have them discuss with that person how thoroughness leads to better decisions. What is one key learning they can incorporate?	• Encourage the person to involve others when situations become more complex or more critically strategic. • Challenge them when you believe they are moving too quickly. Ask insightful questions to uncover where they may have acted impulsively.

Tips for Coaching in a Global Environment

Critical Thinking and Judgment may be practiced or expressed differently within other cultures. This might impact how you approach coaching. Try to keep an open mind, avoid generalizations, and continue gathering data as you gain experience with another culture. Consider these suggestions:

Investigation: Appreciate that Eastern cultures place a higher value on searching inside oneself, while Western cultures emphasize looking outside the self for data and objective analysis. Western leaders are likely to challenge ideas and may feel a need to see or prove things before they can be believed or acted on. Some Eastern leaders may tend to take the truth as a given and may not be comfortable challenging authority or established views.

Analysis: Don't assume that because someone is quiet they are not thinking. They may be sensing the context and working out a way of expression that keeps people comfortable. Some cultures, including many Western cultures, encourage thinking out loud and active discussion of ideas, whereas other cultures emphasize a more reflective, contemplative approach. Certain cultures place more or less emphasis on feelings, values, and relationships in decision-making.

Systems Thinking: Recognize that Western leaders may prefer to take a more linear view with a clear beginning and an end, while Eastern leaders are likely to see things as more circular and interconnected. Eastern leaders are likely to be more holistic in their thinking, while Western leaders are more likely to compartmentalize issues.

Navigation: Recognize that leaders who are working in a non-native language are likely to need more time to digest complex information and formulate their thoughts. Language barriers may also make it extremely difficult to quickly assess critical thinking skills. Eastern leaders may tend to take a longer-term view on issues, even in business. For instance, some Asian organizations have developed 100-year business plans whereas most U.S. businesses struggle to establish three-year plans.

Decision-Making: The type of schooling people have had may affect their approaches to decision-making. For example, children in some educational systems are encouraged to ask questions, challenge assumptions, and think independently. Meanwhile, schools in other cultures may expect students to show deferential respect for teachers and engage in more rote memorization. Ask how people you are coaching learned to think and express their own points of view. Group problem-solving varies greatly from individualistic to collectivistic cultures. As a result, diverse groups may ultimately lead to better results, but it will clearly take more time for global teams to form and work through all aspects of a problem. Recent research suggests that a more collectivistic approach to group problem-solving results in greater decision quality.

A Case Study in Critical Thinking and Judgment

Critical Thinking and Judgment are required to deal with complexity and provide direction for the organization in the face of ambiguity and competing priorities.

As you read about Robert's situation, reflect on what you've learned about Critical Thinking and Judgment in this chapter. How does Robert sound like you or one of your team members? What experiences or tendencies do you share? Finally, consider how you would help Robert demonstrate greater skill in Critical Thinking and Judgment and be successful in his leadership role.

Judging When and Where to Jump

Robert Driver had three decades of success in sales, marketing, and product management roles with several global corporations. While he never considered himself the brightest among his peers, he had learned how to lead and influence people, get things done in a complex organization, and manage a P&L. With his strong commercial orientation, he had repeatedly led successful new product launches, established and maintained strong customer relationships, and driven revenue to meet or exceed growth targets.

Robert had always aspired to lead an independent organization and knew that it was just a matter of time before he would have that opportunity. He was confident that he could handle the increasing demands on his ability and make the tough judgment calls required at the top. At the same time, he had received feedback over the years that he wasn't as analytical as some of his peers and that he tended to move quickly without taking the time to consult with others. When the president of a relatively new business left to join a competitor, Robert lobbied for the role. He got the job thanks in part to having developed good working relationships with the executive management team and his peers. He was eager to make an impact.

Soon after being promoted, Robert held an offsite meeting to discuss the results of a SWOT analysis and put together a plan. The SWOT had revealed significant threats such as an economic downturn, increased global competition, net sales declines, and cyclical petroleum costs that had recently hurt their cash position. The business also had significant opportunities, including the need to integrate acquisitions that had helped fuel growth over the past several years, but were currently contributing to the drag on operating profits. There were also huge growth opportunities if they could find a way to diversify beyond their largest customer, whose orders comprised over 70 percent of their total volume.

Robert quickly found that things were more chaotic and less defined in his new business unit than he had been led to believe or could have imagined. Then things got worse. Thirty days into the plan, their main customer warned him that they were planning to source more closely to their own markets and reduce their dependency on Robert's business as a key supplier. While he needed to act quickly, he decided to hold another offsite to analyze the impact and create a new plan.

Robert found that he needed Critical Thinking and Judgment more than ever, in order to:

- Identify all the potential opportunities and problems in the business.

- Assess and clarify each aspect of the current situation.

- See and make sense of the many interdependencies.

- Prioritize and stay focused through this uncertain time.

- Work with others to generate options, make decisions, and plan a course of action.

Robert's Leadership Development Plan

Following is a sample development plan for Robert Driver. Research on leadership development has shown that leaders learn through experience and that this learning is optimized through the use of an individual development plan that includes new experiences as well as introduces the leader to new conversations and tools. The suggestions included in the previous sections may stimulate your thinking about other possibilities that Robert might pursue.

LEADERSHIP DEVELOPMENT PLAN FOR ROBERT DRIVER
DEVELOPMENT GOAL
Goal: To strengthen my Critical Thinking and Judgment skills
Desired Outcomes—results I want to see from developing this skill
Self: I will have increased confidence in my abilities and be seen as a strong leader and strategist. **Team:** My team will demonstrate a sense of ownership of the direction and contribute to a strong plan. **Organization:** My business will contribute to the bottom line with a plan for creating shareholder value.
Self-Understanding—strengths that I can build on and development needs I can address
Strengths: Effective influencer across the organization; established record of strong results; commercial and financial acumen; global experience **Development Needs:** Can be bold, impatient, and hard charging; independent-minded rather than inclusive under pressure; new in the transition to business unit leader
Business Context—challenges in my business environment that require this skill
The need to diversify sources of revenue in a highly competitive, global environment.

LEADERSHIP DEVELOPMENT PLAN FOR ROBERT DRIVER

DEVELOPMENT ACTIONS

AWAKEN

- Reflect on how I have approached complex situations in the past. Look at what worked as well as times when things did not turn out as I had expected. Note key ingredients of my past success as well as common pitfalls.

- Determine my emotional triggers/topics/issues and when to seek guidance from others.

- Ask what kinds of information I need to make decisions at this time. Establish criteria for evaluating my options.

ALIGN

- Explore alternatives with corporate leadership and gain clarity on strategic intent. Consider the criteria or goals that will ultimately guide my decision-making efforts.

- Create a cabinet of trusted advisors to test my thinking. Solicit others' opinions, practice listening, build off of others' ideas, etc. Include peers plus some external contacts, depending on the nature of the issue.

ACCELERATE

- Assess needs of the business before taking action. Be careful of doing exactly what the customer requests.

- Make a chart of alternatives and assess the risk or cost associated with each.

- Make a list of questions and what I need to know in order to solve a problem correctly.

- Research and understand changing business practices in our customer base.

- Schedule time individually and as a group to think more from a longer-term, broader perspective.

- Before proceeding with a course of action, work through the chain of possible consequences.

DEVELOPMENT SUCCESS FACTORS

Timeline: Within the next six months

Support Needed:

- I will need corporate support for analytics and business intelligence to inform me and my team.

- I will need a corporate-level leader or external mentor to bounce ideas off of and learn from their experiences.

LEADERSHIP DEVELOPMENT PLAN FOR ROBERT DRIVER

Indicators of Success:

- I will have a strong plan for dealing with current business challenges including long-term plans and contingencies.
- My team will feel engaged and involved in the decision-making process and committed to the ultimate plan.
- I will gain credibility with corporate leadership and respect for my thought processes.

An Example of Coaching for Critical Thinking and Judgment

Robert Driver's goal was to strengthen his skills in Critical Thinking and Judgment. Here are some steps Robert's manager could take using the Awaken, Align, Accelerate framework to coach Robert in this area:

AWAKEN	**Increase INSIGHT**	Engage Robert in reflection about how he approached complex situations in the past. Talk about how his emotions and the pressure of the situation may be preventing him from thinking clearly about the best course of action.
	MOTIVATE change	Help Robert understand his preferences for making decisions—is he gathering data or relying on his gut? Is he listening to inputs from others or focused on his ideas? Identify potential priorities for development. Ask about the consequences of not making any changes.
ALIGN	**PLAN goals**	Determine what would enable Robert to handle current and future business challenges more successfully. Focus on what Robert and his team could change to improve their planning and decision-making process. Work together to construct a leadership development plan similar to the sample provided in this chapter.
	ALIGN expectations	Review broader organizational objectives and discuss the need to balance short-term objectives with the longer-term strategy. Recommend that Robert engage shared services to ensure consistent practice with respect to analytics and strategic planning. Ask Robert to keep you informed as he and his team make decisions.
ACCELERATE	**CREATE teachable moments**	Encourage Robert to experiment with new approaches. Propose that Robert reach out to peers, consultants, and external thought leaders to improve his thinking and the thinking of his team. Advise Robert to build a project plan that includes time for him to work with his team and explore more than one alternative. Remind Robert that he ultimately needs to be decisive, set direction, and adjust things over time.
	TRACK progress	Discuss expected outcomes and results. Work with Robert to evaluate progress toward his development goal as well as progress in developing his business plan. Provide feedback based on your own observations. Celebrate milestones.

Results: Measuring Impact

Robert Driver felt a great deal of urgency. He set priorities, stayed focused, and worked through his development plan in less than four months. He experimented with alternative approaches and made progress on improving his Critical Thinking and Judgment. His new skills allowed Robert to:

- Assess the current business situation including the many interdependencies.

- Engage his team in generating options and making decisions.

- Develop a strong plan for dealing with current business challenges.

- Anticipate and prepare for contingencies as well as longer-term opportunities.

- Increase his personal credibility and gain more respect from senior leaders.

ACHIEVING

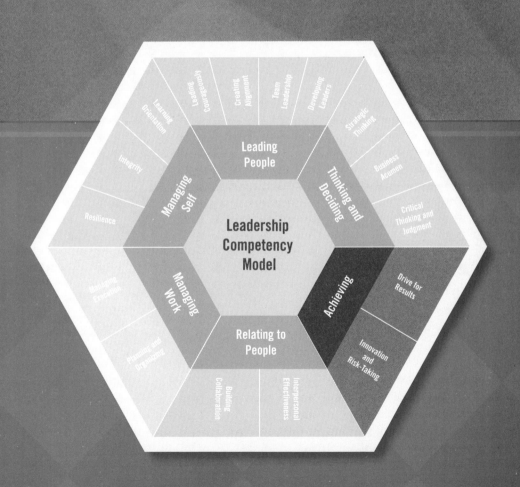

12

Drive for Results

Results-driven leaders demonstrate strong personal drive to accomplish goals and are motivated by challenges no matter how difficult. They establish high standards of performance and convey a passion to achieve results that are above and beyond expectations. They convey a sense of urgency and establish aggressive timelines. They show initiative and set things in motion. They are energetic and determined in the face of setbacks. They maintain a focus on what makes a difference to the success, performance, and profitability of the organization.

Factor	Competency	Core Practice
Leading People	Drive for Results	Drive
Thinking and Deciding	Innovation and Risk-Taking	Expectations
Achieving		Urgency
Relating to People		Initiatve
Managing Work		Determination
Managing Self		

Successful leaders rally their teams and focus their energy on the right things—the goals and activities that will truly make a difference to the performance and success of the organization.

Drive for Results is the starting point for making things happen. Passion, energy, tenacity, a thirst for challenge, and an ability to convey a sense of urgency to get things done are the key ingredients to driving for results. It's also about the choices we make as leaders—the outcomes and goals on which we focus, and the means by which we choose to achieve them. Not surprisingly, people who aspire to leadership roles are typically achievement-oriented and show high levels of ambition, energy, and drive. Especially at senior levels of leadership, Drive for Results often shows up as an overused strength, rather than as a deficit.

When leaders struggle in this area, the problems are often related to execution or a lack of focus on the right goals. In fact, many leaders find managing and maintaining a strong Drive for Results in their employees to be much more challenging than managing their own personal levels of drive, initiative, and persistence. Inspiring a team to achieve a high level of performance when faced with a stretch goal is one of the most difficult (and important) tasks a leader faces.

A results-driven leader demonstrates strong passion, urgency, and determination in moving things forward and accomplishing goals. At the end of the day, the most successful leaders channel their ambition, energy, and initiative toward the right things—the goals and actions that will truly make a difference to the performance, success, and profitability of the business. They bring others along by providing both challenge and support—setting high expectations and holding others accountable while sensitively handling the people side of the equation. Their enthusiasm is genuine and infectious, helping them to rally others around the goal and motivating them to exceed expectations. While vital at every level, how these skills are applied looks differently depending on the leader's level and role in the organization.

How Leaders at Different Levels Drive for Results

	Managers	Function Leaders	Senior Executives
Drive	Encourages team members to embrace new challenges and expect the best.	Drives to exceed goals and deliver outstanding results.	Inspires the organization to drive toward results that improve the top and bottom line.
Expectations	Conveys expectations for hard work to others.	Establishes high standards of performance for self and others.	Ensures goals and objectives are clearly understood throughout the enterprise.
Urgency	Produces high-quality work on time.	Sets aggressive timelines for achieving objectives.	Consistently sets the pace for the entire organization.
Initiative	Sustains the team's momentum and progress.	Takes initiative to get things done.	Empowers function and business leaders to step up and drive results.
Determination	Keeps the team focused on key goals.	Persists towards goals despite obstacles or setbacks.	Infuses the organization with a sense of optimism and determination.

Self-Assessment

To evaluate your effectiveness in Drive for Results, check all boxes below that represent current behavior or performance. Look for patterns: Which core practices represent a development need, a strength, or an excessive use? Recognize that you might have some blind spots. Invite your boss or colleagues to indicate what they have observed in your behavior. Use this assessment to help identify development suggestions that are most relevant to you.

	Development Need	Strength	Excessive Use
Drive	☐ Has inconsistent or uneven personal drive ☐ Avoids committing to stretch goals	☐ Strives to exceed goals and deliver outstanding results ☐ Shows a willingness to do whatever it takes to accomplish objectives	☐ Overcommits and burns out; has little work/life balance ☐ Takes on too many things and becomes distracted and unproductive
Expectations	☐ Is ineffective or inconsistent in conveying performance expectations to others ☐ Is not focused on the right things; directs energy to activities that have only a marginal impact on the business	☐ Inspires others to perform and achieve beyond expectations ☐ Sets the expectation of building a best-in-class team to achieve optimal results	☐ Sets the bar unrealistically high; leaves people feeling like they can't measure up ☐ Loses sight of people and process while relentlessly focusing on results
Urgency	☐ Establishes unrealistic or overly lax timelines for achieving objectives ☐ Does not clarify deadlines or milestones for gauging progress	☐ Insists on aggressive timelines for achieving objectives ☐ Ensures that timelines and milestones are clear and understood	☐ Is overly optimistic; overpromises and underdelivers ☐ Rigidly or blindly adheres to timelines
Initiative	☐ Shows little interest in taking the lead or driving to closure ☐ Hesitates to take initiative	☐ Takes charge quickly to get things moving forward ☐ Confronts problems and issues promptly and directly	☐ Is presumptive and excessively demanding of others ☐ Has difficulty letting others take the lead
Determination	☐ Is easily frustrated or discouraged; shows fatigue ☐ Is easily distracted by new challenges or problems	☐ Demonstrates exceptional stamina and persistence ☐ Remains determined despite obstacles or setbacks	☐ Pushes too hard; goes beyond the point of diminishing returns ☐ Rigidly stays the course; doesn't acknowledge when a plan is not working

Development Suggestions

The following section contains development suggestions for each core practice. Having completed the self-assessment, focus on suggestions that correspond to the core practices you identified as a development need or excessive use. Use these suggestions to create your own development plan, making sure to try one or two from each phase. In addition, feel free to create your own or adapt these to best meet your development needs.

Drive

Drive to exceed goals and deliver outstanding results.

"Big results require big ambitions."

Heraclitus

Awaken potential:

- **Consider what truly motivates you at work.** Is it the thrill of competition and winning? Getting things done? Solving problems with creative ideas? The chance to work collaboratively with others? Be honest about what you are genuinely motivated to do.

- **Examine the fit** between your career and your natural interests, values, and motivation. Do you feel passionate about the work? If the thrill is gone and you've lost your drive, try to pinpoint the problem. Is it the work itself? Your boss? Your fit with the organization? Articulating the problem will help point you toward the solution.

- **Consider what is holding you back,** if this is the case for you. Some people prefer to play it safe and avoid challenges.

- **Use 360-degree feedback** to see whether your Drive for Results has unintended downsides or consequences. Overdrive can inadvertently cause leaders to work in ways that may be counter to the values and culture of the organization.

- **Consider a career assessment** if you're ready for a career change but aren't sure about which direction to go. A skilled career coach can help you identify new possibilities.

Align goals:

- **Focus your energies.** As a leader, you are likely passionate about certain things. Review your goals and priorities with your manager on a regular basis to ensure that you are focused on what matters to the organization.

- **Make sure you focus your energy on the right goals,** and that important but not necessarily urgent initiatives are given adequate attention each week. Prioritize your work and allocate your time based on its value to the organization; communicate this to your team as well.

Accelerate performance:

- **Learn from others** who you regard as strongly but constructively driven and achievement-oriented. Talk to them about where they get their passion and energy for their work. Can they provide any insights that are motivating or inspiring to you? How do they demonstrate their sense of drive? Do they do anything that you should consider doing?

- **Manage your career.** Talk to your manager at least once a year about your career progress, interests, and aspirations.

- **Determine where you will spend extra effort.** Focus on what the organization needs you and your team to do exceptionally well. Make sure you share this with your team.

- **Identify the skills you need to develop** to get ready for the position you want next. Interview people in the position you want, or people who are one level above you. Ask them to identify the skills they need to be most successful. If you feel you do not have these, ask your manager for an assignment that would help you develop them.

- **Take a chance.** If you tend to be cautious, take some risks by publicly committing to an ambitious goal. If doing this doesn't feel uncomfortable at first, then you aren't pushing yourself hard enough!

- **Solicit ongoing feedback** about your balance between results leadership and people leadership. Recognize that taking care of people should allow you to achieve even better and stronger results.

- **Step back and recharge your batteries** if you've pushed yourself too hard for too long. Start setting reasonable limits to keep the work from completely eroding your personal time, sleep, etc. You may find that you have even more energy to tackle the job.

EXCESSIVE USE

As an example, if you overcommit and try to accomplish everything, you risk burning out. Ask yourself whether you commit to more than you can realistically deliver. Do you push your team to deliver at all costs? Or do you end up meeting some goals and objectives, but not others? The best antidote to over-commitment is to proactively manage expectations with stakeholders at the front end. Ask them how critical the request is. What are the barriers to delivery, and what resources are available? Ask your boss to help prioritize competing commitments.

Establish high standards of performance for self and others.

> *Every achievement, big or small, begins in your mind.*
>
> Mary Kay Ash

Awaken potential:

- **Look for inspiration.** Think about a time when you were inspired to give a major task or project your all and felt proud of the outcome. What inspired you?

- **Be a go-to leader.** Ask your manager whether he/she would come to you with a project or initiative that requires a deliverable of the highest quality and standards. Why might you be someone who is not called upon?

- **Be a champion.** Look around you at leaders who consistently "go for the gold" and rally their team members to deliver outstanding results. Why and how are they successful? Seek them out for advice and insight.

- **Challenge yourself.** Give some thought to whether you hold back and sell yourself (and your team) short. Some people prefer to play it safe and are careful not to commit to anything that might be risky or potentially beyond their reach.

- **Challenge others.** Delve into the barriers that keep you from asking team members and others to go beyond "meets expectations." As a leader, are you hesitant to ask for more from your team? If you work harder than your team does, it may be because you expect more from yourself than you do from them.

Align goals:

- **Focus on critical priorities.** Make a list of the most critical priorities facing your function or division in the next six months. Have a conversation with your manager about the organization's expectations of you and the team in addressing them.

- **Solicit feedback** from your manager, colleagues, and team members regarding the expectations you set. Are you seen as someone who sets a high bar for performance? Or do you expect too little?

Accelerate performance:

- **Maintain high standards.** Hold yourself and the team to high standards for the right things, and check yourself on an ongoing basis. Some leaders find themselves striving for perfection in activities that capture their personal attention but hold marginal value for the function or business.

- **Communicate expectations.** Ask your direct reports if you are clear and consistent in conveying performance expectations. What's obvious to you as a leader may not be so obvious to your team members, and repeated communication may be necessary to keep expectations front of mind for all.

- **Stretch your team.** Don't be afraid to assign stretch goals to your most capable and ambitious team members. Research shows that high-potential talent wants to be challenged and kept at their growing edge.

- **Set challenging but realistic objectives**—what can and cannot be achieved given the capabilities of your team and available resources? Stretch goals may be necessary to meet the demands of the business; they need to be challenging, but not out of reach.

- **Involve your team.** Goals—especially challenging goals—are more likely to be accomplished if they are developed with the people who are responsible for meeting them.

- **Establish measures of success.** Make sure you identify the way you and your team will know if you are on track (or ahead of pace) to meet the goals you have set.

- **Provide feedback.** Make sure you inform your team regularly about the progress they are making. This is especially critical if the effort or results you are expecting are difficult to quantify or measure.

- **Read about people who accomplished seemingly impossible tasks,** either at work or in their personal lives. Read Secrets of Special Ops Leadership: Dare the Impossible—Achieve the Extraordinary by William Cohen (AMACOM, 2005) for stories about military special operations. Make notes about what made them successful and what you could adopt in your own work.

- **Review Chapter 17, "Managing Execution,"** for additional suggestions and recommendations.

EXCESSIVE USE

As an example, if your high standards leave people feeling like they cannot measure up, this can be highly de-motivating, especially if you couple this habit with a tendency to criticize. Try inviting people to set their own standards. Those will be much more motivating.

Set aggressive timelines for achieving objectives.

If I had to sum up in a word what makes a good manager, I'd say decisiveness. You can use the fanciest computers to gather the numbers, but in the end you have to set a timetable and act.

Lee Iacocca

Awaken potential:

- **Evaluate your use of deadlines.** Consider when you feel most energized by your work. How does pressure (or lack of pressure) play a role in your level of engagement with the task?

- **Review successful time management.** Think about the most successful projects you have been a part of. What role did effective time management play in making these efforts successful?

- **Identify barriers.** Think of a time when you failed to move quickly enough to meet a deadline or commitment. What got in the way? Identify what you could have done differently to achieve a better outcome.

- **Analyze past experiences.** Reflect on a situation when a colleague did not complete a task that was important to your goals. How quickly did you respond, and what did you do? What was the impact on your team? The business?

- **Gather feedback.** Ask your team members and colleagues for feedback about whether you consistently set clear timeline expectations with others. Make sure you focus on deadlines in the planning and delegation process. Set deadlines that are specific and ensure that others understand the importance of meeting them.

Align goals:

- **Secure buy-in.** Create annual and quarterly priorities, and clearly tie them to the business strategy and objectives. Get key stakeholder buy-in on proposed timelines to ensure they are both aggressive and realistic.

- **Communicate proactively.** Speak directly with your manager if you are accountable for a significant deliverable on a tight timeframe. Discuss what is needed to ensure success. Do other priorities need shifting? What can you postpone or delegate? What resources do you need?

Accelerate performance:

- **Start with the end in mind** if you find it challenging to sit down and map out a specific work plan. Begin with your delivery date and then work backward to determine the length of time required to accomplish each step. Highlight the milestones or checkpoints you will use to monitor progress.

- **Introduce the discipline of weekly updates on the project plan.** Find what works best for you and the team (e.g., email/electronic file sharing, voice mail, conference call, or face to face).

- **Solicit feedback from team members** when setting aggressive timelines regarding the barriers to success, as well as the resources they will need to deliver on time. Have staff members prepare plans with dates, timelines, and checkpoints. Let them know you expect candor and no surprises along the way. Provide appropriate support and coaching as needed.

- **Include extra time** when numerous stakeholders are involved in a project you are planning. This is especially critical for complex and/or sensitive initiatives.

- **Intervene.** If a project you are leading turns into a struggle to meet the deadline, find out why. Stop the presses, talk to the team, and discuss specifically what needs to happen to get things back on track. Make sure the team understands the criticality of the project to overall goals and objectives.

EXCESSIVE USE

As an example, if you are overly optimistic in setting aggressive timelines, you may experience a lot of slippage. If you tend to over promise and underdeliver, develop project schedules in collaboration with others so they can help you establish achievable timelines. Work to create a reputation in the organization for overdelivering on timelines.

Take initiative to accomplish functional priorities.

> *I have been impressed with the urgency of doing. Knowing is not enough; we must apply. Being willing is not enough; we must do.*

Leonardo Da Vinci

Awaken potential:

- **Identify common factors.** Take stock of situations in which you feel most self-motivated and energized to step up and move things forward. Identify the aspects of the work or situation that draw you to action.

- **Analyze how you approach new challenges and opportunities.** Are you quick to take initiative? Or do you limit your initiative-taking to situations that are squarely in your comfort zone?

- **Look for role models.** Give some thought to leaders you believe set a good example for driving things forward. Consider what behaviors and practices you might try on the job.

- **Think of a time** when you felt overwhelmed with a project to the point that you were uncertain of where to begin. What did you do to get things going and make progress toward your goal?

- **Identify barriers.** Consider barriers that stop you from taking action or getting things done. Is it perfectionism? Fear of looking foolish? Fear of offending others or stepping on toes? If you typically wait to be asked, make the first move instead.

- **Make a realistic appraisal of your commitments,** both inside and outside of work. If you have taken on too much and can renegotiate, do what is necessary to inject some realism into the picture.

Align goals:

- **Clarify opportunities to step up in making decisions.** Talk with your boss to identify the issues the issues or activities to bring forward for approval and the items that he/she can be informed of after the fact.

- **Commit to taking action more quickly with key stakeholders.** Some individuals need a clear and imminent deadline to spur them into action. If you are one to hold back until the last minute, talk with others about how your efforts impact them and the results the team achieves.

- **Match your efforts with overall goals.** Make sure you are taking necessary initiative on the key objectives and priorities that are most important for your function or business.

Accelerate performance:

- **Push yourself** to take on one extra challenge in the next month, something important for the business. Select something that you are passionate about and that best fits your skills and interests.

- **Address anything that is holding you back.** If you have ample time but still aren't tackling some priorities, be honest with yourself about why. Are you putting off some things because they are less enjoyable? Because they may not come easily to you?

- **Take action.** Practice informing after the fact instead of asking for approval first. Write the email or the report or make the call, then inform your manager about what you have done.

- **Do your least favorite activities first,** using your preferred activities as a reward. Set aside specific times of the day or week to do them. Consider delegating them to others who enjoy that part of the work.

- **Keep a progress journal**, noting particularly when you have overcome any hesitancy about making the first move. Audit your actions once per month, noting the impact and outcomes of your efforts.

- **Have courageous conversations.** Make sure team members fully understand what you expect and why if your challenge is getting them to take initiative. Communicate using the "3 C's": clarity (about what you expect), commitment (from them to deliver), and consequences (the potential impact on the business).

EXCESSIVE USE

As an example, if you become demanding and inflexible in driving projects forward, you may experience resistance and turnover that slows you down even further.
If you enjoy taking the lead, be careful about going too far.
Let others take the reins when appropriate. Review the "Structure" and "Empowerment" core practices in Chapter 7 for some suggestions.

Persist toward goals despite obstacles or setbacks.

"Good enough never is."

Debbie Fields

Awaken potential:

- **Recognize what motivates you.** Some people get excited about new endeavors but lose interest once the fun front-end work is done. What about you? What keeps you going through tough times?

- **Analyze your success.** Think about a long-term project that you successfully completed. Evaluate what enabled you to stay on track and maintain progress over time.

- **Assess your persistence.** Evaluate what happens when things don't proceed as planned. How do you respond to setbacks and disappointments? A common temptation when faced with problems is to use them as an excuse to procrastinate. Recognize when you begin to get discouraged and lose energy on a project. Make a deliberate effort to step back, get support from others, and regroup so you can tackle the obstacles with renewed energy. Look for mentors who show outstanding persistence, and ask them for advice.

- **Be honest with yourself** about whether you are fully empowering your team to deliver in a self-directed way. Are you inadvertently getting in their way?

- **Ask for feedback** about the effort you are putting into various activities. Do people see you consistently adding value? Are you doing enough to drive things forward? Do you give too much effort to activities that are personally interesting but have questionable importance for the organization as a whole?

Align goals:

- **Act proactively and engage stakeholders early.** Plan ahead, and anticipate the resources or support you will need to make a project successful. If money is involved, prepare a business case (investment/cost-benefit analysis) to support your request and share it with your boss.

- **Categorize commitments and deliverables** based on (a) importance (high versus low) and (b) urgency (high versus low). If you struggle with staying focused on important but not necessarily urgent priorities, try to keep them top of mind. Schedule time each day or week to devote to them, and turn off email and/or phone distractions so you aren't sidetracked by urgent but less important requests.

- **Follow the norms.** Ensure you persist in ways that are culturally consistent with the norms of the organization. While it may be expected that people leading people through change may push them a bit and cause some discomfort, taking that too far can be counterproductive and work against you.

Accelerate performance:

- **Thank people for their efforts.** Take time to personally acknowledge team efforts and show your appreciation. Even a simple "thank you" can have a huge impact. If doing such things doesn't come naturally to you, make a routine practice of thanking and/or giving recognition to someone every day.

- **Take care of yourself.** Regular exercise and sufficient sleep are linked to increased attention and energy levels. Make an extra effort to manage stress and maintain a healthier lifestyle.

- **Focus on what it will take to bring things to completion.** Act swiftly and directly if it becomes apparent that successful completion of a project will require more resources than were originally budgeted or planned. If resources are scarce, be prepared to share some creative ideas and show flexibility about potential solutions. Review the "Resource Management" core practice in Chapter 16 for ways to anticipate and successfully request the resources you need to get the results expected of you.

EXCESSIVE USE

As an example, if you persist too hard without getting results,
you may need to acknowledge that your plan isn't working.
The best leaders know when to stop and change course.

Coach Others on Drive for Results

When coaching others, focus on the core practices that were identified as either a development need or excessive use in the self-assessment at the beginning of this chapter. Identify and adapt any relevant development suggestions. Additional coaching tips are provided in the following table for some adverse leadership behaviors. For more information review Chapter 4, "Coach Others."

Coaching Suggestions

Behavior		Awaken	Align	Accelerate
Drive	*Has unreliable drive*	• Discuss what motivates the person. What changes in the work or organization would help play to the person's motivation? • Try to awaken the person's desires for the future. What does the person want to achieve?	• Try to assign projects that tap the person's personal passions and interests. • Team with human resources to evaluate potential better fit in a role elsewhere in the enterprise.	• Communicate how you see new projects or tasks fitting in with the person's motivation. • Use inspiring language to help the person see how today's efforts can help fulfill his/her goals.
	Avoids stretch goals	• Help the person articulate reasons for playing it safe. What keeps the person from taking on the tough challenges? • Provide some examples of where you have seen the person play it safe. What consequences did you observe?	• Work together to define a stretch goal and put adequate support and resources behind it. • Demonstrate how increased effort and risk-taking could positively impact both the person's and the organization's goals.	• Offer encouragement, remove barriers, and ensure the person gets what is needed to be successful. • Balance challenge with support, ensuring that they are not disproportionate.
Expectations	*Conveys few performance expectations*	• Observe the person in action with his/her team: What's missing? Provide feedback on what he/she can do to convey performance expectations in a compelling way. • Have the person circle back with the team to understand how to be more effective.	• Reinforce the link between deliverables and the organization's success. • Encourage the person to do the same in everyday communication with the team.	• Use multi-rater feedback to check progress and ensure the person is clear and unambiguous about what is needed and expected from others. • Review communication in one-on-ones, providing regular feedback on your observations.
	Does not focus on the right things	• Ask the person to complete a time audit to determine how the person's time is spent. • Ask whether key initiatives are set up for success. Are critical stakeholders engaged and adequate resources available? Are team members skilled and ready to deliver?	• Review together how the person's activities contribute to the broader objectives of the business; point out discrepancies. • Create a plan to better align the person's activities/focus with the business goals.	• Provide appropriate oversight and monitoring to ensure things stay on track; give timely and actionable feedback. • Create an accountability group with several peers to keep each other on track with priorities and goals.

DRIVE FOR RESULTS

Behavior		Awaken	Align	Accelerate
Urgency	*Sets lax or unrealistic timelines*	• Help the person diagnose the problem. Is the person setting timelines? Creating timelines that are unrealistic, or conversely, not ambitious enough? • Share your expectations regarding the timing of deliverables. Model strong goal-setting.	• Ensure that the person seeks input from others who will be affected by his/her timelines, especially those downstream from the person's work. • Pair the person with an internal mentor who is known for creating challenging, but realistic, timelines. Learn how they make decisions about dates.	• Encourage the person to continually re-evaluate the plan, the barriers to success, as well as the resources needed to deliver on time. • Have the person promote challenge from the team when setting timelines. What are they seeing that the person may not?
	Fails to establish milestones	• How does the person currently set milestones? At what intervals? What criteria are used? Who does the person involve? • Have the person review the organization's project planning material and rate himself/herself on skill at each phase. Identify where the person tends to miss opportunities.	• Encourage the person to speak with others involved to build a shared understanding about what needs to happen, when, and by whom. • Have the person work with a skilled colleague who can help take a lofty goal or objective and break it down into component parts.	• Once the work is underway, ask for regular updates so that things stay on track. • Encourage the person to celebrate milestone achievements and small successes with the team.

Behavior		Awaken	Align	Accelerate
Initiative	Does not lead	• Have a conversation about intentions. Did the person truly "miss" the opportunity to lead or was it a deliberate choice? • Review the person's motivation as a leader. Has the person been promoted to a level that requires something in which he/she is not interested? Make sure that role and career paths are aligned with the person's interests and goals.	• Use the "3-Cs" (clarity, commitment, and consequences) to engage and focus the person's attention on the right priorities. • Focus the person's energy on leading a project or initiative where he/she can take charge. Ensure the project is key to departmental or organizational goals to provide visibility.	• Set clear and concise behavioral targets that will make it evident to others that the person's leadership behavior is changing. • Regularly review progress, providing reinforcing feedback, especially when you observe the person making progress.
	Hesitates to take initiative	• Uncover any concerns the person may have about stepping up (e.g., stepping on others' toes, making a mistake, etc.). • Discuss what is holding the person back. Any fears? Give "permission" to make some mistakes along the way.	• Convey how taking more initiative would affect team or organizational goals. Show direct correlation between your expectations of the person and results. • Have the person take leadership of a task team in which other team members are strong drivers. Discuss how the person will stay ahead of their urge to take the lead.	• On significant projects that require taking initiative, make sure you give the person space to find his/her own way. Expect some mistakes and make it okay to learn on the job. Reinforce attempts at change, rather than criticize mistakes. • Review together what the person observes in other strong leaders. What is the person learning from them?

Behavior		Awaken	Align	Accelerate
Determination	Lacks stamina	• Ask questions to understand what's behind the low energy level. Is it stress? Has the person bitten off too much? Is the person discouraged by setbacks or problems? • Talk together about how the person is taking care of himself/herself. Encourage talking to external resources such as a personal trainer, nutritionist, or EAP, as necessary.	• If the person is trying to do too much, encourage leveraging others and devoting energy to those issues and activities where the person can uniquely add value. • Have specific discussions about prioritization. Make sure the person understands what is necessary vs. what is nice to have.	• Team with human resources to provide necessary resources, remove barriers, and remind the person how to use vacation time and manage work-life balance. • Recognize the person when you see him/her demonstrating resilience during a challenging time.
	Loses focus	• Determine why the person loses focus. Does the person become distracted by opportunities? Is attention stretched in too many directions? • If lack of interest is part of the problem, help the person think creatively about how to get less-preferred tasks done.	• Encourage the person to manage to a concrete plan, tied back to team or organizational goal achievement. • Prioritize together projects that are integral vs. secondary. Ensure adequate resources are assigned to critical projects and not removed as others arise.	• Regular status updates are critical. Remind the person to keep key priorities top of mind and delegate tasks to maintain progress. • Help the person to minimize distractions by planning time away from the office or phone/email distractions to spend quality time on prioritized projects.

Tips for Coaching in a Global Environment

Drive for Results may be practiced or expressed differently within other cultures. This might impact how you approach coaching. Try to keep an open mind, avoid generalizations, and continue gathering data as you gain experience with another culture. Consider these suggestions:

Ambition: Recognize that a focus on individual achievement is a decidedly Western cultural concept. Learn all you can about the culture of the individual with whom you are working. Is it collectivistic or individualistic? Does it promote cooperation and team performance, or individual achievement and recognition? Be aware that these elements will determine what constitutes acceptable and effective leadership in those cultures. Be careful not to assume a person lacks drive just because someone is less assertive in sharing individual accomplishments, ambitions, or goals for the future. Have a conversation about what achievement looks like in your culture and in that individual's culture.

Expectations: Consider that the notion of stretch goals is less common outside the United States. It is notably less common in Asia. There, people who are asked to set their own goals are likely to establish realistic rather than ambitious objectives. Doing so may help them avoid the embarrassment of a goal that is not achieved, thereby saving face for themselves and others. Under-promise and over-deliver may be considered sage advice.

Urgency: Keep in mind that the notion of time is treated differently in different cultures. The most industrialized and economically developed countries have a strong future orientation and tend to operate at a fast pace—think Japan, the United States, and most of Western Europe. In contrast, some Mediterranean, Arab, Latin American, and Native American cultures are more likely to encourage taking one's time before getting down to business. Depending on the background of the individual, "tomorrow" may not be taken literally.

Initiative: Help the individual understand your expectations for stepping up and driving results. Make sure that your communications are clear and unambiguous. The formality of reporting structures and the requirement to seek approval before taking independent action can vary. Some departments, functions, and entire organizations can be more rule-bound than others. Meanwhile, in cultures that tend to encourage more initiative (i.e., doing what it takes to get things done), going outside reporting channels may be judged efficient.

Determination: When you see someone driving too hard and being too "chain of command" in management style, have a conversation about your expectations for enhancing engagement or empowering others. You may need to provide training for individuals who are open to learning other ways to lead.

Drive for Results is required to move things forward and accomplish goals. Drive for Results is what gets things going and keeps them moving forward despite challenges, distractions, and setbacks.

As you read about June's situation, reflect on what you've learned about Drive for Results in this chapter. How does June sound like you or one of your team members? What experiences or tendencies do you share? Finally, consider how you would help June demonstrate greater skill in Drive for Results and be successful in her leadership role.

Pushing People for Performance

June Lee recently changed leadership roles within her company. An experienced director who was ready for a new challenge, she took a lateral move when a similar position opened up in a different division. There was widespread support from both senior leaders and peers for June to make this move. With her no-nonsense approach and keen intellect, June was highly regarded by all. She relished new challenges and was known for rolling up her sleeves and getting things done with a determined, can-do attitude. June was tireless, and her teams consistently outperformed other teams.

She embraced her new role with the same vigor and enthusiasm she brought to her other positions. However, she quickly learned that her new team was not the high-performing group of players to which she was accustomed. For the first time in her career, June found herself working with a struggling team. The previous director had not set a high bar for performance. Although a few people had promise, several were significantly underdelivering, resulting in missed deadlines and several unhappy internal customers. June made some immediate staffing changes with the support of human resources. Even with these moves, June had some work to do to bring this team to a new level of performance and to meet customer expectations.

June was surprised that her senior-level managers looked to her to clarify her expectations and action plans. Several appeared satisfied to do just enough to stay on track with their individual goals and deliverables. June did her best to empower and motivate them with incentives, but she became increasingly frustrated with their laid-back attitudes and overall lackluster results. As her first sixty days on the job drew to a close, June pushed harder and harder, and eventually issued an ultimatum: failing to meet plan was not an option; things had to improve…or else. She shifted into high gear with "take no prisoners" status meetings to tightly manage the priority initiatives in her area.

One month later, her most talented senior manager announced that she was taking a job in a different division. This departure was followed by others. June was perplexed. She thought she was doing what was necessary to make things right with customers, but instead she had alienated her strongest performers and frightened the rest into submission. With support from her manager and human resources, plus some learning from multi-rater feedback, she began the work of examining the unintended impact of her driver style, and became more attuned to what was really needed to bring out the best in her team.

June found that she needed Drive for Results more than ever, in order to:

- Understand the impact of her personal ambition and strong drive for results on others.

- Stay focused on people and process as well as results.

- Motivate and inspire others to meet commitments and exceed expectations.

- Find ways to gain buy-in and get others to take the lead in driving results.

- Demonstrate stamina and persistence in turning things around in her division.

June's Leadership Development Plan

Following is a sample development plan for June Lee. Research on leadership development has shown that leaders learn through experience and that this learning is optimized through the use of an individual development plan. A successful plan includes new experiences and introduces the leader to new conversations and tools. The suggestions included in the previous sections may stimulate your thinking about additional possibilities for June's development.

LEADERSHIP DEVELOPMENT PLAN FOR JUNE LEE
DEVELOPMENT GOAL
Goal: To channel my Drive for Results in positive and productive ways
Desired Outcomes—results I want to see from developing this skill
Self: I will be more effective at achieving results through the team and will be more satisfied with the job.
Team: My reports will feel well led, motivated, and engaged and will have the satisfaction and confidence that comes with being part of a successful team.
Organization: High-quality results will be delivered on time, meeting customer needs.
Self-Understanding—strengths that I can build on and development needs I can address
Strengths: Leveraging my drive and initiative along with my personal execution skills.
Development Needs: Achieve results through the team, motivate rather than push them to deliver.

LEADERSHIP DEVELOPMENT PLAN FOR JUNE LEE

Business Context—challenges in my business environment that require this skill

My group is behind schedule delivering "on time" to internal customers.

DEVELOPMENT ACTIONS

AWAKEN

- Study colleagues who impress me—like Gloria and Ben—who rally their teams to high levels of performance.
- Use multi-rater feedback to understand my impact on my team and the stakeholder groups within the organization.
- Take stock of my hot buttons and the situations in which I get into overdrive mode, pushing others too hard. Write down what the trigger factors have been so I can anticipate them and act differently next time.

ALIGN

- Have a town hall meeting to bring the team together and talk openly about the current state and where we need to go. Ask Pete to co-facilitate this with me. He's trusted by the team and will help them open up.
- Talk to customers to get their perspective of my group's service to them—what's worked well, how we've fallen short.
- Review all project plans with my direct reports within the next week; ensure that they are realistic and well-aligned with key priorities.
- Use clarity, commitment, and consequences to lay the foundation for results with my direct reports. Make sure they understand what I expect and why, secure their commitment individually, and reinforce the importance of "no surprises."

ACCELERATE

- Resume my routine of going to the gym at least three days per week. For one week (for starters), I will commit to sleeping seven to eight hours each night and eating regular meals (a bag of chips doesn't count).
- Have team members take turns leading weekly status updates and learn to bite my tongue. Get them into the habit of holding each other accountable rather than looking to me.
- Collect additional customer feedback after thirty to forty-five days to gauge signs of improvement.
- At least once each morning, make a point of showing appreciation to a team member.
- After forty-five days, take an honest look at individual performers on improvement plans; consult with human resources.

LEADERSHIP DEVELOPMENT PLAN FOR JUNE LEE		
DEVELOPMENT SUCCESS FACTORS		

Timeline: Within the next six months

Support Needed:

- Feedback from trusted others (including Pete) about my leadership impact.
- Help from my boss with aligning resources with key priorities and deliverables.
- Continue partnering with human resources to size up and understand my talent.

Indicators of Success:

- Customer satisfaction—high quality, on-time results with no surprises.
- We have a reputation for being a high-performing team; peers see my team as a good source of talent for open positions.
- Engaged and satisfied team members; no more unwanted turnover.
- I am spending less time on direct, hands-on management; I can trust the team members to take initiative.

An Example of Coaching to Drive for Results

June Lee's goal was to temper her own Drive for Results and build that capability in others. Here are some steps June's manager could take using the Awaken, Align, Accelerate framework to coach June in this area:

AWAKEN	**Increase INSIGHT**	Share candid feedback and observations about June's impact in her "blind spot" areas—how her efforts have missed the mark. Probe June's reactions to her multi-rater feedback. Help her use the feedback to gain greater self-awareness and understand her impact on others.
	MOTIVATE change	Encourage June to visualize and reflect on what kind of leader she wants to become. Ask what she is motivated to change. Explore the consequences of not making any changes; discuss consequences for her personally as well as her team.

ALIGN	**PLAN goals**	Brainstorm possibilities for channeling her tremendous Drive for Results in more positive and productive ways that would engage other people rather than turning them off. Focus on what she could change in her day-to-day behavior. Work together to construct a leadership development plan similar to the sample provided in this chapter.
	ALIGN expectations	Work with June to evaluate her team and ensure she has the right people in the right roles. Her expectations of them may not be realistic. If so, some restructuring may be warranted. Focus on observing June's interactions with people on her team. Provide feedback afterward about how she influenced others positively or negatively. Coach her on what it might take to build a more engaged, performance-oriented culture.
ACCELERATE	**CREATE teachable moments**	Continually challenge June to inspire and empower rather than push her team. Encourage her to experiment with new leadership behaviors—such as showing more appreciation to team members. Help her reflect on successes, mistakes, and learnings in order to build new habits and sustain changes.
	TRACK progress	Meet twice per month to debrief her approach and the results. Help June evaluate progress toward her goals. Discuss what kinds of changes will be visible to others. Encourage June to invite feedback and ask others to support the changes they see. Acknowledge and reinforce her efforts.

Results: Measuring Impact

In characteristic fashion, June Lee attacked each of the activities in her development plan and finished early. It took longer, however, for her to bring others around. People on her team noticed that June was behaving differently, but were unwilling to trust the changes in the beginning. Over time, she was able to convince them that the changes were real. Her new skills allowed June to:

- Understand the ramifications of her strong drive for results on others.

- Realize that she needed to care about people and process as well as results.

- Discover how to gain buy-in and get others to take the lead in driving results.

- Turn relationships around by engaging people and trusting team members to take initiative.

- Eliminate unwanted turnover and recover her reputation for leading high-performing teams.

13

Innovation and Risk-Taking

Innovative, risk-taking leaders bring novel thinking to bear on issues. They welcome and enjoy the new and unfamiliar. They support experimentation and intelligent risk-taking to develop new processes, products, and businesses. They also continually look for ways to improve how work gets done. They encourage out-of-the-box thinking and support imaginative ideas, especially in the context of disciplined innovation processes. They appropriately challenge the status quo, examine assumptions, and embrace new approaches.

Factor	Competency	Core Practice
Leading People	Drive for Results	Exploration
Thinking and Deciding	Innovation and Risk-Taking	Experimentation
Achieving		Improvement
Relating to People		Creativity
Managing Work		Challenge
Managing Self		

Customers have a world of choices at their fingertips. Leaders who create sustainable results listen to their customers and try new things to meet their needs. In the past, leaders were taught to think about stability in building organizations. Conventional management wisdom was rooted in long-term goals and decision-making systems established to support stainability versus innovation. Now that information moves at the speed of light and changes in traditional value chains happen overnight, the best leaders build organizations that are agile and efficient in trying new things.

Looking into the future, it's clear that Innovation and Risk-Taking will become even more essential to success. Great leaders will improve the organization's ability to listen and respond to customers in ways that are flexible, creative, and efficient. They will build a culture of learning and knowledge-sharing where people are encouraged to try new things, learn from mistakes, and seek continual improvement. The most skilled leaders have clear processes for surfacing ideas, filtering them for timeliness and relevance, and testing business potential against disciplined decision-making criteria.

Leaders need to continually look for industry best practices, fresh talent, and new ways of doing things to help the company stay ahead of competitors. Innovation and Risk-Taking can be enhanced by making small changes in personal routines and organizational processes. More senior leaders need to experiment with ideas and concepts that could pay significant returns in order to meet the expectations of more stakeholders. The five core practices of Innovation and Risk-Taking and how they vary by level are shown in the following table.

How Leaders at Different Levels Innovate and Take Risks

	Managers	Function Leaders	Senior Executives
Exploration	Continually looks for new ways of doing things.	Pursues new ideas and possibilities to stimulate business results.	Discovers and drives new business opportunities.
Experimentation	Encourages experimentation and innovation.	Models experimentation and learning from trying new approaches.	Pushes hard for experimentation around new processes, products, or businesses.
Improvement	Facilitates continuous improvement in quality and productivity.	Focuses on ways to improve existing processes, products, or services.	Explores places to maximize innovation in the organization.
Creativity	Welcomes new, original, or unconventional approaches.	Encourages and rewards creativity and innovative thinking.	Cultivates imagination, resourcefulness, and ingenuity throughout the organization.
Challenge	Appropriately questions the way things are done.	Examines assumptions and challenges the status quo.	Actively challenges assumptions embedded in the business model.

13

INNOVATION AND RISK-TAKING

Self-Assessment

To evaluate your effectiveness in Innovation and Risk-Taking, check all boxes below that represent current behavior or performance. Look for patterns: Which core practices represent a development need, a strength, or an excessive use? Recognize that you might have some blind spots. Invite your boss or colleagues to indicate what they have observed in your behavior. Use this assessment to help identify development suggestions that are most relevant to you.

	Development Need	Strength	Excessive Use
Exploration	❑ Avoids new and unfamiliar business directions ❑ Ignores the cost/benefit ratio; pursues unprofitable options	❑ Actively seeks out new possibilities and opportunities for the business ❑ Consistently explores ways to increase profits and/or reduce costs	❑ Neglects closure in constant search for new possibilities ❑ Pursues change for change's sake; acts on new ideas even when established approaches may be most cost-effective
Experimentation	❑ Does not encourage or reward experimentation or risk-taking ❑ Avoids trying new approaches for fear of failure or making mistakes; de-values learning	❑ Pushes for innovation and risk-taking to develop new processes and products ❑ Maximizes learning from experimentation and trying new approaches	❑ Advocates revolutionary changes without bridging to where people are now ❑ Implements new approaches without vetting pros and cons from previous experiments
Improvement	❑ Resists or is closed to new ways of thinking about issues ❑ Is content with established ways of doing things	❑ Consistently makes suggestions for better ways of doing things ❑ Motivates self and team to continuously be improvement-minded	❑ Offers constant stream of ideas and corrections that exhausts people; does not filter new ideas ❑ Minimizes what is working; puts excessive focus on novel approaches
Creativity	❑ Rejects or dismisses innovative ideas too quickly; de-values creative thinking ❑ Overvalues practicality	❑ Models and rewards creative and innovative thinking ❑ Inspires imagination and ingenuity	❑ Supports wild ideas that aren't practical or feasible ❑ Misses opportunities to explain ideas or connect the dots for others
Challenge	❑ Rarely or never challenges assumptions ❑ Fails to question the status quo	❑ Is willing to examine and challenge deeply-held assumptions ❑ Effectively challenges the status quo; questions whether the way things have always been done is truly the best way	❑ Challenges everything about the status quo in a relentless, tiresome way ❑ Questions everything rather than putting a stake in the ground or defending good ideas

ACHIEVING

238

Development Suggestions

The following section contains development suggestions for each core practice. Having completed the self-assessment, focus on suggestions that correspond to the core practices you identified as a development need or excessive use. Use these suggestions to create your own development plan, making sure to try one or two from each phase. In addition, feel free to create your own or adapt these to best meet your development needs.

Exploration

Pursue new ideas and possibilities to stimulate business results.

> *I have not failed 700 times. I have failed once. I have succeeded in proving that those 700 ways will not work. When I have eliminated the ways that will not work, I will find the way that will work.*

Thomas Edison

Awaken potential:

- **Reflect on your natural level of curiosity.** Are you curious about how things work? Do you frequently ask "Why?" or "How?" about areas outside of your realm?

- **Check your assumptions.** Think about your function or area of the business, and identify an area where you tend to make assumptions about why things are the way they are. Identify two people who might have different perspectives about that area and ask them to share them with you.

- **Track your quest for new ideas.** Make a list of all the external sources of information you regularly access for new ideas. Take ten minutes to reflect on your last week. Identify how much time you spent seeking new information and ideas to inform your thinking.

- **Seek feedback** about your receptivity to new ideas. Ask your manager, peers, or direct reports whether your team is generating new business opportunities through exploring new ideas.

Align goals:

- **Involve your team** in reviewing key business goals for the year. Ask, "What new information do we need to ensure we meet our goals?" Identify key customer, competitor, or industry areas that are changing rapidly, and dedicate resources to research areas of opportunity or risk to your business.

- **Vet new ideas.** Establish simple criteria that can be used consistently to consider all ideas. Invite people from other functions to participate. Evaluate results.

Accelerate performance:

- **Expose yourself to new ideas.** Participate in events that will stretch and challenge your thinking. Attend a thought leadership conference on trends in your industry, or a meeting of the World Future Society or other futurist group; take a class or workshop; join a networking group with professionals from different fields or an industry group to learn about best practices in your area. Then share highlights with your team and identify ideas that can be implemented.

- **Use your calendar strategically.** Set aside specific time every week or month to read new things, visit other companies, or search out new ideas to help you explore innovation and make changes to increase profitability.

- **Commit time to ideate.** Determine the best time of day for you to commit twenty minutes to review and seek new ideas, a time when you are least likely to be interrupted and when your thinking is expansive. Schedule this time weekly.

- **Promote learning and development activities** for your staff to stretch their perspectives on business problems or opportunities. Have them report learning to the team and discuss some applications.

- **Reward others for new ideas.** Build a company-wide reward and recognition system to encourage people to contribute ideas.

- **Find an external mentor** who can help you broaden how you think about your function or business.

- **Become a disciplined note taker.** Write down every new idea and assemble a journal of new ideas you generate. Regularly review it to evaluate ideas that went nowhere, ones that got implemented, etc.

EXCESSIVE USE

As an example, if you pursue new ideas even when standard approaches may be most cost-effective, you may need more focus on achieving results. The core practice "Goal Orientation" in Chapter 17 contains some ideas on balancing this important trade off.

Model experimentation and learning from trying new approaches.

> *Discoveries are often made by not following instructions, by going off the main road, by trying the untried.*

Frank Tyger

Awaken potential:

- **Evaluate your work style and daily habits.** Experimentation involves breaking with tradition or routine. When was the last time you deliberately broke from the routine?

- **Reflect on your approach to new ideas.** Monitor the topics of conversation in your next round of one-on-one meetings with your direct reports. Do you encourage experimentation or subtly discourage new ideas or variances from the norm?

- **Observe your manager's approach to new ideas.** Analyze whether your manager encourages or stifles experimentation. Do you follow that pattern, or do you have a different approach? What happens when someone on your team tries something new without telling you? Is that a good thing or a bad thing from their perspective?

- **Assess your experiences.** Examine what particular experiences have created the most learning for you as a leader. How was experimentation involved?

Align goals:

- **Encourage experimentation.** Hold a specific discussion with your team about where experimenting with new processes could improve effectiveness. Invite them to make suggestions.

- **Gather success stories.** Ask peers about experiments that added unique value to their businesses or cultures. Use those stories with your team to highlight the need for continual improvement through experimentation.

Accelerate performance:

- **Encourage creativity in others.** Read *Leading Innovation: How to Jump Start Your Organization's Growth Engine* by Jeff Degraff and Shawn Quinn (McGraw-Hill, 2007) for ideas about how to encourage creativity and innovation at all levels in your organization.

13

INNOVATION AND RISK-TAKING

- **Observe research and development in action.** Spend a day with leaders in research and development. Ask them how they approach their work, and discuss options with them for applying their daily thinking to your job.

- **Demonstrate your commitment to experimentation.** Import one new management process or innovative idea on a regular basis to help people understand your commitment to experimenting for the purpose of Innovation and Risk-Taking.

- **Gain customer perspective.** Discuss possible pricing options with several customers; bring back the data for a conversation with your team.

- **Consult other leaders.** Discuss the experimentation process with other leaders. Identify interesting processes or ideas that may be beneficial for your organization.

- **Identify opportunities for experimentation** that you can initiate as an example for others. Debrief specific projects or assignments with direct reports through a lens of experimentation. Discuss specific options that were or were not tried.

- **Create an experiment within your team** by identifying a project where two separate approaches could be considered. Generate a hypothesis to test. Ask what further experimentation could be pursued.

- **Break routine in meetings.** Change the order of where people traditionally sit in management meetings to see what effect this has on the discussion. Debrief afterward, and tell the team why you experimented.

EXCESSIVE USE

As an example, if you advocate revolutionary changes without bridging to where people are now, people may be confused or threatened. Review the "Change" section in Chapter 6, "Creating Alignment," for some suggestions about managing change.

Focus on ways to improve existing processes, products, or services.

> *It was not so very long ago that people thought that semiconductors were part-time orchestra leaders and microchips were very, very small snack foods.*

Geraldine Ferraro

Awaken potential:

- **Reflect on your approach to change management.** Do you approach your leadership through the lens of successfully leading change? Ask what you are willing to change about yourself and your business to consistently get better results.

- **Examine your typical reaction** when others propose new ideas. Do you criticize ideas, or do you try to identify the potential positives? Type "positive psychology" into your search engine to learn more.

- **Ask colleagues for feedback** on how frequently and effectively you challenge the status quo. Do you offer suggestions for improvement or focus on what is broken and expect others to find solutions?

- **Find a role model.** Identify an excellent example of someone who is constantly seeking improvements. Articulate why you think that person is effective. Analyze the similarities and gaps in your leadership.

Align goals:

- **Assess your organization.** Evaluate your organization's processes, products, and services with your team. Rate each on a scale of one to five with five being excellent and one indicating that significant improvement is needed. Prioritize how you will address areas that were ranked three or lower over the next year.

- **Engage employees at all levels** to focus on reducing costs and improving processes throughout the organization. Encourage them to identify inefficiencies and learn from mistakes. Install processes such as suggestion systems for continuous improvement.

- **Set goals for improvement.** Require that each direct report has a goal to improve how things are done in one area of the business that is critical to overall business success. Include this in the performance review process.

- **Engage others in process improvement.** Join or initiate a cross-functional task force to identify organizational processes that could be improved to meet customer demands more quickly and effectively. Quantify the cost of doing nothing and the potential financial benefit of improvement.

Accelerate performance:

- **Listen to the voice of the customer.** Meet with key customers, and ask for feedback on how your organization could improve or better serve them. Discuss the feedback with your team.

- **Use Six Sigma practices.** Read *The Six Sigma Handbook: A Complete Guide for Greenbelts, Blackbelts, and Managers at All Levels* by Thomas Pyzdek (McGraw-Hill, 2000). Share and discuss this with your team.

- **Cultivate a culture of continuous improvement** by creating mechanisms for employees to shop or research your competitors. Build processes to take action on suggestions. Make changes visible.

- **Celebrate improvement.** Establish a management discipline with your team to identify and celebrate achievements that involve improving anything in the business, such as cost savings, making meetings more effective, or finding new ways to delight customers.

- **Explore new technologies and "green" practices** that could improve profitability and position your organization differently. Work to deliver products and services more flexibly and ecologically.

EXCESSIVE USE

As an example, if you offer a constant stream of ideas and corrections, people may become defensive and won't know where to focus their attention. Next time you identify a better way to do something, lead into the conversation by appreciating how or why it is the way it is.

Encourage and reward creativity and innovative thinking.

"Mindless habitual behavior is the enemy of innovation."

Rosabeth Moss Kanter

Awaken potential:

- **Imagine creativity in action.** Develop a picture in your mind of an "out-of-the-box" thinker—someone who brings a fresh perspective and creativity to work. Ask yourself, "How might that person approach my situation?"

- **Seek feedback on your creativity.** Do others consider you to be a creative problem-solver? Ask them what is the most creative thing that they have seen you do and why.

Align goals:

- **Use brainstorming.** Schedule and execute a brainstorming session to approach a cross-functional problem in fresh, innovative ways. Follow the rules of effective brainstorming: (1) do not evaluate ideas; (2) all ideas are good in brainstorming and wild ideas are encouraged; (3) quantity of ideas takes precedence over quality of ideas; and (4) people should feel free to build on the ideas of others.

- **Learn from competitors.** Discuss with your team the competitors you collectively envy for their brands and how they approach the market. Ask, "What would it take for us to surpass them?"

- **Inspire ideas.** Ask your direct reports, "If time, energy, and money were not inhibitors, what would you do tomorrow to help us be wildly successful?" Create incentive systems that reward creative thinking.

Accelerate performance:

- **Incorporate "design thinking" into your team.** Design thinking is a structured approach to creativity that can help an organization see new opportunities, connect deeply with customers, and transforms insights and data into actionable ideas that have business impact. It is the approach that organizations like Apple, Starbucks, Google, and others have adopted to spur innovation. To learn more about the discipline of design thinking, read Change by Design by Tim Brown (HarperCollins, 2009).

- **Implement creative thinking tools and techniques.** For example, read about mind-mapping techniques. Use white boards to document important conversations about changes in your business.

- **Benchmark outside your organization.** Organize friends from other industries and businesses into a study group and visit each other's companies. Ask questions, and look closely into how they approach their customers. Pose problems, coach, and consult with each other on how to approach your businesses differently.

- **Trade top people.** Discuss with a business friend the opportunity to exchange an executive for two days. Invite the executive to participate in meetings and share observations and ideas.

- **Meet in unusual venues.** Schedule your team to meet in different spaces within and outside your company walls—break the routine. Visit a public library or art museum for an executive team retreat.

- **Use provocative analogies.** Create an analogy that shows how your business is like a different activity. Explore similarities and differences to gain a new perspective. For example, how is managing a team like herding cats?

- **Stretch yourself through the arts.** Take a painting, sculpture, or pottery class to get more in touch with other ways of expressing ideas. Learn more about how creative, expressive people think and approach their worlds. Invite an orchestra conductor, sculptor, or artist to speak at a leadership retreat.

- **Be a photographer.** Review coffee-table books with spectacular photography. Imagine how you would photograph the work of your company. Assemble photo journals of your most exciting work and customers.

EXCESSIVE USE

As an example, if you support wild ideas that aren't practical or able to be implemented, you run the risk of jeopardizing your credibility and reputation.
Ask people to develop a business case for their proposals. Assess the likelihood of success before offering your support.

Examine assumptions and challenge the status quo.

> *Only those who dare to fail greatly can ever achieve greatly.*

Robert F. Kennedy

Awaken potential:

- **Learn more about your style of risk-taking** by completing one of many personality tests such as the Myers-Briggs Type Indicator® or Hogan Personality Inventory. This will help you learn about how you naturally interpret and react to challenge, risk, and new ideas.

- **Examine your reactions to new ideas.** Keep notes about how you react and respond when others are discussing new ideas. Do you encourage the discussions or shut them down?

- **Weigh consequences.** Reflect on questions such as, "What am I unwilling to change about my business, especially during difficult times?" "What changes have we made previously to improve our business?" "What is the worst thing that could happen by challenging a colleague on something important?" Level with yourself about the opportunity for positive and negative consequences.

- **Seek feedback** from a mentor or colleague about when he/she has seen you resist new ideas or shut down creativity. Take note of when and think about why. Were there good reasons or not?

Align goals:

- **Make a fresh start.** Begin planning for the next quarter with a clean sheet of paper. Focus on what's most important to drive the business forward. Then compare that list with the commitments you've made previously. How do they match up? What does or doesn't need to be changed for you to be more competitive?

- **Make innovation a goal for everyone.** Set one goal with each direct report that relates to a practice or system in your company that the person will challenge or improve. Be specific. Set team goals that promote Innovation and Risk-Taking at the individual and company levels.

Accelerate performance:

- **Find a role model.** Identify someone you personally saw challenge the status quo for the benefit of the person's mission. Articulate how that person was successful, and assess yourself against that model.

- **Challenge the status quo.** Ask each member of your team to articulate the sacred cows—investments or systems they believe are untouchable. Record each sacred cow on a single sheet of paper, put them in a hat, and draw them out one at a time for discussion.

- **Think like the competition.** Invite your team to discuss competitive threats. Ask, "If you left our company tomorrow and wanted to compete with us, what would you do to ensure you succeeded?"

- **Benchmark best practices.** Compare and contrast how other businesses approach problems and opportunities.

- **Keep a journal.** Make notes about new ideas you have supported and rejected. Examine them for patterns. Identify best practices to implement.

- **Map the risks** you are currently considering in both your personal and professional life. Rank them from least risk to greatest risk, along with potential positive and negative consequences. Discuss this chart with a friend or colleague. Challenge yourself to find ways to embrace higher-risk activities.

- **Develop a mentoring relationship** with someone to see your business through a fresh set of eyes.

EXCESSIVE USE

As an example, if you challenge everything about the status quo in a relentless, tiresome way, you may develop a reputation as a critic and not be invited to key meetings. Learning about Appreciative Inquiry may help you to focus more on the positive aspects of the status quo.

Coach Others on Innovation and Risk-Taking

When coaching others, focus on the core practices that were identified as either a development need or excessive use in the self-assessment at the beginning of this chapter. Identify and adapt any relevant development suggestions. Additional coaching tips are provided in the following table for some adverse leadership behaviors. For more information review Chapter 4, "Coach Others."

Coaching Suggestions

Behavior		Awaken	Align	Accelerate
Exploration	Plods along with an internal, myopic focus	• Ask the person to calculate the amount of time spent in the past month focusing internally vs. externally. Identify opportunities to take a broader, external lens. • Push everyone on your own team to ask externally focused questions to force powerful discussion.	• Encourage the person to secure more time with customers. Schedule the person to accompany you or others on customer visits, or to attend an industry trade show. • Encourage the person to debrief these activities with the team and some key peers to discuss their learning and the potential impact on the business.	• Assign the person to collect at least ten insightful items gleaned from customers or competitors for discussion with the team. Debrief these during your one-on-one. • Propose that the person visit another company to examine their business for best practices and bring the learning back to the team.
	Plays it safe; is overly cautious	• Discuss prior personality data about the person's natural orientation for risk. What would feel risky to the person? • Ask the person to remember a time when he/she regretted not being bolder. How might the outcome have been different?	• Propose that the person discuss Innovation and Risk-Taking with a peer or mentor. Ask what could be game-changers for the person. • Encourage the person to involve and solicit input from a wide mix of people, some with non-traditional ideas.	• Create a think tank to generate and advocate new ideas for your team or organization. Include the person, and debrief periodically. • Mutually agree on one change in routine the person will try for one week. Debrief the experience.

Behavior		Awaken	Align	Accelerate
Experimentation	Is overly safe and conservative	• Review and celebrate the milestones of the person's leadership. What significant changes have occurred under his/her watch? • Discuss who the person models leadership after. Is the person safe or bold in his/her leadership agenda?	• Propose that the person engage peers in a conversation about opportunity cost. What gains have been sacrificed by playing it safe? • Encourage the person to ask for feedback on where he/she felt the organization could have been more aggressive. What were the consequences of holding back?	• Discuss specific areas of the job today that may benefit from experimentation within the next week or month. Identify where being more courageous may benefit the project or initiative. • Develop a plan to make that happen, and publicize the plan to hold the person accountable and encourage external reinforcement.
	Is afraid of failure; doesn't take chances	• Discuss an opportunity where you want the person to be more aggressive. Give permission to fail as well as succeed. • Suggest that the person ask himself/herself what is the worst thing that could happen if this experiment fails. Is the consequence really that severe?	• Host a team discussion about what changes would be made if there was a free day where no negative consequences would happen. • Pair the person up with a colleague who is more aggressive, creating a balanced decision-making team.	• Recommend starting a small beta test on a new way of accomplishing an old task. Monitor for results and then celebrate success and failure. • Propose providing feedback to peers or team members when the person feels they are being safe. Ask them to do the same.
Improvement	Has a closed mind	• What items/issues (e.g., sacred cows) is the person willing to defend at all costs? Why are these so important? Discuss your own items as well. • Brainstorm a list of people you both respect for their ideas. Ask what they do to keep their ideas fresh, but on point.	• Share your list of untouchable items with the team. Declare open season on improvement. Encourage people to have that discussion with their own teams as well. • Find out what untouchable items others believe should be challenged.	• Empower a task force to study the impact of investing in one significant improvement. • Articulate the criteria necessary to implement the improvement. Help the person use the criteria to choose one with which to move forward.

Behavior		Awaken	Align	Accelerate
Improvement	*Appears stuck in a rut; prefers established practices*	• Invite the person to discuss what topics arise over and over again without any solutions. What factors are contributing to this? • Identify a recent event in which the person accepted the status quo. Provide some alternatives you saw to that decision.	• Suggest the person research the recurring problem with help from a peer in a different area, or someone outside the company. • Have the person bring back one of the ideas to discuss with the team. Encourage the person to leverage the team to propose a solution.	• Take the team on a field trip to another company to learn how it approaches similar problems. Have the person collect the observations others had during the visit. • Encourage the person to bring in an external thought leader to get others thinking differently. Discuss what type of expert would be most helpful to the organization.
Creativity	*Rejects innovative ideas as too impractical*	• Articulate the last really good idea you considered. Ask the person you are coaching to do that. What happened to those ideas? • Review an idea that you valued but the person felt was too impractical.	• Articulate criteria for ideas you'd consider for funding. Make them known to team members. Ensure you are linking them to strategic imperatives, promoting the alignment of innovation and current strategy. • Create an incentive or contest for innovation. Demonstrate support for new thinking.	• Appoint the person to host a series of brainstorming sessions to surface ideas. • Challenge the person to bring at least one bold idea to you each month. Spend time during your one-on-one to review these.
	Derails brainstorming by critiquing ideas	• Help the person assess his/her own rules of engagement when others are brainstorming. When does the person choose to engage? • Provide the person feedback on a specific event in which you observed him/her stifling creativity by critiquing ideas. What were the factors at hand? What consequences resulted?	• Propose that the person ask a trusted colleague to share what he/she thinks the person's contributions are to brainstorming sessions. • Invite the person to create a personal contract to be accountable for keeping an open mind, and not shooting the messenger of a crazy idea.	• Serve as a role model. Keep a publicly visible list of the best ideas brought forward by the team. Celebrate contributions in staff meetings and other communication. Create and communicate brainstorming rules for the team or organization. • Have the person practice a "Listen first. Talk second" mantra. Provide immediate feedback when he/she gets others off track.

Behavior	Awaken	Align	Accelerate
Challenge — *Rarely challenges others*	• Ask the person what is happening in the business with which he/she doesn't agree. How would going in a different direction benefit the organization? Its strategy or goals? • Debrief together what prevents the person from communicating feedback to others.	• Help the person identify other leaders who are driving initiatives that create a source of disagreement. Discuss what aspects of their leadership styles allow them to challenge, while also advancing, the cause. • Identify a person who models appropriate challenge. Have the person observe how that person influences others.	• Suggest that the person study how to have high impact conversations; identify and initiate a direct discussion to state his/her opinion. • Debrief the conversation together to evaluate successes and challenges. Make this a regular part your one-on-one meeting.
Accepts the status quo and prefers mainstream approaches	• Work together to evaluate the strategy being pursued in your organization. Will a steadfast commitment to this strategy accelerate the organization past your key competitors? • Based on your observations of the person's behavior, identify one thing the person can do differently to bring innovation to their own leadership agenda.	• Raise this issue in one of your staff meetings. Invite the person and his/her peers to comment on the same question. • Convey how risk-taking is a key part of the organization's values and success, both past and future. Align it with a current value or strategy.	• Build options for how you might perform better against competitors with riskier, more innovative approaches. • Assign the person to select one option on which to execute within the next quarter, and then communicate the plan to others for accountability.

Tips for Coaching in a Global Environment

Innovation and Risk-Taking may be practiced or expressed differently within other cultures. This might impact how you approach coaching. Try to keep an open mind, avoid generalizations, and continue gathering data as you gain experience with another culture. Consider these suggestions:

Exploration: It is important to understand cultural context, especially around risk-taking. Before you ask people from other cultures to take chances, try to understand how Innovation and Risk-Taking have been encouraged (or not) where they have worked. Ask for examples about how Risk-Taking has been rewarded (or punished). Show how innovation has contributed to organizational progress and results.

Experimentation: Discuss how other leaders have approached risk-taking in that culture. Ask the person you are coaching to observe some leaders in the business for one month, paying particular attention to what kinds of risks are taken in the workplace. Discuss the potential positive and negative impacts of investing time, energy, and money in such risks, and how that may be different from the person's current approach or way of thinking.

Improvement: It's important for leaders to define terms and be clear about their expectations when it comes to innovation. Innovation may look like imitation in some cultures—and can translate into an even stronger advantage for companies that are fast followers.

Creativity: Michael Kirton's research suggests that all people are creative and can solve problems. However, people tend to approach problems differently—either as adaptors (who are motivated to improve the system to make it better) or as innovators (who want to change the system and make it different). Conflict frequently arises over the goals for change as well as the process. This type of conflict is not a unique cultural phenomenon, but can be exacerbated by cultural issues. When leaders coming into different cultures attempt to make changes, they are often dealing with local leaders who have a great deal of investment in the status quo. That is particularly true where cultures accord great prestige and authority to local leaders who have worked their way up in the local organization. Such leaders may be personally threatened by any talk of change, whether it is heralded as innovation, improvement, or risk-taking. Review the chapter "Creating Alignment" for ideas about creating sustainable change.

Challenge: The type of education people have had may affect their willingness in this area. For example, independent thinking and creative expression is encouraged in some countries more than others. Children in those educational systems also learn to question and challenge assumptions. Meanwhile, schools in other cultures may expect students to show deferential respect for tradition and engage in more rote memorization. Ask how people you are coaching learned to think and express their own points of view. Find out whether questioning authority was encouraged in their cultures.

Companies that dominate their industries for decades are highly vulnerable to competitive threats as customer needs change. Leaders in such organizations often need to reinvent product development processes and increase tolerance. They may also need to create a shift in complacent corporate cultures in order to ensure long-term prosperity.

As you read about Brenda's situation, reflect on what you've learned about Innovation and Risk-Taking in this chapter and consider how you would help Brenda demonstrate greater skill in Innovation and Risk-Taking and be successful in her leadership role.

Realizing the Risks of Not Innovating

Brenda Thomas was an established leader in a billion-dollar company that had dominated the industry for three decades. In their glory years, each of three business units consistently realized double-digit sales growth. Their success came without any disciplined processes for listening to customer opinions or needs. Each business unit operated independently, with customers purchasing their high-quality products separately through different sales people and with different service/support teams. However, smaller, more nimble competitors began to enter the market with new and integrated solutions that addressed multiple customer needs with compelling pricing. Feedback from customers suggested that these new competitors "listened better" and truly understood their needs. For the first time ever, Brenda's business predicted negative sales growth and declining operating margins.

Brenda was a self-described analytic, with a careful and meticulous decision-making style. The company stressed operational efficiency, and her style of leadership was consistent with the culture. Brenda did not see herself as overly creative or much of a risk-taker. However, she recognized that the competitive threats required a fundamental shift in understanding the needs of the customer. She organized a listening team to systematically ask customers about their experience, including what competitive choices they were considering. Brenda was encouraged that the findings seemed to be within their reach. They simply needed to take fresh ideas to the market faster.

By studying some of the most effective innovators, Brenda learned that at least 100 ideas are needed to identify approximately ten feasible innovations. From those ten, most companies expect only one to pay off significantly. The first challenge was to encourage front-line supervisors to collect new ideas from their customers. These team members needed to feel safe in sharing the ideas with company leaders. As the ideas began to flow, Brenda leveraged her analytical, disciplined style to create a stage-gate process where all ideas were run through four distinct decision-making filters: (1) relevance to the ideal customer; (2) development timeframe to impact the market; (3) return on capital within production capabilities; and (4) level of excitement generated from internal and external stakeholders.

Team members soon began to discover that the stage-gate process was sensible and effective. When ideas didn't make it to the next level, they weren't considered a failure. Rather, saying "no" to an idea was celebrated as a successful outcome—a win for their operational efficiency culture because no valuable time would be wasted pursuing ideas that were unlikely to have the desired impact.

Brenda's Leadership Development Plan

Following is a sample development plan for Brenda Thomas. Research on leadership development has shown that leaders learn through experience and that this learning is optimized through the use of an individual development plan. A successful plan includes new experiences and introduces the leader to new conversations and tools. The suggestions included in the previous sections may stimulate your thinking about additional possibilities for Brenda's development.

LEADERSHIP DEVELOPMENT PLAN FOR BRENDA THOMAS
DEVELOPMENT GOAL
Goal: To strengthen and imbed Innovation and Risk-Taking in the culture
Desired Outcomes—results I want to see from developing this skill
Self: Spend the majority of my time focused on "outside-in" leadership, seeking input and insight from customers and competitors to make business decisions.
Team: Create a climate where customer and competitive feedback is expected, and the information makes us more adaptive, responsive, and competitive.
Organization: Everyone in the company who works with customers will feel free to share their learning from customer insights in ways that are respected and energizing.
Self-Understanding—strengths that I can build on and development needs I can address
Strengths: My disciplined, careful style is an asset as long as I create a climate where marketplace feedback is free-flowing and people are well-equipped to use that information to improve the business quickly.
Development Needs: Creativity and risk-taking
Business Context—challenges in my business environment that require this skill
Competitors are taking market share with new ideas and flexible options that are motivating to our customers. We can win at this game if we can work together to leverage our talent and our resources.

LEADERSHIP DEVELOPMENT PLAN FOR BRENDA THOMAS

DEVELOPMENT ACTIONS

AWAKEN

- Be realistic about what made our business and me personally successful. Ask myself what I am willing to do differently to be even more successful in the face of better competition.
- Learn to embrace challenging conversations about our assumptions without getting defensive.
- Look for one new idea every day that would benefit our customers.

ALIGN

- Share my personal development plan with my manager and team so they are aware of my leadership objectives.

ACCELERATE

- Evaluate how much time I'm spending internally versus externally focused. Build a master plan for how I will spend my weeks, months, and quarters, with at least sixty percent of my time focused on outside-in thinking.
- Build a "What great ideas do we have from our customers?" agenda item into my regular team meetings.
- Meet with at least one front-line supervisor per month to ask for insights from interactions with customers.
- Schedule four meetings with key customers each quarter to ask for their feedback.
- Build specific messages about innovation, creativity, and risk-taking into all my company-wide communications.
- Work with my team to develop a reward and recognition system that encourages customer feedback and idea-sharing.
- Review and refine the stage-gate process twice monthly to ensure the best ideas are being explored and implemented efficiently and effectively.

DEVELOPMENT SUCCESS FACTORS

Timeline: Within the next six months

Support Needed:

- Direct reports to respect my need for more outside-in input and allow that time to stay on my calendar.
- My family to understand that increased business travel is a necessity to continue the prosperity of the company and our livelihood.

Indicators of Success:

- Employee engagement scores will improve, including scores from my staff.
- Customer retention and sales average will improve.
- Competitors are imitating us, instead of the other way around.

ACHIEVING

An Example of Coaching for Innovation and Risk-Taking

Brenda Thomas' goal was to strengthen her skills in Innovation and Risk-Taking. Here are some steps Brenda's manager could take using the Awaken, Align, Accelerate framework to coach Brenda in this area:

AWAKEN	**Increase INSIGHT**	Provide feedback using your own observations. Help Brenda gain greater self-awareness and understand her impact on others, especially through the ways she communicates to the organization. Discuss new avenues of reading, networking, discussion groups, webinars, or conferences that could provide new perspectives on how Brenda might accomplish results differently.
	MOTIVATE change	Review the most powerful and important experiences of Brenda's career—noting the value of learning from mistakes and trying new things. Identify current performance gaps and potential priorities for development. Ask about the consequences of not making any changes.
ALIGN	**PLAN goals**	Ask Brenda what would enable her to manage the stage-gate process more successfully. Focus on what she could change to increase her strategic impact and influence in the organization. Work together to construct a leadership development plan similar to the sample provided in this chapter.
	ALIGN expectations	Start a dialogue about what topics Brenda thinks are off limits for particular leaders; discuss the perceived consequences for surfacing those topics. Discuss Brenda's goals with the corporate planning team (peers) to encourage them to assist Brenda in developing stronger Innovation and Risk-Taking skills that will benefit everyone. Ensure that organizational systems (e.g., incentives) are well aligned with the behavior Brenda is hoping to embed in the culture.
ACCELERATE	**CREATE teachable moments**	Help Brenda experiment with trying new things. Encourage Brenda to host a meeting of peers from other companies or industries to discuss a business problem. Ask how they would approach the problem from their perspective. Engage in a hypothetical conversation about the best way to perform critical business tasks if Brenda had the opportunity to start the business from scratch tomorrow.
	TRACK progress	Discuss expected outcomes and results. Encourage Brenda to invite feedback and ask other people to support the changes they see. Discuss what kinds of changes in the culture should be visible to others. Work with Brenda to evaluate progress toward her goals. Express appreciation for her efforts.

Results: Measuring Impact

Brenda Thomas used her development plan as a platform for developing others on her team as well. The "great customer ideas" portion of her meeting agenda was widely publicized and adopted as a best practice by other leaders in the organization. After one year, Brenda was pleased with the progress she had made. Her new focus and improved skills allowed Brenda to:

- Inspire others by building messages about Innovation and Risk-Taking into her communications.

- Develop a reward and recognition system that encouraged customer feedback and idea-sharing.

- Refine the stage-gate process to ensure the best ideas were being explored and implemented.

- Improve employee engagement scores as well as customer retention and sales.

- Discover that competitors had begun imitating them, instead of the other way around.

RELATING
TO PEOPLE

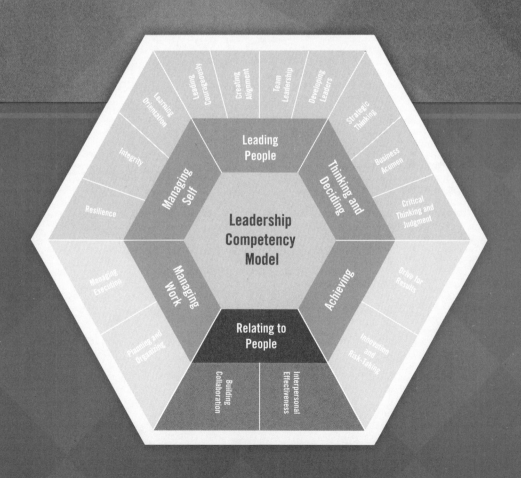

14

Interpersonal Effectiveness

Interpersonally effective leaders interact and communicate directly with others, through multiple layers of the organization, and externally with a variety of partners and stakeholders. They are approachable and considerate. They effectively elicit the right information from others. They tend to listen more than talk. They respect different perspectives and welcome contributions from everyone on their teams.

Factor	Competency	Core Practice
Leading People	Interpersonal Effectiveness	Empathy
Thinking and Deciding	Building Collaboration	Approachability
Achieving		Respect
Relating to People		Listening
Managing Work		Communication
Managing Self		

Nice guys sometimes finish last in sports, but not in business. Most people don't want to work for abrasive bullies. Exit interviews reveal that people don't leave companies, they leave bad bosses. Meanwhile, the primary reason leaders plateau in their careers is a lack of interpersonal skills. The good news is that all leaders can improve their Interpersonal Effectiveness. Even small changes can pay big dividends, keeping followers engaged and more committed to getting results.

Interpersonal Effectiveness does not mean liking everyone equally or avoiding conflict. Communicating respect and building healthy relationships enables leaders to increase participation, overcome resistance, and complete important projects successfully. Leaders who initiate difficult conversations and handle them with finesse can achieve breakthrough results in working with others. Without this, followers may shut down, drift away, or quit.

Everyone in an organization deserves to be treated with consideration and respect. Effective leaders pay attention to how results are achieved and ensure that human contributions and sacrifices are appreciated. By modeling and encouraging others to be interpersonally effective, more senior leaders can build this into the DNA of the organization. While Interpersonal Effectiveness is important for all leaders, the most effective behaviors vary by level, as illustrated in the table below.

How Leaders at Different Levels Display Interpersonal Effectiveness

	Managers	Function Leaders	Senior Executives
Empathy	Is attuned to the feelings of others.	Shows genuine consideration for others.	Makes others feel understood, accepted, and valued.
Approachability	Is friendly and approachable.	Displays interest and responsiveness in interacting with others.	Connects with others quickly, naturally, and genuinely, putting others at ease.
Respect	Demonstrates respect for others' perspectives and contributions.	Expresses respect and appreciation for differences.	Builds and supports a diverse and respectful culture.
Listening	Asks questions and listens with genuine interest.	Expands dialogue by listening actively and asking insightful questions about key facts and assumptions.	Models effective listening skills and exchange of ideas throughout the organization.
Communication	Articulates ideas clearly when speaking and writing.	Communicates effectively across organizational levels.	Is able to adapt communication and interpersonal style to a wide range of audiences.

Self-Assessment

To evaluate your Interpersonal Effectiveness, check all boxes below that represent current behavior or performance. Look for patterns: Which core practices represent a development need, a strength, or an excessive use? Recognize that you might have some blind spots. Invite your boss or colleagues to indicate what they have observed in your behavior. Use this assessment to help identify development suggestions that are most relevant to you.

	Development Need	Strength	Excessive Use
Empathy	☐ Is distant or impersonal in interactions with others ☐ Fails to demonstrate insight or communicate understanding of others' thoughts and feelings	☐ Conveys warmth and interest in others' wants, needs, and concerns ☐ Makes others feel understood, accepted, and valued	☐ Aligns too quickly with others; makes mistakes in judging people ☐ Does not show enough objectivity about others; appears naïve and easily taken advantage of
Approachability	☐ Is impatient and treats others unfairly or inconsistently ☐ Acts in ways that are off-putting; creates distance from others	☐ Draws people to him/her through verbal and nonverbal signals that convey interest and receptivity ☐ Is responsive when others make requests	☐ Is too patient with others; reinforces dependencies ☐ Is constantly available and unable to create appropriate boundaries
Respect	☐ Is insensitive to people whose backgrounds or ways of doing things differ from his/her own ☐ Acts dismissive toward others	☐ Is highly attuned to and values differences and diversity ☐ Is actively inclusive of others regardless of differences	☐ Appears to play favorites or treat people inconsistently due to over sensitivity to differences ☐ Seeks too much approval; acts deferential
Listening	☐ Talks over or interrupts others ☐ Spends more time talking than listening and fails to draw others out; asks ineffective or too few questions	☐ Listens actively by accurately summarizing and paraphrasing to check for accuracy in understanding ☐ Asks open-ended questions to draw out information and convey interest	☐ Uses imbalanced communication; lacks give and take ☐ Asks too many questions; fails to offer own point of view
Communication	☐ Is effective at communicating to only a narrow range of audiences ☐ Is difficult to follow when speaking or communicating ideas; is not articulate	☐ Skillfully adapts interpersonal style and communcation methods to the needs of audience ☐ Communicates with a wide range of audiences across organizational levels	☐ Tells people what they want to hear; never takes a stand; pulls punches ☐ Craves recognition and strives to gain attention; likes to hear himself/herself speak

Development Suggestions

The following section contains development suggestions for each core practice. Having completed the self-assessment, focus on suggestions that correspond to the core practices you identified as a development need or excessive use. Use these suggestions to create your own development plan, making sure to try one or two from each phase. In addition, feel free to create your own or adapt these to best meet your development needs.

Empathy

Show genuine consideration for others.

"Wherever there is a human being, there is an opportunity for kindness."

Seneca

Awaken potential:

- **Learn about empathy.** Empathy is the ability to truly see things from another person's perspective. Being able to put aside your own needs to really listen and understand another individual's ideas or concerns leads to deeper connections and trust between people. Where do you want to develop deeper connections and trust?

- **Seek feedback** about the extent to which you show understanding and appreciation of others' needs or concerns. Ask for examples. Invite suggestions about how you could improve.

- **Expand your awareness about differences.** Learn how your leadership style differs from others. For example, take the MBTI or another inventory to explore personality differences.

- **Focus on similarities.** It is much easier to be empathetic when you can find a strong connection to the other person or find the areas in which you are similar. Focus attention on similarities between yourself and those around you. What do you notice?

- **Study empathy in action.** Observe leaders who easily create positive connections with others. Notice the styles and behaviors that contribute to their success. Assess your own style against those models. Interview someone you admire who has a special touch with people. Compliment that person's behavior, and ask for tips to help you create the same effect.

- **Increase your mindfulness.** Pay attention to the different kinds of feelings you experience and what feelings are associated with various situations. Your ability to open up your heart and understand another person's perspective often starts with focusing on your own feelings.

Align goals:

- **Examine the link among empathy, trust, and performance.** Evaluate your relationships with key stakeholders. Where could better relationships lead to improved performance and results? Discuss your observations with your manager.

- **Focus on specific groups or individuals.** Talk with your manager about which relationships are important for you to improve and why. Expand your circles of relationships beyond those that are the most comfortable.

- **Use empathetic conversations to improve alignment.** Read *The Communication Catalyst: The Fast (But Not Stupid) Track to Value for Customers, Investors, and Employees* by Mickey Connolly and Richard Rianoshek (Dearborn, 2001).

Accelerate performance:

- **Step into another perspective.** Attend a meeting with the intent to observe the discussion from another person's perspective. Take notes about what benefits and threats are implied to that person in the decisions being discussed.

- **Circle back.** Whenever you have a more difficult, intense, or even emotional meeting with someone, get in the habit of circling back to check in. Ask about how the individual is feeling currently; simply show your interest. Listen for what his/her takeaways were.

- **Prepare specific questions to initiate conversations** that will help you establish a connection with individuals. Include questions such as how people are feeling about their jobs, not just questions about what progress they are making or *what* they are doing. Meet over coffee or lunch to ask someone a sincere "How's it going?" question … then listen.

- **Tune in to others.** For example:

  - **Pay attention to nonverbal cues.** Watch for discrepancies between what people say and what their nonverbal behavior tells you. Determine what messages might be conflicting and why.

  - **Avoid interrupting.** Give people their moment. Don't rush to give advice. Don't change the subject.

  - **Restate what you hear** to allow people to correct any misperceptions.

  - **Act on your intuition.** When a colleague is visibly off center, say something such as, "You seem to be upset. Is there anything I can do to help?" Demonstrate empathy and offer to help in ways that are meaningful.

- **Be authentic.** Allow yourself to be vulnerable, especially when people have shown their trust to be vulnerable with you. Match their intensity when expressing your own feelings. Be genuine and sincere in your comments.

- **Learn more about expressing yourself.** Read *How the Way We Talk Can Change the Way We Work: Seven Languages for Transformation* by Robert Kegan and Lisa Laskow Lahey (Jossey-Bass, 2001).

EXCESSIVE USE

As an example, if you fail to maintain objectivity, you may appear weak or naïve. Others may take advantage of you. Review the core practice "Independence" in Chapter 5 for suggestions on ways to balance consideration for others with expressing an objective, bold point-of-view.

Approachability

Display interest and responsiveness when interacting with others.

"You can make more friends in two months by becoming really interested in other people than you can in two years by trying to get other people interested in you."

Dale Carnegie

Awaken potential:

- **Learn how others view your approachability.** Ask someone you trust to give you feedback, especially if you do not know how others perceive you. Do others believe you welcome interactions?

- **Analyze traffic patterns.** How and where do you spend your day? How often is your door closed? Do you have open time on your calendar so people can find you? Do people queue by your office? Do you eat lunch at your desk? How much do you walk around to connect with people where they are? The higher your position in the company, the more others may not seek you out because they don't want to bother you.

- **Monitor body language.** Body language can greatly affect perceived approachability. Pay attention to what you are doing with your hands, arms, and legs, as well as your facial expressions and physical distance from others. Observe the physical appearance of others—dress, posture, presence, and poise. How does their appearance improve or detract from their approachability? How does this apply to you?

- **Consider others' frame of reference.** When you managed others at lower levels in the organization, you may have been highly approachable. You were more like the others on your team. Your title and position could create barriers to others approaching you. While you may view yourself as approachable, don't assume that others know it or have the same perception.

Align goals:

- **Develop a rationale** for how becoming more approachable will help you meet your goals. Share your intention with others on your team, and ask for their support.

- **Map your stakeholder interactions.** Decide where more interaction with peers and customers could help you improve overall performance. Evaluate what form(s) of contact will further your goals. Develop a plan to increase and maintain contact with key stakeholders.

- **Consider the power of your attention.** Think about the goals and initiatives that you are working on now. Who is central to success? Figure out actions you might take to stay closer to them and more approachable.

Accelerate performance:

- **Build more interaction into your day.** Schedule time to connect with people. Take a quick break to check in with people. Walk the hallways just to say hello. Invite people to join you for coffee or tea. Meet with people more often in their work spaces than yours.

- **Use intentional body language.** For example:
  - **Maintain an open posture.** Don't cross your arms, even if you're cold.
  - **Make eye contact** when engaged in conversation.
  - **Smile,** even when you don't feel like smiling. Try to be positive and cheerful.

- **Increase communication channels.** Give people as many different options to contact you as possible, even if you prefer email. Mirror your communication to theirs—answer emails with emails, texts with texts, and phone calls with phone calls; then reply within hours, not days. Build in more opportunities to connect with people. Keep your office door open as much as possible. Use a "Do not disturb" sign when you have important tasks that require your full attention—then open the door when you are done.

- **Listen more.** Ask more. Get others to tell you more by being an active questioner. Ask questions to draw people out. Don't interrupt. Listen for common points of interest. Develop ice-breaker questions to use with people you don't know, such as, "What do you do for fun?" or "Tell me about your role and contribution to this project."

- **Express appreciation.** Make a point of thanking people for their input or ideas; let them know their contributions are valued. Finish all meaningful conversations by saying, "I really appreciate the chance to connect." Make a habit of going out of your way to help people feel good about themselves.

- **Don't complain.** Complainers attract other complainers. End your conversations on a positive note and say thanks. Do your best not to engage in complaining, even when others instigate it.

- **Keep it short.** Keep your communications succinct so people learn that interacting with you is rewarding and valuable, instead of boring and not worth the time.

- **Surrender the spotlight.** When others are sharing personal stories, avoid the temptation to upstage them with a better story of your own.

- **Learn about boss whispering.** Read *Taming the Abrasive Manager: How to End Unnecessary Roughness in the Workplace* by Laura Crawshaw (Jossey-Bass, 2007).

EXCESSIVE USE

As an example, if you find a constant stream of people at your door,
you may be taking on too many of their problems and subtly reinforcing their dependency.
Create some boundaries, and limit your availability.
Encourage people to solve their own problems instead.

Respect

Express respect and appreciation for differences.

"To get the most from the people you manage, you have to treat them the way they want to be treated."

Terry R. Bacon

Awaken potential:

- **Learn about respect through the lens of disrespect.** Recall a time when you felt disrespected. Analyze what happened and how you felt. Is it possible that you have done something similar to other people? Develop criteria for what it takes for you to feel respected. Assess your own behavior against that list, and identify changes you could make to improve how you show respect.

- **Stop disrespect.** Reflect on required meetings and activities that you believe are a waste of time. Analyze how you behave in those meetings. Take the meetings off your calendar if it makes no sense for you to be involved. Find out from others why they want you there. Evaluate how well you are doing in respecting others' time.

- **Build your repertoire.** Notice how people treat each other in their work. Make notes about what feels right to you and what doesn't feel right. Seek out movies, books, or personal experiences to observe and analyze how people from different backgrounds, cultures, and countries are treated in everyday situations.

- **Gauge your cultural openness.** Think about individuals from other cultures or backgrounds with whom you interact. What have you really done to learn about their values, customs, preferred ways of working, or culture? Respect starts with a genuine interest in learning.

Align goals:

- **Find out what people want.** Read *What People Want: A Manager's Guide to Building Relationships that Work* by Terry Bacon (Davies-Black, 2006). Debrief with your direct reports. Discuss how everyone could use this information to achieve higher productivity and better outcomes with their teams.

- **Target people from other areas** of the organization you want to get to know better, whose performance impacts your team. Ask for a meeting. Try to learn more about their roles and goals. Discuss how to leverage their perspectives and contributions to improve overall results.

- **Identify benefits of diversity of perspective and thought.** On major decisions or projects, consider how much richer the solutions or actions might be by having a breadth of ideas and perspectives in the mix. Identify how drawing out and respecting divergent views can lead to better results.

Accelerate performance:

- **Model respect for inclusion and diversity.** Build a team with diverse backgrounds and perspectives. Ensure everyone has input to decisions. Spend more time with people on your team to foster trust, respect, and open communication.

- **Plan for participation.** Prepare for meetings. Send agendas and information items ahead of time. Make sure you bring a clear purpose and rationale for why everyone is included in the meeting and what is expected.

- **Engage everyone.** Make sure everyone gets heard in important discussions. Deliberately engage quiet or introverted employees and let them know you value their perspectives. Develop strategies for reining in highly extroverted individuals. Maximize the participation of everyone around you. Ensure that diverse ideas and opinions are being expressed and acknowledged.

- **Embrace opposition.** Seek out and openly engage others who hold opposing views. Try to identify common goals. Brainstorm ways you can work together to achieve your objectives.

- **Stay fully present in conversations.** Avoid multitasking when on conference calls or in meetings. Practice active listening by mirroring posture, tone, and pace. Paraphrase or summarize what you hear so the other person can correct any misunderstandings.

- **Foster a culture of appreciation.** For example:
  - **Praise others publicly whenever possible.** Copy managers if you praise someone via email.
  - **Say thanks.** Write personal thank-you notes.
  - **Criticize others in private; face to face is preferable.** Avoid criticizing others when they are not in the same room. Resist the urge to give advice unless it is solicited.
  - **Accept compliments with a thank you.** Don't shrug them off.
  - **Introduce people you know to others.** Emphasize their strengths and why you think people will benefit from networking with each other.

EXCESSIVE USE

As an example, if you act overly deferential, you may lose respect yourself. Don't be afraid to express disagreement and share your own point of view.

Listening

Expand dialogue by listening actively and asking insightful questions about key facts and assumptions.

"A good listener is better than a good talker."

Chinese proverb

Awaken potential:

- **Learn about listening** and interacting with others. Read *People Skills: How to Assert Yourself, Listen to Others, and Resolve Conflict* by Robert Bolton (Touchstone, 1986). Try some of the exercises in this classic book.

- **Reflect on the importance of being "listened to."** Everyone has the same need for respect and validation. When people on your team approach you with a problem, they aren't always looking for you to solve it. They may just want you to listen.

- **Monitor your talk/listen ratio**—especially if you tend to dominate interactions. After a meeting or conversation, compare the percentage of time you spent talking, to the percentage of time you spent listening. Ask a trusted colleague for his/her perception as well. Develop tactics to increase your listening time (e.g., force yourself to take notes).

- **Identify people who test your patience,** who behave in ways that make it difficult for you to listen. Reflect on what gets in the way of your listening effectively. Try to reframe those relationships to appreciate their perspectives and listen with more generosity.

Align goals:

- **Tune into all of your customers.** Have lunch with internal customers as well as external ones. Ask about their requirements and expectations, and probe for their underlying needs. Listen for what is not being said as well as what is being expressed.

- **Determine where there are pockets of lower morale.** Morale and job satisfaction are correlated with customer satisfaction and business outcomes. Go to the departments or work teams that are struggling, and simply ask questions and listen. You can be a key to building their morale and performance.

Accelerate performance:

- **Set expectations for input.** Begin important meetings by sharing your intentions. Consider saying, "You're all here because you have ideas and opinions that are central to our moving ahead or finding a great solution. It's important for me to hear what you have to say."

- **Listen with your eyes as well as your ears.** Practice giving people your complete attention. Stay fully present. Don't default to reading your text messages or emails. Notice when your attention wanders, and bring yourself back. Later figure out what caused that and what you can do.

- **Use more questions** including phrases such as, "Please tell me about..." or "Describe for me..." to obtain information. Use open-ended questions to allow others to expound on important thoughts. Probe for additional details about what they are saying (e.g., "How does that work?" or "What else could we try?") rather than adding your own perspective or changing the subject.

- **Drum out interrogation.** Using numerous questions that can be answered "yes" or "no" shuts down communication. Avoid numerous "why" questions—they can cause defensiveness or make the other person feel uncomfortable.

- **Converse so others will feel heard.** For example:
  - **Plan questions** to elicit information in which you are interested.
  - **Probe with questions** such as, "How is this important to you?" and "What do you hope will happen?" to broaden the discussion and build upon ideas.
  - **Don't interrupt.** Let the other person finish speaking before you offer a response.
  - **Clarify and confirm your understanding** of what others have said. Ask questions to ensure you have understood them correctly.
  - **Paraphrase and summarize key points.** Practice summarizing, in one or two sentences, the core meaning of what you hear from others.
  - **Ask for feedback** after important conversations.
- **Resist the temptation to provide unnecessary direction.** If people bring you a problem and ask what to do, ask them, "What do you think?" or "What do you recommend?" You will probably find that you can support their recommendations. As you take time to listen, you will develop stronger relationships as well as learn more about their thought processes.

EXCESSIVE USE

As an example, if you ask too many questions and fail to present your own ideas, you may not be adding enough value in conversations. Alternate between asking questions and offering your own point of view to move the conversation forward and keep it balanced.

Communication

Communicate effectively across organizational levels.

> *Great leaders are almost always great simplifiers, who can cut through argument, debate, and doubt to offer a solution everybody can understand.*
>
> General Colin Powell

Awaken potential:

- **Learn about using communication to lead.** Read *Great Communication Secrets of Great Leaders* by John Baldoni (McGraw-Hill, 2003). Baldoni explores the communication styles of a number of the world's most influential leaders and explains what they do to develop, deliver, and keep their message fresh, meaningful, and impactful.

- **Ask others for feedback** on the clarity and impact of your voicemail and email messages. Brainstorm ways you can improve.

- **Capture attention.** Try to remember a time when someone clearly tuned out and didn't stay focused on what you were saying. How did you feel? Reflect on why that person might have drifted away. How could you have communicated in a more compelling way?

- **Look for role models.** Identify several people who are effective communicators. Notice how they modify their communication styles to adapt to their audiences (e.g., faster, slower, more energy, more details, stories). Critique their effectiveness for your own learning—privately, of course. Analyze their styles, and set goals to improve your own communication. Track your progress in a journal.

- **Record yourself,** and listen to your speaking style. How much do you vary your volume, pitch, and cadence? Are you interesting to listen to? At what level do you communicate—overly detailed or overly abstract?

Align goals:

- **Identify your communication challenges,** including people with whom you have difficulty interacting. What contributes to those difficulties? How does your handling of those challenges impact your performance? How could improved communication produce better results?

- **Paint a picture for people.** Strive to understand the needs and goals of your stakeholders. Begin all stakeholder communications with context. Tell them what's in it for them. Consider who your intended audience is, and present yourself in ways that are relevant and understandable from their points of view.

Accelerate performance:

- **Craft your communications.** Make sure your message flows in a logical manner, is accurate, and contains content relevant to the target audience.

- **Tailor your approach** to different stakeholders to maximize effectiveness. Become more skilled at recognizing and managing your nonverbal behavior.

- **Anticipate questions** from stakeholders related to your presentations or other key messages. Plan ahead for frequently asked questions and likely sources of resistance or confusion.

- **Prepare for confrontations.** Read *Crucial Confrontations: Tools for Resolving Broken Promises, Violated Expectations, and Bad Behavior* by Kerry Patterson, Joseph Grenny, Ron McMillan, and Al Switzler (McGraw-Hill, 2005). Apply these principles in conducting high-stakes conversations.

- **Perfect your message.** Try the following:

  - **Listen to your phone greeting** and re-record if you aren't satisfied with how it sounds.

  - **Leave yourself a voicemail** to practice speaking clearly. Practice a few times until you are satisfied with how you have framed and delivered a message.

  - **Do more storytelling.** Tell personal stories to engage your audience and help them remember key points.

  - **Use videotape to practice important presentations.** Watch yourself and make notes on strengths to leverage and areas for improvement.

  - **Compare notes.** Ask a colleague to take notes at a meeting where you both can attend. Write a recap and then compare your notes. What did you discover? Who captured key points most effectively?

  - **Hire a coach** to help you assess your effectiveness and improve your leadership presence and effect.

  - **Get input or feedback** from others before sending particularly critical emails.

  - **Solicit help from a trusted colleague** to ensure your emails, letters, and presentations are error-free.

  - **Read sensitive emails twice before sending.** Would you be comfortable if they got forwarded to the entire world?

- **Avoid taking advantage of less able communicators.** Instead of dominating conversations, use frequent pauses, ask questions to involve others, and challenge yourself to do more listening than talking.

EXCESSIVE USE

As an example, if you crave recognition and over communicate to gain attention, people may question your motivation. They may delete your emails without reading them or avoid having conversations with you. Practice being more deliberate and concise.

Coach Others on Interpersonal Effectiveness

When coaching others, focus on the core practices that were identified as either a development need or excessive use in the self-assessment at the beginning of this chapter. Identify and adapt any relevant development suggestions. Additional coaching tips are provided in the following table for some adverse leadership behaviors. For more information review Chapter 4, "Coach Others."

Coaching Suggestions

	Behavior	Awaken	Align	Accelerate
Empathy	*Is distant or impersonal*	• Ask how often the person reaches out informally to connect with others. • Provide feedback on how you have seen the person's distant style affecting others.	• Provide examples of how developing good personal connections could help the business strategy or goals. • Determine a specific project or initiative where relationships are vital to success.	• Create a Relationship map of key stakeholders to further develop or strengthen relationships. • Have the person identify key people and articulate how to connect with them each week for three months.
Empathy	*Fails to see other perspectives*	• Frequently ask the person to consider how others are likely to feel about situations. • Discuss who else might have a perspective on his/her idea. What might they offer that the person cannot?	• Suggest that the person circle back to seek feedback from people affected by his/her decisions. • Provide a specific scenario where seeking feedback from others may facilitate successful achievement of a goal.	• Suggest that the person ask others to share their feedback (pros and cons) about an idea or initiative. • Discuss strategies to create win/win scenarios that incorporate the ideas of others.
Approachability	*Is impatient*	• Ask the person to watch for situations that cause feelings of impatience. What about those situations tends to trigger impatience? Why? • How does the person typically react, (verbally or nonverbally)?	• Identify a specific goal or initiative in which moderating impatience will pay off. • Determine a plan of action for when it will be important to focus on patience, (e.g., what venues or meetings).	• Help the person recognize when it is important to pause and withhold judgment before reacting. • Provide some alternative means of mitigating the impatience, such as breathing or writing, rather than reacting.

Behavior		Awaken	Align	Accelerate
Approachability	*Acts in ways that are off-putting*	• Provide specific examples (based on your own observation if possible) of times when the person made you or someone else feel uncomfortable. • Identify the consequences that could have been avoided.	• Identify a time when the person was excluded from a project team because others did not feel comfortable. What were the consequences to the business goal or effort? • Create a plan for the person to do some interviews with key stakeholders. Help the person write the interview questions, talk about strategies to make it safe, and then debrief findings.	• Reinforce the person for actions that attract others and make them feel comfortable. • Encourage the person to drop by people's offices to simply check-in and ask how they are doing.
Respect	*Is insensitive to differences*	• Ask the person to articulate at least one thing admired about each colleague. How does the person build on their strengths to create better strategy or execution? • Provide feedback on when the person appeared less tolerant than you would hope. What were the consequences you observed?	• Task the person with building a project team that leverages people with complementary strengths. Review together why each team member was included. • Identify at least one other team member the person might consider including. Challenge the person's assumptions on how this person may affect the goal or initiative.	• Discuss strategies to make sure the person is using others' time in meetings wisely, along with ways to make sure people are feeling appreciated. • Assign the task of voicing admiration (e.g., a specific example) to someone weekly. • Have the person share something new and interesting learned from colleagues.
	Acts dismissive	• Ask the person to rate own strengths and weaknesses related to inclusion. How does the person involve others in decision-making? How well does he/she provide feedback? • Point out specific examples of phrases or nonverbal behavior the person uses that could alienate people.	• Have the person identify one thing needed from others (e.g., help or expertise) that will help him/her accomplish organizational goals. • Identify a particular meeting or venue in which inclusion will help the team achieve greater success.	• Brainstorm ways to provide feedback, offering suggestions about how the person can change verbiage or tone to provide candid feedback without making others defensive or defeated. • Suggest the person include a positive statement when responding to others, even if he/she does not agree with their ideas.

Behavior		Awaken	Align	Accelerate
Listening	Talks over or interrupts	• Provide feedback when you observe the person talking over others. Are there specific individuals for whom this occurs most often? Use your interactions and meetings to point out in the moment instances of this behavior. • Model positive behavior in your regular interactions. Make sure you provide positive reinforcement when you observe the person showing restraint.	• Use a specific meeting to practice having patience with peers. Debrief how it felt to hold back, when the person wanted to interject and didn't, and why he/she felt the urge to at the time. • Offer feedback on how you observed restraint, facilitating more alignment or inclusiveness during the meeting, providing an opportunity for stronger results.	• Work with this person to establish specific goals (e.g., do not talk over others during conversations). Practice a "listen first, talk second" mantra. • Develop a cue or signal when you observe this behavior. Suggest that the person also do this with a trusted peer or direct report who may have visibility during other meetings.
	Asks ineffective or too few questions	• Have the person paraphrase something back to you to see how well the person can listen and repeat important messages. • Provide feedback on the types of questions that may help facilitate conversation rather than stifle it (e.g., how vs. why).	• Identify specific stakeholders who need to be listened to differently from others. Make a link to how they impact business goals or success. • Identify a peer or another leader within the organization who asks great questions. Why is that person effective? Have the person observe and model that person.	• Demonstrate the power of open-ended questions and listening in powerful ways by modeling this behavior in key situations. • Debrief meetings together when you see the person doing this well. Discuss what the person is able to accomplish that might not have been done before.

14

Behavior		Awaken	Align	Accelerate
Communication	*Communicates to a narrow range*	• Probe to understand why the person communicates better or more frequently with some people than others. Discuss how it might be beneficial to communicate with wider audiences. • Brainstorm with other people or groups who would benefit from more (or different) communication, especially those whose roles are upstream or downstream.	• Identify people who are tangential to the person's team, yet have specific roles in facilitating the success of the team and the achievement of their goals. • Identify who could be a good role model or mentor for this person. Make an introduction and encourage them to discuss communication strategies.	• In your one-on-one meetings, review together how the person has broadened the circle of communication. Who has the person recently reached out to? With what result? • Review together how the person is adapting his/her style based on the audience. Provide feedback when you witness the person being adaptive.
	Is not articulate	• Critique a presentation or document to provide suggestions for more crisp, succinct, or powerful ways to convey thoughts. • Provide real-time feedback during your meetings about how the person could speak more crisply, even during one-on-one interactions.	• Ask the person to seek feedback from another key stakeholder about his/her impact during discussions or presentations. • Identify who excels at this within the organization (e.g., communications team or department). Have that individual discuss his/her model of delivery with the person.	• Role play difficult situations, and rehearse options for responding. • Provide regular feedback on progress and challenges you see in the person's communication style and delivery.

Tips for Coaching in a Global Environment

Interpersonal Effectiveness may be practiced or expressed differently within other cultures. This might impact how you approach coaching. Try to keep an open mind, avoid generalizations, and continue gathering data as you gain experience with another culture. Consider these suggestions:

Empathy: Learn all you can about the culture of the individual with whom you are dealing. Is it a collectivistic culture or an individualistic one? What do leaders in that culture do to show genuine consideration for others? Anticipate differences. People may have different expectations and comfort regarding talking openly about feelings and emotions. There are also vast differences about appropriate behaviors such as eye contact, informal language, humor, and intimacy—all of which relate to interpersonal effectiveness. Also remember their needs and motivations may be very different from your own.

Approachability: Developing personal relationships is often fundamental to—and may need to precede—developing and maintaining business networks in someone else's culture. Be alert to conversational openings provided by your host. In some cultures, social invitations represent requests to discuss business issues. Evening socialization may be expected. Some after-work interactions may be an extension of work where people feel more comfortable expressing their opinions. Someone's unwillingness to participate in after-work rituals may signal a lack of approachability.

Respect: Some cultures are more formal, and respect is typically accorded to senior members despite their official role or actual performance contribution. The use of formal titles (or Mr./Mrs.) is one means of showing respect in some cultures. Don't be too quick to call people by their first names. Ask how they would like to be addressed.

Listening: Active listening techniques (e.g., maintaining eye contact) may be useful, but may not be appropriate everywhere. People in some cultures learn to avoid eye contact as a way to show respect. Listen for what is not being said. Just because people say "yes" to your requests does not mean they are committed to any particular action. They may simply be acknowledging that they heard you. Paraphrasing and summarizing what you hear is particularly important when working with people in other cultures.

Communication: Leaders may need to over-communicate in both languages when working with cross-cultural teams. Help the person understand your expectations for speaking up or speaking out. Beware of making assumptions that, just because someone is quiet in team meetings, they are not an effective leader. That person may be struggling with the challenge of trying to communicate effectively in a non-native language. Adapt your communication style when coaching. If necessary, speak more slowly; simplify your vocabulary—and avoid idioms and slang. Take time to confirm important coaching suggestions in writing.

A Case Study in Interpersonal Effectiveness

Most organizations discover a point in time when they need to bring in outside executive talent to address a strategic need. External executive hires typically enter the new organization with some fanfare and hopes for their special contributions. Even though key employees may have been involved in the hiring decision, these new players often face skepticism, or even resentment, from work colleagues or team members. Without effective interpersonal skills, new leaders can quickly turn a challenging situation into an internal revolt.

As you read about Stephanie's situation, reflect on what you've learned about Interpersonal Effectiveness in this chapter and consider how you would help Stephanie demonstrate greater skill in Interpersonal Effectiveness and be successful in her new leadership role.

Dealing with Derailment

Stephanie Brown was recruited to lead a key IT department in a large manufacturing company. She was brought in specifically because she had led similar technology transformations twice—once in a company three times the size of the firm she was joining. During her interviews, colleagues found her to be exceptionally astute about industry dynamics. They were impressed with her drive, suggestions of game-changing solutions, and how she led work teams. Her new assignment was to build a high-performing team to change critical business information systems and reduce technology costs to the company by fifty percent in three years.

Stephanie started off on the wrong foot in her first few meetings. During the time she had been between jobs, she had created a long, intricate plan for change. In that first meeting, her team members were overwhelmed with the pace, intensity, and level of detail she expected. Inadvertently, she sent an "I know more than you do" message. Over the next two months, she seemed to become less and less open to input. She even became defensive when they asked her clarifying questions. Her team began holding meetings before and after Stephanie's meetings to compare notes and strategize on how to protect their own projects. By the third month, there were rumors of Stephanie compiling a list of people she intended to replace.

Stephanie's manager, the CIO, knew something wasn't quite right and that things were starting to go off track after only 100 days. The interview team and recruiter had been impressed with Stephanie's calm, cool demeanor. She was prepared, enthusiastic, and thorough in describing her previous experiences with transformation. After just a few weeks on the job, she had presented a well-defined plan for transforming her area in twelve to eighteen months. Why was she derailing?

Stephanie also realized that something was off track. She was terribly frustrated by the lack of progress and discouraged with how much resistance she was encountering. Feeling isolated, she wondered why the new plans seemed so difficult for her team to understand. In discussing her experiences with human resources, Stephanie learned that her team members perceived her as arrogant, as not interested in their ideas and, at times, disrespectful. She was shocked initially, but recovered enough to commit to addressing her blind spots around her interpersonal skills.

Stephanie's Leadership Development Plan

Following is a sample development plan for Stephanie Brown. Research on leadership development has shown that leaders learn through experience and that this learning is optimized through the use of an individual development plan. A successful plan includes new experiences and introduces the leader to new conversations and tools. Suggestions included in previous sections may stimulate your thinking about additional possibilities for Stephanie's development.

LEADERSHIP DEVELOPMENT PLAN FOR STEPHANIE BROWN
DEVELOPMENT GOAL
Goal: To strengthen my Interpersonal Effectiveness
Desired Outcomes—results I want to see from developing this skill
Self: Better working relationships with my team **Team:** Greater collaboration and sense of engagement **Organization:** Progress against our overall IT transformation goals
Self-Understanding—strengths that I can build on and development needs I can address
Strengths: Persistent leader; detail-oriented; strong planning and execution skills; results-oriented and enthusiastic about making things better; ask great questions and remember details well **Development Needs:** Make more time to connect with direct reports; listen to their ideas; take more of a genuine interest in their proposals; ask more questions about their feelings
Business Context—challenges in my business environment that require this skill
Competitive pressures and the constant need to do more with less within IT; there have been silos before within the various IT departments; we need greater collaboration overall to achieve our common goals; greater trust would help us be more productive.
DEVELOPMENT ACTIONS
AWAKEN - Participate in a 360-degree feedback process through human resources to learn more about my impact. - Talk to my peers about what others have done to be accepted more quickly in the organization. - Contrast the culture I came from with the one I am in now; how does this culture require different behavior from my previous one?

LEADERSHIP DEVELOPMENT PLAN FOR STEPHANIE BROWN

ALIGN

- Talk with my boss about what he sees in terms of my integration and what measures he is using to gauge my success.
- Share my objective of being a better listener with my team. Own my initial behavior and my intentions for improvement. Ask for their support.
- Work with someone in human resources who I can talk to about how I am integrating into the organization.

ACCELERATE

- Buy at least one book on listening skills and set weekly goals for myself for implementation.
- Use open-ended questions more: "Tell me about" or "What do you hope does not change?"
- Focus on being present and concentrate on what others are saying; listen for understanding, not for proving my point.
- When someone challenges my ideas, ask questions for clarification—don't just explain my own logic and ideas.
- Avoid using "yes, but" answers. Find one thing to acknowledge and then state another thought, (e.g., "So you believe that strongly; here are some other thoughts I have.").
- Avoid "should" statements and "why" questions. The former sounds condescending and the latter comes across as interrogation.

DEVELOPMENT SUCCESS FACTORS

Timeline: Within the next six months

Support Needed:

- Regular feedback from my team members and my manager
- Time to reflect on my behavior immediately after meetings (engage assistant in calendar management)

Indicators of Success:

- People will ask to be part of our department and our change initiative.
- Positive morale—in me and my team members; we have more fun in our work.
- Team will collectively own key decisions and feel responsible for our targeted outcomes.
- The follow-up 360 shows people believe we are achieving results—and they feel listened to and respected.

An Example of Coaching for Interpersonal Effectiveness

Stephanie Brown's goal was to strengthen her skills in Interpersonal Effectiveness. Here are some steps Stephanie's manager could take using the Awaken, Align, Accelerate framework to coach Stephanie in this area:

AWAKEN	**Increase INSIGHT**	Review Stephanie's 360-degree feedback results and ask what messages she heard in the feedback from key stakeholders. Ask how this feedback compared to other feedback she has received in the past. Have Stephanie paraphrase something to see how well she can listen and repeat important messages.
	MOTIVATE change	Focus on options and choices. Identify what Stephanie is motivated to change. Identify current performance gaps and potential priorities for development. Make sure Stephanie realizes the consequences of not improving her skills in this area.
ALIGN	**PLAN goals**	Focus on what she could change to improve her relationships with people on her team. Ask what she would spend time working toward and follow through on. Work together to construct a leadership development plan similar to the sample provided in this chapter.
	ALIGN expectations	Explore the need to increase buy-in from others in implementing her change plan. Encourage her to share highlights from her 360-degree feedback with people who responded and ask them for suggestions about what she could do differently. Monitor Stephanie's interactions during meetings and discuss your observations.
ACCELERATE	**CREATE teachable moments**	Encourage Stephanie to experiment with new approaches. Help her identify specific people who need to be listened to with more respect. Demonstrate the power of open-ended questions and listening in powerful ways. Brainstorm some ways that Stephanie can help people feel listened to and more appreciated. Assign her the task of voicing her admiration (e.g., a specific example) at least once a week. Invite her to share something 'new and interesting' she learned from colleagues.
	TRACK progress	Work with Stephanie to evaluate progress toward her goals. Discuss what kinds of changes will be visible to others. Encourage her to invite additional feedback and ask other people to support the changes they see. Express appreciation for her efforts.

Results: Measuring Impact

Stephanie Brown came to view her development plan as a way to build and sustain new habits. She didn't try every action step, and she found some activities were more helpful than others. However, she made tremendous progress on improving her Interpersonal Effectiveness. Her new skills allowed Stephanie to:

- Build stronger relationships with her direct reports, who now feel that she is respecting and listening to them.

- Use their input to revise her plan for changing the company's information systems.

- Improve the overall morale in her team.

- Empower people to own key decisions and feel responsible for outcomes.

- Reduce technology costs even more than she had anticipated.

15

Building Collaboration

Collaborative leaders build, maintain, and leverage a network of good relationships. They demonstrate that maintaining effective working relationships is a priority for the organization. They engage the right people at the right time to build cooperation, and encourage and expect employees at all levels to work together effectively with others across organizational boundaries. Skilled at resolving conflict, they focus on overarching goals and are able to facilitate win-win solutions.

Factor	Competency	Core Practice
Leading People	Interpersonal Effectiveness	Networking
Thinking and Deciding	Building Collaboration	Engagement
Achieving		Cooperation
Relating to People		Partnership
Managing Work		Conflict Management
Managing Self		

Every leader has struggled at one time or another to build the support necessary to drive an important initiative. Building Collaboration means the ability to engage and partner with other leaders in shared pursuit of organizational goals—wherever they live or whatever language they speak at home. Great leaders learn to collaborate with people who work with different styles, bring different perspectives, and excel at many different skills. Building Collaboration requires an insatiable appetite for learning from others and an ability to leverage a wide network. The most collaborative leaders know how to create healthy tension and resolve conflicts effectively. They shape win-win outcomes and build healthy lifelong working relationships. With the complexity of how work gets done today across geographies and areas of expertise, collaboration is a survival skill.

Leaders need to engage and partner with others for a number of reasons—collaboration facilitates good planning, decision-making, alignment, innovation, and commitment to the pursuit of organization goals. All leaders need to operate with a mindset where seeking out opportunities to build agreement and share information, best practices, and resources is the norm rather than the exception. At more senior levels, the most effective leaders understand that active engagement across functions and business lines is the best way to ensure both their individual success and the success of the entire enterprise. The five core practices of Building Collaboration and how they vary by level are described in more detail in the following chart.

How Leaders at Different Levels Build Collaboration

	Managers	Function Leaders	Senior Executives
Networking	Builds and maintains excellent relationships with other leaders.	Establishes and leverages a network of relationships across the organization.	Creates opportunities for people at all levels to build relationships.
Engagement	Improves or enhances relationships with other teams.	Engages and works with other functions for the good of the organization.	Promotes everyone's involvement in achieving the goals of the organization.
Cooperation	Offers genuine assistance to others.	Models the importance of working cooperatively with others.	Solicits opinions and input from others when developing solutions.
Partnership	Makes integration among groups a priority.	Creates partnerships to achieve business goals.	Requires and maintains a collaborative culture. Sets the tone for effective collaboration between internal and external partners.
Conflict Management	Seeks win-win solutions.	Addresses and resolves disagreements constructively.	Addresses even the toughest conflict in an open and straightforward manner.

To evaluate your effectiveness in Building Collaboration, check all boxes below that represent current behavior or performance. Look for patterns: Which core practices represent a development need, a strength, or an excessive use? Recognize that you might have some blind spots. Invite your boss or colleagues to indicate what they have observed in your behavior. Use this assessment to help identify development suggestions that are most relevant to you.

	Development Need	Strength	Excessive Use
Networking	☐ Maintains a small number of close-knit relationships; ineffective or uninterested in networking ☐ Interacts with members of his/her network only when making requests of them	☐ Actively establishes and leverages a broad network of relationships within the organization ☐ Looks for opportunities to connect with others and contribute to the success of those in his/her network	☐ Builds too wide a network to effectively maintain relationships ☐ Spends so much time networking that own needs and priorities are ignored
Engagement	☐ Operates in isolation from others in the organization; manages own group like an island ☐ Creates adversarial relationships with other functions; is overly opinionated and outspoken	☐ Consistently involves other functions in discussions, decisions, and plans to ensure the whole organization is successful ☐ Actively communicates a vision and direction to build opportunities for synergy across functions	☐ Involves the wrong people (or too many), losing the focus of decisions and plans. ☐ Fails to advocate for the interests of own group; doesn't step up as a leader
Cooperation	☐ Ignores or minimizes the need to work effectively with others ☐ Allows or condones a lack of cooperation between people and across functions or groups	☐ Models cooperation and inspires others to work together to produce results ☐ Recognizes and rewards cooperative behavior of own team members and others	☐ Advocates harmony so strongly that he/she appears too quick to compromise ☐ Consistently takes a back seat role in cross-functional initiatives; is overly collaborative at the expense of standing up for the needs of own area
Partnership	☐ Fails to develop relationships with key stakeholders outside the organization (e.g., suppliers and customers) ☐ Ignores opportunities to explore partnerships with groups in other parts of the organization	☐ Builds strong, collaborative relationships and alliances with groups outside the organization ☐ Identifies and/or creates opportunities for collaboration across organizational boundaries	☐ Spends too much time being externally focused at the expense of building relationships internally ☐ Aligns too closely with other groups, losing the sense of loyalty to own organization
Conflict Management	☐ Avoids conflict ☐ Is unable to resolve conflict in most cases	☐ Skillfully resolves conflict by concentrating on overarching goals and business-focused outcomes ☐ Acts as a neutral third party to help others reach win-win solutions	☐ Intervenes unnecessarily to mediate conflicts that could be resolved by others ☐ Preempts disagreements by inappropriately minimizing differences in point of view

Development Suggestions

The following section contains development suggestions for each core practice. Having completed the self-assessment, focus on suggestions that correspond to the core practices you identified as a development need or excessive use. Use these suggestions to create your own development plan, making sure to try one or two from each phase. In addition, feel free to create your own or adapt these to best meet your development needs.

Networking

Establish and leverage a network of relationships across the organization.

It's all about people. It's about networking and being nice to people and not burning any bridges.

Mike Davidson

Awaken potential:

- **Identify the purpose and benefits of networking.** For example, the more you learn about what someone is doing, the more you might realize there are possibilities of doing some things more effectively together. With the advent of LinkedIn, Plaxo, Facebook, Twitter, and many other forms of social networking, people have more and more ways to connect and maintain those connections. Research various options. Which of those vehicles might best suit your own needs and interests?

- **Make a list of the people you most frequently leverage.** How many people are on your list? Are they from multiple functions in the organization or just within your own function? Evaluate the value of the relationships on the list. What would it take to get more out of your network and build more valuable relationships?

- **Examine how you tend to approach your work.** Leaders need to use their networks. Do you close your door and keep things to yourself, or do you look for ways to involve others who might have an interest in what you're working on?

- **Reflect on your own behaviors.** Relationships are important at all levels. Look at how you interact with your peers before and after meetings. Do you invite small talk and opportunities for others to get to know you, or do you arrive late, leave early, and focus only on the business at hand? Ask a trusted colleague for feedback on how accessible you seem to others.

Align goals:

- **Ensure you have the right network.** Ask your boss for names of people who you should get to know or add to your network. Share your network list with several colleagues. Ask for their suggestions about key people to get to know.

- **Identify critical stakeholders for your key priorities.** Note what kind of relationship you have with each person (e.g., if you know each other well, have worked together before, are acquaintances, haven't actually met). Plan how to get them on board with your initiatives.

- **Identify peers in other functions** who might be impacted by your success or failure. Review your division's key performance goals for interdependencies among your function and those of your peers. Review the core practice "Coordination" in Chapter 6 for ways to engage others in discussions of shared, interdependent, and independent goals.

Accelerate performance:

- **Broaden your interactions.** Get to know the organization outside your own division, and learn what opportunities there are to build new relationships.

- **Invite colleagues from other areas to lunch or coffee.** Ask what energizes them about their work. Share information about your key goals and what excites you about your work. Use this time to maintain relationships and build momentum for your objectives.

- **Act on your key priorities/people list.** Set up specific times to talk with others about your goals. Map out the key stakeholders for your critical initiatives and make sure you are leveraging their influence.

- **Co-sponsor initiatives.** Talk to your peers about task forces, committees, or projects you could co-sponsor. What are their ideas about where and how you could collaborate more actively?

- **Expand your network.** If you'd like your network to be more extensive, ask a peer with a large internal network to tell you how he/she developed and has maintained that network. Ask colleagues to introduce you to people in their networks who might have an interest in the work of your organization or function.

- **Use political skills to influence, motivate, and win support.** Read the book *Political Skill at Work* by Gerald Ferris, Sherry Davidson, and Pamela Perrewe (Davis-Black Publishing, 2005) to learn more about why political skills are so important in business and how to enhance your impact.

- **Extend your influence.** Look for opportunities to place your direct reports on cross-functional project teams or lend them to projects outside your area which will be developmental for them.

EXCESSIVE USE

As an example, if you spend so much time networking that you do not attend to performance issues on your own team, you may be perceived as overly political. Establish goals for networking so you will be more intentional about those activities. Leverage this strength to help other people learn how to network. Meanwhile, don't neglect your own team.

Engagement

Engage and work with other functions for the good of the organization.

> *Let us realize that engagement and detachment aren't opposite—the more engaged we become, the more detached we will have to be.*
>
> Deepak Chopra

Awaken potential:

- **Assess your level of engagement.** Rate your relationships with key stakeholders in other functions on a ten-point scale. Identify people with whom you want to build stronger relationships, and plan how to engage them in common goals.

- **Evaluate your influence on others.** Reflect on the aspects of your work and business you feel strongly about. How do you express your views with others? How often do you ask for their views?

- **Compare yourself to others.** Think about a time when peers in other functions engaged you in an issue. How did they approach you? What did they do to gain your interest or commitment? Would their styles or approaches work for you?

- **Ask peers for feedback** about your involvement on cross-functional projects as well as your impact in meetings—especially after meetings where you spoke a lot. Do this periodically.

Align goals:

- **Take the lead on joint planning processes** with other function leaders. Engage peers outside your function in think-out-loud discussions about the overall business direction and goals for their areas when developing strategy and identifying goals for your area.

- **Review change plans with peers** before implementing a change to your area's structure or to a process that is likely to impact other functions. Frame agenda items for cross-functional meetings in the context of the overall organization direction. Review the chapter "Creating Alignment" for more suggestions about managing change.

Accelerate performance:

- **Ask "Who else cares about this and why?"** as you set key goals for your function to remind yourself to engage others who are impacted by your decisions. Develop the practice of inviting comments from peers, including those in other divisions, when considering significant business decisions or changes.

- **Prepare a process map for your function's work.** Identify which areas are upstream and which are downstream from your outputs. How much do you involve your peers in those functions in decisions you make regarding your own area?

- **Organize show-and-tell meetings for peers** in other functions that are upstream or downstream of the work of your function. Use these meetings to encourage everyone to share information about new initiatives, changing priorities, etc.

- **Assign direct reports** to cross-functional project teams as development opportunities. Consider assembling cross-functional project teams to take on process improvements and other needed internal initiatives.

- **Use others' time wisely.** When inviting peers from outside your division for meetings, ask yourself whether they should be involved in the decisions and actions taken during the meeting or if they should just be aware of the situation. Consider finding alternative ways to keep non-decision-makers informed.

- **Use email judiciously.** Before clicking "Reply All," ask yourself if everyone on the "Send" list really cares about the email you are about to send. What kind of reactions or responses do you expect from recipients?

EXCESSIVE USE

As an example, if you spend too much time supporting other areas, you may fail to advocate for the needs of your own department. Ask your manager for feedback about the appropriate balance. You may need to rethink your priorities.

Cooperation

Model the importance of working cooperatively with others.

People who work together will win, whether it be against complex football defenses, or the problems of modern society.

Vince Lombardi

Awaken potential:

- **Evaluate your working relationships.** Try to imagine the way you work with others. What picture comes to mind? Do your relationships operate smoothly like shifting gears on a well-tuned bike or do they grind like worn-out brake pads?

- **Get feedback.** Inquire about how colleagues perceive your relationships with other people. How do they describe you as a leader? Are you seen as cooperative or competitive? Supportive or critical? How much do others enjoy working with you— and vice versa?

- **Ask others what kinds of leaders they admire.** Who could be your role model in the area of cooperation? What steps does that person take to work effectively with others? How does that person model and promote collaboration? What specific behaviors can you emulate?

Align goals:

- **Discuss how to promote more cooperation.** Ask your manager to help you identify where cooperation is most important to the success of the business among individuals and teams in these areas.

- **Consistently define roles and responsibilities** for each member of a task force or project team you oversee. Clarify strategy and desired outcomes with your colleagues to ensure they are focused on organizational values and goals.

- **Align systems to encourage cooperation.** Talk with human resources about how compensation plans or other organizational systems tend to promote competitive behavior—and how those systems could be changed to encourage more cooperation and improve business results.

Accelerate performance:

- **Create a map of your internal network** to identify your most important stakeholders. Who is critical to your success in achieving business objectives over the next year? These can be senior managers, peers, direct reports, distributors, customers, or whomever. Identify which relationships need the most improvement and develop an action plan.

- **Assess your team members.** Which members are the most cooperative when colleagues ask for support? Least cooperative? What are you doing to model and reinforce cooperative behavior? How could you do more to show your appreciation and reward cooperation on your team?

- **Promote a positive, supportive work environment.** How do you show your appreciation for a job well done? How often do you praise the accomplishments of others? How often do you celebrate team achievements? How do you promote and maintain harmony in your team? Consider how you could further emphasize the importance of cooperation.

- **Plan an off-site team event** that will incorporate activities that require people to cooperate with each other. Afterwards, debrief performances and identify how each activity paralleled an actual process in the workplace. Discuss lessons learned and what people will do differently at work. Follow up later to inquire about how things are going, and reinforce progress toward greater cooperation.

- **Review Chapter 14, "Interpersonal Effectiveness,"** for some suggestions on how to improve your working relationships with others.

EXCESSIVE USE

As an example, if you advocate harmony too strongly, you may compromise too quickly. Work at becoming more comfortable managing disagreements or developing more assertiveness to help you articulate your needs and expectations of others. Although working through conflicts can be painful, it can also lead to better outcomes. See the "Conflict Management" section in this chapter for additional ideas. Also review Chapter 5, core practices "Assertiveness" and "Independence" for ways in which you can strengthen the language you use to communicate your needs and interests to others.

Partnership

Create partnerships to achieve business goals.

> *You can't stay in your corner of the forest waiting for others to come to you; you have to go to them sometimes.*
>
> A.A. Milne

Awaken potential:

- **Consider abundance.** Think about how you view organizational resources and marketplace opportunities. Do you see them as scarce commodities to be won, or as communal property to be used to their best advantage?

- **Identify what matters to you.** Make a list of your personal standards for success. Do they encourage you to compete with stakeholders or seek opportunities to work together?

- **Analyze your interactions.** Look at how you view and interact with internal and external stakeholders. Do you tend to look for opportunities to showcase your expertise, or do you look for opportunities to learn from others and share best practices?

- **Assess trust levels.** Discuss with your team where your function needs to build more trust with stakeholders inside and outside the organization. Trust and credibility are foundational elements that enable collaboration. How can you build more trust and credibility with suppliers and customers?

- **Ask for feedback from colleagues** on what you do that promotes partnering, and what you do that impedes it. Ask for suggestions about what you could do differently.

Align goals:

- **Think bigger.** Talk with your manager about what you see others doing in the marketplace and how these activities fit with your organization's strategy. Discuss what opportunities might exist for achieving successful strategic relationships with other organizations.

- **Identify partnership opportunities.** Ask your manager to identify key areas in the organization where opportunities might exist to partner with outside groups to enhance your organization's capabilities. Develop strategies to engage your peers in those areas to ensure that potential partnerships will benefit overarching business goals.

Accelerate performance:

- **Learn more about strategic alliances.** Read books like *Partnering Intelligence* by Stephen M. Dent (Intercultural Press, 2004) that address the important aspects of partnership development and provide tools for building strong alliances for your organization.

- **Organize opportunities** for you and your external stakeholders to discuss new initiatives or best practices in your industry. Initiate conversations with key external stakeholders to tackle issues that impact your respective organizations. Invite these external stakeholders to discuss their business priorities during your staff meetings.

- **Share best practices with others.** Identify best practices in your function or organization that could be applied to other organizations or industries. Speak at conferences. Ask how your other external stakeholders are doing business. Attend industry trade shows, and look for synergies with other groups.

- **Cross-pollinate talent.** Talk with other leaders about trading employees for certain projects or initiatives to give them learning opportunities in other areas of the business. Consider exchanging talent with other organizations such as non-profits to expand your employees' exposure to different leadership challenges.

- **Encourage others to partner.** Keep a journal about how you coach people on your team to partner with others. How often do you empower through your coaching, rather than direct? How much independence do you encourage? How often do you ask something like, "Who else could work on this with you?"

EXCESSIVE USE

As an example, if you involve too many people, initiatives may lose focus. Recognize that over involvement can sometimes be worse than under involvement, especially when time is such a precious commodity for everyone. Strive for the right balance. Identify the people who really need to be included in meetings—or those who need to be consulted on decisions—and limit your outreach to those individuals.

Conflict Management

Address and resolve disagreements constructively.

> *Every fight is on some level a fight between differing 'angles of vision' illuminating the same truth.*
>
> Mahatma Gandhi

Awaken potential:

- **Assess your orientation toward conflict.** List all the words and images that come to mind when you think about the word "conflict." Then think about your initial response in conflict situations. Do you try to avoid conflict at all costs? Or do you recognize and accept that conflict is an inevitable part of doing business?

- **Reflect on a conflict situation that you handled well.** What did you do or say that was effective? How did the other person respond? Reflect on a conflict situation you handled poorly or that wasn't resolved the way you had hoped. What did you do or say that was ineffective? How did the other person respond? What would you do differently next time?

- **Identify your triggers.** Try to remember situations at work when you became irritated with others. What triggered your reaction? Make a list of your most common triggers.

- **Take a conflict styles assessment** such as the Thomas-Kilmann Conflict Mode Instrument (TKI—available on CPP's website: www.cpp.com) to gain insight into your typical approach as well as alternative ways of dealing with conflict.

Align goals:

- **Separate your needs from your wants.** Be clear with yourself about your business goals, objectives, and priorities. In a conflict situation, make an honest assessment of what you actually *need* versus what you *want* from the resolution. Present your needs in an open, unemotional way.

- **Clarify others' needs and wants.** In conflict situations, ask questions to help all parties separate their wants from their needs. When you perceive a possible conflict with a colleague, listen and ask for clarification of his/her point of view and paraphrase what you heard before stating your own position.

Accelerate performance:

- **Practice viewing conflict as an opportunity** to learn more about others' points of view and gain greater insight into business issues outside your area. Read *Capitalizing on Conflict* by Kirk Blackard and James W. Gibson (Davies-Black Publishing, 2002) for ideas for developing an organizational culture that minimizes and manages conflict and optimizes organizational performance.

- **Use the results of your conflict styles assessment** to outline a plan for developing a more versatile approach to handling conflict.

- **Develop self-management techniques for your most common triggers** (see above). Employ them before you respond emotionally to those triggers. For example, taking a deep breath or counting to ten (i.e., pausing before making an angry retort) might help you manage your temper and offer a calmer response.

- **Use "I" statements versus "you" statements** to describe your reaction to your triggers (e.g., "I was surprised by that question; I felt unprepared and on the spot."). Avoid blaming others.

- **Choose neutral language** when stating your point of view on an issue rather than language that makes judgmental comparisons or creates a condescending tone. Instead of looking for the one right solution to a problem, brainstorm a range of possibilities that could promote shared interests.

- **Separate people from issues in conflict situations.** Help people focus on the issues.

EXCESSIVE USE

As an example, if you intervene unnecessarily to mediate conflicts that could be resolved by others, practice standing back and allowing people to work out their own issues.

Coach Others on Building Collaboration

When coaching others, focus on the core practices that were identified as either a development need or excessive use in the self-assessment at the beginning of this chapter. Identify and adapt any relevant development suggestions. Additional coaching tips are provided in the following table for some adverse leadership behaviors. For more information review Chapter 4, "Coach Others."

Coaching Suggestions

	Behavior	Awaken	Align	Accelerate
Networking	*Is not interested in networking*	• Ask about the person's networks. • Encourage the person to expand their thinking about the work of the team. • Help create diagrams that show how others outside the area are related to the person's key goals.	• Encourage the person to find opportunities to discuss mutual goals with people on his/her network diagram. • Pair the person with a mentor who strongly leverages internal relationships to learn some secrets about networking.	• Facilitate introductions to people who the person doesn't know who should be in his/her network. • Create a relationship map, and hold the person accountable for meeting with others.
Networking	*Interacts only when making requests; uses people*	• Offer feedback based on your own observations (e.g., "You only call when you want something"). • Ask the person how others might feel when this happens. • Provide concrete examples of when reaching out, not just in the time of need, may have helped.	• Propose that the person engage in candid conversations with others who might have felt used by this person in the past. • Circle back with several stakeholders. Identify new opportunities for ad hoc meetings.	• Encourage the person to establish mutual exchange relationships. • Identify several places where the person needs to reciprocate.
Engagement	*Creates adversarial relationships; "burns bridges"*	• Ask for the person's perceptions of any burned bridges that may exist. • Discuss negative consequences of continuing this behavior (e.g., people may be unwilling to commit resources to his/her projects).	• Recommend that the person go to those who have been negatively impacted by them and ask for forgiveness (but only if the person is willing to admit culpability and propose building a different kind of relationship). • Leverage allies to help re-build bridges and change perception. Identify who might help.	• Coach the person on developing a plan to repair broken relationships. • Observe the person in meetings, and provide immediate feedback regarding behavior that might create adversarial perceptions.

Behavior		Awaken	Align	Accelerate
Engagement	*Operates in isolation*	• Work together to identify a few trusted advisors who will give the person balanced feedback on his/her participation in cross-functional initiatives. • Identify a time when someone went it alone and they felt a more collaborative approach would have improved results. How did they feel?	• Encourage the person to invite others from outside the area to attend meetings about projects or initiatives that are relevant to their goals. • Have them dialogue with a colleague who prioritizes investment in relationship development. Debrief their learning from this conversation.	• Suggest that the person develop a strategic story for his/her function to use to talk about how his/her function is linked to and supports other areas of the organization. • Model bringing in other stakeholders into key meetings. Discuss how their input creates effective solutions.
Cooperation	*Ignores the need to maintain relationships*	• Ask the person to identify areas of the organization or specific initiatives in which he/she has interest and may add value through experience or knowledge. • Discuss where they feel their relationships are the strongest? When would they see them needing to improve? Why?	• Help the person find ways to get involved and incorporate this work into performance goals or development plans. • Seek understanding from a colleague who invests in relationships. Why do they prioritize the effort?	• Partner the person on an assignment with someone whose expertise differs but is integral to producing successful results. • Reinforce: recognize when they effectively involve others. Take time to inquire who they are involving.
	Condones a lack of cooperation	• Help the person reflect on the impact of his/her behavior. Ask what kind of an example the person is setting for others—and what kind of example the person wants to set. • Reflect on when they felt others weren't cooperating. How did this prevent or delay success?	• Propose that the person introduce the topic of cooperation at a team meeting and have his/her team brainstorm what is working well vs. not in terms of cooperation with other functions. • Work with the team to apply their learning with one function as a pilot. Debrief the results together.	• Meet with the person every two weeks to discuss progress in this area. Ask what obstacles the person is encountering and help find solutions. • Actively seek feedback from the leader of the other function. What do they see changing?

Behavior		Awaken	Align	Accelerate
Partnership	*Fails to develop relationships with internal stakeholders*	• Review key relationships together. Who are the person's allies? Adversaries? Why? • Identify relationships the person would like to strengthen. What would this accomplish?	• Encourage the person to enlist a small team of colleagues to consider opportunities to enhance operations; suggest that he/she ask a colleague to co-lead the effort. • Have them observe how others enlist internal stakeholders. Identify two new ways to do so.	• Build internal networking into the person's development goals. • Encourage and support the person in meeting with others to develop relationships outside of meetings.
	Fails to develop relationships with external stakeholders	• Propose that the person target up to three external relationships to strengthen. • Identify one relationship where you believe attention is due. Discuss why it is important to focus more energy there.	• Propose that the person target up to three relationships to strengthen. • Create an "accountability group." Challenge each other to keep up with building key relationships.	• Create a plan for cultivating relationships using deliberate meetings, lunches, etc. • Encourage the person to use business meetings with others to advance relationships.
Conflict Management	*Avoids conflict*	• Help the person identify issues or situations that trigger negative reactions. • Learn the Thomas-Kilmann model of conflict resolution to better understand their natural style and other alternatives.	• Help the person view situations and conflict from different perspectives. • Pair them with someone with an alternate conflict resolution style. What can they learn from them?	• Brainstorm alternative approaches to responding to triggers. • Practice leveraging a less natural resolution style that is highlighted by Thomas-Kilmann.
	Is unable to resolve conflict	• Discuss conflicts that are currently unresolved. • Explore the potential impact of allowing the conflicts to go unresolved.	• Propose that the person should not allow conflicts to remain unresolved. If problems cannot be addressed at the current time, he/she should propose a process (and time) for dealing with them in the near future. • When they feel stuck encourage them to seek feedback from others on potential means of resolution.	• Suggest that the person read *Getting to Yes* by Roger Fisher and William Ury (Penguin, 1991) for suggestions on how to focus on common goals. • Encourage the person to keep a journal of actions they have taken to resolve conflicts and the lessons they learned. Debrief quarterly, if not more often.

Tips for Coaching in a Global Environment

Building Collaboration may be practiced or expressed differently within other cultures. This might impact how you approach coaching. Try to keep an open mind, avoid generalizations, and continue gathering data as you gain experience with another culture. Consider these suggestions:

Networking: Learn all you can about the culture you are interacting with. Recognize that developing social and personal relationships is fundamental to—and may need to precede—developing and maintaining business networks in their culture. Recognize that people from other cultures may have different expectations and degrees of comfort regarding open conversation about feelings and emotions. There are also differences in the behaviors that are considered appropriate such as eye contact, informal language, humor, and intimacy, all of which can be related to building collaborative relationships.

Engagement: Be careful not to assume that a person is not engaged if they remain quiet at meetings. Have a conversation about leadership and exchange ideas about what effective leadership and engagement looks like in your culture and in that individual's culture. People may need to over-communicate if they are working with people using multiple languages in the workplace, especially if they want to engage everyone. Adapt your communication style when working with people who are communicating with a non-native language. If necessary, speak more slowly, simplify your vocabulary, and avoid idioms and slang. Paraphrase and summarize your key points.

Cooperation: Be aware that independent initiative is valued differently in various cultures. In some, it is appropriate and rewarded. In others, collaboration is more the norm in getting things done. There may be differences in the extent of relationship and trust building that is required before things get done in some cultures. Don't impose your sense of urgency on situations that require more time to build the relationship before you can progress.

Partnership: Have a frank discussion about the challenges, obstacles, and benefits of getting people to work together cross-culturally. Be alert to conversational openings that your partners provide. In some cultures, social invitations represent requests to discuss business issues.

Conflict Management: Addressing conflict up-front isn't effective in all cultures. Don't assume that lack of directness means lack of ability or interest in resolving differences. The use of a third party who is familiar with the situation may be more comfortable and effective in resolving conflicts.

A Case Study in Building Collaboration

Building Collaboration requires a leader to participate with and involve others, promote cooperation, build partnerships, and resolve conflicts. Overusing the strengths that often propel one to positions of leadership (e.g., drive, passion, and independence) can be a leader's downfall if they are not balanced with the ability to gain support and commitment from others. The higher you advance in an organization, the more critical the need for working with and through others. Without effective collaboration, a leader's reach and scope will quickly become quite limited, as will his/her ability to obtain results.

As you read about Dawn's situation, reflect on what you've learned about Building Collaboration in this chapter. How does Dawn sound like you or one of your team members? What experiences or tendencies do you share? Finally, consider how you would help Dawn demonstrate greater skill in Building Collaboration and be successful in her leadership role.

Building Bridges and Buy-in

Dawn Jones rose quickly to head the Supply Chain function of the largest business unit in her company. She had a reputation for being bright, assertive, driven, and independent—she was willing to do what it took to get results for her business unit. Dawn's function was known for having implemented some innovative approaches that not only resulted in cost savings, but also strengthened relationships with key suppliers. As the organization continued to grow, it looked for ways to streamline its Supply Chain by integrating best practices across business units. A monthly meeting of Supply Chain leaders was established to discuss innovations in the field and determine what could be brought into the organization. Dawn believed she had a lot to bring to the table.

Dawn put together a brief presentation of elements she felt had made the most significant impact on streamlining her own Supply Chain function. She shared her presentation at a meeting of Supply Chain leaders from the company's five largest business units. She was a little surprised by the cool reception she got, but chalked it up to her colleagues' aversion to change; several had been managing Supply Chain functions in organizations that had been acquired.

Believing she just needed more time to explain her ideas, Dawn approached her peers in one-on-one meetings. She figured this would give her the opportunity to address individual questions about how her ideas could work in their divisions. They listened to her but still didn't show the enthusiasm she expected. Even Julia, a friend and fellow Supply Chain leader, seemed cool during their meeting. Marty, who had come in with one of the acquisitions, was almost sarcastic when he said, "Great ideas, I'll give them some thought."

Reflecting on the individual meetings she'd had with her peers, Dawn realized that this was the first time she'd talked at any length with most of the other Supply Chain leaders.

Dawn recognized that she needed to Build Collaboration to:

- Gain credibility with her peers.

- Develop solid working relationships outside her division.

- Contribute effectively to the direction the organization was taking on Supply Chain.

- Repair the damage her first approach had inflicted.

Dawn's Leadership Development Plan

Following is a sample development plan for Dawn Jones. Research on leadership development has shown that leaders learn through experience and that this learning is optimized through the use of an individual development plan. A successful plan includes new experiences and introduces the leader to new conversations and tools. The suggestions included in the previous sections may stimulate your thinking about additional possibilities for Dawn's development.

LEADERSHIP DEVELOPMENT PLAN FOR DAWN JONES
DEVELOPMENT GOAL
Goal: To strengthen my skills in Building Collaboration
Desired Outcomes —results I want to see from developing this skill
Self: I will gain credibility with my peer group. **Team:** My team will benefit from improved results and stronger relationships built on trust. **Organization:** Division Supply Chain function leaders will openly share and integrate best practices.
Self-Understanding —strengths that I can build on and development needs I can address
Strengths: I am competitive and like to win. I have high energy and an ability to get things done. Efficiency is important; I don't have time to waste. I enjoy being part of a team when it produces results. **Development needs:** Establishing personal relationships, building collaborative partnerships with key stakeholders, and overcoming impatience when listening to others, especially when I doubt the usefulness of their contributions.
Business Context —challenges in my business environment that require this skill
Sharing best practices among divisions, implementing consistent practices, and continued efforts to trim costs through streamlining business processes.

LEADERSHIP DEVELOPMENT PLAN FOR DAWN JONES

DEVELOPMENT ACTIONS

AWAKEN

- Ask Jim, whom I've worked with for several years, for feedback on my overall impact with peers.

- Talk with colleagues and direct reports about how I have implemented changes in my division. What did I do that helped build the commitment I needed from my own team and from colleagues? Did I really have true support?

- Determine the actual extent of my network in the organization. Am I building relationships with the right people? What have I done to reach out to peers in the organizations we've acquired? Do peers reach out to me?

ALIGN

- Ask Julia for suggestions about what I can do to build and rebuild relationships with the other Supply Chain leaders.

- Have a conversation with my boss about his expectations for my Supply Chain leadership.

- Develop a Network Map (see Appendix) that reflects both my current network and the network I need to have. Identify specific actions that I will take to build the network I need to have.

ACCELERATE

- Listen more than I talk, actively solicit others' ideas, and draw people out with open-ended questions.

- Set up one-on-one meetings with Supply Chain peers in other divisions and focus on learning about their operations and what works for them rather than bringing my own ideas.

- Build time into my calendar for lunch or coffee with people on my Network Map (see Appendix) and leave the agenda open.

- Look for opportunities to involve members of my team in cross-divisional projects to help them expand their own networks and learn more about innovations in other functions.

- Coach my direct reports on developing their own Network Map (see Appendix).

DEVELOPMENT SUCCESS FACTORS

Timeline: Within four to six months

Support Needed:

- Julia's willingness to provide candid feedback when she thinks I am driving my own point of view too hard.

- My boss' continued clarification of results and expectations.

Indicators of Success:

- Interactions with peer Supply Chain leaders and others will be more collegial; conversations will be dialogues in which I learn as well as share information.

- Feedback from my manager and peers will indicate notable improvement in soliciting input and involvement, and asking more questions.

- People will provide positive feedback about the team.

- The team will experience improved results, better relationships, and more effective decision-making. **NOTE**: One indicator of success might be more conflict if divergent viewpoints are more openly shared.

An Example of Coaching to Build Collaboration

Dawn Jones' goal was to strengthen her skills in Building Collaboration. Here are some steps Dawn's manager could take using the Awaken, Align, Accelerate framework to coach Dawn in this area:

AWAKEN	**Increase INSIGHT**	Brainstorm how Dawn could have been more effective in sharing her ideas about streamlining the Supply Chain. Encourage Dawn to consider completing a 360-degree feedback survey. Look together for any gaps in her perceptions. Help her understand the impact and implications of her behavior, especially on peers.
	MOTIVATE change	Ask what Dawn wants to change. Help her reflect on what has led to her success in gaining buy-in from others in the past. Identify potential priorities for development. Explore the consequences for her personally as well as her division of not making any changes.
ALIGN	**PLAN goals**	Work with Dawn to identify her most important stakeholders. Focus on what she could change to improve her credibility with peers. Build internal networking into her development goals. Ask which goals she will spend time working toward and following through on. Work together to construct a leadership development plan similar to the sample provided in this chapter.
	ALIGN expectations	Discuss your expectations for Dawn as well as what expectations her peers might have. Establish a task force yourself or encourage Dawn to enlist a small team of colleagues to look at opportunities to enhance overall Supply Chain Operations. Suggest that she ask one of her colleagues to co-lead the effort. Observe Dawn's interactions in meetings. Provide feedback afterward about her impact on others.

ACCELERATE	CREATE teachable moments	Help Dawn target particular peer relationships to rebuild, and experiment with trying new approaches. Encourage and support her investing time to meet with others to develop relationships outside of meetings focused on business goals or project work. Debrief some of the interactions she has with others, and talk about what she learns.
	TRACK progress	Discuss expected outcomes and results. Work with Dawn to evaluate progress toward her goals. Discuss obstacles, and brainstorm additional possibilities. Acknowledge and celebrate her efforts.

Results: Measuring Impact

Dawn Jones made rapid progress on her plan during the first few months, fueled by her desire to repair some broken relationships. She found that some activities were more helpful than others and didn't try every action step. However, she made progress on becoming more collaborative. Her new skills in Building Collaboration allowed Dawn to:

- Establish more collegial relationships and gain credibility with Supply Chain peers.

- Develop better working relationships with a variety of key stakeholders.

- Solicit input and involve others in a genuine way when planning projects.

- Improve decision-making and results while working on a variety of different project teams.

- Contribute to the streamlining of Supply Chain operations.

MANAGING
WORK

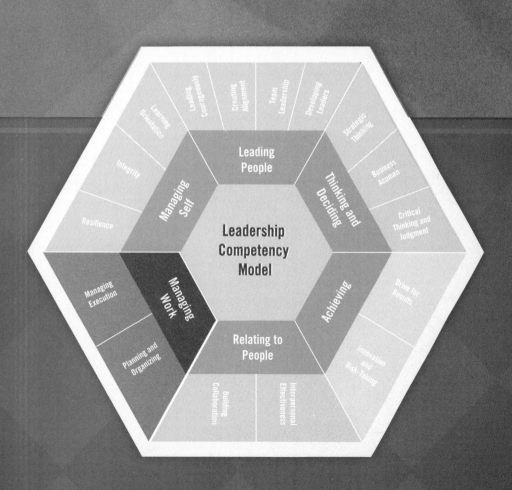

16

Planning and Organizing

The most successful leaders make time for longer-term and strategic planning. They anticipate and think ahead. They are clear about priorities and tie plans and activities to business goals. They are effective at translating strategies into concrete action plans. They involve others and develop plans that are integrated and aligned with the organization's strategy. They do the work necessary to ensure that others have the plans and resources they need to get things done.

Factor	Competency	Core Practice
Leading People	Planning and Organizing	Forward Thinking
Thinking and Deciding	Managing Execution	Prioritizing
Achieving		Planning
Relating to People		Participation
Managing Work		Resource Management
Managing Self		

Leaders who master the competency of Planning and Organizing create success by enabling themselves and others to effectively bring process into situations where it is absent. Planning and Organizing includes proactively defining the strategic direction and then determining what goals and activities should be accomplished, by whom, when, and at what cost. Whether planning for a two-hour department meeting or setting goals for the next three years, effective leaders convey confidence in the path necessary to accomplish what is expected of them and their teams. Failure to effectively plan can create problems and rework, requiring more time and effort to fix than would have been necessary to develop a good plan in the first place. Great leaders enhance their ability to execute successfully by making time for strategic thinking, developing plans, setting priorities that are integrated and aligned with the organization's strategic direction, and engaging staff in planning activities, as well as through thoughtful and timely communication.

Organizing is the process of defining the tasks to be accomplished, then determining the needs of each job. It is vital that the leader is able to delegate authority and responsibility to capable individuals, align resources to reach specific goals, and design the organizational relationships needed for success. Leaders who are skilled in organizing their groups and working their plans will increase their probability of success and enhance their capacity to adapt effectively in today's complex environment.

Solid planning skills characterize effective leadership organization at all levels in an enterprise. Leaders need to think ahead, consider the future impact of business plans, and engage in planning. It is important for leaders to show skill in applying solid thinking to longer-term issues, translating ideas into action plans, and helping others to actualize their ideas. At more senior levels, the type of planning and organizing and time horizon that a leader must focus on expands as the leader's scope of responsibility increases. While Planning and Organizing is important for all leaders, the most effective behaviors vary by level, as illustrated in the table on the next page.

How Leaders at Different Levels Plan and Organize

	Managers	Function Leaders	Senior Executives
Forward Thinking	Anticipates and prevents problems from occurring.	Maintains a longer-term perspective when developing plans.	Thinks about what is beyond the planning horizon.
Prioritizing	Links unit's activities to business goals.	Establishes clear priorities that align with broader organizational goals.	Persistently focuses on the most critical priorities for the business.
Planning	Develops cohesive plans with concrete goals, timetables, and deadlines.	Translates business strategy into action plans.	Ensures that plans align with the organization's strategy.
Participation	Solicits input from others when planning work.	Gains input on plans from key stakeholders.	Insists that plans are made or reviewed by other teams and key stakeholders.
Resource Management	Accurately forecasts and secures resources for projects.	Anticipates needs and utilizes resources effectively to optimize progress on functional goals.	Supports the appropriate resources required to achieve organizational objectives.

Self-Assessment

To evaluate your effectiveness in Planning and Organizing, check all boxes below that represent current behavior or performance. Look for patterns: Which core practices represent a development need, a strength, or an excessive use? Recognize that you might have some blind spots. Invite your boss or colleagues to indicate what they have observed in your behavior. Use this assessment to help identify development suggestions that are most relevant to you.

	Development Need	Strength	Excessive Use
Forward Thinking	☐ Fails to anticipate the impact and consequences of decisions; remains overly reactive ☐ Focuses on the short-term and does not devote time to strategizing for the future	☐ Anticipates and consistently links thinking to long-term issues ☐ Continually emphasizes the need to consider the impact and consequences of plans and decisions	☐ Overlooks short-term needs and practical issues ☐ Devotes too much time to planning at the expense of taking action
Prioritizing	☐ Plans and supports activities that are not linked to business goals ☐ Creates team goals that are ambiguous or vague	☐ Sets priorities based on the business as a whole ☐ Consistently sets goals that rally and unify team members to focus on the most critical priorities	☐ Ignores or fails to improve his/her area by only focusing on overarching priorities ☐ Sets stretch goals that people find unachievable
Planning	☐ Fails to plan or does not put plans into action ☐ Doesn't use plans to guide work or measure progress	☐ Helps others to actualize their strategies and develop specific plans for execution ☐ Establishes a process for reviewing goals and progress and initiating corrective actions	☐ Takes over for others and tells them what to do ☐ Engages in excessive planning activity (involving too much time or too much analysis)
Participation	☐ Develops plans on his/her own or without sufficient input or participation from others ☐ Accepts plans for teams or departments that are not integrated or ignores obvious interdependencies	☐ Includes a wide variety of staff in planning activities—maximizes involvement, input, and participation of others ☐ Ensures that all teams and units consider other teams' plans and priorities	☐ Includes too many people in the planning process so input creates confusion and unaggressive plans ☐ Slows action and progress by over emphasizing the need for harmony
Resource Management	☐ Fails to identify what specific resources are most needed ☐ Does not provide others with the resources they need to move forward	☐ Anticipates resource needs and timing to ensure plans can be implemented ☐ Redeploys resources as needed to optimize efficiency and effectiveness	☐ Over-resources too many activities; promotes inefficiency; allows valuable resources to go to waste ☐ Provides lavish resources without establishing accountability for results

Development Suggestions

The following section contains development suggestions for each core practice. Having completed the self-assessment, focus on suggestions that correspond to the core practices you identified as a development need or excessive use. Use these suggestions to create your own development plan, making sure to try one or two from each phase. In addition, feel free to create your own or adapt these to best meet your development needs.

Forward Thinking

Maintain a longer-term perspective when developing plans.

Don't let yesterday take up too much of today.

Will Rogers

Awaken potential:

- **Ask questions** about where the organization has been, where it is, and where it needs to go. How has it evolved over time? What factors caused this evolution? How have you considered this context in developing plans for your function?

- **Review your company's vision, mission, and core values.** How might you engage your employees and other key stakeholders in a discussion about your organization's strategic direction? Where do they identify opportunities to tweak the functional plans based on where the market is trending?

- **Mentally rehearse the steps in your business plan.** Use your imagination to visualize steps being taken. What steps need to be added? What problems can you anticipate that must be prevented? Where are likely obstacles or roadblocks? How should you prepare for these?

- **Assess how much of your time is spent on strategic thinking and planning** for your function. What is preventing you from doing more? What can be done to reallocate some of your time for doing this?

- **Bring a long-term perspective to planning.** Review Chapter 9, "Strategic Thinking," to learn about a simple tool for understanding your business context and for ways to continuously challenge and update your thinking about your business and industry.

Be particularly conscious of where strategy development shifts to translation into an action plan.

Align goals:

- **Anticipate problems you may encounter** in executing your strategy because of misalignment of internal systems, structure, style, skills, or staff. What might inhibit your success in achieving your goals? What preventive actions might be important for your high-risk situations?

- **Plan for the unexpected.** Conduct a "what if" exercise to anticipate possible issues, changes, or demands that might affect your future plans. Consider problems and pitfalls that have happened during similar projects in the past. What can you learn from those experiences? Work with others to identify specific steps that can be taken to overcome potential obstacles.

- **Check with others.** Consult your peers to discuss how they are interpreting the trends that will influence your organization, how they see the future, and the problems and challenges they anticipate will occur.

Accelerate performance:

- **Conduct formal scenario planning.** Read *Scenario Planning: Managing for the Future* by Gill Ringland (Wiley, 1998). In what ways might you apply scenario planning to your strategic planning activities? For a good illustration of how Royal Dutch/Shell developed and applied the techniques of scenario planning, read *The Art of the Long View* by Peter Schwartz (Doubleday, 1991).

- **Encourage taking risks to create more growth opportunities.** Review Chapter 13, "Innovation and Risk-Taking," for ways to create and encourage your team to try experiments. Good experiments are low risk, quick, and easy, and focused on increasing your learning about what could work. Plant a few seed ideas to key staff that they might explore further or take a chance on. Give them permission to be courageous.

- **Examine external factors** such as market environment, economic forces, technological influences, governmental/legal variables, and others to guide your thinking with a view to the future. Synthesize information about challenges, issues, and opportunities that can be used to set priorities. Identify and reach out to someone who could provide you with additional insights into your industry.

- **Assess customer satisfaction.** Conduct surveys or focus groups to gain insight from the voice of the customer and incorporate these findings into your plans. Hold a team session to discuss how your plans may need to be adapted due to this new information.

- **Become a futurist.** Periodically make time to study and think about the future. Imagine how the work of your team and your organization will play out over a longer time horizon.

- **Set aside time to discuss the future with your staff.** Find ways to encourage your team to look at problems from all possible angles and question inherent assumptions. Continue to expand their time horizon, getting them thinking further ahead.

EXCESSIVE USE

As an example, if you devote too much time to anticipatory planning, you may not be accomplishing enough tangible results. Reflect on the time and level of detail you put into planning; is it proportionate to the amount of action you take and the results you achieve?

Prioritizing

Establish clear priorities that align with broader organizational goals.

Three Rules of Work: Out of clutter, find simplicity. From discord, find harmony. In the middle of difficulty lies opportunity.

Albert Einstein

Awaken potential:

- **Complete a time study.** Track the time you spend on various activities over the next week or month. What percentage of your time was devoted to activities that have a long-term payoff? Are any critical tasks that align directly with business goals not getting their fair share of attention?

- **Learn to prioritize.** Read *First Things First* by Stephen Covey, Roger Merrill, and Rebecca Merrill (Simon & Schuster, 1994).

- **Reflect on how you spend your time.** Continually ask, "What is the best use of my time right now?"

Align goals:

- **Discuss your organization's priorities with your manager.** How might you better align your function's objectives and actions with these priorities? Identify places where he/she believes you are spending time that may not be critical at this time.

- **Develop criteria to establish and assess your function's priorities.** How might you use your long-term goals to create concrete, short-range actions that will take you in the direction you wish? How are your direct reports' priorities aligned with your function and organization?

- **Develop goals jointly with your staff** that will motivate them and optimize their capabilities. Have them create the initial drafts on their own with guidance to ensure that they are aligned with overall function goals. Use their drafts as conversation starters and a place to begin joint goal development.

- **Ensure goals and objectives are clear and feasible.** Is everyone committed to achieve the same outcomes? Are individual responsibilities clear? Make sure you have identified how and when you will measure success.

- **Incorporate goals into the performance management and incentive process.** Meet regularly to review progress. What other approaches will help you continually review goals and scheduled actions? How will you reward for the successful completion of key employee and team goals?

Accelerate performance:

- **Create SMART goals** (specific, measurable, attainable, relevant, and timely). Evaluate your current list of goals and determine the ways in which your function's goals need to be strengthened or clarified. Challenge yourself and your team members to put goals into this framework. Create tools for reinforcing this framework.

- **Plan time to work on complex tasks without interruption.** Block out your calendar to signal planning time. Return calls or answer emails before you start the tasks. Ask others not to interrupt you for a certain period of time (except in an emergency). If you are interrupted, enforce the limit you have set; find other options to address the issue (e.g., working off-site). Protect your planning time.

- **Assess both short and long-term goals weekly.** Schedule time each day to work on top priorities. Review how the previous week went and what needs to change.

- **Centralize your schedule,** and keep all your appointments, to-do lists, and work plans in one location. Publicize your calendar to your team. Encourage them to do the same. Use calendars as a time study to determine if the team is putting the right focus and energy into the right priorities.

- **Avoid procrastinating.** Delaying unpleasant tasks tends to make them even less appealing, so tackle them as soon as possible to get them off your to-do list. Start each day by tackling one from the unpleasant list.

- **Set, communicate, and enforce deadlines.** Determine the final deadline, and set milestones for each step of the project. Clearly communicate these to everyone involved. If problems arise, ask people to inform you as soon as possible, and make necessary adjustments to milestones.

- **Use backward planning.** Planning things in reverse, from the end state to the present, helps ensure you create clear goals and responsibilities. Rank key steps so you will focus on the most important items first.

EXCESSIVE USE

As an example, if you set goals that people find unachievable, you may exhaust some people and discourage others. Try to set more realistic goals by involving them in the goal-setting process.

Planning

Translate business strategy into action plans.

"Planning is bringing the future into the present so that you can do something about it now."

Alan Lakein

Awaken potential:

- **Emphasize strategic thinking.** Read *Strategic Thinking: A Four Piece Puzzle* by Bill Birnbaum (Douglas Mountain, 2004). How can you continually emphasize strategic thinking and planning for your function?

- **Translate your thoughts and ideas into clear action plans.** Talk with key stakeholders to determine how well they are able to interpret the plans you lay out. How can you communicate more effectively so others share your vision?

- **Analyze how you help others actualize their ideas.** What venues have you created to do this? How can this be strengthened?

- **Reflect on your approach to delegation.** Do you balance accountability with authority or do you hold back on the freedom others need to use their skills and knowledge to take effective action?

Align goals:

- **Build a foundation.** Read *Morrisey on Planning, a Guide to Strategic Thinking: Building your Planning Foundation* by George Morrisey (Jossey-Bass, 1995). Conduct regular, formal planning meetings. Assemble a team to establish criteria for monitoring measures, identifying gaps, and initiating corrective actions. Review goals and progress. Address discrepancies promptly.

- **Develop an implementation plan.** Outline others' responsibilities once you have agreement and clarity about strategic priorities with key stakeholders. Have them develop action plans for how to accomplish their parts and review as a team.

- **Make sure the outcomes of various action plans are clear.** Communicate what needs to be done by whom, when it should be finished, and to what degree of quality or detail. Ask others how you can most effectively communicate relevant information to them. Ensure measures of success are shared and aligned.

- **Observe individuals who manage their time wisely.** Leverage them as internal resources or mentors on this topic. Ask about their approaches and how they would prioritize some issues you face. Ask them about an instance when they missed an opportunity to have an important impact on business results. What lessons did they learn from that experience?

Accelerate performance:

- **Invest time in strategic planning.** Debrief your learnings and share your ideas with your manager.

- **Learn the "urgent versus important" concept** in Stephen Covey's *The Seven Habits of Highly Effective People* (Free Press, 1989). "Important" means a task needs to be done, while "urgent" means it must be done immediately. Knowing the difference between the two will make prioritizing easier. Review and prioritize goals in order of importance and urgency and eliminate any non-essential items.

- **Examine the issue from all sides** when developing a plan or making a key decision. Write out a list of benefits and risks for each stakeholder across a time spectrum that looks at both the present and the next two to five years.

- **Sequence individual action steps before writing out a plan.** List the steps individually on sticky notes and sequence the pieces of paper. The visual nature of this exercise can help ensure that the flow and order of events/tasks are correct. To complete the exercise, write out the whole plan in sequential order and share it with the team for review and finalization.

- **Be concrete and specific in providing direction.** It is important to be able to tell others exactly what you want from them, what kind of output or product you expect them to produce, and when you want it. Help them understand the big picture and not just their individual parts. Watch for any tendency to give only a general idea or leave a minimal email. Take individual differences into account, remembering some people will need a more explicit and detailed set of expectations before they can comfortably begin their work.

EXCESSIVE USE

As an example, if you get overly involved in planning activities, you may be too hands-on rather than empowering to others. Experiment with new behavior of having your team members develop initial planning drafts. Manage the planning process by monitoring results rather than developing plans.

Participation

Gain input on plans from key stakeholders.

*Tell me, I may listen. Teach me, I may remember.
Involve me, I will do it.*

Chinese Proverb

Awaken potential:

- **Learn about your organization's business calendar cycle** (e.g., company business planning, budgeting, performance management). What are important dates and events to keep in mind during your planning activities? How can you set aside time with your team throughout the year to engage them in planning activities?

- **Reflect on your approach to planning for your function.** Whom do you include? Is anyone missing? Are there people who don't need to participate, but just need to be informed? Check in with employees to see how they feel about their involvement in the planning process. What changes would they propose for their own involvement?

- **Determine what planning activities you can delegate.** Review the overall planning process and cycle. How can you break large tasks into manageable pieces and delegate them to those who can do them most readily? Keep in mind that delegating is different from simply assigning people a task that is already a part of their normal job requirements. When you delegate, you give someone one of your tasks but you maintain control and responsibility.

- **Evaluate how you delegate authority and accountability.** If you delegated more, could that free you up for more strategic thinking and create a more participatory environment in your function? What might you take on that would be excessive today?

Align goals:

- **Assess your function's strategic priorities.** What interdependencies are needed across systems, structure, style, staff, and skills to effectively execute these priorities? Review the core practice "Coordination" in Chapter 6 for ways to ensure your part of the organization is aligned internally as well as with peer functions across the organization.

- **Identify what functions are upstream and downstream from yours.** How do you engage those peers in planning? Do you jointly look for synergistic opportunities? Where do roles overlap? How do you handle involvement and planning participation on these topics/issues?

- **Talk with key stakeholders about your function's direction.** Ask about their strategic agendas, and look for opportunities to work together to achieve greater results. Share your plans with others who may have a stake in the outcomes. Ask how realistic your timeframes are and what obstacles may be encountered. If necessary, make modifications to reflect the input of others.

- **Develop a rhythm for your planning activities.** Set and review your strategic priorities with your direct reports and others to ensure progress is being made and interdependencies are discussed. Ensure they understand the corporate calendar and how these meetings intersect with key enterprise timelines.

Accelerate performance:

- **Stick to your delegation program.** Identify the right people for the right responsibilities. Don't always give tasks to the strongest, most experienced, or first available person. Avoid "reverse" delegation. Leverage your learnings from *Leadership and the One Minute Manager: Increasing Effectiveness through Situational Leadership* by Ken Blanchard (William Morrow, 1999) to ensure you are delegating effectively.

- **Ask team leaders to develop action plans** for their projects and share them with each other. Establish a routine process to check their progress against the action plans and reinforce accountability as a group.

- **Establish an individual follow-up schedule.** Design and implement a series of follow-up meetings to monitor individual progress and determine any need for assistance. This can help you adapt your level of involvement and the degree to which you need to be directive versus supportive.

EXCESSIVE USE

As an example, if you include too many people in planning, you may create confusion and slow progress. Involve the right people, and clarify everyone's role and responsibilities before moving forward with the planning process.

Resource Management

Anticipate needs and utilize resources effectively to optimize progress on functional goals.

"The greatest achievement of the human spirit is to live up to one's opportunities and make the most of one's resources."

Marquis de Vauvenarques

Awaken potential:

- **Analyze how your function creates value.** Read *Strategy Maps: Converting Intangible Assets into Tangible Outcomes* by Robert Kaplan and David Norton (Harvard Business Press, 2004).

- **Assess your current talent supply against work demands.** How many and what types of jobs and skills are needed to meet the performance objectives of the function? How can you make assignments that reflect staff members' strengths as well as ensure they are in roles that help address their development needs?

- **Analyze how you link planning and budgeting processes.** Do you set a number before you identify key strategic priorities? Do you overvalue the head count measure in your equation?

Align goals:

- **Identify the resources required to excel.** Determine the timing and resources needed to complete your priorities during your function's strategic planning process. What areas are critical to executing your function's strategy? Partner with human resources on your findings to ensure you have the right people in the right roles.

- **Be flexible and creative when budgeting for resources.** Look at needed resources and ask yourself if this is the most efficient, effective, and practical way to meet objectives. Are you allocating enough staff time to key priorities? Are you maximizing the potential contribution of each individual? How can you help remove some of the noise of non-essential priorities to ensure a focus on those that are vital to the organization's strategic goals?

- **Review relevant project plans when allocating resources.** Identify potential overlaps or competition for resources. Communicate openly and often with individuals and groups who own resources you need.

- **Monitor the need for resources.** Ask team members across functional areas about progress and resource requirements. If available resources are not adequate to meet plan objectives, rethink your options. How might you be flexible and creative? Bring together a cross-functional group to brainstorm how issues can be resolved.

Accelerate performance:

- **Map out the anticipated flow of projects**, including requirements for completing each phase. Estimate the amount of time participants will need and look for possible conflicts. How do your current resources align with these plans?

- **Coach project leaders to identify shared goals** and the resources needed to accomplish them. Help those leaders identify ways they can ensure each project has appropriate resources while being mindful of individual and overall team needs.

- **Be prepared to answer tough questions** when requesting resources. Be specific in communicating your needs. Create a cost/benefit analysis and timeline indicating when you will need specific resources. Hold yourself accountable for the ROI (return on investment) of your resource planning.

- **Establish checkpoints to monitor progress against goals.** Ask team leaders and members how things are going, and listen closely to both the tone and content of their replies. If you see patterns in their responses, you may want to call a meeting to clarify issues and modify plans.

- **Facilitate more cross-training in your area.** Use less important tasks as opportunities to cross-train, and help staff build strengths in weaker areas. Rotate responsibilities to balance workloads as needed.

EXCESSIVE USE

As an example, if you provide too many resources, some may go to waste.
Do more to evaluate the opportunity cost of providing additional resources,
and try to maximize your ROI.

Coach Others on Planning and Organizing

When coaching others, focus on the core practices that were identified as either a development need or excessive use in the self-assessment at the beginning of this chapter. Identify and adapt any relevant development suggestions. Additional coaching tips are provided in the following table for some adverse leadership behaviors. For more information review Chapter 4, "Coach Others."

Coaching Suggestions

	Behavior	Awaken	Align	Accelerate
Forward Thinking	*Is too short-term focused*	• Suggest reading Covey's *First Things First*. • Engage the person in contingency planning. Ask about possible issues, changes, or demands that might affect the person's priorities and plans.	• Review strategic priorities together, and ask what interdependencies exist across systems, structure, style, staff, and skills that impact effective execution of those priorities. • Suggest that the person talk to peers as well.	• Work on a three-year timeline together or assign it as homework. • Recommend developing and sharing a long-term plan with the person's team; have the team brainstorm obstacles that could occur over the next three years.
	Manages by crisis—"Fire, Ready, Aim"	• Review the person's calendar together, asking how he/she is spending time. • Ask questions about what kinds of crises tend to occur, and when/how the person gets involved. Probe for root causes of any crises that occur regularly. • Ask what the person has learned about managing by crisis, and what he/she wants to do differently.	• Brainstorm and analyze the impact on other functions when the person manages by crisis. • Encourage the person to make a public declaration about wanting to make a change and communicating what will be different (e.g., scheduling time for planning that won't be interrupted).	• Help the person imagine and create a planning rhythm (e.g., weekly team meetings on hot issues, quarterly half-day meetings on strategic plan, and one-on-one time with each of the person's direct reports). • Ask questions about current opportunities in executing the business strategy. Help the person identify some benefits of being more organized in addressing those opportunities.

Behavior		Awaken	Align	Accelerate
Prioritizing	*Confuses activity with productivity*	• Look together at how goals are being set, how activities are tied to goals, and how results are being measured. • Use a framework (e.g., the 5S or 7S models) to diagram activities and identify roadblocks or misalignments.	• Recommend empowering the team to have conversations with key stakeholders about how well their needs are being met. • Review data together, and discuss how activities are connected to results.	• Support the person in creating a scorecard with items such as increasing revenue, reducing costs, building capacity or taking less time. • Reinforce focus on the right activities by regularly updating and reviewing the scorecard.
Prioritizing	*Sets unclear goals*	• Recommend that the person survey stakeholders about the clarity of goals. • Propose reading *Five Dysfunctions of a Team* (Jossey-Bass, 2002) by Patrick Lencioni to understand the importance of goal clarity in becoming a high-performing team. • Help the person understand how to develop SMART goals for the department.	• Encourage the person to clarify his/her goals with others. • Review the person's goals and objectives, and discuss how they can be strengthened using the SMART format. • Ask for examples of how the person has aligned department objectives and actions to organizational priorities.	• Redefine goals using the SMART framework. • Institute a practice of regular discussion about goals and build this into his/her planning process. • Coach the person to make repeated references to goals at every meeting. • Brainstorm a visual symbol or mascot that could remind the person about specific goals.
Planning	*Has vague or nonexistent plans*	• Introduce the person to some people who do planning exceptionally well to learn what they are doing. • Assign the person to do an audit of his/her planning process. Compare this to what the organization is doing.	• Discuss interdependencies, where the planning process (or lack thereof) impacts other functions. • Coach the person to facilitate a session with his/her group to build and commit to a planning process.	• Ask the person to investigate project management tools (e.g., Gantt charts) that could be implemented. • Approve training in project management. Encourage the person to select people with that competence.

	Behavior	Awaken	Align	Accelerate
Planning	*Doesn't adapt plans to changing conditions*	• Collect and analyze data about progress; determine whether the person is hitting key milestones. • Ask the person to identify what obstacles are occurring, what is interfering with execution. • Help the person identify possible ways to get people to recommit to achieving results.	• Encourage the person to engage with direct reports regarding what analysis and action is needed to overcome impediments to plans. • Remind the person that leaders must set clarity for decision-making authority and limits of analysis (e.g., use the 80/20 rule to decide when to act).	• Coach the person to (1) institute a planning discipline, (2) establish a norm of action orientation, and (3) drive the discipline of planning and ongoing learning followed by adjustment. • Encourage the person to create a culture of learning from mistakes.
Participation	*Plans in a vacuum*	• Review any employee engagement data that might be relevant. • Encourage the person to conduct discovery interviews to identify unintended negative consequences of failing to create a line of sight. • Show the downside of failing to capture input from others; if people are discouraged, they may leave the team—and that could throw plans off target.	• Suggest that the person partner with others to facilitate a planning process and engage more people in the process. • Discuss how the person builds alignment with goals. • Ask the person for ideas about getting staff more involved in planning. Reinforce why employee involvement, input, and participation are important for buy-in and development.	• Establish some structure around the planning process. • Use responsibility charting to look at who needs to be responsible, accountable, consulted with, or informed—and how. • Have the person identify two or three things to do over the next six months to ensure plans are effectively integrated in his/her teams and work unit.
	Operates in silos	• Reflect together on possible interdependencies and who can affect or is affected by the group's plans, both upstream and downstream. Assess gaps, and decide whether to include them in the planning process or not. • Get feedback from people in other silos.	• Suggest the team connect with others to learn what's happening in other areas; discuss dilemmas and identify priorities. • Propose that the person invite leaders in other areas to participate in his/her planning process.	• Ask the person to describe how he/she talks about the area's strategic direction. Point out connections to other areas. • Work together to establish cross-silo priorities and planning processes. Ensure cross-functionality is built into the planning process at all levels.

Behavior		Awaken	Align	Accelerate
Resource Management	*Fails to identify resource needs*	• Ask what resources the person needs to be effective. • Help the person understand that resource planning is broader than workforce planning—it also includes things like IT and capital budget planning.	• Suggest that the person work with his/her team to conduct a SWOT or analyze supply vs. demand factors and gaps related to the business plan. • Create a plan to close the gaps.	• Propose a review of current resources against the business plan. • Build an assessment process into the annual planning process. • Check regularly to see what progress has been made.
	Under-resources priorities	• Discuss the person's role in helping the team and the overall operation run smoothly. • Ask where people are currently spending their time and how resources are being used against priorities. • Ask how the person identifies resources the team needs, how assignments are made, and how the person considers other teams' plans and priorities.	• Engage the person in a discussion about your priorities. Explore how he/she sets priorities, and how those are aligned with your priorities. • Recommend that the person read Chapter 6, "Creating Alignment," for some suggestions about creating more alignment around priorities and sharing resources.	• Suggest that the person read *Leadership and the One Minute Manager: Increasing Effectiveness through Situational Leadership* by Ken Blanchard. • Ask the person to discuss the readiness of his/her staff to take on greater challenges and how to delegate work to draw upon the strengths of staff members.

Tips for Coaching in a Global Environment

Planning and Organizing may be practiced or expressed differently within other cultures. This might impact how you approach coaching. Try to keep an open mind, avoid generalizations, and continue gathering data as you gain experience with another culture. Consider these suggestions:

Forward Thinking: Recognize that people from other cultures may view "time" differently from you. Their approach to advance planning or setting goals and milestones may be much looser than your own. Sometimes their approaches may be more structured. Learn about their circumstances and check your assumptions before offering suggestions.

Prioritizing: People in some cultures view goals as commitments and don't like to set stretch goals they might have trouble achieving. Explain the benefits of stretch goals (e.g., higher results are achieved even when the goals aren't met) and provide lots of personal encouragement. When leaders in some cultures have difficulty saying no to requests, their workloads may become unmanageable. You may need to help them set priorities—as well as coach them on how to decline requests or delegate tasks they don't need to perform themselves.

Planning: Cultures (as well as companies) differ in the extent to which they use top-down versus bottom-up planning and goal-setting. These differences can impact the annual budgeting process, planning assignments, and the level of involvement participants expect. You may find other differences in planning such as the following:

- Standard planning protocols in multinational organizations may be unfamiliar to some cultures. People may need more explicit and regular communication to establish agreed-upon goals and then to confirm those commitments.

- Some cultures may have a more disciplined and rigorous approach to planning than your own. If so, you may need to help people develop more flexibility in their approaches to contingency planning.

- Some cultures are more laid back than others. People from such cultures may not have much experience with structured planning and organizing. Simple things you take for granted (e.g., creating a to-do list or meeting agenda) may be unfamiliar to some. Find out the person's level of comfort and expertise with structured planning; help him/her learn and develop additional skills step by step.

Participation: Teamwork may operate much more naturally, more seamlessly, in other cultures—especially in cultures with a group rather than individual orientation. Participation in planning may not have to be invited or scheduled in such cultures—it may already be happening naturally. When leaders or people on their teams are working in a non-native language, the leader may need to over-communicate in both languages when doing planning that involves others.

Resource Management: The availability of key resources will also impact planning and organizing. Some countries lack sophisticated infrastructure, so work may be organized and done differently from the way it is done in your own country. Differences in the level of mechanization and transportation logistics may need to be factored into the planning process—as well as different holidays. Keep these differences in mind as you are coaching people and brainstorming alternatives. Check your assumptions before offering suggestions.

A Case Study in Planning and Organizing

Planful, organized leaders make time to think and plan for the long term. They anticipate and think ahead. They are clear about priorities and tie activities to business goals, then translate ideas into concrete action plans. The best leaders involve others and develop plans that integrate and align with the organization's strategy. In fact, they ensure that others have the plans and resources they need to get things done.

As you read about Jane's situation, reflect on what you've learned about Planning and Organizing in this chapter and consider how you would help Jane demonstrate greater skill in Planning and Organizing and be successful in her leadership role.

Fighting Fires

Jane Smith was respected in her organization for her institutional knowledge, insights, and ability to get things done. People appreciated her ability to create a collegial workforce, manage projects, and lead with an informal style. When the functional leadership role in her department became vacant, Jane's manager Tom promoted her because of her past experience, attention to detail, and strong performance as a project manager. The new role was a stretch for her, because she now had accountability for leading and managing a function with five direct reports and eighty associates.

After six months in the new role, Jane was struggling to keep up with the volume and was working harder than ever. In her six-month performance review, Tom expressed concern about how her transition was going—especially in setting goals, prioritizing projects, and completing tasks with her team in a timely manner. He also shared that some people had complained that she wasn't showing up for meetings or returning phone calls. Jane acknowledged that she had little time for planning, as she was overwhelmed with the number of meetings and emails, volume of work, and daily demands on her time. She told Tom that she prioritized her work activities based upon deadlines and the "hottest fire" of the day. He replied, "This style of prioritization may be creating an impression for others that you procrastinate, operate in the moment and don't think or plan ahead."

In the same discussion, Tom pointed out the need to reduce overhead costs and improve service quality. He challenged Jane to be more proactive in demonstrating ROI for her function. He asked her to submit a personal plan in two weeks for how she could better manage her time and priorities. Tom also emphasized the need for her to develop a strategic plan for her function that would include overall direction-setting, prioritization of important opportunities, and identification of key performance indicators that could influence stakeholders and demonstrate her function's value.

Jane found that she needed to develop skills in Planning and Organizing more than ever in order to:

- Increase credibility and convey confidence in her own leadership as well as her team's.

- Effectively manage competing demands for her time.

- Demonstrate the difference between important and urgent tasks to key stakeholders.

- Delegate authority and responsibility to her direct reports instead of doing the work herself.

- Engage her leadership team in planning the goals and activities to be accomplished.

- Articulate to key stakeholders within the organization how her function could add value.

Jane's Sample Development Plan

Following is a sample development plan for Jane Smith. Research on leadership development has shown that leaders learn through experience and that this learning is optimized through the use of an individual development plan that includes new experiences as well as introduces the leader to new conversations and tools. The suggestions included in the previous sections may stimulate your thinking about other possibilities that Jane might pursue.

LEADERSHIP DEVELOPMENT PLAN FOR JANE SMITH
DEVELOPMENT GOAL
Goal: To strengthen my Planning and Organizing skills.
Desired Outcomes—results I want to see from developing this skill
Self: Increase credibility and effectively manage competing demands on my time.
Team: Delegate authority and responsibility instead of doing the work myself or getting mired in detail.
Organization: Engage staff in planning activities and identify the strategic direction for the function.
Self-Understanding—strengths that I can build on and development needs I can address
Strengths: Knowledge of the organization; ability to make connections at multiple levels; project management skills; approachable style.
Development Needs: Setting goals, prioritizing projects, delegating work to others, completing tasks in a timely manner, and keeping up with daily demands on my time without getting stressed.

LEADERSHIP DEVELOPMENT PLAN FOR JANE SMITH

Business Context—challenges in my business environment that require this skill

Reduce overhead costs, improve service quality, be more proactive, and demonstrate value.

DEVELOPMENT ACTIONS

AWAKEN

- Read Stephen Covey's *First Things First.*
- Reflect on where my time is going by analyzing my activities over the past month. Summarize key findings.
- Prepare a personal plan for managing time and priorities; submit to Tom as requested.
- Identify what will be needed to prepare a strategic plan for my function.

ALIGN

- Review development plan with staff and other key stakeholders. Ask for input.
- Communicate to staff the changes I am implementing to get organized, including DO NOT DISTURB time on Mondays, Wednesdays, and Fridays from 7:30 to 9:00 am. This will be time to organize myself, plan my response to commitments, delegate tasks to others, etc.

ACCELERATE

- Talk with my assistant about the steps she can take to be a more effective gatekeeper.
- Schedule weekly one-on-ones with reports. Change open-door policy and save information for weekly meetings.
- Partner with human resources to develop strategic planning agenda and session. Share agenda with my manager.
- Educate direct reports on planning process and SWOT analysis. Discuss how feedback would be used.
- Hold a strategic planning offsite involving a wide variety of stakeholders.
- Discuss with the team a process for engaging and communicating the strategic plan with key stakeholders. Brainstorm ways to ensure the strategic plan is being executed and progress assessed.

DEVELOPMENT SUCCESS FACTORS

Timeline: Within the next six months

Support Needed:

- Coaching and ongoing feedback from my manager on strategic planning, setting priorities, and managing time.
- Feedback from direct reports and staff on changes being implemented to get more organized.
- Partnership with human resources to design and facilitate strategic planning session.

Indicators of Success:

- Personally, feel less stressed and not overwhelmed with daily demands on my time. Have improved work/life balance.

- Ongoing feedback from manager, staff, and stakeholders indicates improved priority-setting and time management.

- Strategic plan for function is developed, communicated, and executed.

- Feedback from key stakeholders indicates improved understanding of the value of our function.

An Example of Coaching for Planning and Organizing

Jane Smith's goal was to strengthen her skills in Planning and Organizing. Here are some steps Jane's manager could take using the Awaken, Align, Accelerate framework to coach Jane in this area:

AWAKEN	**Increase INSIGHT**	Help Jane understand her own tendencies and preferences (e.g., does she prefer to work alone or involve others? Is she more spontaneous or planful?). Discuss the implications of these preferences, and how they might be viewed by others. Encourage Jane to complete a 360-degree feedback survey. Look together for any gaps in her perceptions and help her understand the impact and implications of her behavior on others.
	MOTIVATE change	Focus on options and choices. Identify what Jane is motivated to change. Help her reflect on what has led to successful project management in the past. Explore the consequences of not making any changes; identify consequences for her personally as well as her projects.
ALIGN	**PLAN goals**	Review Jane's proposal for how she will manage her time and priorities. Identify what Jane could change to improve her approach. Work together to construct a leadership development plan similar to the sample provided in this chapter.
	ALIGN expectations	Discuss organizational alignment with Jane, highlighting your strategic direction and priorities. Focus on observing Jane in action to see how she makes commitments and delegates work to others (or not). Provide immediate feedback to reinforce progress or help her see opportunities where she could have been more effective.

ACCELERATE	**CREATE teachable moments**	Review the strategic planning agenda with Jane, and provide your insights. Discuss Responsibility Charting with Jane, identifying where this could help her and others on her team. Conduct role-plays to help Jane practice telling her strategic story in a compelling way. Introduce Jane to Bill Todd, who might be a good mentor in this area.
	TRACK progress	Track Jane's progress toward her goals. Evaluate increased effectiveness, and measure progress toward outcomes and results. Discuss what kinds of changes will be visible to others. Encourage her to invite additional feedback, and ask people to support the changes they see. Acknowledge and celebrate her efforts.

Results: Measuring Impact

Jane Smith worked through her development plan in parallel with the other plans that Tom had requested. She found some activities were more helpful than others and slowly made progress in becoming more organized. Her new Planning and Organizing skills allowed Jane to:

- Better manage the competing demands on her time.

- Improve her work/life balance.

- Delegate authority and responsibility to direct reports instead of doing the work herself.

- Develop and implement a strategic plan for her function.

- Demonstrate the value of her function to key stakeholders.

17

Managing Execution

Execution-focused leaders know how to get things done in a complex organization. They establish clear goals and set aggressive timelines for meeting objectives. They drive organizational performance by helping others clarify and understand their roles, responsibilities, and accountabilities. They delegate leadership responsibility to others to satisfy customers' needs, support strategy, and ensure successful achievement of results. They intervene when necessary, remove obstacles, follow-up, and follow through.

Factor	Competency	Core Practice
Leading People	Planning and Organizing	Organization Know-how
Thinking and Deciding	Managing Execution	Accountabiltity
Achieving		Delegation
Relating to People		Goal Orientation
Managing Work		Follow Through
Managing Self		

Does your culture thrive on accountability? Or does great strategy go nowhere because execution stalls? An organization's ability to execute strategy is often the difference between superior performance and floundering or inconsistent results.

Managing Execution, or the art of getting things done in complex organizations, is important for leaders at all levels, from the CEO to front-line supervisors. Everyone plays a role, but leaders at more senior levels are ultimately accountable for what's achieved—or not. Quickly and effectively translating strategy into results is especially critical today with the fast pace of change and increasing customer demands and expectations. To stay competitive and profitable, organizations must be both nimble and sophisticated in how they deliver their products and services to the market. This is where the rubber hits the road. Compelling strategies are nothing but missed opportunities without disciplined execution, and this makes all the difference between success and failure. Great leadership today requires accountability; a passion for doing things right the first time; and solid, practical judgment about how to get things done.

Effectiveness at any level is dependent on a leader's ability to clearly communicate a strong accountability message and provide clarity without being overly prescriptive about how results are achieved. More senior leaders need to ensure clarity of roles and responsibilities down two levels or more within their functions and make the linkages to function and business strategy clear to employees. It is important to identify the most critical business indicators that drive performance and ensure that the right strategy, people, and systems are in place and aligned to create a culture of execution. By driving clarity in their own roles, effective leaders work to create alignment across various functional priorities to support the overall business strategy. While the ability to manage execution is important for all leaders, the most effective behaviors vary by level, as illustrated in the following table.

How Leaders at Different Levels Manage Execution

	Managers	Function Leaders	Senior Executives
Organization Know-How	Helps team members understand and appreciate the organization's way of doing things.	Knows how to get things done in a complex organization.	Helps others navigate a complex organization to accomplish results.
Accountability	Holds team members accountable for achieving performance goals.	Establishes the performance required from others to achieve desired function outcomes.	Holds the leadership team accountable for business performance on a regular basis.
Delegation	Delegates and assigns work to others in an insightful manner.	Values getting things done through others.	Directs short-term actions in a manner that supports longer-term strategy.
Goal Orientation	Monitors progress towards goals and follows up as needed.	Ensures progress is being made towards the right goals.	Focuses others on achieving goals that satisfy external stakeholders.
Follow Through	Follows through on promises and commitments.	Drives things to closure by following up and following through.	Ensures accountability systems and processes exist to sustain consistent execution.

MANAGING EXECUTION

Self-Assessment

To evaluate your effectiveness in Managing Execution, check all boxes below that represent current behavior or performance. Look for patterns: Which core practices represent a development need, a strength, or an excessive use? Recognize that you might have some blind spots. Invite your boss or colleagues to indicate what they have observed in your behavior. Use this assessment to help identify development suggestions that are most relevant to you.

	Development Need	Strength	Excessive Use
Organization Know-How	☐ Doesn't know how to leverage the people and resources of the organization ☐ Is confused by the complexity of the organization so actions are stalled or ineffective	☐ Expertly knows how to get things done in a complex organization ☐ Anticipates and removes organizational barriers that impede success	☐ Taxes the organization and takes on too much; cannot say "no" ☐ Appears overly political in maneuvering execution and influencing results
Accountability	☐ Is vague in communicating about roles, responsibilities, and accountabilities for accomplishing objectives ☐ Doesn't take personal accountability for short-term performance	☐ Helps other leaders understand and expand their roles, responsibilities, and accountabilities for driving performance ☐ Drives short-term actions in support of the business strategy and profitability	☐ Is overly prescriptive about responsibilities and accountabilities ☐ Refuses to deviate from planned strategy; misses opportunities to enhance performance
Delegation	☐ Relies too much on own effort to get things done; unable to fully let go of the need to handle tasks alone ☐ Cannot focus on top priorities because effort is spread too thin	☐ Consistently relies on others to achieve results ☐ Provides others the support they need to act independently	☐ Overrelies on others without providing sufficient direction or guidance ☐ Delegates critical tasks that should be retained
Goal Orientation	☐ Rarely or inadequately measures or monitors progress toward goals ☐ Doesn't model or promote goal-directed behavior; consistently misses milestones	☐ Establishes good processes and systems to monitor performance ☐ Establishes clear goals and actively anticipates issues to ensure progress	☐ Creates complex monitoring processes requiring too much effort ☐ Intervenes too frequently; tends to disempower others
Follow-Through	☐ Doesn't close consistently; fails to complete things due to obstacles, lack of follow-through, or not following up ☐ Gravitates to the next new idea and neglects current projects that may be off-track	☐ Ensures quality by follow-up and following through ☐ Gives both new and existing projects appropriate effort and attention	☐ Drives for closure prematurely; compromises quality of results ☐ Manages performance in a manner that only supports short-term results; intervenes too often or unnecessarily

Development Suggestions

The following section contains development suggestions for each core practice. Having completed the self-assessment, focus on suggestions that correspond to the core practices you identified as a development need or excessive use. Use these suggestions to create your own development plan, making sure to try one or two from each phase. In addition, feel free to create your own or adapt these to best meet your development needs.

Organization Know-How

Know how to get things done in a complex organization.

> *If you have knowledge,*
> *let others light their candles with it.*
>
> Margaret Fuller

Awaken potential:

- **Learn about excellent execution.** Read *Execution: The Discipline of Getting Things Done* by Larry Bossidy and Ram Charan (Crown Business, 2002), especially the first and third chapters. Identify gaps in your organization's people, strategy, and operations processes, and the impact on execution. What behaviors do you need to develop?

- **Analyze your successes and failures.** Reflect on your successes and areas where you failed to meet or exceed business objectives for the previous year. For successes, identify the top three factors that contributed to success. In the cases where expectations were not met, what barriers did you encounter and how could you have handled those better? What activities should you have said "no" to? As you apply these insights to your current activities, consider whether people are doing anything that is not high priority in achieving goals.

- **Think about how you respond when faced with complexity.** Do you narrow your focus or think big picture? Get inspired or become overwhelmed? Seeking feedback from several key stakeholders may help provide you with outside perception of how well you handle complexity as well.

- **Inventory the resources at your disposal.** Are you utilizing all known resources? Engaging team members and getting work done through others? The "Resource Management" core practice in Chapter 15 will provide you with additional ideas for ways in which you can identify resources and options outside your own area for accomplishing your goals.

Align goals:

- **Recognize your political environment.** Identify areas where organizational politics may hamper your team's ability to achieve goals. Seek counsel from those who know key players to strategize approaches to circumventing politics.

- **Find a successful role model or mentor.** Identify someone in the organization who consistently surpasses expectations and gets things accomplished. Become a keen observer of how he/she overcomes obstacles and responds to setbacks. Ask that person to share what works and see what you can apply to your situation.

Accelerate performance:

- **Balance your focus.** Recognize that staying focused on long-term strategy while attending to operational issues is required to reach desired outcomes. What situations cause you to tighten your focus on "trees" at the expense of seeing the "forest"? Identify specific areas in which you wish to practice this and then make it known to others, creating a team of supporters who can help hold you accountable.

- **Plan to navigate complexity.** Have a candid conversation with your manager about your business objectives. Identify areas where more concerted planning or effort is required to address complexities and ask your manager for ideas on how to navigate or overcome these. Together create a plan to work through the issues identified.

- **Identify obstacles.** Make a list of the people, processes, and structures that make achievement of your objectives difficult. Prioritize the top three to four and make an action plan for how to address them.

- **Enlist others to remove barriers.** Engage your team of direct reports in a solution-oriented discussion of key obstacles to achieving business objectives. Create a clear action plan at the end of the meeting and ensure each direct report has a meaningful action related to driving business results.

- **Apply learning from every week's performance.** At the end of each week, reflect on your progress toward your business objectives at a high level. Identify the key conversations and actions you need to take the next week to keep the organization focused and moving forward. Schedule time on your calendar for those actions. Reflect on how you did at the end of the week and repeat.

EXCESSIVE USE

As an example, if you take on too much yourself, this may hamper your ability to deliver. Do you know when to say "no" and when to stretch yourself? Ask colleagues for feedback.

Establish the performance required from others to achieve desired function outcomes.

> *It is not only what we do, but also what we do not do, for which we are accountable.*

Molière

Awaken potential:

- **Recognize the value of clarity.** Reflect on a situation where you were unclear about what was expected of you, or where your role was ambiguous. How did this impact your motivation? Your performance? What did you need to be successful?

- **Seek feedback** on the clarity of your communications. Ask your manager and colleagues whether you are direct and upfront or too indirect. How does your style impact others' clarity about their responsibilities? What do they believe you could do to improve this?

Align goals:

- **Get feedback on execution.** Ask colleagues and superiors for feedback about how well your people execute in the organization. Identify areas where more clarity is required or where your people can expand their impact. Discuss these areas with direct reports.

- **Conduct a talent review of your people** to identify those with the potential to expand the breadth of their roles and responsibilities. Identify specific areas where people can take on more, and discuss their willingness to do so.

- **Provide strategic context.** Structure one-on-one meetings with direct reports to include a review of long-term strategic goals which will provide context for monthly operational updates. Set an expectation for direct reports to articulate how their requests, projects, or initiatives support the business strategy or improve profitability.

- **Link short-term actions to long-term goals.** In developing new business strategies, explicitly link short-term actions to strategies and communicate the linkages consistently. Reinforce communication about those linkages whenever results are reviewed with your team and key stakeholders. When making tradeoffs between competing interests, clearly articulate the rationale behind decisions within the context of the business strategy.

- **Coach for big-picture thinking.** Ask direct reports to articulate the business strategy and key outcomes then have them talk about how the work they are doing will help achieve the strategy. The fluency and accuracy of their descriptions will serve as feedback about their line of sight, and how well they understand their roles.

Accelerate performance:

- **Learn about creating metrics.** Read *The Balanced Scorecard: Translating Strategy into Action* by Robert Kaplan and David Norton (Harvard Business Press, 1996). Create a Balanced Scorecard with your team to link strategy and operations. Align your team's Balanced Scorecard with your manager's. Review critical measures with your team on a regular basis.

- **Conduct responsibility charting** to clarify roles and responsibilities. With your team identify the most critical actions, decisions, or activities you need to accomplish. Then discuss and clarify who is Responsible for the activity, who can Approve the activity or decision, who must be Consulted or provide support, and who must be kept Informed (this technique is referred to as "RACI").

- **Assign work to employees based on their skills and abilities.** Use your talent review to identify and generate potential opportunities for staff members. Challenge associates to take the initiative to get involved with projects that expand their skills and experiences. Provide encouragement and support for both learning and progress.

- **Talk about results and outcomes** in concrete terms with your staff and tie them to the business strategy. Review progress quarterly. Provide specific, reinforcing feedback and recognition to direct reports when their actions have a direct, positive impact on business objectives.

- **Learn how to communicate a strong accountability message.** For example, articulate the positive as well as negative consequences of meeting commitments; act swiftly to reward or correct performance.

EXCESSIVE USE

As an example, if you tend to be overly prescriptive, ask your direct reports to articulate their understanding of their roles, responsibilities, and accountabilities. Listen; don't interrupt to clarify. Discuss areas of alignment and identify gaps in expectations. Provide clear examples to support how you see their roles or responsibilities differently. Focus on outcomes rather than process.

Value getting things done through others.

> *"Never tell people how to do things. Tell them what to do and they will surprise you with their ingenuity."*

General George S. Patton, Jr.

Awaken potential:

- **Determine why you do or do not delegate.** Reflect on the kinds of tasks and activities you gravitate toward. Now, consider your role and identify the highest priority areas of focus. Where is there alignment? Misalignment? Analyze whether there are some high-value activities you never seem to have enough time for. What is the potential benefit to the business of your spending more time in these activities?

- **Reflect on how you delegate.** Review a situation where you provided direction to others on a specific project. How did you assess whether your expectations were clear? What could you have done differently to further clarify your expectations?

- **Participate in a multi-rater feedback process** to determine your strengths and challenges in effectively delegating and getting results through others. What themes emerge from this process?

- **Consider how you like to be delegated to**—how much direction do you require? What barriers are there to seeking further clarification? How have your preferences and assumptions shaped your approach to delegating to direct reports?

Align goals:

- **Articulate your leadership role clearly for your team.** What do you see as your critical areas of focus? Where will you be more involved? Less involved? What decisions require your input? By publicizing this, you are not only identifying specific priorities and helping others to know what is most critical, but also giving your team "nagging rights" when you overstep your boundaries.

- **Make goals compelling** for others by establishing their relevance to their individual efforts. Translate the business goals into implications for the specific roles and responsibilities of direct reports.

- **Create ownership.** Conduct a team session to identify key areas of responsibility integral to executing the business strategy. Come to agreement on who owns what and why. Create a scorecard to track progress monthly.

17

MANAGING EXECUTION

Accelerate performance:

- **Provide big-picture context.** Help others structure their work by sharing your overall goals and priorities. By identifying issues such as timeliness, quality, customer buy-in, or cost-effectiveness as primary considerations, you can help others make informed decisions about their own work and ensure they are aligned with desired results.

- **Model good delegation.** Identify tasks or responsibilities that you failed to divest from previous roles. If there is no strategic reason to retain them, identify who else you trust to take these on and create a delegation plan.

- **Learn to develop people.** Review the "Feedback" core practice in Chapter 8 for ways you can enhance the capability and capacity of team members to step up to additional, more challenging assignments.

- **Provide authority with responsibility.** When delegating work, sit down with the employee and ask for his/her approach to the project. Ask, "What else can I tell you?" or say, "Tell me what you understand your part in this to be." Use this opportunity to reinforce that the person has the capability and authority to manage the project. Focus on communicating the "why" before the "what."

- **Coach for independence.** Focus on removing barriers to others' work (if they want your help with that) vs. doing the work yourself. Help others think through their approaches, if necessary. Ask questions such as, "How might you approach this problem? What obstacles have you considered?" Provide suggestions to facilitate their learning vs. giving them the solution.

EXCESSIVE USE

As an example, if you over rely on others without providing sufficient guidance, make a habit of asking, "How can I best support you to be successful? What do you need from me?" When delegating work, proactively reach out and ask, "How is XYZ going? What obstacles are you facing? What successes have you had?"—even if they are not coming to you with clarifying questions.

Goal Orientation

Ensure progress is being made toward the right goals.

*"Slaying the dragon of delay is no sport
for the short-winded."*

Sandra Day O'Connor

Awaken potential:

- **Determine how you monitor now.** Conduct a calendar review for the last month. Identify the percentage of your time spent measuring or reviewing progress toward goals. What would be the impact of more time spent in these activities?

- **Learn from experience.** Try to remember a time when you intuitively knew that a project was off track. How could you or others have done a better job of measuring progress and keeping the project moving forward? Where can you apply these insights to a current project?

- **Recognize what prevents you from monitoring effectively.** Identify your personal barriers to measuring and monitoring performance. Are there skills or preferences that support or work against your effectiveness in overseeing the results of others?

- **Identify how active participation can motivate.** Consider how you like your performance to be measured and monitored. What does your manager do (or not do) to keep you motivated and inspired? What would people on your team say about you?

Align goals:

- **Create a dashboard.** Develop a simple yet powerful panel of key indicators and review them regularly with your team. MDA's Performance Dashboard is included in the Appendix as an example.

- **Clarify expectations.** Meet with each direct report and set clear expectations about what kinds of performance data you need to see and when. Hold them accountable for meeting those expectations.

- **Agree on "nagging rights" with your team.** How will members hold each other accountable? What venues or processes will you create to do so?

- **Align your assumptions with others.** List some important assumptions about quality, speed, and innovation that guide your work. Discuss and align these with the assumptions and expectations of your manager and those of your team.

- **Leverage organization systems.** Identify the key measurement tools and monitoring systems your organization uses to track progress toward business objectives. How can you leverage these to provide better tracking data?

Accelerate performance:

- **Set high standards.** Describe your organization's value promise to its customers. Evaluate your group's performance. Share positive customer feedback to reinforce the importance of meeting high standards. Balancing challenge and realism is important to setting effective goals—motivating your team to push themselves out of their comfort zones, but not to get discouraged.

- **Identify performance milestones.** Looking ahead on your calendar, identify key dates in the business cycle when you will assess progress toward goals. Work backward to identify the points in between where you will need to check progress and make adjustments if needed. Create a review process by which to evaluate.

- **Check early and often.** Add a standing agenda item to one-on-one meetings with your direct reports to identify their progress toward annual goals and strategize moving forward to overcome setbacks. Don't let day-to-day operational concerns overtake this agenda item! Do MBWA (management by walking around) on a weekly basis; talk to people about what's happening to head things off early.

- **Preempt problems.** Tell others that you want them to inform you about problems before a major crisis erupts. Don't "shoot the messenger" (i.e., punish people who bring you bad news). Instead, thank them for spotting the problem and express appreciation for their courage in speaking up. Encourage them to come up with at least one solution. Recognize those who are proactive in this regard.

- **Provide timely feedback** when results don't measure up to expectations. Coach your managers to address performance issues swiftly and support them when needed. Use a method such as DESC (describe, effect, solution, consequence) to give feedback in order to minimize defensiveness.

- **Find a mentor.** Identify someone in the organization who has good foresight and is proactive in intervening to keep execution on track. Ask that person to coach you in this area. Review with him/her some upcoming situations in which you anticipate challenges to help determine alternative approaches.

EXCESSIVE USE

As an example, if you create an overly complex monitoring process, people may stop inputting data if they decide that it requires too much effort. If that happens, you won't be able to trust the information. Ask for ideas about how you can simplify your current monitoring process.

Drive things to closure by following up and following through.

Those who are blessed with the most talent don't necessarily outperform everyone else. It's the people with follow-through who excel.

Mary Kay Ash

Awaken potential:

- **Learn from surprises.** Think about a situation where you were "blindsided" by an obstacle or setback at work. Identify what questions you could have asked early in the process to foresee the danger ahead.

- **Evaluate your follow-through.** On a scale of one to ten, assess your personal discipline in closing the loop with others. Why do you give yourself that rating? What would you need to do differently to increase your score? What prevents you from demonstrating those behaviors?

- **Recognize what distracts you.** If you are one who is strongly drawn toward the new and exciting, you may be neglecting more routine, but important follow-up tasks. What impact is this preference having on results?

- **Understand your natural preferences.** Take the *Myers-Briggs Type Indicator (MBTI®)* instrument and review your preferences along the Judging/Perceiving continuum as they relate to needs for clarity and closure.

- **Ask for feedback** about how well you follow up and close the loop. Do you involve yourself too much? Not enough? Solicit others' ideas for how you could improve.

Align goals:

- **Plan time for follow-up.** Review your calendar for a typical week and identify the best times of the day and week for dedicated follow-up and follow-through activities. Protect this time on your calendar.

- **Support others' follow-up.** Ask direct reports what actions you can do to support them in meeting their goals. Follow up immediately to demonstrate your commitment to helping them be successful.

- **Seek mentoring** from a highly effective executive in this area. Probe into how this leader manages time and prioritizes what is most important each day.

Accelerate performance:

- **Focus on weekly results.** At the start of each week, make a list of actions required to bring closure in important areas. Set specific goals for what you or your team will accomplish. Refer to this list throughout the week to keep you focused on attending to these areas.

- **Finish what you start.** Make a list of open items on your desk including what is needed for completion. Review the list and build a plan for completing your tasks.

- **Document your commitments.** Carry a journal with you throughout your day and make note of promises you make to others to support their work and areas where you need to follow up. Review and act on these items weekly.

- **Recap action steps from important meetings** and send to attendees, or assign this task to someone. Set a positive example by ensuring your action items are completed in a timely manner.

- **Start meetings with unfinished business.** Review previous meeting recaps for action items at the start of meetings. Identify actions taken, items that remain unaddressed, and ones that are no longer relevant.

- **Identify an accountability partner** in your community to hold you accountable for your intentions to improve your follow-up. Many leaders find an "accountability group" rewarding, as there are colleagues holding you accountable for results who don't have emotional ties to the goals you need to achieve.

EXCESSIVE USE

As an example, if you drive for closure prematurely, you may compromise the quality of results. Conduct an after-action review after completing important projects to evaluate what went well and what could have been done differently.
Apply the lessons you learn to your ongoing projects.

Coach Others on Managing Execution

When coaching others, focus on the core practices that were identified as either a development need or excessive use in the self-assessment at the beginning of this chapter. Identify and adapt any relevant development suggestions. Additional coaching tips are provided in the following table for some adverse leadership behaviors. For more information review Chapter 4, "Coach Others."

Coaching Suggestions

Behavior		Awaken	Align	Accelerate
Organization Know-How	*Goes it alone*	• Discuss how full the person's plate is and his/her limits. What price is the person paying for taking on too much work or doing it alone? • Share your observations of a time you saw the person take charge of a project at the expense of his/her well-being or another priority. What could have been done differently?	• Recommend reaching out to several peers to better understand their goals and priorities. • Collaborate to prepare an "influence map" to identify key stakeholders. Who else might the person involve in the future?	• Propose engaging in joint planning with peers; identify opportunities to support each other. Also ask what support you could provide. • Use a personal gauge to determine how full the person's plate is. Ask where new assignments or upcoming tasks may fall or how they may affect the quality of his/her work.
	Underestimates complexity	• What are the person's checks and balances for understanding the facts and dynamics of new initiatives or projects? How does the person regularly gather others' insight? • Debrief a recent project where the person underestimated the complexity. What were the consequences? What opportunities were missed?	• Identify people who are effective at working the system to get things done. Encourage the person to learn about their approaches. • Help the person create a "cabinet" of key advisors with whom to review ideas or decisions. Stress the importance of being vulnerable and testing ideas even when they aren't perfect.	• Diagram what might be happening behind the scenes. Talk about the organizational dynamics you see from your perspective. • Make it a point to incorporate regular discussions on organizational dynamics in your one-on-one meetings.
Accountability	*Sets accountability vaguely*	• Engage the person in a conversation about business strategy. Ask the person to talk about several recent decisions he/she made and explain how the course of action supported the strategy. • Have the person use an accountability matrix to map who is accountable for what on the team.	• Recommend that the person conduct role clarification discussions with direct reports to identify areas of agreement and disagreement around key areas of responsibility. • During that meeting, review the person's own team accountability matrix. How aligned is the team with the person's allocation? What needs to change?	• Have a "skip level" meeting with the person's reports to find out how clear they are about their roles and responsibilities. Share feedback and identify actions to drive clarity. • Coach the person on communicating clear expectations. Ask for recaps of important meetings and conversations.

17

MANAGING EXECUTION

349

Behavior		Awaken	Align	Accelerate
Accountability	*Focuses too heavily on short-term performance*	• What causes the person to focus on the short term? Ask what you do that inadvertently reinforces this behavior. • Identify actions and behaviors necessary to ensure long-term performance. Compare current performance and assess the gap.	• Together examine current incentives and the performance management system. How are they are tied to long-term performance? • Create a task team for the person to co-lead which works to tie incentives to growth over a longer time frame, (e.g., two years).	• Establish an expectation for performing longer-term behaviors. Help the person assess the team against those expectations as well. Create appropriate intervals to discuss together. • Challenge the person when you see him/her making tradeoffs that only favor the short term. Seek to understand what is driving this behavior and help the person to resolve it.
Delegation	*Cannot let go*	• Discuss what work the person typically delegates to others vs. retains. How is this determined? Help the person identify any underlying assumptions about what work gets delegated. • Together review each of the person's team members. What are their strengths? Development needs? Examine in particular the person's level of trust. What has led to this?	• Have the person review his/her current to-do list during a team meeting and ask if anyone else could complete any of the tasks. • For tasks that others can complete, ask about the pros and cons of transferring this duty. For tasks that others cannot do, review what would be needed to delegate certain aspects.	• Ensure the person has rigorous development plans for each direct report. • Practice and debrief the person's coaching sessions with team members. How is the person moving them forward and building trust in their skills and abilities?
	Is spread too thin	• Review the person's calendar together to identify key priorities and discuss how time is spent. • Discuss an appropriate workload with the person regarding what is reasonable and most typical. What causes him/her to exceed those expectations? What do you do to reinforce that behavior?	• Ensure the person can tie his/her own efforts to broader strategic imperatives. Which tasks can the person eliminate that do not support the most strategic priorities? • Ask the person to find a role model—someone who effectively manages a high work volume. Have the person talk with the mentor about his/her secrets of success.	• Coach the person in establishing better work/life balance. Encourage the person to make family or other personal needs a priority (e.g., ensure the person uses vacation time). • Help the person identify people on his/her team who can handle particular tasks. Hold the person accountable for delegation.

	Behavior	Awaken	Align	Accelerate
Goal Orientation	*Is too hands-off*	• Discuss how effective team leaders balance involvement with empowerment. • Ask how the person would benchmark his/her own behavior and what feedback the person has received.	• Help the person facilitate a team session. Ask where the team might want the person more involved on current projects. Determine a work plan to do so. • Ask if there is a particular place where the person would appreciate your involvement as well.	• Debrief a project that didn't go very well. Ask how similar behavior may be impacting current projects. • Formulate a plan for the person to be more involved in monitoring performance.
	Misses milestones	• Review the previous year's goals. Ask what obstacles the person faced and how he/she overcame them to get results. • Review planning and organization processes. Ask how better planning and the use of milestones could have helped.	• Brainstorm how missing milestones might be impacting the work of other teams. • Encourage the person to seek feedback from key peers and ask for suggestions about what could be done differently.	• Help the person develop a stage-gate process and check how it's being implemented. • Help the person develop a Performance Dashboard (a sample is included in the Appendix).
Follow-Through	*Has poor follow-through*	• Ask the person to assess how well he/she follows up and follows through on commitments. • Debrief a regret the person has about his/her own execution. What does the person believe got in the way?	• Ask the person to present the current status of projects he/she manages. How would the person rate progress—red, yellow, or green? • Calibrate expectations around project timelines and what success looks like. Ensure there are plans in place to execute.	• Together, read and debrief *First Things First* by Stephen Covey (Simon and Schuster, 1994). • Help the person identify several self- and time-management techniques to improve how he/she brings closure.
	Gravitates to the next new thing and neglects current projects	• Have the person "think out loud" about an area under his/her purview where quality or speed is integral. • Ask the person to brainstorm issues that may arise which could negatively affect results (especially if the person neglects this project).	• Provide feedback about how well the person's results meet quality, innovation, and speed expectations. • Debrief a recent project and identify what the person could do differently to enhance results next time.	• Ask the person to put together a scorecard to measure key indicators of business results. • Provide coaching to help the person position and utilize the scorecard.

Tips for Coaching in a Global Environment

Managing Execution may be practiced or expressed differently within other cultures. This might impact how you approach coaching. Try to keep an open mind, avoid generalizations, and continue gathering data as you gain experience with another culture. Consider these suggestions:

Organization Know-How: Understanding cultural differences and knowing the ins and outs of how to get things done in different geographies is imperative to Managing Execution. The know-how you have developed over your career might be based on experiences you've had working in large, sophisticated organizations which invested in developing their leadership talent. You may now be managing and coaching people in other cultures who had significantly different experiences. For example, some leaders on your team may not have been trained in time management or project management. They may not have been exposed to some fundamental leadership concepts such as empowerment, much less flexing their leadership styles depending on the readiness of followers for empowerment rather than direction. Ask what kind of leadership or management training they have had during their careers. You might want to invest in sending them to a management training course rather than coaching them on basic skills.

Accountability: There are major differences in how people treat the concept of "time" in other cultures. For example, someone who says "mañana" may not be committing to finishing something "tomorrow"; instead, it may simply mean that the person will deal with it sometime in the future. This phenomenon impacts Managing Execution more than some other areas of leadership. The way leaders in some cultures communicate about expectations may be more subtle and less direct than is typical in Western cultures. Since they may also address performance issues indirectly, learn how people are being held accountable. Adapt your coaching as necessary.

Delegation: Just because people say "yes" to your requests, it does not necessarily mean they agree. They may simply be acknowledging that they heard you. Even if they agree, that doesn't mean they are committed to execution. Confirm people's understanding about your expectations when assigning and delegating work, including their understanding about deadlines. If the person you are coaching is having trouble getting things done through others, probe to understand how assignments are being communicated and confirmed.

Goal Orientation: Some cultures tend to encourage entrepreneurial behavior and initiative, while other cultures tend to be more rule-bound. The formality of reporting structures and the requirement to seek approval before taking independent action can vary. Establishing goals, milestones, and checkpoints can be helpful to monitor progress. You may need to coach leaders to check in more often and do more active monitoring with people in some cultures in order to accomplish the desired outcomes in a timely manner.

Follow-Through: The amount of relationship- and trust-building that is required before things get done also varies among cultures. Recognize that some projects may require more time for completion, especially when people on the team have different levels of experience and may be working in a non-native language. People may need to proceed slowly at first in order to work more efficiently later. Once there is understanding and agreement about the process to be followed, execution can often happen more quickly. If deadlines or results are in jeopardy, leaders may need to check whether their own sense of urgency is shared by others—and coach accordingly.

An execution-focused leader knows how to get things done in a complex organization, establishes the performance required from others to achieve desired outcomes, gets things done through others, directs and monitors progress toward goals, and achieves results by removing obstacles and following up.

As you read about Greg's situation, reflect on what you've learned about Managing Execution in this chapter and consider how you would help Greg demonstrate greater skill in Managing Execution and be successful in his leadership role.

Managing the Matrix

Greg Lawson assumed a senior leadership role at his law firm when he was promoted to practice group chair overseeing the Commercial Group—the largest and fastest-growing area of the business. The role was created when the firm reorganized into a practice group structure—the second attempt within four years to find the most optimal structure to manage talent and drive accountability for business development. The firm had moved to a practice group structure in response to market changes and increased competitive pressure—firms that excelled in client management were snatching up market share; the landscape had changed which necessitated a new focus on client management, collaboration, and business development.

With his unparalleled subject matter expertise and a track record of strong client relationships, Greg seemed to be the perfect choice to lead the group of highly intelligent and independent attorneys. However, Greg was unaware of just how much he needed to change his approach to leading others as the firm as a whole grappled to understand and adapt to its new structure. Initially, Greg embraced the aspect of his role that required him to consult with more junior lawyers on their cases and provide expert advice; he enjoyed mentoring and leveraging his deep experience to guide more junior attorneys. He was a wealth of information and had the respect of all, in part because of his diplomatic and humble interpersonal style. However, the Executive Committee was clear that they expected him to not only mentor, but actively manage practice group leaders and drive accountability for results through the new structure.

Greg personally struggled with the responsibility as practice group chair that required him to hold his leaders accountable for developing and executing annual business plans; he resisted monitoring attorneys and expected them to be self-directed. His hands-off approach and reluctance to have tough conversations when partners failed to meet internal deadlines left him feeling frustrated, and business plans were incomplete or sub-par. Meanwhile, the partners struggled with lack of direction and clarity about their new roles in the practice structure—they needed a strong leader to provide clear expectations and help them grow in their leadership roles.

As pressure from the Executive Committee to drive business results through practice group development increased—and apathy among the partners threatened their retention—Greg knew that he had to rethink his role and learn new skills to drive execution and hold others accountable to achieve business results.

Through coaching, Greg realized that he needed to focus more on Managing Execution in order to:

- Clarify his leadership role and communicate it to the firm, particularly to the partners. Clarify the role and responsibilities of the group's partners, specifically in regard to holding them accountable.

- Proactively address marginal performance to align talent to business objectives.

- Learn how to use his substantial credibility to hold others accountable, not just lend his technical expertise.

- Drive short-term actions to support the strategy and improve profitability of the practice group; coach people in developing effective plans/measures to achieve objectives.

- Create monitoring and accountability systems to support his ability to track progress and reward achievements.

Greg's Leadership Development Plan

Following is a sample development plan for Greg Lawson. Research on leadership development has shown that leaders learn through experience and that this learning is optimized through the use of an individual development plan. A successful plan includes new experiences and introduces the leader to new conversations and tools. The suggestions included in the previous sections may stimulate your thinking about additional possibilities for Greg's development.

LEADERSHIP DEVELOPMENT PLAN FOR GREG LAWSON

DEVELOPMENT GOAL

Goal: To strengthen my skills in Managing Execution

Desired Outcomes—results I want to see from developing this skill

Self: I will have clarified my leadership role and feel comfortable proactively managing the performance of others.

Team: My team will demonstrate a sense of accountability and goal orientation to drive strong action.

Organization: My business will have solid monitoring and accountability systems in place to support the challenging expectations we have for team members.

Self-Understanding—strengths that I can build on and development needs I can address

Strengths: Technical expertise, strong credibility, diplomatic style, humility.

Development Needs: Lack of tough-mindedness, hands-off approach, reluctance to hold others accountable, new in the transition to practice group chair.

Business Context—challenges in my business environment that require this skill

The need to develop and execute strong business plans across the enterprise.

DEVELOPMENT ACTIONS

AWAKEN

- Reflect on how I have approached accountability in the past. What factors prevent me from being as tough-minded as I need to be?

- Identify someone within the organization who exemplifies results orientation. Observe that person's behavior to learn potential new ways of handling tough situations. Ask myself what do they do that I am afraid to?

ALIGN

- Clarify my leadership role and communicate it to the firm, particularly to the partners. Clarify the role and responsibilities of the group's partners, specifically in regard to holding them accountable.

- Identify another leader of a non competing professional services firm to discuss his/her strategy for holding others accountable in this role. Leverage this mentoring relationship to review tough situations and practice courageous conversations. Find a way to return the favor.

LEADERSHIP DEVELOPMENT PLAN FOR GREG LAWSON

ACCELERATE

- Proactively address marginal performance by creating an accountability group within the partner community. Set incremental incentives around completion of a strong business plan.

- Drive short-term actions to support the strategy and improve profitability of the practice group by reviewing each partner's progress monthly. Create and share a dashboard of results to motivate others to achieve set goals.

- Leverage my own experience to coach people in developing effective plans/measures to achieve objectives.

- Team with human resources leaders to create monitoring and accountability systems increasing our ability to track progress and reward achievements.

DEVELOPMENT SUCCESS FACTORS

Timeline: Within the next six months

Support Needed:

- I will need human resources support to help create a monitoring and accountability tracking system.

- I will need a non-competing professional services firm leader as an external mentor to bounce ideas off and learn from his/her experiences.

Indicators of Success:

- Partners within the firm will report that I am holding them accountable for strong results, and organizational measures reflect this.

- I will feel more comfortable driving accountability throughout the organization by having the tough conversations necessary.

- The organization will have an accountability system in place to help reinforce this behavior change across the firm.

An Example of Coaching for Managing Execution

Greg Lawson's goal was to strengthen his skills in Managing Execution. Here are some steps Greg's manager could take using the Awaken, Align, Accelerate framework to coach Greg in this area:

AWAKEN	**Increase INSIGHT**	Ask Greg what is going well vs. poorly with his new responsibilities as practice group chair. Look at the firm's history with driving results from this leadership role. Reflect on how that might be impacting people's expectations and perceptions about Greg's performance.
	MOTIVATE change	Review annual goals. Ask Greg what he would need to do differently to stretch his goals by ten percent. Ask Greg what might happen if he asked others this question. Explore the consequences of not making any changes; identify consequences for him personally as well as the firm.
ALIGN	**PLAN goals**	Ask Greg what would enable him to handle his new role more successfully. Focus on what he could change to improve his performance. Work together to construct a Leadership Development Plan similar to the sample provided in this chapter.
	ALIGN expectations	Calibrate expectations around project timelines and what success looks like for strong business planning to occur. Ensure there are plans in place to execute. Periodically during the planning cycle ask Greg to present the current status of the business planning in the firm. How would he rate their progress, red, yellow, or green? Why?
ACCELERATE	**CREATE teachable moments**	Coach Greg in creating monitoring and accountability systems to track progress and reward achievements. Ask Greg about his ideas for improving the profitability of the practice group. Discuss options for holding other partners more accountable for developing and executing annual business plans. Practice the tough conversations.
	TRACK progress	Discuss expected outcomes and results. Work with Greg to evaluate progress toward his goals. Express appreciation for the steps he is taking to improve accountability.

Results: Measuring Impact

Greg Lawson took almost six months to work through his plan. He didn't try every action step, and he found some activities were more helpful than others. However, he made tremendous progress on improving his own skills and increasing accountability within the firm. His new skills in Managing Execution allowed Greg to:

- Clarify partner roles and responsibilities and to hold partners accountable for results.

- Create monitoring and accountability systems to track progress and reward achievements.

- Drive accountability throughout the firm.

- Have tough conversations as needed.

- Initiate short-term actions to improve profitability.

MANAGING
SELF

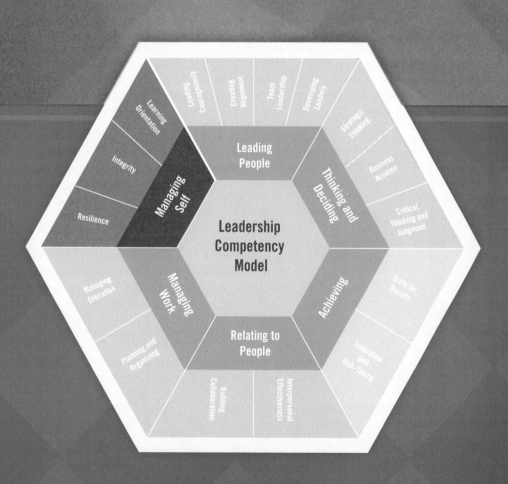

Leadership Competency Model

Managing Self — Resilience, Integrity, Learning Orientation

Leading People — Leading Consistency, Creating Alignment, Team Leadership, Developing Leaders

Thinking and Deciding — Strategic Thinking, Business Acumen, Critical Thinking and Judgment

Achieving — Drive for Results, Innovation and Risk-Taking

Relating to People — Interpersonal Effectiveness, Building Collaboration

Managing Work — Managing Execution, Planning and Organizing

18

Resilience

Resilient leaders demonstrate healthy self-acceptance and convey confidence. They readily adapt and adjust to changes and challenges. Highly resilient leaders often turn crises into opportunities—they remain calm and constructive. They maintain a sense of optimism and provide encouragement for others. They also recover quickly from setbacks or disappointments and help others do the same.

Factor	Competency	Core Practice
Leading People	Resilience	Confidence
Thinking and Deciding	Integrity	Adaptability
Achieving	Learning Orientation	Composure
Relating to People		Optimism
Managing Work		Recovery
Managing Self		

Change. Loss. Competitive threats. Deadlines. Tight budgets. Job security. Anxiety. Balancing the demands of work and home. Sound familiar? Resilience can help leaders overcome daily challenges as well as manage business through difficult times such as the financial meltdown of 2008 or the dotcom boom/bust a decade earlier. Change and periodic crises are inevitable. Organizations need strong leaders who can survive daily turbulence, thrive in times of uncertainty, and navigate rapid change to create new business opportunities.

Resilience is often a learned skill that develops over time. It may become embodied once people achieve senior leadership roles, yet it can always be improved. Executives who effectively model Resilience can have a dramatic effect on employee engagement and organizational performance. They can enhance employee commitment, satisfaction, and morale by establishing a resilient tone and atmosphere. Following are the five core practices of Resilience.

How Leaders Show Resilience

	Managers, Function Leaders, and Senior Executives
Confidence	Balances healthy self-confidence with appropriate humility.
Adaptability	Adapts to changes and challenges.
Composure	Handles stress in a calm and constructive manner.
Optimism	Remains optimistic in the face of obstacles or problems.
Recovery	Recovers quickly from setbacks or disappointments.

Self-Assessment

To evaluate your effectiveness in Resilience, check all boxes below that represent current behavior or performance. Look for patterns: Which core practices represent a development need, a strength, or an excessive use? Recognize that you might have some blind spots. Invite your boss or colleagues to indicate what they have observed in your behavior. Use this assessment to help identify development suggestions that are most relevant to you.

	Development Need	Strength	Excessive Use
Confidence	❑ Displays feelings of insecurity ❑ Is prone to worry, doubt, and second-guessing decisions	❑ Conveys a strong but appropriate sense of self-confidence ❑ Is free of significant doubts or insecurities	❑ Portrays an aura of invincibility ❑ May come across as arrogant or narcissistic
Adaptability	❑ Is immobilized by or slow to adjust to change or surprises ❑ Is overly rigid, structured, and controlling	❑ Anticipates and is prepared to change, adapt, or compromise when required ❑ Turns crisis situations into opportunities to restructure and improve processes	❑ Changes plans too often—shifts from one thing to the next too quickly ❑ Doesn't finish things and tends to leave things open-ended
Composure	❑ Is discouraged easily ❑ Becomes flustered and unfocused when faced with difficulties	❑ Is constructive, effective, and helpful to others in stressful situations ❑ Remains calm and even-tempered	❑ Is overcontrolled and unexpressive ❑ May come across as lacking passion or energy
Optimism	❑ Allows skepticism or negativity to dampen his/her outlook ❑ Conveys pessimism, worries, or fears that discourage others	❑ Maintains a highly positive, optimistic outlook that conveys hope ❑ Encourages others to believe in their ability to succeed	❑ Is overly aggressive or ambitious in underestimating the difficulties and likely roadblocks to success ❑ Ignores criticism and overestimates own talents
Recovery	❑ Lets feelings of disappointment linger ❑ Complains about "what might have been" rather than creating new opportunities	❑ Does not personalize or view setbacks as permanent or pervasive—and helps others do the same ❑ Bounces back and redirects energy into productive pursuits	❑ Glosses over setbacks and disappointments ❑ May come across as not making mistakes or learning from them

Development Suggestions

The following section contains development suggestions for each core practice. Having completed the self-assessment, focus on suggestions that correspond to the core practices you identified as a development need or excessive use. Use these suggestions to create your own development plan, making sure to try one or two from each phase. In addition, feel free to create your own or adapt these to best meet your development needs.

Confidence

Balance healthy self-confidence with appropriate humility.

The ultimate measure of a man is not where he stands in moments of comfort and convenience, but where he stands at times of challenge and controversy.

Martin Luther King, Jr.

Awaken potential:

- **Assess where your confidence comes from.** Make a list of the tasks or activities where you are most confident in your performance. How do you express that confidence?

- **Reflect on when and where you feel least confident.** Identify the last time you might have shown insecurity or a lack of confidence. What situations trigger confidence issues, including interactions with particular people? Where do you need to show more "tough love"?

- **Ask colleagues for feedback.** Inquire about the way you show confidence (or not) when expressing your point of view. You may have some habits you are not aware of, such as speaking softly, using too many "uhs" or "ums," or coming across as tentative rather than assertive.

- **Record yourself practicing an upcoming presentation.** With your eyes closed, listen to how you sound. What do others hear? Would you sound confident to them?

Align goals:

- **Inspire confidence in achieving results.** List the greatest business challenges that you anticipate over the next six to twelve months. Identify where you will need to display confidence in addressing those challenges and how that might impact outcomes. Put together a 100-day action plan. Share the plan with your manager. Ask for feedback. Then share your plan with others on your team.

- **Identify others who need to develop more confidence.** Help other leaders on your team identify where they are most and least confident. Provide feedback and coaching to help people express themselves with greater confidence.

Accelerate performance:

- **Find a mentor.** Think about someone with whom you have worked who showed exceptional self-confidence without arrogance. Ask that person to become your mentor.

- **Minimize excessive self-criticism.** Many people are their own worst critics. Self-criticism helps us correct mistakes, learn, and develop. However, irrational or excessive self-criticism, can erode one's confidence. Take appropriate pride in your accomplishments and accept the compliments others give you. Learn to build your self-confidence while you are also learning to become better.

- **Analyze the sources of power you have.** Most leaders have a good amount of "position power." However, if they overuse or misuse it, they can be viewed as lacking confidence. The most successful leaders blend their position power with "personal power" (i.e., the credibility one has based on effort, expertise, commitment, and interpersonal style). Make sure you are using both position and personal power as much or more when you are making requests or providing direction so that you are not seen as insecure, arrogant, or unnecessarily domineering.

- **Be a role model during challenging times.** Acting decisively and being proactive in resolving issues can convey confidence. Review Chapter 5, particularly the core practice "Courage," to provide you with practices for enhancing your confidence and ability to step up to be a courageous and visible leader when the going gets tough.

- **Anticipate problems.** Look ahead and develop contingency plans so that you can be prepared for emergencies or surprises, and ready to react or respond rather than showing hesitation or confusion.

- **Work with a communications coach** to strengthen your voice quality or gestures for impact. Or, work with an executive coach to improve your executive presence.

- **Increase your chance of success.** Pessimism can get in the way of your taking timely action on issues. Review the "Optimism" section of this chapter for ways to develop and sustain a more positive belief in your ability to get results, even in the face of setbacks and obstacles.

EXCESSIVE USE

As an example, if you portray yourself as invincible or come across as arrogant, you may be turning off or alienating some of your stakeholders. People may be reluctant to provide feedback or tell you when your ideas are off-course if they fear that you will be defensive or scornful. You may be missing out on vital information that could make your business even more successful. Humility is a powerful practice that encourages others to provide honest feedback and help when needed. Review Chapter 20, "Learning Orientation," for ways to develop an appropriate level of humility that will help you demonstrate your interest and willingness to partner with others for shared success.

Adaptability

Adapt to changes and challenges.

If you don't like something, change it. If you can't change it, change your attitude. Don't complain.

Maya Angelou

Awaken potential:

- **Draw a "career lifeline"** to graph the emotional ups and downs you have experienced over the course of your leadership journey. When/where did you experience the greatest highs? Lows? What have you learned about coping with changes and role transitions?

- **Consider taking the MBTI®.** Use this resource to better understand your personality style and preferences. Find out what role your personality plays in your flexibility and openness to possibilities (P=Perceiving) or your preference for structured and planful activities (J=Judging).

- **Evaluate how you typically react to changes and challenges.** If you find it difficult to adapt to change, your behavior may stifle the creativity and resourcefulness of other people. If you tend to become stressed during periods of change, review the "Composure" section later in this chapter.

- **Reflect on the culture in your organization.** How do people deal with adversity and unexpected changes, including top leaders? If your culture has become calcified, read *RELAX It's Only Uncertainty: Lead the Way When the Way is Changing* by Philip Hodgson and Randall White (Pearson, 2001) for tips about enablers and restrainers that you can use to analyze and transform your culture.

Align goals:

- **Engage key stakeholders.** Talk with your manager about how to engage important stakeholders in your change efforts. Confirm how your change initiative fits with the broader goals of the organization—and how those changes will help the organization achieve greater results.

- **Over-communicate!** Keep others informed as you adapt and change your plans. It's important to communicate regularly and engage in honest conversations, especially when you don't have all the answers in times of change. Help people see how changes are linked to business outcomes.

- **Evaluate the adaptability of people on your team.** Does anyone tend to become paralyzed or fall into "analysis-paralysis" mode? Who tends to be resistant to change or slow to adjust/adapt? Provide feedback and coaching to help people manage ambiguity and increase the speed of decision-making.

Accelerate performance:

- **Follow a structured process** to initiate changes. Review the core practice "Change" in Chapter 6 for some suggestions about managing change.

- **Assemble a cross-functional task force** to recommend restructuring options in response to shifting conditions. Focus on core capabilities, streamline operations, and "get the right people on the bus."

- **Seek advisors** who can help you discover opposing views and new opportunities, then sift through options to find the right choices. Identify people who can serve as trusted sounding boards.

- **Reframe challenges.** View these as opportunities to restructure and improve processes. Crisis periods can be a perfect time to challenge "sacred cows" or orthodoxies (i.e., practices that seemed immune to criticism in the past). Enlist others to help you identify possibilities for winning scenarios.

Composure

Handle stress in a calm and constructive manner.

One cool judgment is worth a thousand hasty counsels. The thing to do is to supply light and not heat.

Woodrow T. Wilson

Awaken potential:

- **Keep a journal.** Record what kinds of things tend to cause stress reactions for you. Do you feel anxiety about deadlines? Do you become nervous before speaking? How does your body react when you are engaged in arguments? Does anxiety affect your productivity or your relationships with others?

- **Evaluate your typical reactions to stress.** Do you keep "cool, calm, and collected" and engage in rational thinking, or are you prone to panic? Do you over-react to unexpected events? It's time to develop better coping strategies if your behavior creates chaos for yourself or others.

- **Learn to manage your energy.** Read *The Power of Full Engagement: Managing Energy, Not Time, Is the Key to High Performance and Personal Renewal* by Jim Loehr and Tony Schwartz (Free Press, 2003). Visit their website to take the Full Engagement Self Profile™—a free assessment of physical, mental, emotional, and spiritual behaviors related to energy management.

Align goals:

- **Acknowledge the importance of managing stress** in producing sustained results. Seek out peers or senior leaders who could serve as sounding boards in critical situations, especially people who could offer reassurance that you are on the right track.

- **Help people respond constructively to stress.** Conduct skip-level meetings to stay in touch with what is happening at all levels. Focus people on things they can control. Provide feedback and coaching to people who need to maintain a more balanced perspective and focus on key priorities (e.g., execution and performance), especially in times of stress.

Accelerate performance:

- **Look for role models.** Watch the movie *Apollo 13*. Pay attention to mission director Gene Kranz.

- **Strive to complete projects early** to avoid last-minute rushing around. Establish milestones and checkpoints so there will be no surprises—especially on major projects.

- **Count to ten before responding** if you tend to "lose your cool" and become upset during arguments. Save draft emails to review before sending. Do not type messages using all capital letters, as that may convey anger.

- **Spend five minutes in meditation daily.** Clear your mind of clutter. Focus on becoming calm.

- **Watch the pacing.** Pace yourself in your daily calendar. Ensure there are enough "white space" opportunities for you to think and catch your breath, allowing downtime and preventing yourself and others from feeling rushed.

EXCESSIVE USE

As an example, if you are overly poised and never show any stress,
others may view you as a super-human who cannot relate to what they are going through.
Don't be afraid to show your vulnerability. Open up to others. Talk calmly and reflectively
about what you are experiencing. People will relate to you more easily—and be more
inclined to open up to you as well.

Optimism

Remain optimistic in the face of obstacles or problems.

"Hope is like a road in the country; there was never a road, but when many people walk on it, the road comes into existence."

Lin Yutang

Awaken potential:

- **Test your own optimism.** Read *Learned Optimism: How to Change Your Mind and Your Life* by Martin Seligman (Vintage; 1990, 2006). Take the quiz in the third chapter.

- **Seek feedback on the way you are communicating** about the current business situation. What kinds of messages are you conveying through your words and actions? How are people receiving those messages? Do they see you being positive and upbeat without being overly optimistic?

- **Look for positive role models.** Who exemplifies a "can do" attitude even when the odds are against them? Try to observe them in action. Which of their behaviors can you adopt?

- **Use "Appreciative Inquiry" methodology** to find out what people value and appreciate about your organization (i.e., the positive core—what gives life to your organizational culture). How can you use that insight to keep people engaged during difficult times?

Align goals:

- **Conduct a force field analysis.** Identify positive vs. negative forces in the environment—forces that may enable your team to succeed on a particular initiative, and forces that could threaten that success. How can you maximize the potential for success and neutralize or eliminate potential threats in order to achieve more sustainable results?

- **Promote optimism on your team.** Who exemplifies a "glass half full" vs. a "glass half empty" approach? How does that orientation come through in the comments they make at meetings? Provide feedback and coaching to help people be more optimistic.

Accelerate performance:

- **Provide vision and hope while telling the unvarnished truth.** Focus on the future while adapting your strategy to deal with short-term challenges. Communicate with clarity how you see the way forward.

- **Identify ten outcomes that would represent wild success.** Write them down. The simple act of identifying these impossible possibilities could trigger your imagination to see challenges and opportunities in a new light. Review the list each month to see which ones have been achieved.

- **Praise people's efforts.** Use positive feedback to reinforce the effort you want to see. If you are plagued by an "inner critic" or if someone on your team tends to play that role, identify ways to silence or neutralize that voice, or channel it in a way that doesn't disrupt or derail progress.

- **Practice story-telling to highlight accomplishments.** Acknowledge others' progress, even small successes, in order to build excitement and momentum.

- **Recognize the value of going with the flow.** Rather than trying to swim upstream, identify how you can build on others' efforts. Focus especially on leveraging and capitalizing on their momentum.

EXCESSIVE USE

As an example, if you ignore criticism or disregard objections, you may alienate some people you need to bring on board. Invite people to raise objections. Make sure people feel safe expressing their concerns. Strive for realistic rather than unbridled optimism.

Recovery

Recover quickly from setbacks or disappointments.

When you get into a tight place and everything goes against you, never give up then, for that is just the place and time that the tide will turn.

Harriet Beecher Stowe

Awaken potential:

- **List the most significant hardships and setbacks** you have experienced personally and professionally. How did you recover? How long did it take? What strategies did you use? What support did you receive? What did you learn? How would you handle them differently in the future?

- **Look for patterns in your own response to adversity.** Read *Adversity Quotient: Turning Obstacles into Opportunities* by Paul Stoltz (John Wiley, 1997). Complete the Adversity Response Profile (ARP) Quick Take™ in the fourth chapter.

- **Assess your firm's mindfulness.** Read *Managing the Unexpected: Resilient Performance in an Age of Uncertainty* by Karl Weick and Kathleen Sutcliffe (Jossey Bass, 2007). Learn how high-reliability organizations discover and correct problems before they escalate.

Align goals:

- **Be realistic in confronting your present circumstances.** Provide a balanced, rational perspective. Help others clearly recognize what the organization is facing. Adjust goals if necessary, and hold people accountable for doing what it takes to achieve their objectives.

- **Prevent performance problems from escalating.** Ask everyone on your team to develop personal scorecards to measure performance and progress. Discuss those scorecards on a regular basis (e.g., monthly) in order to deal with setbacks before they get out of hand. Provide feedback and coaching.

Accelerate performance:

- **Organize a field trip** for your team to visit an organization that emerged from setbacks even stronger than before. What did leaders learn from that experience? How can you apply some of those lessons to the current situation you are experiencing? Challenge your team to be role models in this area.

- **Model the behavior** of someone in your organization whom you view as resilient and optimistic, and who recovers well from setbacks or disappointments. How does he or she behave? What does the person say? Incorporate what you see into your style to strengthen your own personal sense of resilience.

- **Examine your way of making sense out of difficulties and disappointments.** Pessimists tend to view these as permanent, unchangeable, and pervasive, and tend to personalize or blame themselves for causing these situations. Optimists believe that most difficulties are temporary or situational, and typically do not see themselves as the cause. When discussing setbacks with your team, make sure you are approaching issues from an optimist's perspective. Study the work of Martin Seligman (referenced earlier in this chapter) to learn more.

- **Establish an "early warning system"** to anticipate potential problems and manage them before they get out of control.

- **Show empathy.** When others encounter setbacks, you can help them recover and move forward by demonstrating empathy. Chapter 14, "Interpersonal Effectiveness," provides specific practices for demonstrating empathy.

EXCESSIVE USE

As an example, if you gloss over setbacks and disappointments rather than investing effort to learn from your mistakes, you may be missing out on a huge source of learning for yourself and others. Conduct after-action reviews with your team to evaluate what was done well and what could have been done differently to produce an even better outcome.

Coach Others on Resilience

When coaching others, focus on the core practices that were identified as either a development need or excessive use in the self-assessment at the beginning of this chapter. Identify and adapt any relevant development suggestions. Additional coaching tips are provided in the following table for some adverse leadership behaviors. For more information review Chapter 4, "Coach Others."

Coaching Suggestions

Behavior	Awaken	Align	Accelerate
Is insecure	• Talk together about when and where the person feels least confident. Ask what situations trigger confidence issues. • Discuss how improved confidence could stimulate more trust and confidence in others.	• Invite the person to share the greatest business challenges he/she anticipates over the next six to twelve months; discuss how they might impact results. • Work together to identify role models for healthy self-confidence. Who within the organization could the person model or learn from?	• Serve as a sounding board while the person makes plans to try new approaches. Conduct role-plays to help the person practice conveying confidence. • Provide (more) positive feedback to recognize specific accomplishments and increase the person's confidence.
Second-guesses decisions	• Ask the person to share several recent decisions where his/her mind was changed as new information emerged. Provide feedback based on your own observations and their implications. • Suggest keeping a log of key decisions. What information does the person need to make decisions? What new information might change his/her decision?	• Discuss the implications of second-guessing on business outcomes and relationships with others, especially one or two peers who have been impacted by the person's decisions. • Encourage the person to vet important decisions with the team. Invite them to critique assumptions and discuss impact on results.	• Have the person review upcoming decisions with you during one-on-one meetings. As you discuss, help the person look for ways to improve decision-making. • Recommend that the person review the core practice "Decision-Making" in Chapter 11, suggest that he/she identify one or two behaviors to adopt and practice. Set a specific time to follow up on the effectiveness of the behaviors.

Confidence

	Behavior	Awaken	Align	Accelerate
Adaptability	*Immobilized by change*	• Debrief how the person handled recent changes. What were your observations of the person's behavior? • Discuss the value of being proactive rather than reactive. Share some personal experiences that helped you in this area.	• Discuss how change may lead to accomplishing current strategic goals and/or improved business results. • Encourage the person to involve the team in developing a vision for what the organization could become in three years; review potential contingencies and prepare a change plan.	• Ask what changes might be occurring in the next months. Help the person figure out how to prepar those changes. • Use a series of "what if?" questions to anticipate s possible scenarios.
	Overly rigid and controlling	• Ask how the person thinks others perceive him/her, including what feedback the person has received. Follow up with a multi-rater feedback assessment if more data is needed. • Probe to understand the person's motivation and what is truly needed for control.	• Help the person understand the impact of his/her behavior on the team and organization over time, as well as the benefits of making some changes. • Encourage the person to collect data about how time is spent—and evaluate whether it fits with priorities.	• Invite the person to revie Chapter 16, "Planning ar Organizing," and Chapter "Managing Execution," a reflect on implications of excessive use as well as opportunities they propos to be more empowering. • Ask the person to work w the team to clarify decisi making responsibility.
Composure	*Gets discouraged easily*	• Help the person identify reactions to stress and what triggers discouragement. • Probe to help the person realize how self-talk may drain energy and prevent taking action. • Help the person recognize emotional and physical reactions to stress so he/ she can avoid being a victim.	• Suggest that the person engage others and help everyone feel more accountable for progress—along with seeking support and encouragement so the person won't feel so alone. • Reinforce the need for keeping a balanced perspective and focusing on key priorities in order to achieve results.	• Help the person identify positive cues to remember what has beer accomplished in the past self-talk can change to " possible." • Schedule periodic "pep talks" to inquire how thir are going and provide encouragement.

Behavior		Awaken	Align	Accelerate
Composure	*Over-reacts when faced with difficulties*	• Explore what happened the last time the person faced difficulties. Ask what occurred, how the person handled the situation, how others reacted, what was learned, and what could have been done differently. • Help the person identify triggers along with options for conveying a "can do, this will pass" reaction.	• Explore how non-productive reactions can negatively impact business results. • Find a mentor who could help the person develop in this area by providing guidance about possibilities that may not have been considered.	• Ask what messages the person wants to convey in both talking about disappointment as well as presenting constructive options for what is possible. • Stress the importance of physical exercise for a healthy mind and body. Propose that the person develops a physical routine and encourages their team to do the same.
Optimism	*Is skeptical*	• Suggest that the person complete a multi-rater feedback assessment to learn how skepticism impacts their problem solving and affects others on the team. • Ask what leadership impact the person wants to have, and how that could lead to better business outcomes.	• Propose that the person identify others who need to be more optimistic—and suggest they work on developing this skill together. • Have the person interview key stakeholders to gain understanding of how questioning the beliefs or credibility of others conveys a lack of trust.	• Encourage the person to "go public" with trusted colleagues about intentions so that other people can help and provide ongoing feedback. • Highlight specific language or non-verbals that exemplify the person's skepticism. Help to provide an alternative tone or words to change perception.
	Conveys pessimism	• Provide feedback based on your own observations of recent examples. What consequences came from the person's behavior? What could have been achieved if the person had behaved differently? • Discuss how believing in the worst-case scenario—coupled with talking about what could go wrong and how things could fail—tends to drain other people's hope.	• Ask what contributions of people on the team the person is most proud of. Help the person recognize that people on his/her team are skilled and valuable and suggest that he/she tell them so more often. • Point out that progress, no matter how small, can be used to build excitement and a sense of momentum for the team toward their achievement of strategic goals.	• Explore ways to capitalize on the team's momentum and convey more positive messages. Identify specifically what impact you believe that might have on results. • Suggest using "Appreciative Inquiry" to find out what people value and appreciate about the organization (i.e., what gives life to the culture).

Behavior		Awaken	Align	Accelerate
Recovery	*Lingers over disappointment*	• Ask about the last time the person made a mistake or was disappointed in his/her own performance. How did the person feel about the situation? How did he/she react? What impact did the reaction have on others? • Help the person understand the need for leaders to set a good example in moving forward and conveying hope despite disappointments.	• Challenge the person to prevent performance problems from escalating. Suggest that the person work with the team to develop personal scorecards for everyone. Then deal with missed milestones before they become setbacks. • If goals need to be adjusted, ask the person to communicate the new objectives to team members and hold them accountable. Ensure that the person's language reflects how aligned the goals are with organizational strategic imperatives.	• Work together on developing an "early warning system" to anticipate possible problems going forward. • Check in periodically to see how the person is doing and make sure the person is not sliding backward. Encourage preparing for routine one-on-one meetings by checking the pulse of key team members.
	Complains about "what might have been"	• Have the person do a self-assessment on the team's mindfulness. How well does the team anticipate what might occur and plan for it? • Help the person rate and identify any performance problems on the person's team. Explore how those may be impacting overall business results.	• Have the person organize a field trip to a business that turned around and find out what actions leaders there took. Have the person to present findings to the team or peers. What can they learn from this? • Brainstorm possible role models—people who faced setbacks and moved on without complaining. How is the person's style similar or different? Who might the person connect with to review how to anticipate more effectively?	• Brainstorm options for how the person's team might discover and correct problems before they escalate. • Insist that the person take action and not put off having critical conversations about performance.

Tips for Coaching in a Global Environment

Resilience may be practiced or expressed differently within other cultures. This might impact how you approach coaching. Try to keep an open mind, avoid generalizations, and continue gathering data as you gain experience with another culture. Consider these suggestions:

Confidence: The appearance and expression of confidence may be different elsewhere. For example:

- Leaders in some cultures may lack appreciation for the role that individual aspirations can play in achieving career or business success. Or they may not value individual over group performance. People may need extra support from you in identifying ambitions and/or setting personal goals.

- It is important to understand the cultural context around risk-taking. Ask for personal stories about how risk-taking has had a positive or negative influence on the career of the person you are coaching.

- The formality of reporting structures and the requirement to seek approval before taking independent action can vary. Some cultures tend to encourage more initiative than others—while some departments, functions, and entire organizations can be more rule-bound than others. People may need encouragement to develop and express confidence in tackling change.

Adaptability: When you see behavior that may be too controlling (rather than adaptable), have a dialogue about what your expectations are for empowering the team. You may need to provide feedback, coaching, or training to individuals who need to learn other ways to lead.

Composure: The degree of composure may be misjudged because people from different cultures sometimes express emotions differently. They may have very different expectations and degrees of comfort regarding open conversation about feelings and emotions. Pay attention to the assumptions you are making.

Optimism: Some cultures tend to emphasize positivity and optimism more than others. For example, setting "stretch goals" is a much more comfortable activity in the USA than in cultures where people are uncomfortable with the fear of failure. It may be difficult for people from some cultures to buy into an optimistic approach without receiving extra support and encouragement.

Recovery: People in some cultures expect their companies—or their managers—to play a more paternalistic role in helping people and their families navigate challenging circumstances. Check out what expectations may exist. Negotiate for the support you are willing to provide.

A Case Study in Resilience

The expression "When the going gets tough, the tough get going" takes on new meaning during economic downturns. Leadership challenges often include restructuring to reduce costs while dealing with both planned and unplanned turnover. Such times can be difficult and stressful for leaders, especially people who are transitioning into new roles and feeling somewhat vulnerable themselves.

As you read about Tom Garcia's situation, reflect on what you've learned about Resilience in this chapter and consider how you would help Tom demonstrate greater skill in Resilience and be successful in his leadership role.

Operating With Optimism

Tom Garcia was hired away from a competitor to lead an ailing business unit on the West Coast. The business there had gone through a lot of changes in the five years since being acquired by Tom's new company. Tom was told that his mission was to improve the profitability of the business unit or it would be sold. He was excited to have the opportunity, but also somewhat anxious given the challenges he foresaw. He was accustomed to leading successful groups, and this was his first turnaround situation.

Tom started by meeting one on one with everyone on his team as well as key people throughout the organization. He worked with an integration coach to help him understand his day-to-day leadership style and career-derailing behaviors, and how his core values and goals play roles in the kind of environment he creates and how he works with others. He created a development plan to keep himself focused on staying positive and refraining from his tendency to be overly critical.

After assessing the organization, Tom established initial priorities and worked to gain buy-in from his executive team for the restructuring he determined was necessary. He was in the middle of this process when an economic recession sent shock waves throughout all industries, and the bottom dropped out of Tom's business. Several major customers cancelled orders, while others delayed payments.

The orderly restructuring that Tom had planned suddenly became moot as he contemplated the need to make drastic cuts to bring costs in line with projected revenues. Tom began putting pressure on the head of sales to bring in other business. The organization was in turmoil as rumors surfaced that it might be sold or have some of its functions absorbed by other business units. Tom's own job was in jeopardy as he recognized that headquarters might run out of patience.

Tom found that he needed to build Resilience more than ever, in order to:

- Convey confidence in his own leadership as well as in his team.

- Engage his people in anticipating and adapting to possible changes.

- Stay calm and help others manage through this stressful time.

- Remain open to challenge and feedback from headquarters.

- Convey optimism that they could survive the present situation.

- Help others rebound from the current setback.

Tom's Leadership Development Plan

Following is a sample development plan for Tom Garcia. Research on leadership development has shown that leaders learn through experience and that this learning is optimized through the use of an individual development plan. A successful plan includes new experiences and introduces the leader to new conversations and tools. The suggestions included in the previous sections may stimulate your thinking about additional possibilities for Tom's development.

LEADERSHIP DEVELOPMENT PLAN FOR TOM GARCIA
DEVELOPMENT GOAL
Goal: To strengthen my overall Resilience
Desired Outcomes—results I want to see from developing this skill
Self: Increased ability to cope and remain focused   **Team:** Increased engagement and contribution   **Organization:** Increased productivity and profitability
Self-Understanding—strengths that I can build on and development needs I can address
Strengths: Track record of success in the industry; willingness to listen and involve people; decisiveness   **Development Needs:** Handling stress and dealing with pressure from headquarters; managing my tendency to be overly critical
Business Context—challenges in my business environment that require this skill
Coping with economic recession, sharp decline in orders from key customers, and organization in turmoil; must improve the profitability of the business.

LEADERSHIP DEVELOPMENT PLAN FOR TOM GARCIA

DEVELOPMENT ACTIONS

AWAKEN

- Revisit assessment findings regarding potential derailers during times of difficulty, as well as my leadership style. Note ways that I may contribute to the stress of the business unit, when I am at my worst.

- Reassess the business given the current financial situation. Assess existing goals vs. current reality. What people, structure, and processes need to be adjusted? What can and cannot be controlled?

ALIGN

- Partner with manager to determine how objectives have changed; determine course of action with contingencies.

- Ask manager what success would look like from the perspective of corporate leadership.

ACCELERATE

- Create regular and frequent opportunities to communicate with my team, both as a group and one-on-one to share what is known and provide an outlet for concerns and questions. Expect my direct reports to do the same with their teams.

- Communicate a clear message to team regarding what has changed, what will stay the same, and the new vision overall. Help the team focus on priorities. Minimize disorientation by being clear about expectations, vision, and direction.

- Determine what is in my control and focus energies there. Be clear about what is not in my control and let go.

- Identify ways to de-stress and determine regular opportunities to engage.

- Talk with peers and others outside the organization to share stories and exchange ideas.

DEVELOPMENT SUCCESS FACTORS

Timeline: Within the next six months

Support Needed:

- Clear and frequent information/communication from manager.

- Clear expectations/goals from executive team.

Indicators of Success:

- Turnover is minimized.
- Productivity is maximized despite changes.
- The team is engaged despite upheaval.
- The team is clear about expectations and vision.
- I am managing the business and team in a way that supports my well-being and effectiveness.

An Example of Coaching for Resilience

Tom Garcia's goal was to strengthen his skills in Resilience. Here are some steps Tom's manager could take using the Awaken, Align, Accelerate framework to coach Tom in this area:

AWAKEN	**Increase INSIGHT**	If Tom has shared his tendency to be overly critical of others in the past, ask what progress he is making in this area. Ask about the last time Tom made a mistake or was disappointed in his own performance. How did he feel about the situation? How did he react? What impact did his reaction have on others?
	MOTIVATE change	Identify what Tom is motivated to change—for himself and for his team. Find out how he prefers to learn. Explore the consequences of not making any changes; identify consequences for him personally as well as for his team.
ALIGN	**PLAN goals**	Identify possibilities for change that would enable Tom to handle current challenges and future uncertainty more successfully. Focus on what he could change as part of his restructuring plan. Work together to construct a leadership development plan similar to the sample provided in this chapter.
	ALIGN expectations	Encourage Tom to clearly communicate what his business unit is facing. Ask what Tom is doing to get his entire team involved in dealing with the current situation. If he is operating with a hub-and-spoke style, help him identify some alternatives. If it becomes necessary to adjust goals, expect him to communicate the new objectives to his team and hold them accountable.

ACCELERATE	**CREATE teachable moments**	Suggest that Tom read *Good to Great* by Jim Collins (HarperBusiness, 2001) for stories about how some leaders were able to change their businesses by "telling it like it is" and getting everyone committed to a new direction. Work with Tom on developing an "early warning system" to anticipate possible problems going forward.
	TRACK progress	Discuss expected outcomes and results. Work with Tom to evaluate progress toward his goals. Encourage him to invite additional feedback and ask other people to support the changes they see. Acknowledge and celebrate his efforts.

Results: Measuring Impact

Tom Garcia completed his development plan in less than three months, since it was so tightly linked to what he needed to do anyway. He made progress in improving his Resilience—and helped others on his team increase their Resilience as well. He knew that it would be important to help people handle ongoing changes in the VUCA environment (in a world characterized by volatility, uncertainty, complexity, and ambiguity). These new skills allowed Tom to:

- Clarify his vision and expectations for the team and communicate with hope and optimism.

- Stay calm and remain open to challenges from headquarters.

- Help others rebound and engage people in adapting to changes.

- Minimize turnover and maximize productivity despite several rounds of restructuring.

- Manage the business in a way that supported his health and wellness.

19

Integrity

High-integrity leaders demonstrate principled leadership and an uncompromising commitment to the highest standards of professionalism and ethical behavior. They lead with a clear sense of well-developed personal values and standards. They act as custodians of the organization culture and model admirable corporate citizenship in their behavior. They display consistency in their actions and build trust. Others view them as trustworthy, authentic, and credible. They are concerned with equity and are fair in their treatment of people. They accept responsibility for their actions and promote accountability.

Factor	Competency	Core Practice
Leading People	Resilience	Ethics
Thinking and Deciding	Integrity	Values
Achieving	Learning Orientation	Trust
Relating to People		Fairness
Managing Work		Responsibility
Managing Self		

Integrity is the currency that builds long-term followership. With success comes bigger challenges and larger temptations, and followers are watching leaders every step of the way. Business scandals with Enron, Bernie Madoff, and the banking crisis have heightened our awareness of the importance of transparency. High-integrity leaders are willing to work in a fishbowl, submitting themselves to the scrutiny of others. They shape culture by influencing behavior in accordance with the organization's values. By walking the talk with their actions, they set the tone and establish guidelines for what's acceptable.

When it comes to Integrity, the fewer gray areas the better. Actions that are not consistent with the espoused values of the organization raise doubts in the minds of followers and erode culture. It doesn't take long for observant followers to detect blatant self-interest or a hollow façade. Great leaders model authentic leadership in service of the best interests of the organization and all its stakeholders. Leaders with high Integrity are naturally inspiring to followers, and attract and retain great talent for their organizations. Imagine reading the morning newspaper featuring you on the cover: what would the quotes from your followers say?

Leaders need to demonstrate Integrity to effectively shape the culture, maintain the organization's values, and set the tone for what's expected. Leaders at every level who operate with Integrity demonstrate trustworthiness, fairness, and personal responsibility, as well as an uncompromising commitment to ethical and values-based behavior. Leaders' actions (or inaction) set tone and context for how others in the organization are expected to behave. Although Integrity does not vary by level, at more senior levels of leadership, it can be assumed that there are more people watching the leader's actions—both internally and externally—which magnifies the risk of getting off-track. The five core practices of Integrity are described in more detail below.

How Leaders Demonstrate Integrity

	Managers, Function Leaders, and Senior Executives
Ethics	Commits to high standards of ethical behavior.
Values	Demonstrates a commitment to the organization's values.
Trust	Builds trust by being candid and consistent.
Fairness	Treats others fairly and equitably.
Responsibility	Takes responsibility for own actions, including mistakes.

Self-Assessment

To evaluate your Integrity, check all boxes below that represent current behavior or performance. Look for patterns: Which core practices represent a development need, a strength, or an excessive use? Recognize that you might have some blind spots. Invite your boss or colleagues to indicate what they have observed in your behavior. Use this assessment to help identify development suggestions that are most relevant to you.

	Development Need	Strength	Excessive Use
Ethics	☐ Has professional standards and values that are unclear, relative, or overly self-serving ☐ Acts in ways that are inconsistent with relevant professional standards and ethics	☐ Demonstrates a commitment to his/her values and professional standards, even if there could be negative personal repercussions ☐ Openly discusses professional values and standards with others	☐ Expresses values in an absolute, black-and-white way ☐ Thinks and acts in terms of absolutes and is unwilling to compromise; shows intolerance for gray situations
Values	☐ Cannot articulate what he/she values; often unable or unwilling to take a stand ☐ Acts in ways that are inconsistent with the organization's espoused values	☐ Constructively raises and helps others think through values-related issues ☐ Builds commitment to the organization's culture and values in others	☐ Pushes own values on others; tells them what to do or makes (personal) decisions for them ☐ Blindly subscribes and adheres to the organization's values and culture; is overly conforming
Trust	☐ Does not walk the talk; says one thing, does another ☐ Acts and reacts in an unpredictable manner, which raises doubts about his/her motives	☐ Can present the unvarnished truth to others in a way they can accept and understand ☐ Is consistently reliable and dependable	☐ Communicates with such candor that others are hurt or embarrassed, especially in public ☐ Does not adapt; loses credibility by ignoring the complexity or fluidity of situations
Fairness	☐ Shows favoritism and preferential treatment of others ☐ Adopts exclusive or uncommon people practices that are not consistent with practices in other areas of the organization	☐ Models equitable treatment of others; is able to expand or deepen others' understanding of fairness and equity ☐ Takes action to change practices that have inconsistent or inequitable impact in the workplace	☐ Is rigidly rule-oriented and inflexible—never allows exceptions ☐ May overlook individual needs in an attempt to treat everyone equally
Responsibility	☐ Blames others or makes excuses when he/she makes mistakes; takes credit for the work of others ☐ Consistently attributes problems to uncontrollable circumstances; assumes little personal responsibility	☐ Accepts responsibility for the actions of his/her team and things that happen on his/her watch ☐ Reviews mistakes objectively—seeks to create solutions rather than assign blame	☐ Lets others "off the hook" by taking sole responsibility for problems ☐ Apologizes unnecessarily for uncontrollable problems

Development Suggestions

The following section contains development suggestions for each core practice. Having completed the self-assessment, focus on suggestions that correspond to the core practices you identified as a development need or excessive use. Use these suggestions to create your own development plan, making sure to try one or two from each phase. In addition, feel free to create your own or adapt these to best meet your development needs.

Ethics

Commit to high standards of ethical behavior.

Character is much easier kept than recovered.

Thomas Paine

Awaken potential:

- **Reflect on significant learning experiences in your life,** both successes and failures. What lessons did you learn from those experiences? How have those lessons shaped your approach to leading people and managing your business? Identify personal values that have been formed or reinforced through these significant experiences.

- **Write down your personal leadership principles and values.** Keep the list short—just three to five succinct statements. Why are these so important to you? What has helped shape these? Display the list prominently in your office for you and others to see.

- **Walk the line.** Remember a time when you were tempted to do something you knew was wrong. What prompted you to stay true to your values? Think about a time you saw someone else cross a line you would not have. What did you do?

- **Reflect on how you deal with ambiguity.** Try to remember several situations in which you had to deal with uncertainty or ambiguity, when the direction wasn't clear. How comfortable did you feel? Were you open to different points of view and possibilities or did you try to clarify by artificially sorting issues into either-or categories? How important was being right to you? Did it get in the way of your ability to influence and gain commitment from others?

Align goals:

- **Review your organization's code of ethics.** Do you have one? What areas have particular application to your function's work? Periodically review the code of ethics with your team. Talk about situations they may encounter that could put them to the test.

- **Discuss ethical behavior.** Look for opportunities to discuss expectations and concerns about ethical behavior. For example, debrief a recent controversial decision with your team. Evaluate the ethical dimensions of this decision.

- **Check your own behavior for consistency.** Work with your human resources partner to survey employee perceptions about your leadership behavior and its consistency with the organization's values. Identify strengths to leverage and create an action plan to address gaps. Communicate your plans to employees in a transparent and timely manner.

Accelerate performance:

- **Make it safe to talk about ethics.** Create a team climate conducive to honest conversations about ethical dilemmas people have faced. Give them permission, and encourage people to take risks in raising their questions and concerns. Share ethical dilemmas of your own and how you resolved them.

- **Use the newspaper test.** When facing challenging situations, ask yourself, "Would I be happy about seeing my picture in the paper next to a description of what I'm about to do?" Engage in proactive conversation to discuss the pros and cons of various approaches.

- **Keep an open mind** when dealing with others whose principles and standards differ from yours. Look for ways to learn from them and to find mutually acceptable possibilities. Be willing to have the discussion when others prefer alternative approaches.

- **Prepare for being tested.** Identify situations that challenge your commitment to acting in accordance with your personal principles. Next time you anticipate being in a similar situation, write out the principle that might be challenged and several specific things you will do or say to reinforce the principle being tested.

- **Coach others.** Develop an original case study for discussion with your team based on an incident you observed during your career. Provide them with several alternatives from which to choose and together evaluate the ethical ramifications of each decision.

- **Establish an ethics officer in your group.** Empower this person to provide others with resources that could support living the organization's values. Ensure that the person is well supported and that you lead by example in using the resources provided.

As an example, if you express your values in an absolute way and show intolerance for gray situations, people may see you as rigid or inflexible and be afraid to bring their dilemmas to you. Try to show more compassion for people who have different beliefs and standards from your own.

Values

Demonstrate a commitment to the organization's values.

"Don't compromise yourself. You are all you've got."

Janis Joplin

Awaken potential:

- **Complete a values assessment** to identify your own motivations and guiding values. Reflect on how your values influence the way you motivate others and the team climate you create.

- **Examine how you act on your values.** Think about a time when doing the right thing might have resulted in your losing a sale, missing an opportunity, annoying a customer, etc. What process did you use to decide on the action to take? Who did you consult, if anyone? What alternatives did you consider? What made you hesitate?

- **Analyze your reputation in the organization.** How are you viewed by peers and direct reports? Would their descriptions of how you operate be consistent? Would their descriptions match your intentions?

- **Might or right?** Try to remember when you have thought or said something like, "It's the principle of the thing" to explain your decision. Were you standing up for what was right or trying to get your own way?

- **Identify role models.** List some people you admire. What do you admire them for? What insights does this give you into your own values and principles?

Align goals:

- **Link performance goals to organization values.** Make a review of your organization's mission and values statements a standard part of your business planning process.

Demonstrate connections to decisions and choice points you are making based on these values.

- **Take an external perspective.** Visit your organization's website and look around, pretending you are a first-time viewer. How well does it convey the organization's values to customers and other visitors? What are the key themes or message you take away? Is this what your organization wants to be known for?

- **Review your own values against those of the organization.** Are they consistent or competing? What do you need to do to get them more aligned? Make a concerted effort to reinforce those values when speaking to your team and others in the organization.

- **Periodically check yourself against your espoused values.** When have you compromised your beliefs to "keep the peace" with leaders in other functions? How did that sit? What did you or the organization gain or lose by doing so?

Accelerate performance:

- **Learn more about principled leadership.** Read *Authentic Leadership: Rediscovering the Secrets to Creating Lasting Value* by Bill George (Jossey-Bass, 2003). The former CEO of Medtronic discusses the importance of purpose, values, heart, relationships, and self-discipline for leaders who want to create healthy corporations.

- **Identify values in action.** Actively engage others in conversations about the organization's espoused values. Share real examples of those values in action. Build these stories into your communications with direct reports.

- **Examine your organization's cultural norms.** Which ones promote effective behavior and high-quality results? Establish norms in your area that reinforce the best aspects of the organization's culture.

- **Be courageous** and open about where you see organizational values and business decisions not always aligning. Create an environment where challenging those who are near the line is welcomed rather than approached tentatively or with skepticism.

- **Take time to learn the values of each member of your team.** Knowing what motivates them is critical to your ability to lead them to their best performance and most engaged state. It's likely that you may not share all of the same values. Initiate conversations for alignment.

- **Actively seek out divergent views** to ensure healthy challenge in dialogues. Shared values and assumptions can create cohesion in a team, but can prevent the group from testing their assumptions. Select a few advisors who generally see the world differently from you or your team. Find ways to incorporate them into your decision-making.

Trust

Build trust by being candid and consistent.

> *The glue that holds all relationships together—including
> the relationship between the leader and the led—is trust,
> and trust is based on integrity.*

Brian Tracy

Awaken potential:

- **Learn about your trust level.** Reflect on times when you have received helpful feedback about trust. What insights did you gain? How did it help you enhance your effectiveness as a leader? How can you do the same for others?

- **How would others describe you as a leader?** Would they describe you as candid? Would they say they could predict your reactions to issues, or would they say it would depend on your mood? How often have you held back from openly expressing your point of view because it differed from mainstream thinking or because you were concerned that others would disagree?

- **Assess your reputation as a leader**—do people feel that you do what you set out to do? Do others see opportunities for success by getting on board with your initiatives? How central to your organization's culture is being trustworthy and credible? How does your credibility impact your ability to be effective in the organization?

- **Analyze your follow-through on commitments.** How aligned are your actions with your intentions? How often do you fail to follow through on commitments because your plate is too full? Are there people who might be wondering if you have forgotten a promise? Make a habit of providing quick, regular, informal progress updates to everyone who is counting on you for something. Excellent execution requires commitment and follow-through from others. Make sure to set a good example.

Align goals:

- **Establish and communicate clear priorities** to help others produce timely and effective results. Be candid in explaining the hierarchy of priorities, and let people know when those priorities shift.

- **Practice no surprises** by doing what you say you will do—and by saying what you will do. As soon as you think you may not be able to deliver on a commitment, talk with each person involved and work together to set a new timeframe or find alternatives to getting the work done.

Accelerate performance:

- **Learn about leadership credibility.** Read *Credibility: How Leaders Gain and Lose It, Why People Demand It* by James Kouzes and Barry Posner (Jossey-Bass, 2003). Identify one or two specific behaviors to work on, and create a plan to do so. Share this plan with a colleague or two to invite feedback.

- **Respect others' styles.** Think about the interpersonal styles of your direct reports before giving them feedback. Work to modify your approach in a way that respects their preferences without compromising the message.

- **Encourage candor with your responses to others' honesty.** Practice active listening, thank people for their feedback, and appreciate their courage in speaking up. Don't shoot the messenger.

- **Be upfront.** To build trust with others, be clear about where you stand and what you want in your work relationship. Ask others to do the same and try to agree on the ways in which you will work with each other to be most productive. For additional information about strategies to build trust, read *The Empowered Manager* by Peter Block (Jossey-Bass, 1987).

EXCESSIVE USE

As an example, if you communicate with such candor that others are hurt or embarrassed, let go of the notion of being brutally honest. Honesty fosters constructive change. However, brutality triggers defensiveness and resentment.

Fairness

Treat others fairly and equitably.

Keep in mind that the true measure of an individual is how he treats a person who can do him absolutely no good.

Ann Landers

Awaken potential:

- **Analyze your relationships with people on your team.** Are there some individuals with whom you enjoy working more than others? Think about whether you provide different assignments or development experiences because of that preference, and how that might look to others.

- **Evaluate your people decisions.** Reflect on the significant decisions about people you have made over the past six months. Do you see any themes in your decisions or do you approach each decision in isolation? Consider whether you are treating everyone in your group consistently.

- **Appraise your appraisal standards.** Think about the styles of the people you lead, especially if anyone tends to push your buttons (i.e., irritate or aggravate you). Consider how this might be impacting your assessment of that person's performance.

Align goals:

- **Identify red rules and blue rules.** Work with your team to identify your organization's "red rules" (absolutes) and "blue rules" (rules related to process that sometimes can and should be broken, depending on the circumstances). Discuss how these rules are communicated. Talk about how your team can use "blue rules" to empower staff and build appropriate flexibility into your operations.

- **Compare your people practices to those of your peers.** If practices in your area are extremely different (e.g., more rigid or more relaxed), consider how this might impact others' perceptions of your fairness. Engage your team in a discussion about what people practices they would like to change.

- **Align your requirements for promotions.** Look at the standards you have set for promotion in your area. How similar or different are they from other leaders' or the organization's standards? Are there obvious and legitimate reasons for the differences, or could they be perceived as arbitrarily too high or too low?

- **Review your rules.** Periodically check in with peer leaders about rules and practices in your respective areas to ensure consistent treatment of employees across the organization. How might you together shape how the organization moves forward consistently and fairly?

Accelerate performance:

- **Use your head *and* your heart.** Before making significant decisions, make a habit of considering both business and people implications by thinking through each separately. Look for competing issues and inconsistencies before deciding.

- **Reveal your decision-making process.** When communicating decisions, particularly those that others may not like, share the process by which you made your decision and the factors you considered—in addition to the decision itself. Sometimes the "whys" help bring context and understanding.

- **Match assignments with interests.** Meet with each of your direct reports to understand their interests and aspirations as well as their strengths and development needs. Look for ways to adjust work assignments to reflect what you learn.

- **Coach people as individuals.** When having conversations with direct reports about performance, focus on how their skills, strengths, and development needs compare to the requirements of their jobs rather than how they compare to each other. Work together to help each person realize his/her true potential.

- **Separate style from substance when reviewing performance.** Ensure that you recognize the excellent work of others even if it wasn't done the way you would have handled it.

- **Send a clear and consistent message about performance.** Clearly communicate and consistently reinforce your standards for effective performance. When rewarding or recognizing performance, reiterate the standards that have been met. When taking corrective action, reiterate the standards that have not been met.

EXCESSIVE USE

As an example, if you overlook individual needs in attempting to treat everyone equally, your best performers may not feel valued. Be sure to express appreciation for their efforts.

Responsibility

Take responsibility for his/her own actions, including mistakes.

"Correcting someone else's mistakes is a lot easier than facing your own."

Bill George

Awaken potential:

- **Review how you handle your mistakes.** Think about errors in judgment or other business mistakes you have made. Did you react with embarrassment and try to minimize what happened—or did you identify the mistake for what it was, admit it, and move on?

- **Analyze how you react to the mistakes of others.** Do you treat these as lessons learned and allow the person to recover—or do you continue to bring up the mistakes as cautionary tales or use them to limit the person's opportunities to grow?

- **Assess your reputation.** Complete the Leadership Reputation Exercise in the Appendix to identify what actions you want to become known for as a leader and to help you think through how you want to be perceived inside and outside your organization. A copy of this exercise is included later in this guide.

Align goals:

- **Take responsibility.** Remember that leaders retain ultimate accountability for the performance of their functions and teams. How does your ownership of team outcomes impact your leadership and ability to be successful?

- **Set clear expectations.** Ensure that everyone, especially new people, understands the norm for accountability in your organization. Use your next team meeting to have individual team members talk about their experiences with team accountability. What do they think the rules are? How do you together reinforce them?

- **Hold others accountable** for their actions without protecting them from mistakes or allowing them to fail unnecessarily. Evaluate what prompts you when you jump in. Discuss with others your tendencies and when they might appreciate a more systematic or consistent approach.

Accelerate performance:

- **Conduct after-action reviews** to discuss what happened on particular projects. Invite everyone who was meaningfully involved in the project to participate. Review each major stage and ask what could have been done differently to complete the project more efficiently or make it even more successful. Capture important lessons learned and apply them to current and future projects.

- **Establish a personal board of directors** consisting of people outside your organization who can provide you with candid views about important issues and honest feedback on your behavior.

- **Model responsibility** by openly admitting mistakes and taking active steps to move on. Own your actions.

- **Take responsibility in public, coach in private.** When members of your team make mistakes, accept responsibility as the leader. Provide feedback and coaching for those team members in private rather than surfacing the issues publicly, which may be inappropriate.

- **Treat mistakes as learning opportunities.** Give people permission to try. When others make mistakes, work with them to find learning opportunities that can be applied as quickly as possible. As a leader, provide second chances for employees who have made mistakes to demonstrate your trust, help them apply learning, and regain confidence in their skills and abilities.

- **Communicate your reasoning** behind decisions and actions you take. Help others understand what factors you consider and how they impact the outcome. This not only helps them make better decisions in the future, but also gives them the context of the "why" today.

EXCESSIVE USE

As an example, if you let people "off the hook" by taking too much responsibility for problems, they will not learn the right lesson. Hold them accountable for resolving problems created by their actions.

Coach Others on Integrity

When coaching others, focus on the core practices that were identified as either a development need or excessive use in the self-assessment at the beginning of this chapter. Identify and adapt any relevant development suggestions. Additional coaching tips are provided in the following table for some adverse leadership behaviors. For more information review Chapter 4, "Coach Others."

Coaching Suggestions

	Behavior	Awaken	Align	Accelerate
Ethics	Acts selfishly	• Arrange for the person to get feedback from key stakeholders, through multi-rater feedback or interviews. What do others believe the person does that may be selfish? • Suggest that the person identify where selfishness gets in the way of being successful. Are there any triggers that may lead to this behavior?	• Encourage the person to share feedback and personal reflections with others, and ask them for suggestions about what the person could do differently. • Help identify a mentor who is recognized as selfless. Have them meet to examine new ways of exploring the topic.	• Propose that the person ask a trusted colleague to help observe and provide feedback when this occurs. • Have the person come to you or a mentor when a potential trigger is identified. Review together the options for further action before proceeding. Help review the tradeoffs of those options.
	Violates professional ethics	• Assign the person to research ethical standards and practices in your industry. Discuss what the person learns along with what is expected in your area. • Ask the person to reflect on his/her standards for ethical behavior and identify situations where these standards were challenged. Discuss these together.	• Have the person present the findings to his/her peers. Where are there similarities and/or gaps between current organizational leadership and industry standard? • Establish an expectation that gray area decisions must be reviewed by others before implementation. Identify a core group of stakeholders to act as that panel.	• Coach the person to identify ways to demonstrate more flexibility while maintaining personal standards and acting in an ethical manner. • Have the person bring decisions that may approach "the line" in advance to your one-on-one meetings.

Behavior		Awaken	Align	Accelerate
Values	*Operates in a values vacuum*	• Conduct a values clarification exercise to clarify values and motivations. • Discuss examples of the organization's espoused values in action. What difficult decisions have been made to uphold the values?	• Assign the person to collect feedback about what others expect. • Identify situations where company values were maintained as well as where the company fell short. Discuss what action was taken to realign actions with values.	• Encourage the person to be mindful of the values component in making decisions. • Help the person identify what to do to make his/her behavior more consistent. Build in a regular review process.
	Acts in ways that don't reflect organizational values	• Discuss the organization's espoused values. Which are most important? Which are often overlooked? • Help the person examine his/her values and identify how they align with those of the organization— or not.	• Suggest that the person talk about the organization's values in a team meeting and then brainstorm ways to support those values. • Have the person seek feedback from team members on when he or she might have strayed from these values.	• Propose that the person engage in a regular discussion with a trusted colleague about how their values are expressed. • Discuss the "fishbowl phenomenon" and the importance of operating with transparency, especially in senior leadership roles.
Trust	*Doesn't follow through*	• Have the person reflect on how well he/she is trusted within the organization. What actions contribute to that trust? What might the person be doing that prevents trust? • Ask the person what commitments he/she has made in the past six months—and how many have been broken.	• Add an experiential component to the next team off-site that highlights trust. Debrief learnings with the entire team. Then talk privately with the person about the experience later on. • Encourage the person to seek feedback from key stakeholders about walking the talk and how it impacts trust.	• Ask the person to keep a journal of overt commitments and what was done to fulfill them. Recommend that the person "publish" intentions to enhance accountability. • Coach the person to identify ways to ensure actions are consistent with intentions.

19

INTEGRITY

Behavior	Awaken	Align	Accelerate
Trust *Is unpredictable; lacks consistency*	• Help the person figure out what might be at the heart of the unpredictable behavior (e.g., loses interest, is highly excitable). • Offer your own observations about behavior you have seen in team meetings. Ask the person to imagine how that behavior was viewed and interpreted by others.	• Identify an internal model of consistency and resilience. What characteristics or behaviors define his/her reputation? Have the person select one or two behaviors to mirror and experiment with. • Seek feedback from key stakeholders on the impact of the person's unpredictability. How does it affect their perception of the person's leadership?	• Ensure the person's attempt at behavior change is overt and transparent. Have the person ask others to provide immediate feedback when they see his/her behavior escalating. Monitor progress and help the person seek ongoing feedback. • Ensure that those brave enough to give feedback are taken care of. Help prevent any negative ramifications of being courageous.
Fairness *Plays favorites*	• Suggest that the person look through his/her sent items. Who gets the most emails? How is the discrepancy justified? • Provide your own observations on instances in which certain talent may have been isolated or not leveraged properly. What drove the person to do so?	• Introduce the topic of fairness in one of your own team meetings. Discuss challenges of recognizing and responding to individual needs. Invite the group to discuss what leaders can do to treat their people more consistently. • Look together at how people are being assigned, and at which people are chosen for the best projects.	• Ask the person to suspend assumptions about people. Suggest that the person learn about their interests and use that data rather than personal preferences in making assignments—and then provide that rationale to others. • Create a plan to spend more informal time with those lower on the trusted list. Facilitate comfort level by ongoing conversation and understanding.

Behavior		Awaken	Align	Accelerate
Fairness	*Adopts exclusive or uncommon people practices*	• Audit the common norms and practices across the organization. How does the person champion those processes? Where does the person stray? To what consequence? • Help the person identify situations to act more consistently while treating people as individuals. How would the team benefit?	• Suggest that the person work with the team to review the results of the most recent employee engagement survey. Look at what issues were identified and how they were addressed. • Pair the person with the human resources business partner to review current people practices. Have them meet routinely to review new or potential changes. Make the person a part of the evolution by having them serve on a task team.	• Look together for ways to increase consistency. Coach the person to be clear in communicating expectations. • Acknowledge that it may be important to take a stand and communicate that "this is the way it is" even when it may not be the way the person has always done it.
Responsibility	*Points fingers at others*	• Ask the person if he/she has had experience working with someone like that, and how it felt. • Ask the person what tends to trigger the reaction. Does everything trigger a defensive reaction or only highly visible mistakes?	• Recommend conducting an after action review with the team to look at what could have been done differently. • Have the team read *The OZ Principle* by Roger Conners, Tom Smith and Craig Hickman (Prentice Hall Press, 1998) and debrief it as a group.	• Coach the person to look at what part he/she played when things went wrong. Provide immediate feedback when this happens. • Be consistent with identifying above the line or below the line behavior. Build that language into the team's vocabulary.
	Makes excuses for own mistakes or shortcomings	• Examine situations where excuses have been made, and look together at what might be causing the problem. • What has prompted excuses in the past? Does the person feel powerless? Help the person make a realistic appraisal about what forces are controllable vs. uncontrollable.	• Set clear expectations for accountability together, ensuring the person focuses on the process and owns the result. • Recommend that he or she review situations with the team and get help sorting through what is and is not controllable.	• Help the person understand how to delegate responsibility and authority to others while retaining accountability for overall performance and results. • Encourage the person to declare that "the buck stops here" more publicly and more often.

INTEGRITY

Tips for Coaching in a Global Environment

Integrity may be practiced or expressed differently within other cultures. This might impact how you approach coaching. Try to keep an open mind, avoid generalizations, and continue gathering data as you gain experience with another culture. Consider these suggestions:

Ethics: Be clear about your expectations for speaking up or speaking out, especially when it comes to ethical issues. Many companies have established clear rules about doing business. Sarbanes-Oxley governs corporate conduct in the United States. Practices in some countries may be different (e.g., bribery and respecting copyrights and other forms of intellectual property). Some development suggestions presented earlier in this chapter call for making many aspects of Integrity more clear and explicit. Such explicit communication might seem strange to people who come from a high context culture, where many things are left unsaid. It is important to understand cultural context, especially around what might be involved in taking a risk to stand up for what is right. Ask for personal stories about how personal risk-taking has had a positive or negative influence on the person's career.

Values: Take time to learn the values and business norms of other cultures, especially when you are coaching people who come from different cultural backgrounds. Ask about their cultural values and ways of demonstrating Integrity. Discuss together how those values can be respected at work. Other cultures may value different kinds of behaviors. For example, independent initiative is valued and rewarded in some cultures. Collaboration is more the norm in how things get done in others. In some, absolute obedience to authority is expected.

Trust: It may take time to build trust with people you are coaching for them to be comfortable sharing their needs and motivations. People from other cultures may have very different expectations and degrees of comfort regarding open conversation about feelings and emotions. There are also different perceptions about behaviors such as eye contact, informal language, humor, and intimacy—all of which may be related to establishing and maintaining trustful relationships. Recognize that in some cultures it is considered disrespectful to criticize or share negative feedback about a person in a leadership position. Be cautious about the directness of your feedback as you work to build trust. Some cultures are less forthright than others, and this may prevent some people from hearing the point you are trying to make.

Fairness: Learn all you can about the culture of the individual with whom you are dealing. Do the cultural norms tend to favor entitlement or fairness and equity? Some leaders may operate from a quid pro quo mentality (e.g., "you take care of me, and I will take care of you") and give special treatment to some stakeholders at the expense of others. Such customs and treatment may be difficult for people in other cultures to understand—and may be highly resistant to change.

Responsibility: People in some cultures view goals as commitments, and don't like to set stretch goals that they might have trouble achieving. Different expectations about performance commitments (e.g., meeting particular project milestones) may impact what you are coaching the leader to perform—as well as impacting the coaching process itself. People may need more explicit and regular communication to establish agreed-upon goals and commit to taking action. Recognize that not all cultures have the same expectations for how leaders respond to and take accountability for mistakes.

A Case Study in Integrity

Integrity requires you to effectively commit to high standards of ethical behavior, express your values and commitment to the organization, build trust by being candid and consistent, treat others fairly and equitably, and take responsibility for your actions. As you read about Jack's situation, reflect on what you've learned about Integrity in this chapter. How does Jack sound like you or one of your team members? What experiences or tendencies do you share? Finally, consider how you would help Jack demonstrate greater skill in Integrity and be successful in his leadership role.

Walking the Walk as Well as the Talk

Jack Moore had worked in a variety of senior director roles over the years. He was recently promoted to SVP, Supply Chain, to work for Frank Johansson. Frank wanted Jack to drive performance in the supply chain organization because he had a reputation for having what it takes to get things done. Sustainability was a personal passion for Jack, and he was excited to finally have the authority and staff to implement some major green initiatives. Several people on his team, specifically Ellen and Brian, were familiar with and supportive of Jack's ideas. In fact, they had joined the company because they believed in Jack's vision. Others on his team were people he had known as colleagues, but not well.

Jack started by sharing a high-level vision of how he wanted to "green" the supply chain function. He talked about his excitement over having such a capable team, then assigned Ellen and Brian to lead a variety of new green-oriented projects. When Jack told his boss about the new green initiatives, he expected Frank's support. Instead, he found out that Frank was quite conservative—and saw green initiatives as costly and trendy. He told Jack that he wanted him to "stick to the knitting" rather than disrupt current relationships with their key suppliers. Jack decided to go ahead anyway, figuring he could win Frank over once several projects were successful and demonstrated results. He took Ellen into his confidence and plotted a stealth strategy with her.

Over time, Brian noticed that Ellen's projects were getting more time and attention from Jack along with more resources. When Brian approached Jack about this, he was told that his own projects were still key priorities—and that it would be "full speed ahead" once key suppliers were on board. Brian started to receive other assignments that competed with the green projects for his time. Brian saw that Jack was spending much more time with Ellen. He worried that Jack was losing confidence in his capabilities but didn't know why.

During mid-year reviews, Brian told Jack that he was hoping to go somewhere where he could add more value. Several others expressed concern that there was a lot of activity in Ellen's area, but no results. They questioned whether Jack was following through on everything he had committed to. People felt that he had sold out by not pursuing his green agenda with more vigor—and they felt betrayed. They were also confused.

Jack realized that his decision to assign the stealth projects to Ellen made it seem to Brian like he was playing favorites. He also realized that they might have gone too far in maneuvering behind Frank's back—and that it was probably time to tell Frank what was going on, especially since Ellen's projects weren't getting the traction he had expected. Jack's behavior had raised doubts in the minds of several people about what information Jack was sharing and what he was not sharing.

Jack found that he needed Integrity more than ever, in order to:

- Demonstrate his commitment to his values, even if there could be negative personal repercussions.

- Openly discuss his beliefs with Frank and help him think through the issues.

- Present the unvarnished truth to others in a way they could accept and understand.

- See the danger of overlooking individual needs and the importance of equity.

- Accept responsibility for the things that happened on his watch and then move things forward.

Jack's Leadership Development Plan

Following is a sample development plan for Jack Moore. Research on leadership development has shown that leaders learn through experience and that this learning is optimized through the use of an individual development plan that includes new experiences as well as introduces the leader to new conversations and tools. The suggestions included in the previous sections may stimulate your thinking about other possibilities that Jack might pursue.

LEADERSHIP DEVELOPMENT PLAN FOR JACK MOORE
DEVELOPMENT GOAL
Goal: To strengthen the expression of my Integrity
Desired Outcomes—results I want to see from developing this skill
Self: I will be seen as a leader with Integrity who values each team member and provides consistent opportunities for contribution.
Team: Each member of my team will be clear about our business priorities—and how he/she contributes to our results.
Organization: Supply Chain will be a more effective and efficient business partner within our organization.

LEADERSHIP DEVELOPMENT PLAN FOR JACK MOORE

Self-Understanding—strengths that I can build on and development needs I can address

Strengths:

- I am committed to building and maintaining a high-performing team.
- I have effectively coached and developed direct reports in previous leadership positions.
- I believe I am fair in my dealings with others and intend to do what it takes to demonstrate that.
- I am willing to accept responsibility for my behavior and the impact it has had on others in the organization.

Development Needs:

- I have a lot of ideas for how we can improve; I tend to communicate them in the moment vs. talking about how they connect to initiatives already in progress.
- I like to brainstorm and let others run with ideas. It's easier for me to do this with people whose work styles I know.
- Projects are more interesting to me during planning than when they are in the day-to-day development stage.

Business Context—challenges in my business environment that require this skill

There is increasing pressure on profitability. Current economic conditions require that all parts of the organization reduce costs. The Supply Chain organization could contribute significantly to reduced costs.

DEVELOPMENT ACTIONS

AWAKEN

- Meet with appropriate stakeholders to acknowledge mistakes in how I approached the green initiative. Get feedback from them on how I could have handled things differently.
- Have a candid conversation with my manager. Identify what I need to do to win back his trust.
- Have a candid conversation with the Supply Chain team. Share my personal pledge with the team.

ALIGN

- Have an all-staff meeting to review current and planned initiatives; work as a team to set priorities.
- Make the case for the green initiatives with my manager and other important stakeholders.
- Establish regular review meetings with superiors on the progress of supply chain initiatives. Let our accomplishments speak for themselves.

LEADERSHIP DEVELOPMENT PLAN FOR JACK MOORE

ACCELERATE

- Share my development goals with others. Ask trusted colleagues for periodic feedback.
- Solicit regular feedback from my team regarding areas of concern: consistency, fairness, ethics, trust, and responsibility.
- Review my progress with my manager in regular one-on-one meetings.
- During quarterly reviews, discuss engagement and development as well as results with my direct reports in the context of the organization's strategic initiatives.
- Contract with an outside consulting firm to conduct a thorough multi-rater feedback survey process in order to monitor the perceptions about my leadership. Share the results with my manager and my team.

DEVELOPMENT SUCCESS FACTORS

Timeline: Within the next six months

Support Needed:

- Ongoing feedback from my direct reports about my follow-through on initiatives.
- Feedback from individual direct reports on their engagement and whether they are being stretched by assignments.

Indicators of Success:

- Agreement about priorities for the supply chain organization up and down the organization.
- All direct reports will feel they are valued members of the supply chain team focused on meaningful initiatives.
- Key projects will be completed in a timely manner.
- Manager will express trust in my leadership, and someday recognize the importance of green initiatives.

An Example of Coaching for Integrity

Jack Moore's goal was to strengthen his skills in Integrity. Here are some steps Jack's manager could take using the Awaken, Align, Accelerate framework to coach Jack in this area:

AWAKEN	Increase INSIGHT	Brainstorm other ways he could have handled the situation rather than resorting to stealth. Invite Jack to analyze and reflect on his leadership reputation. Suggest that Jack invest time getting to know more about the interests and capabilities of his team members.
	MOTIVATE change	Focus on options and choices. Identify what Jack is motivated to change. Explore the consequences of not making any changes, including the impact on his personal reputation or credibility with his team.
ALIGN	PLAN goals	Ask Jack what can be done to rescue and repair the current situation. Focus on what he could change to improve his reputation and credibility. Work together to construct a leadership development plan similar to the sample provided in this chapter.
	ALIGN expectations	Suggest that Jack talk with his team about what is most important to him in achieving results for the organization. Encourage Jack to share what he learned in mid-year reviews about his leadership practices. Challenge him to commit to change the way he communicates priorities.
ACCELERATE	CREATE teachable moments	Propose adding a review of projects and priorities to Jack's regular staff meetings to help maintain a consistent focus and clearly communicate changes when needed. Ask Jack to take stock of outstanding commitments before agreeing to take on more. Talk about the implications of trying to be too accommodating of others' requests. Coach Jack on providing feedback to others through a respectful dialogue.
	TRACK progress	Discuss what kinds of changes will be visible to others. Ensure that Jack communicates with stakeholders. Encourage him to invite additional feedback and ask other people to support the changes they see. Acknowledge his efforts.

Results: Measuring Impact

Jack Moore took almost six months to work through his plan. He came close to losing his job when Frank learned about the stealth projects. However, he was saved by the timing. When several newspaper articles showcased what other local companies were doing to green their supply chains, the CEO asked Frank what they were doing in this area. Thanks to Jack's initiative, Frank had a story to tell. His new Integrity skill set allowed Jack to:

- Operate with greater transparency.

- Be more courageous in presenting the truth to others.

- Help Frank think through the issues and get alignment for supply chain priorities.

- Keep Brian from transferring to another division.

- Complete important green projects in a timely manner.

20

Learning Orientation

Learning-oriented leaders are self-aware and open to feedback and observations concerning their style and effect. They value what they don't know, acknowledge that others have more expertise in their respective areas, solicit input, and are willing to learn. They avoid functional prejudice and can see issues from different perspectives They reflect on and learn from their mistakes. A drive for personal mastery is reflected in their priorities and they actively pursue personal growth and improvement.

Factor	Competency	Core Practice
Leading People	Resilience	Self-Awareness
Thinking and Deciding	Integrity	Humility
Achieving	Learning Orientation	Openness
Relating to People		Mastery
Managing Work		Reflection
Managing Self		

Not to be confused with intelligence or agility, Learning Orientation is more attitude than aptitude. It is limited only by one's openness to new experiences and personal growth. A solid Learning Orientation enables individuals to not only learn from others but also to benefit from their own experiences. Great leaders continually evaluate their successes and failures and develop a sense of mastery necessary to sustain success at every level. They balance this mastery with humility—the recognition that they are not infallible and can benefit from others' ideas, talents, and contributions.

An orientation toward learning begins with curiosity and the inclination to ask questions. To be successful, leaders must learn to solicit and act on feedback from others without becoming defensive. As important as it is to celebrate successes, it is equally important for them to capitalize on the learning opportunities that come with mistakes. Leaders who can cultivate openness to new ideas and perspectives, acknowledge personal shortcomings, and treat mistakes as chances to learn are much more likely to grow personally and professionally on the job. Their teams benefit as well. Great leaders consistently learn from their experiences as they move into successively larger leadership roles. The five core practices of Learning Orientation are described in more detail below.

How Leaders at Different Levels Show Learning Orientation

	Managers, Function Leaders, and Senior Executives
Self-Awareness	Demonstrates a clear grasp of his/her own strengths, limitations, and development needs.
Humility	Accepts and acts on feedback from others.
Openness	Actively considers others' ideas and suggestions.
Mastery	Displays a desire to gain new knowledge and skills.
Reflection	Reflects on experience and learn from mistakes.

Self-Assessment

To evaluate your Learning Orientation, check all boxes below that represent current behavior or performance. Look for patterns: Which core practices represent a development need, a strength, or an excessive use? Recognize that you might have some blind spots. Invite your boss or colleagues to indicate what they have observed in your behavior. Use this assessment to help identify development suggestions that are most relevant to you.

	Development Need	Strength	Excessive Use
Self-Awareness	❏ Fails to invite constructive feedback from others ❏ Lacks insight into own strengths and weaknesses; has unrecognized blind spots	❏ Remains open to challenge and constructive feedback ❏ Acknowledges strengths and weaknesses in a matter-of-fact manner	❏ Invites too much feedback; may come across as insecure ❏ Shares too much personal insight with others
Humility	❏ Overestimates own talents and skills; needs to be seen as an expert ❏ Minimizes or disregards constructive input from others	❏ Demonstrates humility, truly values people who know more, and displays a willingness to seek others' expertise ❏ Actively solicits input from others in a variety of settings and contexts	❏ Is overly humble and self-effacing; does not inspire confidence ❏ Seeks too much input or guidance and comes across as lacking confidence or self-assurance
Openness	❏ Remains closed to or argues with ideas or perspectives that differ from his/her own ❏ Shows function prejudice or insists on seeing things from the perspective of the familiar function	❏ Routinely looks at things from a variety of perspectives; actively considers the ideas and opinions of others ❏ Promotes to others the importance of valuing and learning from different areas or functions	❏ Continually seeks out other perspectives and may be overly agreeable or deferent ❏ May not advocate strongly for or invest enough time in own area
Mastery	❏ Resists the notion that he/she could benefit from further development—or makes it a low priority ❏ Appears content with what he/she already knows and may seem disinterested in new learning	❏ Makes personal development a high priority; seeks out stretch assignments and learning experiences ❏ Stays abreast of the latest developments and best practices in the field, industry, or business	❏ Constantly seeks new experiences and seems more interested in personal development than delivering results ❏ Achieves depth at the expense of breadth; expertise may be excessively narrow
Reflection	❏ Doesn't pause to learn from past experiences—successes, failures, or both ❏ Fails to recognize mistakes and blames others when things go wrong	❏ Mindfully reflects on experiences; shares own learnings and helps others learn from their experiences ❏ Owns mistakes and acknowledges opportunities for improvement	❏ Tells too many war stories and seems overly self-focused ❏ Ruminates over mistakes and has difficulty letting go or moving on

Development Suggestions

The following section contains development suggestions for each core practice. Having completed the self-assessment, focus on suggestions that correspond to the core practices you identified as a development need or excessive use. Use these suggestions to create your own development plan, making sure to try one or two from each phase. In addition, feel free to create your own or adapt these to best meet your development needs.

Self-Awareness

Demonstrate a clear grasp of his/her own strengths, limitations, and development needs.

Knowing others is intelligence; knowing yourself is true wisdom.
Mastering others is strength; mastering yourself is true power.

Tao Te Ching

Awaken potential:

- **Start with your strengths.** Create a list of your greatest strengths as a leader. Consider how those have helped you become the leader you are today. How have your strengths changed or developed over the course of your career? What situations (including interactions with particular people) draw forth your best qualities?

- **Learn from others' experience.** Think about the leaders who have been most successful in your organization. What leadership strengths have you seen garner the best results in your organization? What leadership weaknesses have hindered executives in your company? How can you leverage your strengths and develop your limitations to achieve the results you want?

- **Examine your weaknesses.** Develop a list of your limitations as a leader (e.g., weaknesses, challenges, development needs, areas for growth, vulnerabilities). How have you identified and overcome limitations in the past?

- **Assess your openness to feedback.** Remember a time when you were NOT open to challenge or constructive feedback from others. What was the situation? What did you do? How did people react? What would you do differently next time? Where can you leverage this insight in working with others on a current project?

- **Ask colleagues for feedback,** or arrange for a multi-rater review process. How do the results match up with your expectations? Do you have some blind spots you didn't anticipate? What other methods could you employ to learn about your abilities and limitations?

Align goals:

- **Ask your boss for critical feedback** about your strengths and development needs. How does that assessment align with your self-assessment? Were there any surprises? Does your manager have any suggestions for addressing your growth areas? How does your profile of strengths and development needs fit with the goals and objectives for the business?

- **Identify your greatest business challenges** over the next six to twelve months. How will you leverage your strengths to address those challenges? Where might your limitations get in the way? How can you compensate for those? Put together a 100-day action plan to address those with a sense of urgency. Share your action plan with your manager. Ask for feedback. Then share it with others on your team.

- **Hold critical conversations with the right people.** Develop a stakeholder map, and figure out how to more fully engage key stakeholders to support you in accomplishing your development goals and business objectives.

Accelerate performance:

- **Find a mentor or coach.** Identify someone who has an exceptional grasp of his/her strengths and limitations. Ask that person to serve as your coach or mentor in this area. Ask how that person does self-monitoring.

- **Revisit your development plan on a regular basis.** Are you making progress on your developmental needs? Incorporate your findings into a revised and updated plan.

- **Recognize what you can change and accept what you can't.** If you can't—or won't— then look for ways to compensate for personal limitations that negatively affect your performance.

- **Become a champion** for learning and development. Consider what it would mean to be a role model in this area. Who could *you* mentor in this area? Help others on your team identify their own strengths and vulnerabilities. Ask everyone to develop personal scorecards to measure performance and progress. Discuss monthly. Coach them.

EXCESSIVE USE

As an example, if you show too much interest in self-assessment or continually seek feedback about your capabilities, you may come across as insecure. Review the "Confidence" section of Chapter 18, "Resilience," for some suggestions about acting with more self-confidence.

Accept and act on feedback from others.

"A single conversation with a wise man is better than ten years of study."

Chinese Proverb

Awaken potential:

- **Reflect on the power of humility.** Consider your experience working with leaders who brag about their own accomplishments. Contrast their behavior with leaders who acknowledge and express appreciation for the contributions of others. Which leader is likely to inspire greater followership? How can you do more to recognize others?

- **Explore your own humility.** Ask yourself how humility plays a role in your own leadership style. Reflect on whether you have a tendency to do things on your own rather than seeking out the expertise of others. Are you more comfortable making proposals or inviting suggestions? Do you seek and welcome input from others?

- **Evaluate your need for recognition.** Consider where your pride of accomplishment comes from. When receiving a compliment, what is your first reaction—taking credit or giving credit to others? Recognize that better solutions can often come from welcoming and increasing the participation of others.

- **Assess your reactions to feedback.** Reflect on a recent experience receiving feedback from someone. Who gave you the feedback? Did you ask for the feedback, or was it unsolicited? How did you react? How did you use the feedback?

- **Analyze your pattern of soliciting feedback.** Who do you typically ask for feedback and about what? How do you know who to ask? How do you incorporate their feedback into your future behavior?

- **Ask your direct reports** about their experiences getting feedback from you. Is it helpful? Is it delivered respectfully? Is it instructional? Is it timely? How could it be more useful? Try to be mindful of their responses and incorporate them into future feedback-giving opportunities.

Align goals:

- **Ask your peers for feedback.** Solicit feedback from your peers as well as your manager about how the organization can best use your talents. Use their comments to set new goals for yourself.

- **Review your personal development plan** with others, especially your manager. From time to time, ask for honest feedback on your progression toward your goals.

Accelerate performance:

- **Talk with your boss** about ways he/she uses feedback to develop. Are there ways you can replicate your boss' experience to get the most out of feedback?

- **Look for possible role models**—people who model humility in leadership. Try to observe and develop greater appreciation for different ways of handling meetings or other interactions (e.g., conflict situations). Experiment with some of those methods to improve your own approach.

- **Implement best practices.** Recognize that established ways of doing things may not be the most cost-effective, productive, or appealing. Tap internal and external expertise for new ideas. Invite others to help you identify and implement changes that would improve the status quo. Read "Level 5 Leadership: The Triumph of Humility and Fierce Resolve" by Jim Collins (*Harvard Business Review,* 2005). How could you incorporate some of those ideas in your own leadership approach?

- **Ask those involved in projects with you for feedback** about the overall project and your role in it. Was it managed well? Were roles clear? Were expectations understood? What would be useful in the future? Review the comments, and be mindful of them at the outset of your next project.

EXCESSIVE USE

As an example, if you are overly humble and self-effacing, you won't inspire confidence in your leadership brand. If you invite too much feedback from others, or in too many situations, you may come across as less self-assured. Practice story-telling to convey your own contributions while recognizing others for their achievements. Review the "Boldness" section of Chapter 5, "Leading Courageously," for some suggestions about acting with more assertiveness.

Actively consider others' ideas and suggestions.

"The real voyage of discovery consists not in seeking new lands, but in seeing with new eyes."

Marcel Proust

Awaken potential:

- **Reflect on the value of openness.** Identify leaders who were stuck in their own approaches and resistant to the suggestions of others. How did that kind of behavior impact your enthusiasm for working with them? How did their lack of openness impact the business? How did that impact other people in your area?

- **Assess your openness to others' ideas.** How do you typically react when someone suggests a competing solution or approach? Are you open to new ideas or do you tend to proceed as usual?

- **Look at how you react to suggestions.** Think back to the last time you rejected or argued against a proposal made by someone on your team. How did you handle that situation? Did you actively evaluate its merits or did you tend to dismiss it (e.g., "that's been tried before") without consideration? What impression did you convey? Did your reaction diminish his/her willingness to make suggestions or offer counter-proposals after that incident?

Align goals:

- **Broaden your goals.** Talk to your manager about your understanding of what you are trying to achieve for the business. Discuss whether there are other ways to think about your value to the organization. What new exposures or challenges might you bring to the organization?

- **Go around barriers to meet your goals.** Consider ways your team seems to be stuck on important goals or objectives. Could a new approach be employed to jump-start productivity or advancement? How might you initiate this process? How could this help ensure you achieve your business outcomes?

Accelerate performance:

- **Show interest in what others are doing.** Consider how new developments in other functions, organizations, or industries could be applied to your own area.

- **Expand your mind.** Read a broad array of publications from outside your industry. Are there techniques or approaches that are commonplace in another business sector that could be useful in your function area? The core practices "Exploration," "Experimentation," and "Creativity," in Chapter 13, provide a variety of ideas for developing openness to new ideas.

- **Celebrate openness.** Reward creative problem-solving by people on your team, especially when they propose significant improvements. Identify business successes that have resulted from collaboration and compilation of good ideas from leaders in other areas. Ask others to contribute examples from their own experience. Encourage people to look for new and better ways to organize systems and processes.

- **Lead a team brainstorming session** to address a specific problem. Allow everyone to express ideas without interruption or criticism, and evaluate ideas that diverge from standard operations to see if the solution is a new approach.

- **Solicit ideas from other leaders** about a challenge you are facing. Ask how they would address such a challenge in their own areas. Can you employ some of their techniques or modify them to fit your need?

- **Solicit the perspective of other executives.** Look for opportunities to tap into others' experience and expertise, and develop greater openness to ideas that are different from your own.

- **Encourage your team to be more open.** Invite your direct reports to describe how their teams operate. Encourage them to reflect on similarities and differences in their approaches. Ask them to work together to create more efficient, streamlined processes.

EXCESSIVE USE

As an example, if you are overly deferent when seeking information, you may not be doing enough to express your own point of view. You may need to provide more context and acknowledge what your own team is already doing to contribute toward the solution. While openness to the ideas of others is important, others are also interested in your point-of-view. Review the core practices "Independence" and "Assertiveness" in Chapter 5, and identify behaviors that will enhance your effectiveness in stating your point-of-view with more impact.

Mastery

Display a desire to gain new knowledge and skills.

" Unless you try to do something beyond what you have already mastered, you will never grow. "

Ronald Osborn

Awaken potential:

- **Learn from transitions.** Reflect on the job transitions you have experienced during your leadership journey. What have you learned about coping with the challenges of transitions? How has your position changed since you were hired? How is it likely to change in the near future? Create a list of new skills to develop to be successful.

- **Analyze your response to new experiences.** Think about your most recent experience doing something new for the first time. How did you approach that? What did you learn? What would you do differently?

- **Assess your appetite for challenges.** When was the last time you really pushed yourself? How did you approach the most significant business challenges you have faced in your career? What risks did you take? What were the outcomes? What did you learn?

Align goals:

- **Interview your boss about their last role.** Ask them about the most important thing he or she learned when working at your level. What can you glean from your boss' experience? How is it similar or different from yours? What do you need to focus on to ensure your success in your current role?

- **Predict the future by staying current in your industry.** Try to predict what skills you and your team will need to develop in the future in order to be successful. Subscribe to trade magazines to stay current on the latest developments and growth areas in your field. Continually be on the lookout for areas to grow your knowledge, skills, and abilities in ways that align with the strategic direction of your organization.

Accelerate performance:

- **Discover a learning attitude.** Read books on mindful learning to discover how a learning attitude can be taught, such as *The Power of Mindful Learning* by Ellen Langer (Da Capo Press, 1998).

- **Write your own personal development plan,** and actively pursue learning experiences that will help you meet your goals. Share your plan with your manager or a trusted colleague. Ask that person to hold you accountable for developing new skills. Ask him/her to alert you to opportunities for new experiences.

- **Create an active learning environment.** Reward learning initiatives, recognize when someone has developed critical new skills and competencies, and provide opportunities for others to learn in the workplace.

- **Share your learning.** Discuss your most exceptional learning experiences with your peers. What makes those experiences stand out? How can you create meaningful learning experiences for yourself?

- **Inspire your direct reports to learn and develop.** Talk with your direct reports about a professional growth experience you had when you were at their point in your career. Help them identify learning opportunities in their current roles.

- **Attend a development program** that will assist you in building new professional skills; be sure that the program is focused on senior management and that others at your level will be in attendance. Implement new learning from workshops or seminars immediately. Don't just return to business as usual after a development opportunity.

- **Incorporate new experiences into your life outside work.** You can develop a more open Learning Orientation by engaging in new behaviors in your personal life. Take up a new hobby or research a new interest, and try to be mindful of what the learning experience is like.

- **Teach others.** Identify a high-potential direct report and make intentional efforts to mentor that person. Be mindful as you mentor. Monitor what you learn in the process.

EXCESSIVE USE

As an example, if you constantly seek out new experiences or invest in personal development at the expense of achieving results, you may appear overly ambitious. Change your focus to improving your performance and results, and you will acquire new capabilities in the process.

Reflection

Reflect on experience and learn from mistakes.

"The only real mistake is the one from which we learn nothing."

John Powell

Awaken potential:

- **Reflect on mistakes.** Think back to a recent mistake you made. How did you deal with the error? How were others affected? How did you process the incident with them? What did you learn from the situation?

- **Recognize that mistakes can be beneficial** when you learn something from them. Work to process the errors you make, and help your direct reports process their mistakes. What happened? Why did it happen? How can a repeat be prevented?

- **Analyze a process improvement you initiated after making a mistake.** How did that change help your business? Is it likely to have been instituted without an error being made? Conduct a review to find out how the process is working. Ask whether there are opportunities to make other improvements.

- **Focus on the positives.** Being reflective doesn't mean just analyzing mistakes—review your successes as well. What are you doing right? Can what you're doing be applied to other situations?

- **Think about how you respond to others' mistakes.** How do you discuss the situation? What have you done (if anything) to help them learn from their mistakes?

Align goals:

- **Ask your boss about critical mistakes** he/she made when at your level. How did your boss process those mistakes? What did he/she learn from the experience? How can you apply these lessons to your current situation to help ensure success in your role?

- **Create a cabinet of advisors** to review the outcomes of decisions regularly. Examine the choices the organization has made and resulting outcomes. Decide with each other how to approach similar situations in the future.

Accelerate performance:

- **Assess your ability to sense and shape the future.** Read a book such as *Presence: Human Purpose and the Field of the Future* by Peter Senge, Otto Scharmer, Joseph Jaworski, and Betty Sue Flowers (Society for Organizational Learning, 2004). Reflect on the most important questions at the heart of your professional work.

- **Create a reflective environment** that does not see mistakes just as errors but also as learning opportunities. Train your direct reports to analyze their failures and successes; it can sometimes be difficult for people to reflect on mistakes with their bosses. Encourage them to be sounding boards for each other as well as their reports.

- **Ask your boss to debrief about a mistake you made.** Express your desire to learn from the mistake and ask him/her to help you consider alternative approaches that could avoid future mistakes. Your willingness to acknowledge and talk openly about mistakes may impress your manager.

- **Conduct formal after-action reviews** with your team to debrief projects.

- **Identify people to mentor in this area.** Talk with them about the value of reflecting on mistakes. Ask them to process an error they made with you. What was the mistake? Could it have been avoided? What could be done differently next time? Are there other mistakes that might be avoided by reflecting on this one? What was learned by reflecting on the error?

EXCESSIVE USE

As an example, if you continually reflect aloud about prior experiences, you may be boring people with your war stories or sounding like you are living in the past. Shift your focus to ask questions about challenges that others have faced, and help them learn from those experiences.

Coach Others on Learning Orientation

Coaching Suggestions

Behavior	Awaken	Align	Accelerate
Self-Awareness — *Fails to invite feedback*	• Have the person create a list of strengths and weaknesses. Complete your own list for the individual. Include your observations based on what you have seen in team meetings, reports, or other behavior. • Review the lists together and ask what the implications are. Also seek to understand whether the person was surprised by anything on the lists. Why?	• Encourage the person to share the lists with trusted team members or peers. How similarly or differently do they see the person? • Encourage the person to ask how some of the weaknesses could be affecting team performance on strategic goals or project completion.	• Brainstorm tactics for addressing growth areas and leveraging strengths. Create a development plan to promote growth. • Identify a specific new initiative where the person can leverage his/her strengths. Outline specific roles to play in implementing the change. Be clear about why these roles are important and how they play to the person's strengths.
Self-Awareness — *Has blind spots*	• Use a 360-degree feedback tool or interviews to uncover potential blind spots. • Review the concept of Johari's window together. Identify and discuss places where blind spots may affect relationships with others as well as performance.	• Recommend circling back to key stakeholders to thank them and get more context about development needs. • Suggest reviewing 360-degree feedback results together. How similarly or differently did you see the results?	• Brainstorm action steps for the person's development plan. Use the template included later in the Appendix. • Create a plan for getting regular and ongoing feedback to prevent surprises. Identify questions the person could ask others (e.g., "What am I doing that contributes to the problem?").

Behavior		Awaken	Align	Accelerate
Humility	*Overestimates own talent*	• Help the person think about someone with whom he/she has worked who is like this. Ask how the person feels/felt about working with that person. • Recommend reading "Level 5 Leadership" by Jim Collins (*Harvard Business Review*, 2005) about the role humility and fierce resolve play in leading significant change.	• Ask how the person perceives his/her effect on the team or with peers. Ask how this style affects the person's achievement of goals and where the person could empower others to achieve even more success for the team. Encourage the person to circle back with peers to test assumptions. • Coach the person to look for someone to mentor to help that person develop more expertise. What does the person admire about the mentee's humility?	• Suggest that the person identify a new object that could serve as a reminder to stay humble, such as a watch or a pen that can be an overt reminder of humility. • Provide specific and timely feedback when you see the person being successful and humble as well as when you observe the person overestimating him/herself. Be sure to tie your feedback to the success generated or consequences observed.
	Disregards feedback	• Ask about the person's experience getting and giving feedback. Ask where the person welcomes feedback, and what kind of feedback is more difficult to hear. • Discuss how resistance might be perceived by others and how it might affect their behavior. Talk about the valuable role that feedback has played in your own development.	• Suggest that the person ask others about what feedback would be helpful and why. • Work together to identify a trusted peer who could provide perspective on the person's response to changes and feedback in the organization. Offer to debrief difficult conversations or feedback received.	• Help the person determine how changing behavior could positively impact relationships. Recognize that this needs to be a meaningful goal for the person. • Recommend creating a cabinet of trustworthy colleagues to provide regular and ongoing feedback. Push the person to expand the cabinet to include people he/she doesn't have much trust with (yet).

20

Behavior		Awaken	Align	Accelerate
Openness	*Has a closed perspective*	• Help the person understand what triggers his/her reaction. What situations typically prompt this? • Ask what it would be like to try something new or different, especially if it isn't guaranteed to work. Brainstorm other possibilities that may differ from the person's preferred approach.	• Encourage the person to share triggers with others so they will be aware. • Arrange for the person to participate in cross-functional planning meetings for a new initiative. Ask the person to identify one new idea from each meeting that might work in his/her organization.	• Recommend that the person practice listening first, talking second. Provide regular feedback when you see the person living by that mantra. • Suggest that the person empower others to confront him/her when they see closed behavior (e.g., using a code word or gesture as a reminder).
	Shows function prejudice	• Make a case for why it's in the person's best interest to broaden perspective (e.g., "in order to advance, you'll be more influential if others know that you are trying to learn about them"). • Provide feedback on your own observation of an instance or event when the person's functional prejudice created negative consequences.	• Identify some important functions that the person should get to know (e.g., operations learning about sales). • Create a list of key stakeholders with whom to more frequently communicate or collaborate.	• Coach the person to develop a habit of asking "What would sales say?" • Brainstorm a list of specific questions that could come from other perspectives, and encourage the person to make those a part of team discussions.
Mastery	*Resists development*	• Talk with the person about skills he/she wants to develop. Why are those important to the person? How are they important to the business? • Share your thoughts about what skills you feel would be most valuable to the person and why.	• Set specific learning goals that are aligned with current or future strategic organizational goals. Identify progress measures you can monitor together. • Discuss your own development goals together. Demonstrate your own commitment to development.	• Incorporate these new learning goals into the person's development plan. Set specific timelines for review. • Provide the venue to regularly discuss challenges and/or progress during one-on-ones. Set specific meetings just to review development, instead of other business matters.

Behavior		Awaken	Align	Accelerate
Mastery	*Shows complacency*	• Ask "What's in it for you?" to examine the person's current motivation. • Review what the person is currently doing in terms of new people, education, or experiences to push his/her own growth and learning.	• Identify a current problem that might be best addressed by a new approach, then suggest doing this as a team. • Pair the person with a peer who is active in his/her own development. Have him/her review how he/she pushes him/herself to learn and why it is important.	• Recommend inviting a futurist to attend one of the person's staff meetings, then debrief the person's learnings afterward. • Model the behavior of pushing yourself to grow and develop. Be clear about what you are doing to develop yourself.
Reflection	*Fails to debrief past experience*	• Ask the person what's keeping this from happening—lack of interest, discipline, or something else? • Discuss the costs of not debriefing and learning from the past.	• Help the person organize a team meeting or offsite to debrief the outcome of a major project or initiative. • Discuss how to apply those lessons to current operational issues or activities.	• Encourage the person to take ten minutes at the end of each week to identify one new thing learned, whether from a mistake or success. • Create a plan for how the person will apply the learning in the following week.
	Doesn't learn from mistakes	• Be supportive yet direct and talk about past situations where the person seemed reluctant to own the blame. Provide your own observations of how the person's behavior affected others. • Discuss what's getting in the way of taking responsibility for failures, regardless of how small.	• Talk about a mistake you made and how you benefited from being honest with yourself and candid with others. • Help the person understand how honest reflection will help achieve goals by increasing trust and credibility with others.	• Make reflection a regular part of your one-on-one meetings. What can the person do differently to be more effective next time? • Make sure you make it okay for the person to admit to mistakes and failure; avoid overreacting or punishing the messenger.

LEARNING ORIENTATION

Tips for Coaching in a Global Environment

Learning Orientation may be practiced or expressed differently within other cultures. This might impact how you approach coaching. Try to keep an open mind, avoid generalizations, and continue gathering data as you gain experience with another culture. Consider these suggestions:

Self-Awareness: Management and human resources practices are defined with greater specificity in some cultures than others. Competency models and performance standards are not the norm everywhere. Nor is feedback. Some people you are coaching might never have encountered personality testing or multi-rater feedback surveys, or received feedback from managers about their strengths and development needs. Their self-awareness might come from self-perceptions without any reference to standards. If you think someone has a blind spot, use an appropriate competency model to jointly assess the person's strengths and limitations. Ask what feedback was received in the past, and provide guidance about seeking feedback from colleagues. Be cautious about the directness of your feedback, or people may not hear the point you are trying to make.

Humility: Some leaders operate from a place of pride and condescension, conveying arrogance about their own countries/cultures, which makes it seem as though people from other cultures have nothing to teach them. That attitude may not only be disrespectful, but annoying to others. Provide feedback when you notice cultural arrogance rather than humility being displayed. Also watch out for your own possible bias in this regard. For example, if the person you are coaching doesn't speak English well, that doesn't mean he/she doesn't have good ideas or instincts. Adapt your communication style when working with people who are communicating in a non-native language. Check for understanding.

Openness: When leaders are not open to new ideas and experiences, they may struggle when working in cross-cultural situations. Such situations tend to be filled with new and different kinds of people and information. Their preferences for familiar structures or solutions may discourage people from coming to them with new possibilities. Showing bias toward people from their own cultures may also discourage other people from pursuing interactions with them. This situation may be exacerbated in cultures where it is considered disrespectful to criticize or provide negative information to senior members. The mutual avoidance may never get expressed or dealt with, especially when people from different cultures are uncomfortable having open conversation about feelings and emotions. If you see any examples of this, share your observations and ask what is happening.

Mastery: You may not see a drive for mastery in cultures that are more relaxed. Take time to learn about business practices in the other person's culture. Ask what kind of leadership or management training he/she has had during his/her career. You might want to invest in sending the person to a management training course rather than coaching on basic leadership skills. Meanwhile, leaders in some cultures may not have a good appreciation for the role individual aspirations or individual performance can play in achieving career or business success. They may need support from you in setting personal goals and coaching people on their own teams.

Reflection: Reflective practice seems to be less common in some cultures than others. The fast pace of getting things done may discourage people from taking time to reflect. People also have different learning styles. When people from other cultures have difficulty admitting mistakes and show reluctance to be debriefed, it may help to model reflective practice. Share an incident from your own experience and mention what you learned from that experience.

Learning Orientation is about actively pursuing personal growth and improvement that facilitate higher and higher levels of performance. The best leaders approach growth and learning as a lifelong endeavor.

As you read about Steve's situation, reflect on what you've learned about Learning Orientation in this chapter. How does Steve sound like you or one of your team members? What experiences or tendencies do you share? Finally, consider how you would help Steve demonstrate greater skill in Learning Orientation and be successful in his leadership role.

Learning Leadership Lessons

Steve Williams was exceptionally bright. He enjoyed his years in school and fancied himself as a lifelong learner. Gifted with an active mind, he was a quick study. He delighted in reading books about management and applying key principles. His early career progression was more rapid than most. He developed a reputation for sizing up the demands of each new situation and getting people organized to accomplish results. One of his early assignments took him to Shanghai, where he learned to speak some Chinese and fell in love with the culture. He longed for an opportunity to return someday.

His track record came to the attention of others in the industry. Steve was recruited by a competitor to lead their subsidiary in China. He asked to spend time at the company headquarters even before his official start date, so he could begin meeting people and learning about the company's product strategy. After moving to Shanghai, he formulated an initial plan and began by interviewing each of his direct reports. He also organized a series of interviews and site visits to meet people in all parts of the business. He gave everyone on his management team a copy of *The First 90 Days* by Michael Watkins (Harvard Business Press, 2003) to help them understand his approach.

Steve identified some changes he wanted to make, yet understood that his typical fast pace might overwhelm the organization. Thus, he proceeded in a very structured manner, communicating each step along the way so people would know what was happening and why. After identifying some delivery issues, he gave everyone a book on execution to help people expand their thinking about how to get results.

One of his direct reports, Gary, was clearly not on board with the new initiatives. Someone else confided to Steve that Gary had privately expressed skepticism about the changes and had told her to "wait it out" because Steve would move on eventually. Steve was flabbergasted, because he had never received feedback like this before. Gary had always seemed agreeable in meetings and never questioned or challenged his approach during their monthly check-ins. Although Gary wasn't following through on commitments in a timely manner and hadn't read any of the recommended books, Steve had assumed that was due to Gary's having some difficulty communicating in English.

Steve had always prided himself on being an able learner, but he was stumped about how to win over Gary. It dawned on him that Gary's learning style might be different from his own, and that it might take a different approach to help Gary embrace new ways of doing things. However, Steve was reluctant to ask anyone for help because he didn't want to admit that he couldn't handle the situation himself. He knew from previous multi-rater feedback that he had a tendency to become defensive. He wondered what to do.

Steve found that he needed Learning Orientation more than ever, in order to:

- Further understand his style and impact as a leader.

- Display humility and accept constructive feedback.

- Consider ideas and recommendations for improvements from his team.

- Discover new ways to gain information.

- Reflect on his early experience with the new company and chart a new path forward.

Steve's Leadership Development Plan

Following is a sample development plan for Steve Williams. Research on leadership development has shown that leaders learn through experience and that this learning is optimized through the use of an individual development plan. A successful plan includes new experiences and introduces the leader to new conversations and tools. The suggestions included in the previous sections may stimulate your thinking about additional possibilities for Steve's development.

LEADERSHIP DEVELOPMENT PLAN FOR STEVE WILLIAMS

DEVELOPMENT GOAL

Goal: To strengthen my Learning Orientation

Desired Outcomes—results I want to see from developing this skill

Self: I will better understand others' learning styles and modify my approach accordingly.

Team: My boss and direct reports will be more open to trying the changes I want to implement.

Organization: My ability to influence change in my new unit will impact our ability to become more profitable.

Self-Understanding—strengths that I can build on and development needs I can address

Strengths: I am a quick study and like to learn and implement new ideas. I also have experience building buy-in for implementing needed organization change.

Development Needs: I like to learn from business books; I sometimes forget that others have different learning styles. Also, because I am excited by and can see the value in trying new things, I can overlook others' reservations about change.

Business Context—challenges in my business environment that require this skill

The challenges I face in my business environment include price-cutting from competitors that are concerned about our taking market share; transforming China BU to become profitable.

DEVELOPMENT ACTIONS

AWAKEN

- Meet with colleagues to learn about successful changes implemented in the past and what made the process successful.
- Identify changes that have had negative consequences that may be getting in the way of my boss' and direct reports' openness to trying new approaches to the business.
- Find a resource to learn more about learning styles; use this information to modify my approach.

ALIGN

- Meet with Gary to learn more about how he views our business and the opportunities he sees for enhancing our competitiveness. Ask about his experience with previous changes.
- Create a development plan with Gary that focuses on learning from a variety of sources about the future of our industry and market.
- Work with my boss to create a shared vision for the future of our business. Stress opportunities to build on current strengths as a platform for needed changes.

LEADERSHIP DEVELOPMENT PLAN FOR STEVE WILLIAMS

ACCELERATE

- Look for opportunities to involve Gary in small projects with peers who are energized by the change.
- Organize benchmarking opportunities for Gary and others to accompany my boss to visit executives from other industries who my boss respects.
- Ask my boss to serve as a mentor for Gary—and include him on a cross-functional project where he would gain exposure to other parts of the business.

DEVELOPMENT SUCCESS FACTORS

Timeline: Within the next six months

Support Needed:

- People from my network who are willing to benchmark with my boss.
- Feedback from others on whether I am becoming more versatile in my leadership approach

Indicators of Success:

- I will use a variety of approaches to engage others in learning about best practices in our industry.
- Gary will ask for additional opportunities to work on change teams.

An Example of Coaching for Learning Orientation

Steve Williams' goal was to strengthen his skills in Learning Orientation. Here are some steps Steve's manager could take using the Awaken, Align, Accelerate framework to coach Steve in this area:

AWAKEN	**Increase INSIGHT**	Invite Steve to describe how he has approached making changes in the past. Ask him to recall the last time he dealt with resistance and describe what happened. Ask what he learned and how he could apply that learning in working with Gary. Recommend that Steve participate in a multi-rater feedback process to get feedback from everyone on his team.
	MOTIVATE change	Identify potential priorities for developing both Steve and Gary. Explore the consequences if no changes are made. Identify consequences for Steve personally as well as potential consequences for Gary.

ALIGN	**PLAN goals**	Focus on what Steve could change to work with Gary more effectively. Ask what Steve could spend time working toward and follow through on. Work together to construct a leadership development plan similar to the sample provided in this chapter.
	ALIGN expectations	Work with Steve to map key stakeholders for the changes he is trying to initiate. Help him see that there may be others like Gary who are not fully on board, then strategize about what can be done. Ensure that organizational systems (e.g., incentives) are well aligned with the behavior that Steve is hoping to change in Gary.
ACCELERATE	**CREATE teachable moments**	Since Steve likes to read books, suggest that he read *Working GlobeSmart* by Ernest Gundling (Intercultural Press, 2003), especially the part about expats trying to initiate changes that are resisted by people in the local culture. Encourage Steve to create an advisory board to help him steer the changes he wants to make. Recommend that he populate the board with people from different perspectives. Help him experiment with trying new approaches.
	TRACK progress	Discuss expected outcomes and results. Check in more regularly to see what progress Steve is making toward his goals and ask what kind of help he might need (since he may not be comfortable bringing up that topic himself). Encourage him to invite additional feedback and ask other people to support the changes they see. Express appreciation for his efforts to develop Gary's learning orientation.

Results: Measuring Impact

Steve Williams made rapid progress on his plan during the first few months, fueled by his desire to help Gary get on board with the new initiatives. He didn't try every action step, and he found some activities were more helpful than others. However, he made significant progress toward his goals. His new skills in Learning Orientation allowed Steve to:

- Become a more versatile leader.

- Develop Gary to take more initiative in working on changes.

- Engage others in learning about best practices in the industry.

- Invite and consider recommendations for improvement from his team.

- Chart a new path forward for his organization in China.

FINAL WORDS

Congratulations and best wishes as you continue along your journey to great leadership. We hope this guide has provided you with new ingredients and inspired you to create your own recipe for leadership success.

With great leadership, anything is possible®.

Visit **www.mdaleadership.com** for more ideas.

ACKNOWLEDGEMENTS

Many forces came together to produce this book, particularly all of the great consultants at MDA Leadership. It is the product of our collective wisdom and experience over decades of work with leaders at every level in a broad range of sectors and industries. We gratefully acknowledge the thoughtful contributions of Bob Barnett, Chris Bedford, Sandra Davis, Peter Germann, Lisa Gordon, Michael Hepperlen, Jeff Hinds, Katherine Holt, Sarah Murphy, Sharon Sackett, Randy Shimanski, LexAnn Steffens, Joe Volker, Nancy Weidenfeller, Heather Wray-Isquierdo, and Susan Zemke, who each contributed substantially to the creation of one or more chapters based on their particular expertise, interest, and appetite. We also want to thank a number of individuals who helped to organize and edit our early work to make it more clear and accessible: Jean Worrell, who proofread chapters, and David Prin and Sean McDonnell, who brought an external perspective to our work.

Ultimately, there was a core team that we need to thank for carrying this work across the finish line: LexAnn Steffens, whose energy and pragmatic approach to projects like this one was invaluable; Julia Schulte who dedicated her attention to this project and to caring for the many versions of the manuscript; Katherine Holt, who shared her expertise as a global leader in coaching and leadership development, and who was committed to making this the best book of its kind; and Randy Shimanski, who invested endless hours to ensure we produced and launched an outstanding leadership development resource.

We can also say that this guide is better due to the help of our many friends. Over sixty of our colleagues and clients provided input and crucial feedback—which sometimes stung but always helped improve the end product. The following is a list of those whom we can thank for their generous contribution of insight and candor:

Steve Arneson, Ph.D.
Joan Austin
Mary Rygg Bailey
Paul Batz

Tom Bepler
Mary E. Blegen
Margaret E. Bowman-Pensel
Ray Chadwick

Judy Chartrand

Walter T. Chesley

Carol Cummins

Nancy M. Dahl

David Donnay

Lynn J. Davis

Paul Dominski

Joshua S. Ehrlich, Ph.D.

John Goodrich

Douglas R. Gordon

Rhonda L. Gutenberg, Ph.D.

Donald W. Hasbargen

Heather Ishikawa

Gillian P.S. Khoo, Ph.D.

Betsy Koonce

Linda E. Laddin

Mary Elizabeth Lawton

Rae Lesmeister

Linda Livers RN, BS, MA

David H. Marquardt

Mark Messick

Scott Meyer

Shawn Moren

Adair Linn Nagata, Ph.D.

Patrick D. O'Brien

William R. Phillips

Mary Kay Plath

Chris Schwartz

Nancy Siska

Elizabeth B. Stites

Jack Stoltzfus, Ph.D.

John D. Vegas

Randall P. White, Ph.D.

Luann Widener

Virginia Williams

Ellen Wingard

Lastly, we thank our publishing team at Beaver's Pond Press, whose custom and one-to-one approach to working with us so closely mirrored our own client-intimate strategy: Dara Beevas who mentored and advised us through the publishing process, Marly Cornell who edited and massaged our writing, and James Monroe who so readily captured our look and feel.

Although it is often said, this guide was truly a team effort. Each of the individuals who participated in creating this resource demonstrated dedication, energy, and commitment to the goal that is now realized by the publication of this book.

—Scott E. Nelson & Jason G. Ortmeier (Editors)

APPENDIX

Leadership Competency Model

Factors, Competencies, and Core Practices Table

List of Case Studies

Leadership Development Plan Template

Sample Development Tools

FACTOR	TOOL
Leading People	High Performance Environment Survey
Thinking and Deciding	External Environment Analysis
Achieving	Strategic Innovation Worksheet
Relating to People	Networking Map
Managing Work	Performance Dashboard
Managing Self	Leadership Reputation Exercise

Leadership Competency Model

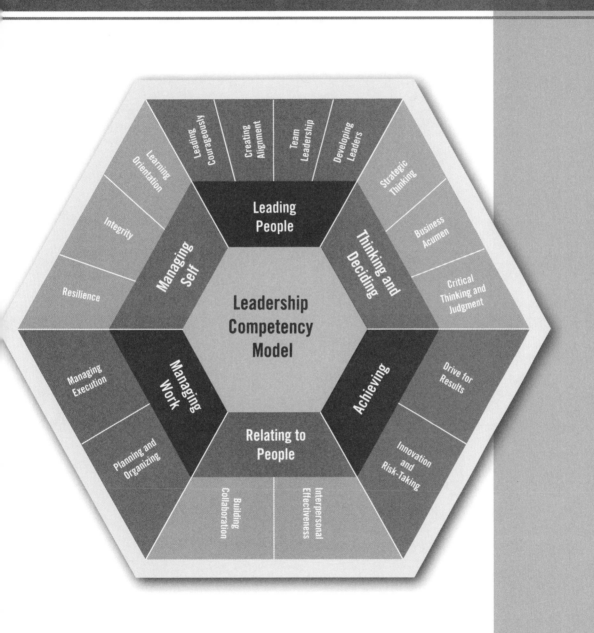

Factors, Competencies, and Core Practices

Factor	Competency	Core Practice
Leading People	**Leading Courageously** Courageous leaders take charge and convey authority in tackling challenges, asserting themselves, pursuing their agenda, and influencing other leaders.	**Authority**: Provide direction without smothering creativity and motivation. **Courage**: Readily take on difficult assignments and challenges. **Assertiveness**: Be direct, assertive, and appropriately tough-minded. **Independence**: Act independently and with conviction. **Influence**: Influence upwards and across the organization.
	Creating Alignment An effective change leader creates alignment by ensuring the structure, systems, people, and processes are aligned in support of organizational goals.	**Direction**: Focus people on the organization's strategies, goals and priorities. **Diagnosis:** Analyze fit between activities and goals to ensure they support and reinforce each other. **Change:** Pursue change plans that align structures, systems, and processes in support of the organization's goals. **Motivation:** Inspire people to make changes and improvements. **Coordination**: Integrate efforts to improve alignment across teams and functions.
	Team Leadership A team leader assembles the right talent, maximizes cross-functional resources, practices group decision-making, empowers others to lead, and builds a sense of team.	**Utilization:** Form productive teams—assemble the best people to meet the function's goals. **Orchestration**: Build teams' capacity by skillfully managing group dynamics. **Involvement**: Involve people in decisions that affect them. **Empowerment**: Give team members real responsibility and authority. **Cohesion**: Build agreement and trust within and across teams.

Factor	Competency	Core Practice
Leading People	**Developing Leaders** A leader who develops others effectively identifies talent, creates a development culture, promotes succession planning, challenges others, and provides coaching and support.	**Talent Assessment**: Identify, hire, or promote top talent to achieve the organization's objectives. **Stretch Assignments**: Provide relevant stretch assignments to develop others' leadership skills. **Development Culture**: Hold leaders accountable for developing talent. **Feedback**: Provide feedback to strengthen leadership skills in others. **Succession Planning**: Conduct regular reviews of leadership planning.
Thinking and Deciding	**Strategic Thinking** A strategic leader brings a broad, longer-term, and informed perspective to bear on issues and problems in order to grow the business and compete in the market.	**Long-Term Perspective**: Bring a long-term perspective to planning and problem-solving. **External Focus**: Demonstrate a well-developed understanding of the external business environment. **Strategic Scope**: Consider the strategic impact of decisions and choices on the business. **Growth Orientation**: Create ideas and strategies to grow the business. **Competitive Advantage**: Promote ways of doing things that increase differentiation and competitive advantage.
	Business Acumen A leader with strong business acumen understands the global environment, business model, and key drivers of the organization, and leverages this understanding to recommend alternatives and measure performance.	**Business Context**: Understand the global business environment. **Operating Models**: Know the organization's business model and how it operates. **Financial Drivers**: Concentrate on key financial drivers and their impact on profit and loss. **Tradeoffs**: Make tradeoffs to support business growth and/or profitability objectives. **Performance Metrics**: Use data to monitor performance and measure results.

Factor	Competency	Core Practice
Thinking and Deciding	**Critical Thinking and Judgment** A leader who thinks critically demonstrates the ability to analyze, synthesize, and manage complex information to develop well-reasoned solutions, navigate ambiguity, and make decisions.	**Investigation**: Investigate underlying issues when solving problems. **Analysis**: Take an analytic approach to complex issues. **Systems Thinking**: Think systemically—see how a decision or action affects other parts of the organization. **Navigation**: Balance the need for action with patience to let ambiguous issues evolve. **Decision-Making**: Make good decisions in a timely manner.
Achieving	**Drive for Results** A results-driven leader demonstrates strong passion, urgency, and determination in moving things forward and accomplishing goals.	**Drive**: Drive to exceed goals and deliver outstanding results. **Expectations**: Establish high standards of performance for self and others. **Urgency**: Set aggressive timelines for achieving objectives. **Initiative**: Take initiative to get things done. **Determination**: Persist toward goals despite obstacles and setbacks.
	Innovation and Risk-Taking An innovative leader explores new ideas, experiments with risks, improves how things are done, encourages creativity, and examines assumptions in challenging the status quo.	**Exploration**: Pursue new ideas and possibilities to stimulate business results. **Experimentation**: Model experimentation and learning from trying new approaches. **Improvement**: Focus on ways to improve existing processes, products, or services. **Creativity**: Encourage and reward creativity and innovative thinking. **Challenge**: Examine assumptions and challenge status quo.

Factor	Competency	Core Practice
Relating to People	**Interpersonal Effectiveness** An interpersonally effective leader interacts and communicates in a manner that demonstrates consideration, care, and concern for others.	**Empathy**: Show genuine consideration for others. **Approachability**: Display interest and responsiveness when interacting with others. **Respect**: Express respect and appreciation for differences. **Listening**: Expand dialogue by listening actively and asking insightful questions about key facts and assumptions. **Communication**: Communicate effectively across organizational levels.
	Building Collaboration A collaborative leader participates with and involves others, promotes cooperation, builds partnerships, and resolves conflicts.	**Networking**: Establish and leverage a network of relationships across the organization. **Engagement**: Engage and work with other functions for the good of the organization. **Cooperation**: Model the importance of working cooperatively with others. **Partnership**: Create partnerships to achieve business goals. **Conflict Management**: Address and resolve disagreements constructively.
Managing Work	**Planning and Organizing** A planful, organized leader anticipates the future and establishes clear priorities by making time to create plans, involve others, and secure resources.	**Forward Thinking**: Maintain a longer (e.g., 2-3 years) perspective when developing plans. **Prioritizing**: Establish clear priorities that align with broader organizational goals. **Planning**: Translate business strategy into action plans. **Participation**: Gain input on plans from key stakeholders. **Resource Management**: Anticipate needs and utilize resources effectively to optimize progress on functional goals.

Factor	Competency	Core Practice
Managing Work	**Managing Execution** An execution-focused leader knows how to get things done by clarifying roles, delegating responsibilities, monitoring progress, and ensuring results.	**Organization Know-How**: Know how to get things done in a complex organization. **Accountability**: Establish the performance required from others to achieve desired function objectives. **Delegation**: Value getting things done through others. **Goal Orientation**: Ensure progress is being made toward the right goals. **Follow-Through**: Drive things to closure by following up and following through.
Managing Self	**Resilience** A resilient leader adapts to changes and recovers from setbacks with composure, optimism, and confidence.	**Confidence**: Balance healthy self-confidence with appropriate humility. **Adaptability**: Adapt to changes and challenges. **Composure**: Handle stress in a calm and constructive manner. **Optimism**: Remain optimistic in the face of obstacles or problems. **Recovery**: Recover quickly from setbacks or disappointments.
	Integrity A high-integrity leader demonstrates trustworthiness, fairness, and personal responsibility, as well as an uncompromising commitment to ethical and values-based behavior.	**Ethics**: Commit to high standards of ethical behavior. **Values**: Demonstrate a commitment to the organization's values. **Trust**: Build trust by being candid and consistent. **Fairness**: Treat others fairly and equitably. **Responsibility**: Take responsibility for his/her own actions, including mistakes.
	Learning Orientation A learning-oriented leader actively pursues personal growth and improvement.	**Self-Awareness**: Demonstrate a clear grasp of his/her own strengths, limitations, and development needs. **Humility**: Accept and act on feedback from others. **Openness**: Actively consider others' ideas and suggestions. **Mastery**: Display a desire to gain new knowledge and skills. **Reflection**: Reflect on experience and learn from mistakes.

List of Case Studies

Chapter	Case Study
5 - Leading Courageously	Influencing Up With Intention
6 - Creating Alignment	Creating a Case for Change
7 - Team Leadership	Trusting in Teams
8 - Developing Leaders	Stretching Successors
9 - Strategic Thinking	Exploring the Competitive Environment
10 - Business Acumen	Accumulating Acumen
11 - Critical Thinking and Judgment	Judging When and Where to Jump
12 - Drive for Results	Pushing People for Performance
13 - Innovation and Risk-Taking	Realizing the Risks of Not Innovating
14 - Interpersonal Effectiveness	Dealing with Derailment
15 - Building Collaboration	Building Bridges and Buy-in
16 - Planning and Organizing	Fighting Fires
17 - Managing Execution	Managing the Matrix
18 - Resilience	Operating With Optimism
19 - Integrity	Walking the Walk as Well as the Talk
20 - Learning Orientation	Learning Leadership Lessons

Leadership Development Plan Template

Write it down! Use this plan to commit to improving your effectiveness as a leader. For more detail on creating an effective development plan, see the beginning of this guide.

LEADERSHIP DEVELOPMENT PLAN FOR ....
DEVELOPMENT GOAL
Goal:
Desired Outcomes—results I want to see from developing this skill
Self: Team: Organization:
Self-Understanding—strengths that I can build on and development needs I can address
Strengths: Development Needs:
Business Context—challenges in my business environment that require this skill
DEVELOPMENT ACTIONS

AWAKEN (Activities for gaining personal insight into my impact as a leader)
    •
    •

LEADERSHIP DEVELOPMENT PLAN FOR ....

ALIGN (Actions for connecting my leadership development goals with my business outcomes)

-
-

ACCELERATE (Experiences, people, and education that will provide new concepts, skills, and knowledge)

-
-

DEVELOPMENT SUCCESS FACTORS

Timeline: Within the next six months

Support Needed: (Who and what I need to effectively implement my plan):

-
-

Indicators of Success:

-
-

Sample Development Tools

Leading People:

High-Performance Environment Survey

The High-Performance Environment Survey is a framework for identifying where organizational systems, processes, and structure present barriers to effective individual and team performance.

It can help you:

- Ensure your structure, systems, and processes support activities that produce results.

- Focus people on organization goals and key priorities.

- Ensure effective cross-organizational coordination.

- Communicate the need for and implement change that improves the alignment between organizational systems, processes, and structure and expectations for individual and team performance.

Directions

- Answer each of the yes/no questions in the survey.

- Note what evidence you have to support your assessment.

- Use the evidence for your affirmative answers to reinforce and strengthen elements that support a high-performance environment.

- Use the evidence for your negative answers to develop a case for change.

- Focus your initial efforts on the first answer that shows there is ambiguity or confusion.

- Consider asking peers and members of your team to complete the survey as a way of engaging others in the case for change and building commitment to specific action to improve your performance environment.

449

High Performance Environment Survey

1. Do current goals and strategies help the organization maintain a favorable position in the marketplace?

    Evidence

    _____

    _____

2. Does management create a clear sense of purpose and direction for the organization?

    Evidence

    _____

    _____

3. Do employees' knowledge, skills, and abilities fit their job requirements and position them to handle the responsibilities they have?

    Evidence

    _____

    _____

4. Are the best people attracted to the organization and meaningfully rewarded for their efforts?

    Evidence

    _____

    _____

5. Are people who need to work together organized (structured) to do so in the best way?

    Evidence

    _____

    _____

6. Are processes for coordinating work, sharing information, and making decisions clear, effective, and efficient?

Evidence

_____

_____

7. Are human resources systems optimally designed to meet the needs of employees and the organization?

Evidence

_____

_____

8. Do managers do an effective job of clarifying objectives, setting expectations, communicating, and coaching employees so their efforts are aligned with organizational or divisional goals?

Evidence

_____

_____

9. Do reward and control mechanisms encourage the behaviors and norms that you want, and that are compatible with the organization's objectives?

Evidence

_____

_____

10. Does competition among units (or individuals) encourage or undermine performance and support for organizational goals and objectives?

Evidence

_____

_____

Thinking and Deciding:

External Environment Analysis

The External Environment Analysis is a framework for identifying and examining the key factors, opportunities, and threats in the external business environment most likely to impact your organization's ability to achieve desired results.

It can help you:

- Identify how key external forces may influence your strategic business decisions.

- Identify potential opportunities for the future.

- Expose potential threats to achieving strategic goals.

- Validate strategic choices.

Directions

- Use the descriptions of each force to identify key factors that are relevant to your industry and business.

- Examine the key factors for new or enhanced business opportunities they may offer.

- Note threats these factors may present to achieving your goals.

- Use your analysis to either validate or make changes in your strategic choices.

Worksheet for External Environment Analysis

External Environment Analysis
Societal: Changes in demographics (age, education, mobility, race, religion, gender, etc.), lifestyles, contemporary culture, consumer tastes, employee expectations, social movements, etc.
Key Factors:
Opportunities:
Threats:
Technological: Impact of new technologies on how our business is done, on customers, on suppliers/vendors; impact of information system technology, etc.
Key Factors:
Opportunities:
Threats:
Economic: Changes in economy (local and national, expansion or recession, etc.), tax structure, money supply, employment, inflation, interest rates, monetary and fiscal policies, etc.
Key Factors:
Opportunities:
Threats:
Environmental: Changes in concern for the earth/environment, environmental regulation, air quality, hazardous waste, etc.
Key Factors:
Opportunities:
Threats:

Political: Changes in regulation, domestic and foreign policy, political trends, state and local laws, court decisions, organization's level of political power, etc.
Key Factors:
Opportunities:
Threats:
Other Relevant Forces: Define for your industry.
Key Factors:
Opportunities:
Threats:

Summary

Most significant opportunities to seize:

_____

_____

Most significant threats to achievement of our goals:

_____

_____

Aspects of my current strategy that need to be reinforced to allow my organization to seize opportunities and mitigate threats:

_____

_____

Aspects of my current strategy that need to change to allow my organization to seize opportunities and mitigate threats:

_____

_____

Strategic Innovation Worksheet

The Strategic Innovation Worksheet provides a clear process for assessing the strategic importance and business potential of new ideas. Remember that the most powerful ideas come from leaders who are equally creative, analytical, disciplined, and courageous.

The worksheet can be completed individually, but is likely to produce the best results when based on a variety of inputs and completed in a team context.

Use this tool to:

- Identify who and what types of customers might be interested in the idea.

- Think about what need or problem the idea proposes to address.

- Create a description of the idea and possible names for it.

- Evaluate the competitive landscape for the proposed idea.

- Link the success of the idea to the strategic goals of the organization.

- Think through issues associated with the proposed product or service.

Directions

Use the worksheet to answer the following:

- Who is the likely buyer for the idea (customer segment)?

- What is the size of the market for this idea (number of potential buyers)?

- What is the need that the idea proposes to fill (statement of primary need, pain, or opportunity)?

- What might we call our idea (name)?

- What does our idea provide (primary benefit statements)?

- Who is the competition (competitive options)?

- How does our idea compete (primary competitive advantages?)

- What do we expect to achieve from this idea (statement of deliverables)?

- How will this idea impact on our business: (list benefits linked to our strategy and goals)?

- What next steps need to be taken to secure funding (from inside or outside the organization) to develop this idea into a viable product or service?

Strategic Innovation Worksheet

This product or service is for (customer segment): _____

There are (number of potential buyers): _____

The need is (state primary need, pain, opportunity): _____

_____

_____

Our product or service (name): _____

Provides (primary benefit statements): _____

_____

Unlike (competitive options): _____

_____

_____

Our product/service delivers (primary competitive advantages):

_____

_____

We expect (statement of deliverables): _____

_____

_____

To have this positive impact on our business (list benefits linked to strategy and business goals):

_____

_____

_____

To get the funding we need to develop this idea into a viable product/service we need to (outline immediate next steps, timing, and accountability):

_____

_____

_____

Networking Map

The Networking Map is a framework to examine the extent of your current network and identify opportunities to build and leverage additional relationships to help you expand your ability to work effectively across organization boundaries.

This helps:

- Identify the variety and strength of your relationships in the organization.

- Highlight gaps in your network and see opportunities to influence more broadly across various functions of the organization.

- Locate people in your current network who can help connect you to others with whom you want to develop relationships.

Directions

- Develop an "elevator speech" (30 seconds) about the mission, vision, and key goals of your function.

- Make a list of the people in your organization with whom you have strong working relationships. Examine the list.
  - Are most of your relationships within your own function?
  - Are there key stakeholders you should know, but don't?

- Draw a map like the one on the following page in order to:
  - Identify the people with whom you have strong relationships with a solid line.
  - Identify the people with whom you have relationships that need to be strengthened with a dotted line.
  - Identify people you would like to add to your network by circling them. Look for connections among these people and those already in your network.

- Make note of actions you will take to strengthen your relationships with people in your network and how you might use your current network to connect to people on your "wish list."

Networking Map Example

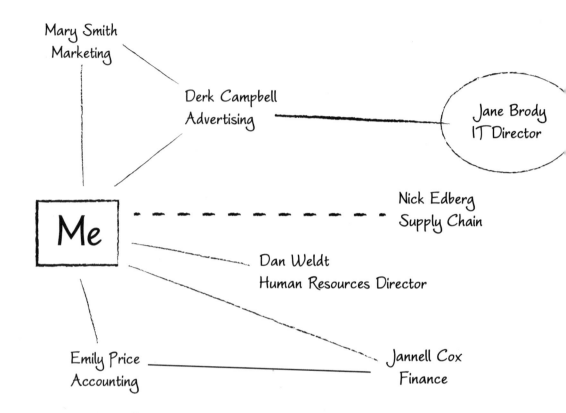

Relationship	Strategy
Strengthen my relationship with Nick.	Invite Nick to coffee to talk about his goals for Supply Chain and what my area can do to support him.
Add Jane to my network.	Find out how well Derk knows Jane. Work together to find a natural way for him to introduce us.
Reconnect with Jannell.	Set up an informal lunch date.

Performance Dashboard

The performance dashboard is a powerful and visually compelling tool that can help you communicate and make timely and well-informed decisions about your business.

This will:

- Present business intelligence about your organization's fundamental health.

- Track key performance indicators integral to execution.

- Improve the quality and timeliness of decision-making.

- Alert you to negative performance trends.

- Identify emerging opportunities to capitalize on.

Directions

- Consider the following as you develop a Performance Dashboard for your function:

  - What indicators accurately measure your progress?
    Identify the operational, financial, people, and other key performance indicators most integral to the business. Identify what indicators tend to be leading and lagging. Which ones most reliably forecast important business trends?

  - Define goals for key indicators that tie directly to the organization's strategy. Specify target ranges for all indicators and ranges of performance that are meaningful, such as what percentage of attainment should be assigned a blue label as significantly below goal.

  - Make your dashboard easy to read and visually compelling.
    Your dashboard should be easy to grasp and allow data to be displayed in impactful ways.

  - Leverage the dashboard as a communication tool.
    Use the dashboard as a tool to inform your team and the larger organization about the state of the business, support the case for change initiatives, and reward achievements.

- Use the example on the following page as a template.

Performance Dash Board Example

20XX Operating Metrics	Q1	Q2	Q3	Q4
Financial Performance Indicators				
Example: Total Revenue Goal	$1,250,000	1,300,000		
Actual	1,376,000	1,261,000		
Operational Performance Indicators				
Example: Average daily production volume	162 units	165 units		
Actual	177 units	145 units		
People Performance Indicators				
Example: % Employees w/ Development Plans	75%	75%		
Actual	44%	69%		
Other Meaningful Performance Indicators				

Key to Color Coding of Actual Results	
Below 90% of Goal	
90 to 100% of Goal	
Above 100% of Goal	

Managing Self:

Leadership Reputation Exercise

Reflect on your current reputation as a leader and to determine if this is the reputation you want or want to change.

This helps you:

- Clarify your values and beliefs about leadership.

- Identify behaviors that demonstrate the values and beliefs you want to be known for.

- Be mindful of your "public image" as a leader.

- Identify and change behavior that tarnishes the leadership reputation you want.

Directions

- Imagine your local newspaper interviewing your direct reports and peers for a story about you as a leader. The story will be featured on the front page of the business section alongside your picture and the name of your organization.

- What will your direct reports say about how they experience you as a leader? How will your colleagues respond to questions about the principles and values you demonstrate in your interactions with them? How would your organization react to seeing your story in print?

- Take some time to reflect on some of the most significant experiences you've had as a leader; peak times when you were very successful and felt good about your accomplishments. Also reflect on the valleys in your leadership career; times when you were unsuccessful or felt uneasy about what you were doing, or reacted in an unthinking way.

- Use the following worksheet to capture your lessons from these experiences and identify the values and principles that guide your actions as a leader.

Leadership Reputation Exercise

Peak Leadership Experience

Reflect on a time when you were at your best as a leader.

1. What was the situation?

   _____

   _____

2. What were you doing that made this a peak experience?

   _____

   _____

3. What do you value most from this experience?

   _____

   _____

4. What characteristics of effective leadership did you demonstrate?

   _____

   _____

Valley Leadership Experience

Reflect on a leadership challenge you feel you did not address appropriately, successfully, or reacted to in an unthinking way.

1. What was the situation?

   _____

   _____

2. What made it challenging?

_____

_____

3. How did you handle the situation? What actions did you take?

_____

_____

4. What might others have inferred about your leadership values and principles from your actions?

_____

_____

5. Given your experience, how would you handle a situation like this in the future?

_____

_____

Summarize your learning from these experiences and the leadership values and principles your actions demonstrated.

_____

_____

Which of these leadership values and principles do you want to consistently demonstrate?

_____

_____

What changes will you make to ensure you maintain the reputation you want to have as a leader, even in challenging and stressful times?

_____

_____